## Praise for *Life Rules*

Ellen LaConte convincingly uses AIDS as a metaphor for the compounding impacts of climate change, peak oil, water and topsoil depletion, overpopulation and economic collapse — a critical mass of problems currently overwhelming the immune system of the planet. Only another critical mass — this one of informed behavior changes toward conservation and localization — can reverse the progress of the disease. This book succeeds in being both comprehensive and inspiring in its diagnosis and prescription.

— Richard Heinberg, Senior Fellow, Post Carbon Institute,
author of *The End of Growth* and *Peak Everything*

If you read just one book about the sickness that threatens the Earth, you cannot choose better than this one. In eminently readable style and with memorable images, LaConte diagnoses the disease and proposes promising responses. She finds seeds of hope without obscuring the imminence of catastrophe. Her message needs to reach a mass audience.

— John B. Cobb, Jr., Professor Emeritus, Claremont School of Theology,
author of *Sustainability: Economics, Ecology & Justice*
(with Herman Daly) and *For the Common Good*

In the world as it operates today, even the most serious politicians persist in pontificating about matters future history will show were irrelevancies and distractions. If there were someone with authority to require all candidates for high public office to read certain books in preparation for the responsibilities they aspire to undertake, Ellen LaConte's *Life Rules* should be high on the list of urgently required reading.

— William R. Catton, Jr., author of *Overshoot* and *Bottleneck*

There are no easy answers to the present challenge of overcoming the obstacles to the survival of our species, but LaConte's book offers the wisdom we need to face up to it.

— James Robertson, Founder, TOES and The New Economics Foundation,
author of *Future Money, Future Work and Future Wealth*

Ellen LaConte is the steward of the kind of holistic mind that we humans were born into but that, amid the myriad fragmentations of mass global society, so many have lost. She applies her elastic intelligence to the most important topic we face: the destruction of life and the means by which we may survive. *Life Rules* is a tour de force and a book to carry with you in the years to come.

— Chellis Glendinning, author of
*Off the Map: An Exploration into Empire and the Global Economy*

Elegant and eloquent ... an important work.

— Derrick Jensen, author of *Endgame, A Language Older than Words* and
*Deep Green Resistance* (with Aric McBay and Lierre Keith)

It is the genius of this book that its hard-hitting diagnosis of our global crisis provides the groundwork for its prescription. What we can and must do for the survival of complex life-forms shines ever clearer, as we follow Ellen LaConte's invigorating portrayal of life's systemic principles. Crackling with intelligence and verve, *Life Rules* immediately became required reading among colleagues in the Work That Reconnects.

— Joanna Macy, author,
*Active Hope: How to Face the Mess We're in Without Going Crazy*

I am SO enjoying every word of *Life Rules* and learning from you. You are carrying the ball now! I will tell many about it and wish you a wonderful new year from my paradise on Mallorca.

— Elisabet Sahtouris, evolution biologist, author of *EarthDance,
A Walk Through Time* and *Biology Revisioned* (with Willis Harmon)

It's as if LaConte googled the world's environmental and economic woes and distilled them down into a construct that we can all easily understand and digest. Critical reading for anyone who cares enough about our planet to try to save it.

—Miles Frieden, Director, Key West Literary Seminar

A very valuable and important book. I will gladly recommend it to colleagues in the Great Work. It anticipates readers' questions and makes the vast complex of present problems comprehensible.

— Herman Greene, Director, The Center for Ecozoic Studies, publisher of *The Ecozoic*

Wonderful summary of what's wrong and what we need to do, not just economically and ecologically, but also politically.... The logic is very persuasive. By the time I put down the book, I was laughing at myself for ever thinking that broad national or global policies would be any use in getting us out of this mess.

— Edmund "Terry" Fowler, author of *From Galileo to the Greens: Our Escape From Mechanical Thinking* and *Building Cities That Work*

While Deep Ecologists explore ways humans can break through to a new level of consciousness in harmony with life, LaConte offers us a compelling reason to provide for ourselves in ways that mimic life: our survival as a species on a livable planet. In a critically challenged world, sustainable means not just Earth-friendly but also lifelike.... A very important attempt to wake us up before our global economy "puts us and life as we know it — as well as itself — out of business."

— John Seed, Founder/Director, Rainforest Information Network, co-author of *Thinking Like a Mountain: Toward a Council of All Beings*

Looking back with more than seventy years of experience, I'm of the opinion that LaConte's conception of democracy, as both characteristic of living systems and the ultimate objective of humanity's political enterprise, is the most inspired and comprehensive I am aware of.

— Lloyd P. Wells, co-founder, The Center for Consensual Democracy, author of *Recreating Democracy: Breathing New Life into American Communities*

*Life Rules* brings fresh clarity and urgency to the serious, complex and interrelated issues and crises that we face as a species to either evolve or perish. Any faith unexamined means another life, another generation, unlived. This book examines those value systems and beliefs that have brought on what some see as the End Time, and offers alternative ways of being and doing that can help our species not only survive, but also evolve. As Albert Schweitzer advised, "Until he extends his circle of compassion to include all living things, man will not himself find peace."

— Dr. Michael W. Fox, veterinarian, author of *Bring Life to Ethics: Global Bioethics for a Humane Society*

There are many books that focus on one aspect of the ecological problems that mankind is generating, but it is rare to find a book like *Life Rules* that looks at the whole picture. It is a sobering read, and leads to the conclusion that there is a systemic problem in our treatment of Gaia that can justly be compared to a disease process. The current individualistic paradigm can be summed up as "Blow you, Jack, I'm all right." Paradigms can change, and Ellen LaConte shows in which direction our present mind-set should move if humanity and Gaia are to recover from the present disease.

— Dr. Richard Lawson, Parliamentary candidate, Green Party UK

This is not just one more cultural, economic and ecological Jeremiad. Rather, LaConte accomplishes a brilliant synthesis of the work of visionary economists, environmentalists and social critics alike. She's done our homework for us. But she's much more than an artful synthesizer of others' work. Her perspective, "big picture" observations, guiding metaphors and incisive, scrappy prose are all her own. She deftly manages to speak to young people and scholars with equal clarity and force. She tells it like it is, but never leaves us feeling helpless. It's rare to find a book that tells the dark truth about our current human and planetary condition while simultaneously motivating us to re-think, re-act and step toward the light. This book does.

— Rebecca Kneale Gould, Associate Professor of Religion and Environmental Studies, Middlebury College, author of *At Home in Nature*

*Life Rules* is a powerful call to action that Americans in particular and all global citizens need to heed for humanity's survival and transformation. Highly recommended.

— Wanda Urbanska, "Simple Living with Wanda Urbanska" (PBS), author of *Less is More* (with Cecile Andrews)

An important book with a compelling argument: that we must be able to see the myriad threats facing the planet, not as discrete problems, but as interconnected issues that must be addressed as a single crisis.

— Walter Fox, Professor of Journalism, Temple University (ret.), *Writing the News: A Guide for Print Journalists*

*Life Rules* shows that more of us are beginning, in the nick of time, to recognize ourselves, our creations and our natural communities and ecosystems as inextricably interdependent. We see that it is no longer OK that our way of life requires that others' ways of life be diminished. It is no longer OK that the preservation of our land, health and jobs requires that others' be destroyed. This book validates those individuals, organizations and movements that are helping to shift the human paradigm from extreme competition, perpetual growth and private gain to cooperation, sustainability and the common good.

— Mary Beth Steisslinger, Integral Systems Biologist,
Global Commons Group, Sky Trust

LaConte sounds depths from which will spring new ways to see cities and buildings become tools for healing our planet. Her book may help to inspire a global movement towards a rediscovery of our sacred commitment to serve as loving Earth stewards.

— Tim Watson, Eco-Restorative architect and teacher,
President, EarthWalk Alliance

LaConte's well-crafted analogies tie together many environmental and economic issues to show why the world is between a rock and a hard place ... and why millions of us need to get up and serve in the world.

— Dwayne Hunn, The People's Lobby; The American World Service Corps,
author of *Ordinary People Doing Extraordinary Things*

In proposing that the earth's rapidly cascading and interlocked symptoms of environmental and social malaise constitute a syndrome analogous to HIV/AIDS, Ellen LaConte aptly explains how we managed to arrive at thresholds that could bring down life as we know it in rapid order. This is a chilling synthesis. But not hopeless.... It comes down, she says, to tending things in the places we live and work. This is the way out — a return to deep local economies nested in limits and potentials given by nature. She has come up with a book that could change the shape of things to come.

— Ted Bernard, Professor, Environmental Studies Program, Voinovich School
of Leadership and Public Affairs, Ohio University,
author of *Hope and Hard Times* and *The Ecology of Hope*

I found LaConte's analogy in re AIDS fascinating.... an approach that may make the earth's crisis more plausible and understandable. It is the kind of analogy that even the simplest among us can understand and may be the kind of marketing "tool" that could catch on in ways other approaches cannot.

— Fred Berger, Vice Chairman (ret.), Hill & Knowlton, Inc.

The key features of LaConte's deeply green vision for the future are economics rooted in sustained commitment to earth, especially to the particular places we live on earth, and politics rooted at the local level in the dialogue of persons in a process she calls "Organic Democracy." Her vision is synchronous with what I believe the Green Party vision must be for its second quarter century.

— John Rensenbrink, co-founder of the Green Party USA, founding director of the Green Horizon Foundation, publisher of *Green Horizon Magazine*

Nothing is more radical and more necessary for this moment of conscious social invention and conscious human evolution than to return life itself to center stage of human political economy and human spiritual cosmology. By doing this here in her book, *Life Rules*, Ellen LaConte is showing the courage, character and wisdom of other leaders whose vision of the possible future changed history. ...

— August T. Jaccaci, Founder of Communiversity, author of *General Periodicity: Nature's Creative Dynamics*

# LIFE
# RULES

### NATURE'S BLUEPRINT
### FOR SURVIVING ECONOMIC AND
### ENVIRONMENTAL COLLAPSE

## ELLEN LaCONTE

new society
PUBLISHERS

Cover design by Diane McIntosh.
Photo: © iStock (theowl84)
Printed in Canada. First printing July 2012.

Paperback ISBN: 978-0-86571-726-8
Ebook ISBN: 978-1-55092-521-0

Inquiries regarding requests to reprint all or part of *Life Rules*
should be addressed to New Society Publishers at the address below.

To order directly from the publishers, please call toll-free (North America)
1-800-567-6772, or order online at www.newsociety.com

Any other inquiries can be directed by mail to:

New Society Publishers
P.O. Box 189, Gabriola Island, BC V0R 1X0, Canada
(250) 247-9737

New Society Publishers' mission is to publish books that contribute in fundamental ways to building an ecologically sustainable and just society, and to do so with the least possible impact on the environment, in a manner that models this vision. We are committed to doing this not just through education, but through action. The interior pages of our bound books are printed on Forest Stewardship Council®-registered acid-free paper that is **100% post-consumer recycled** (100% old growth forest-free), processed chlorine free, and printed with vegetable-based, low-VOC inks, with covers produced using FSC®-registered stock. New Society also works to reduce its carbon footprint, and purchases carbon offsets based on an annual audit to ensure a carbon neutral footprint. For further information, or to browse our full list of books and purchase securely, visit our website at: **www.newsociety.com**

LIBRARY AND ARCHIVES CANADA CATALOGUING IN PUBLICATION

LaConte, Ellen
     Life rules : nature's blueprint for surviving economic and environmental collapse /
Ellen LaConte.

Includes index.
ISBN 978-0-86571-726-8

1. Financial crises. 2. Globalization--Economic aspects. 3. International economic relations. 4. Environmental degradation. 5. Environmental economics. I. Title.

HC59.3.L325 2012          330.9'05          C2012-903821-0

*For*

**James Bitner,** my father, without whose support of every kind I would likely have quit before this book was well begun, who unfailingly makes me proud to be his daughter and to have inherited at least a little of his goodness, generosity and persistence.

**Dolly Hatfield,** my partner, without whose love, wisdom, editorial skills, humor, relentless encouragement and unfailing patience I might have given up on more than just this book.

**Sally Sandler,** my sister and excellent friend and, happily, an extra-ordinarily gifted editor.

**Lloyd P. Wells,** whose renaissance mind, ranging curiosity and genius for democracy were the catalysts for a new way of thinking about the human past and future, and whose enthusiasm and active support for this book have made all the difference.

**Joanna Macy,** who gave *Life Rules* a second life and me the gift of friendship.

**All of you who come after us,** for whom I hope *Life Rules* may serve as an apology for your antecedents' ignorance and excesses, a survival manual and a field guide to good lives lived in a sustainable future.

*If you want to change the world, you have to change the metaphor.*

— Joseph Campbell

*People do not change when we tell them they should; they change when their context tells them they must.*

— Thomas Friedman

*Someone who has been immersed in orthodoxy needs to experience a figure-ground reversal in order to gain perspective. This can't come from encountering just a few heterodox thoughts, but only from a new encompassing architecture of interconnected thoughts that can engulf a person with a different worldview.*

— Jaron Lanier

*There are periods in human existence when the inevitability of a great upheaval, of a cataclysm that shakes society to its very roots, imposes itself on every area of our relationships. At such epochs, all people of good will begin to realize that things cannot go on as they are; that we need great events that roughly break the thread of history, shake humanity out of the ruts in which it is stuck and propel it toward new ways, toward the unknown. ...*

— Pyotr Kropotkin

# Contents

**Acknowledgments** / xiii
**Foreword**, by John Robbins / xv

**Part I: The Real Threat to Life as We Know It** / 1
    Chapter 1: Diagnosing a Critical Condition / 3
    Chapter 2: Symptoms of Critical Mass —
        Making the Connections / 19
    Chapter 3: Discovering the Common Cause / 37
    *HIV and the Viral Global Economy: Powerful Similarities* / 57
    Chapter 4: What's Wrong with a Global Economy? / 59
    Chapter 5: How Did the Economy Get to Be Too Big
        *Not* to Fail? / 83
    Chapter 6: The Prognosis for Global Solutions Is Poor / 101

**Part II: How Life Deals with Critical Mass** / 125
    Chapter 7: Life's Steep Economic Learning Curve / 127
    *Life's Economic Survival Protocol* / 134
    Chapter 8: Life Is Earthonomical, Naturally / 135
    Chapter 9: Life's Earthonomical Communities —
        Prototypes for Deep Green / 141

Chapter 10: Life Is Organically Democratic / 165
*Democratic Earthonomical Communities v. the Pyramidal Global
Economy: Striking Contrasts* / 188
*We Can Do This* / 189


**Part III: Deep Green Methods for Surviving the Global Economy**
*The Heart of the Healing* / 191
Chapter 11:  Mimicking Life's Economics — Improving the Odds
     and Our Lives / 193
Chapter 12: Mimicking Life's Politics — Organically Democratic
     Principles and Practices / 233
Chapter 13: Setting a Good Example / 257
Chapter 14: How to Become Deeply Green / 281
Chapter 15: Precedents for Success / 311
Chapter 16: Dreaming Deep Green, Imagining the Ecozoic / 321


**Endnotes** / 325
**Appendix: Suggestions for Further Reading** / 351
**Index** / 355
**About the Author** / 367

# Acknowledgments

L IFE RULES BENEFITED GREATLY FROM THE SUPPORT given to its previous incarnation (published by Green Horizon Foundation using iUniverse publishing services) by my partner, Dolly Hatfield; John Rensenbrink, Founding Director of Green Horizon Foundation; Herman Greene, Founding Director of The Center for Ecozoic Societies; Miles Frieden, Executive Director of the Key West Literary Seminar; Sally Sandler; August Jaccaci; Timothy Seldes of Russell & Volkening Literary Agency; Susan Schwartz of The Editors' Circle and Tim Watson, Executive Director of the EarthWalk Alliance and lecturer in urban and eco-restorative design at Central Carolina Community College.

It has been most fortunate for *Life Rules* to be chosen for a new edition by New Society Publishers. Working with managing editor Ingrid Witvoet and my fabulous copy editor, Betsy Nuse; my marketing team E.J. Hurst and Sara Reeves; production manager Sue Custance; and designer Greg Green has been, literally, a dream come true. I wrote the first draft with dreams of a New Society future.

For every "original" idea this book may contain there are behind it — coaxing it out of my life experience as a generalist, "gregarious recluse" (in Annie Dillard's terms), intuitive, homesteader, woods-walker, wearer of many hats and perpetual student — scores and more of felicitous and brilliant writers, deep and broad thinkers, social architects and critics, historians, evolutionary and complex systems theorists, scientists, futurists, cultural creatives, activists, innovators, philosophers, spiritual teachers and visionaries in whose work it has its actual origins. Many of them, though not all by any means, are quoted in these pages. I have for several decades been grateful for their intellectual companionship and wisdom, and in some few cases for their friendship and personal encouragement. This isn't my first book. It's probably not my last. But, thanks to them, it is my most significant.

— Ellen LaConte

*If our efforts are fragmented and our victories piecemeal,*
*then clearly we have got to think again and think better.*
*In order to think better, I believe, we are going to have to revive*
*and reinvigorate the tired old idea of context. ...*
*A creature can only live in a context that favors its life.*

— Wendell Berry

# Foreword

By John Robbins

T HERE ARE SOME DAYS that I find it hard to think clearly and calmly about almost anything. In this, I'm not alone. Many people today feel overwhelmed. We are virtually inundated with bad news. Some of our leading scientists feel that we have crossed some kind of threshold, some point of no return. The forces bearing down on us seem to be intensifying. Already there are rampant foreclosures and increasing unemployment. There are the ominous threats of peak oil, climate change, terrorism and pollution. Quite frankly, it's hard to avoid the suspicion that we could see some pretty terrible things in our lifetimes.

We have already entered an entirely new phase in our nation's and our world's economic existence. We have come to the end of the financial world as we have known it.

The idea that the global economy could conceivably collapse is a scary prospect, because we have come to depend so profoundly on the functioning of our economy for just about everything we need. But as Ellen LaConte shows us in her visionary and illuminating book, *Life Rules*, this may actually be just what the doctor ordered. It could be exactly what we need to push us to transition out of an economic system that has become a parasite on the earth, a "sickness," as philosopher Kierkegaard once put it, "unto death."

Is it possible that we could emerge from the disease of our times to find ourselves and our economic life grounded in something far more real, enduring, sustainable and reliable? Is it possible for us to somehow bring our economic life back into alignment with the realities of nature? Might we yet learn to live within the Earth's means? Might we learn to obey, rather than break, Life's rules?

Time will tell. But I think the chances that we might yet evolve in positive and healthy ways through the challenging times to come are greatly increased by the brilliance, clarity and wisdom in this surprisingly hopeful book. Ellen LaConte helps us to understand exactly why the current form of our global economy has led us into such distress, and shows us precisely what we can do, what we must do, if we are to survive and even thrive.

*Life Rules* is more of an alarm clock than a lullaby. If you are looking for escape literature, if you want to be consoled and reassured and sung to sleep, this book probably isn't for you, at the moment anyway. If you want to remain ensconced in denial, that's your right. Denial is the way most of us most often cope, and it's so widespread that we can think of it as normal.

But there's a serious problem with denial. It reduces our capacity to respond. *Life Rules* is all about breaking through the walls of denial precisely so that you and I and millions of us can respond, so that we can be creative and engaged, so that we can clearly understand what we must do and so that we can find in ourselves and in our relationships the power to build a world, a way of life and an economy, on solid ground.

*Life Rules* is an act of genius and a gift of wisdom. As I read this extraordinarily honest and perceptive book, I kept nodding my head, yes, and feeling something deep and powerful awaken in me. This book is powerful medicine.

— John Robbins
*The New Good Life; Diet for a New America*

# Part I

## The Real Threat to Life as We Know It

### What in the world's going wrong:

bankrupt local, regional and national economies

**reduced, overtaxed public and social services**

failing pension plans, banks, lenders and insurers

**degraded and polluted farmland, wetlands, fisheries and forests**

the stark reality of a finite supply of oil, natural gas and coal

**lifestyles, incomes and jobs dependent on all three fuels**

soaring worldwide long-term unemployment, rising costs of living

**fluctuating markets and currencies, floundering credit markets**

crumbling, unsafe infrastructures and inefficient power grids

**insolvent social service, charitable and disaster relief agencies**

increasing shortages of water, minerals, metals and staple foods

**disastrous weather and unpredictable seasons**

globe-trotting viruses, invasive species and ineffective antibiotics

**collapsing ecosystems and Life-threatening species extinctions**

mass migration to cities and relatively prosperous economies

**rising social, racial, ethnic, religious and cultural conflict**

floundering public education and health systems

**inept and corrupt governments**

a widening gap between rich and poor

CHAPTER 1

# Diagnosing a Critical Condition

**Why is so much going wrong everywhere at once?**

The answer is simple, though its implications for us are anything but. We humans are facing what has been variously described as collapse, bottleneck, overshoot, catastrophe, the long emergency and Nature's revenge because we are breaking Life's paramount rule:

**We are living beyond Earth's means.**

Our activities are bankrupting Earth's four-billion-year-old living trust accounts as surely as they are bankrupting most of the Earth's national treasuries.[1] In 2005, the United Nations' Millennium Ecosystem Assessment put our hazardous extravagance in more official terms: "Human actions are depleting the Earth's natural capital, putting such strain on the environment that the ability of the planet's ecosystems to sustain future generations can no longer be taken for granted."[2] Our actions have depleted even more of that natural capital in the intervening years.

Economic, environmental, social and political challenges are the direct and indirect consequences of living beyond Earth's means. And they are neither static nor separate and distinct. On the contrary, they are reinforcing, amplifying and complicating each other and converging in a way that is precipitating a mega-crisis for which we modern humans have no precedent.

- Never in the historic period, going back more than 6,000 years to the first city-states and civilizations, have all of Earth's human communities faced — simultaneously — the real and present danger of being unable to meet most of their people's needs.
- Not since the end of the last ice age 11,000 years ago has the health and continuity of all the living systems on Earth been put at risk by a single global phenomenon.
- Not since archaic bacteria approached the point of exceeding Earth's capacity to support them has a single species been the cause of that Life- and life-threatening phenomenon.

It's not surprising, then, that most of us haven't seen this moment coming and don't yet appreciate the gravity of our circumstances or understand them fully if at all. Not surprising either that most of us, despite our being members of Earth's predominant species, don't yet accept responsibility for the part we're playing in this unfolding tragedy. It's easier, happier — and characteristically human — to deny the seriousness of the fix we're in than to face what it would take to fix it.

Bankrupt governments? Nothing new, we'll find a way out. The end of affordable oil? Not for decades, the skeptics say. Expensive coal, peak natural gas and the ramifications of losing *all* of our cheap fossil sources of energy? Won't happen for centuries, say the no-limits faithful. Global warming, climate change? Fewer than half of us — 26% of Britons, 42% of Germans and barely 50% of people in the US, for example — believe that significant warming or instability is occurring or that we have much to do with it if it is.[3]

Not believing in something doesn't prevent it from happening.

How about Amazon rainforest collapse, warfare over oil and gas in an often open Arctic Sea? Can we imagine Walmart closing, two billion of us homeless and five billion hungry? What if social security systems, insurers and emergency management agencies go bankrupt? How about hundred-year droughts in some places and thousand-year flood cycles in others?

Self-styled realists assure us that these are not logical extensions of what's going wrong in the world already. But what if the realists are wrong? In truth, these scenarios are fantastical. But they are also logical extensions of what's already going wrong in the world, if we don't do something effective about it.

> "The world is on a journey to an unstable destination, through unfamiliar territory, on an uneven road and, critically, having already used its spare tire."[4]

And who is we? In these pages we who will experience this convergence of crises is all of us: humankind. Young, old, rich, poor, male, female — all of us everywhere will suffer a failure to fix what's going wrong everywhere at once. But obviously not all of us are responsible for this mega-crisis. The young and poor and less able in present and past generations have born the brunt of symptoms but do not bear the burden of responsibility. And the deceased cannot help us now except by their wisdom and example. But for reasons that will become clear in the pages ahead, we adult, able humans are all complicit — wittingly or unwittingly, willingly or unwillingly, directly or indirectly — in the creation of Earth's critical condition. Consequently, we adult, able humans are the ones who can do something about it, who can get past denial and create the cure for and alternatives to this critical condition.

But even if we do get past denial of the seriousness of our present circumstances and of worse ones if we don't do something effective, how can we possibly get our minds around a challenge this enormous for which we've had no preparation?

Over 40 years ago media analyst and futurist Marshall McLuhan foresaw this clash of the human mind with too much reality. "When faced with a totally new situation, we tend always to attach ourselves to the objects, to the flavor of the most recent past. We look at the present through a rear-view mirror. We march backwards into the future."[5] In other words, we do more of the same things that brought us to the brink of catastrophe until the catastrophe itself requires us to do something different.

Ignorance and inexperience explain our plight, but they are not permanent conditions and do not require us to capitulate.

The good news, and there is some, is that we adult, able humans are entirely capable of understanding why we are in crisis and of learning how to effectively deal with it.[6] Down through the millennia, when push has come to shove, when there was finally no choice, humans have learned how to work together to survive ice ages and meltdowns, volcanic winters and collapsing civilizations, decades-long droughts, depressions and other disasters. As soft as some of us have become, as exhausted as others of us already are by long years or whole lives of hardship, we are the descendants of those survivors. We can learn how to survive this mega-crisis, too. And we can surely make the process of trying to survive as humane, compassionate and rewarding as we are able. Some portion of us always has.

One way to begin is to acknowledge the fact of the crisis by giving it a name. Giving something unfamiliar an effective name can be the beginning of the end of ignorance — and fear — of it.

## What's in a Name?

We need an evocative, even provocative name for our present mega-crisis so that it gets at least the same level of attention, widespread recognition, support and devotion we give top athletes, pop singers and movie stars.

We have most definitely arrived at or, as Bill McKibben suggests in his newest book with its aptly misspelled title, *Eaarth*,[7] we may have just passed the *tipping point* in the evolution of this crisis after which nothing will be the same. The tippers are anticipated to be the end of cheap oil, an uncongenial climate, a fragile global economy and/or the apocalyptic convergence of all three. But, though McKibben and others believe we've shot past the tipping point already, there is not yet widespread agreement that we have. Most people cling to the belief, or the hope, that if there is to be a tipping point, it's still up in front of us somewhere moving away from, not toward, us.

*Collapse* is the most commonly used term for what's wrong in the world. It's meant to name what comes after the tipping point: the decline and fall of modern industrial civilization. But as I write, collapse is still a prediction. It properly names what will come, and possibly quite soon, if we do not effectively and immediately face up to the real potential for worldwide system failure.

In fact, we have been able to use "collapse" to describe the demise of earlier socio-economic systems and civilizations only long after it was clear they had collapsed. It took the Roman Empire several centuries to complete the process we now call its "fall." Decline was an on-again-off-again affair involving many of the same kinds of challenges we face now except that they took place regionally rather than globally.

**Tipping point?**
**Collapse?**
**Critical Mass!**

It seems to me that *Critical Mass* better suggests the full significance and weight of the collection of crises we are already experiencing. The term critical mass in itself has no positive or negative connotation. Originally used by nuclear physicists to name the amount of fissionable material required to trigger and sustain a chain reaction, it is now used more generally to identify a point in time or in a process when enough of something has been literally amassed that a spontaneous transformation occurs. After critical mass is reached, something new emerges or is created, or a new state of being is achieved.

And unlike the other possible names, Critical Mass can serve a double purpose: It can be used to name not only the crisis but also its cure. Getting through this mega-crisis in a way that doesn't make the Dark Ages look good will require that critical masses of us get our minds around its nature and cause and then deal with that cause.

The something new that follows on the heels of reaching critical mass may by our reckoning be good. Members of the activist cyclists' group Critical Mass deem it good when enough of them gather in a city's streets to stop traffic, making their point about the dark side of our dependence on fossil-fueled transportation and hopefully helping to inspire a widespread transformation to post-carbon (non-fossil fuel) forms of transportation, like cycling.

"I believe that we face a dire and unprecedented period of difficulty in the twenty-first century, but that humankind will survive and continue into the future — though not without taking some severe losses in the meantime, in population, in life expectancies, in standards of living, in retention of knowledge and technology, and in decent behavior."[8]

On the other hand, what comes after critical mass may be something that is by our reckoning disastrous and regrettable, as when plague amasses in so many humans' bodies that it takes the lives of whole communities or when the amount of fissionable material gathered is sufficient to set off a chain reaction in a nuclear weapon.

If it is not dealt with soon and effectively, this critical mass of crises we are facing now will be of the latter sort. It will be *so* disastrous and regrettable from the human perspective that in these pages I will distinguish it from the positive and lesser kinds of critical mass with capital letters in order for us to be constantly reminded how urgent it is that we understand and deal with it.

So, there's a second answer to the question "Why is so much going wrong everywhere at once?"

### We have reached global Critical Mass.

The next step, now that we've got a name for our mega-crisis, is to get our minds around what Critical Mass is and what it's doing to us and our world. We'll do that in this chapter and the next. The second step will be to determine what's causing Critical Mass. *How* are we living beyond Earth's means? That's the subject of the remainder of Part I. Part II offers what I believe is a compelling, perhaps inarguable, context for understanding what it would take to mitigate and get beyond Critical Mass. And Part III explores how we might actually do that.

An emotional roadmap to this book would warn you that Part I is pretty bleak and negative. But rest assured. Part II is inspiring and eye-opening, and Part III is downright optimistic. May our future, starting now, work that way, too!

## Understanding Critical Mass

In his 2007 bestseller *Blessed Unrest*, Paul Hawken observed that one of the reasons most of us have not yet grasped the severity and complexity of the Critical Mass of crises we're facing is that we haven't had anything to compare it to. Referring to the "Gaia hypothesis," (Sir James Lovelock's seminal insight that Life on Earth works in ways that are similar to the way any living organism works) Hawken wrote: "If we accept that the metaphor of an organism can be applied to humankind

[too], we can imagine a collective movement that would protect, repair, and restore that [planetary] organism's capacity to endure when threatened," as it presently is. Hawken proposes that such a movement — of individuals working through non-governmental organizations — would "function like an immune system" and the individuals and organizations in the movement could be thought of as antibodies.[9]

*That's it!* I thought. *A threatened immune system, antibodies ...* That's why we're exceeding Earth's capacity to support Life as we know it.

## Critical Mass is the Earth's equivalent of AIDS.

This insight became more compelling the longer I considered it.

Just as the diverse parts of the immune system are scattered throughout our bodies, Earth's diverse natural communities and ecosystems have in the past worked together to provide the same sort of protective, defensive and healing services for Life as a whole that our immune systems provide for us. That's what James Lovelock and others have meant when they've said that Life learned how to create and maintain the conditions in which it can continue to exist on Earth despite challenges like ice ages and asteroid collisions. Life evolved its own version of an immune system. And our activities are threatening to undermine it.

But, if we're the ones who are compromising Earth's immune system, why haven't we hit global Critical Mass sooner?

For the past 30,000 to 40,000 years, whenever humans arrived on a new continent, we've killed and eaten enough of the largest, slowest mammals we found there to render them extinct within a few thousand years. Their disappearance changed the makeup of ecosystems everywhere we went to the extent that the phenomenon has a name: the Pleistocene Overkill. But mega-fauna (large animal) overkill was the only widespread destruction we were capable of back then, and it happened one region and continent at a time over thousands of years. And after we'd wiped out the mega-fauna, we settled into our new locations. New ecosystems arose around us and settled in, too. We wreaked very little additional havoc until the first civilizations arose around 6,000 years ago. Most indigenous (native) peoples continued to adapt their ways of living to the requirements of their natural surroundings until quite recently. The lives and lifeways of very few indigenous peoples remain unaffected by the global economy, its products and demands.

Civilizations, on the other hand, have always compromised the health and the healing functions of natural and human communities that were within their reach. They have always induced *regional* Critical Mass. But for most of the historic period, the larger planetary immune system (the majority of natural communities and ecosystems, which no civilization had yet compromised) was still intact and functioning. Compromised regional ecosystems eventually recovered, and new ones, adapted to civilizations' trespasses, arose. New, smaller-scale, less excessive human communities developed with them after the offending civilizations collapsed, and for a while these smaller communities lived within Earth's means.

We have only been technologically sophisticated enough to exceed the whole Earth's capacity to support us and to undermine the function of *all* of Earth's natural and human communities — the whole planet's immune system — for the past 100, fossil-fueled, globally industrialized years. And that's just what we've done.

Put simply, then, Critical Mass is attacking Earth's immune system (the methods Life has evolved over four billion years to protect and heal itself) in the same way that AIDS attacks the human immune system (the methods Life evolved over several million years to protect and heal our bodies).

Critical Mass poses the same risk to human survival and Life as we know it that AIDS poses to the lives of the people it infects. If it is allowed to run its course, Critical Mass will lead to a protracted and profoundly unpleasant demise for all but the hardiest, most adaptable forms of life. Life will last, but many of us and other living things won't.

Briefly reviewing how the AIDS crisis has unfolded will help us understand how the Earth's equivalent mega-crisis is

"Let us hope that we will not have to wait for a catastrophe that kills hundreds of thousands or millions before a critical mass in society develops the solidarity and the will to face the problems that confront all of us.... Ours is not a time for despair; it is a time for action. Not short-term remedial action, but action aimed at bringing about fundamental transformation."[10]

presently unfolding and why mitigating and curing Critical Mass must also become our common cause.

## A Brief History of HIV/AIDS and Its Pathology

In the late 1970s, doctors in offices, clinics and hospitals in places as far apart from each other geographically, economically and culturally as the United States, Haiti, Sweden and Central Africa were faced with a mystery. Significant numbers of young men were developing symptoms of infection and disease that ranged from respiratory ailments, lymphomas, blood disorders, anemia and herpes to skin lesions, cancers, fungal and bacterial infections, meningitis, paralyses and tuberculosis.

Despite their caregivers' attempts to mitigate symptoms and treat the diagnosed conditions, and allowing for successes that were often as poorly understood as failures, surprising numbers of the young men on every continent the disease had reached, many of them gay or drug addicts, died. In the course of things, women, children and also men who'd had no homosexual contact or history of street drug addiction were afflicted with the same odd assortment of apparently random illnesses. They too became ill and died. Though some patients were ravaged by multiple illnesses, one after another or several simultaneously, pneumonia was often the immediate cause of death.

Survivors of the first opportunistic infections gradually lost resilience and vigor. After a number of years they became vulnerable to relapse and unusually susceptible to a host of additional infections. And eventually even minor maladies, like the common cold, yeast infections and cat scratches could prove life threatening. No conventional diagnoses untangled the snarl of symptoms. No conventional protocols effectively treated them.

In 1981 "a number of theories were developed about the possible cause of these opportunistic infections and cancers. Early theories included infection with cytomegalovirus, the use of [recreational drugs called] 'poppers,' and 'immune overload'... Knowledge about the disease was changing so quickly that certain assumptions made at this time were shown to be unfounded just months later."[11]

By 1980 this medical mystery occupied the minds and seriously frustrated the staffs of health care establishments on five continents: North America, South America, Europe, Australia and Africa, where the virus was presumed to have originated. By the mid 1980s, cases of the disease had emerged in port cities along the coast of China. Medical practitioners and researchers in institutes, hospitals and national health organizations around the world had begun by then to compare notes. And by 1982 a few threads were untangled from the snarl.

The mystery condition was not a random collection of unusually potent single diseases. It was a syndrome. The wildly diverse illnesses were neither discrete nor unrelated. Nor was any one of them the primary cause of death. Rather they were mutually reinforcing manifestations of a single highly contagious disease with a single unifying pathology: immune system failure. Every one of the patients had a seriously compromised immune system. Their bodies were not resisting or fighting off infections or preventing their recurrence. Each kind of infection was taking full advantage of these patients' weakened, unprotected condition.

What was more disheartening for both patients and caregivers was that each new or recurrent infection amplified others, competed with them for medical attention or even interfered with or counteracted their treatment. The syndrome's particulars varied from patient to patient, but they apparently shared a common source and produced the same results: debilitation and death due to the body's utter defenselessness.

The implication was clear: Relieving symptoms would continue to be important to a patient's overall health and well-being. But treating the diverse illnesses and infections that constituted the syndrome without at the same time addressing its cause — whatever it was that was disabling and shutting down patients' immune systems — could only buy patients time. It would not prevent inevitable disabling and probable death. And it would not prevent the spread of the disease. Millions, perhaps hundreds of millions of lives were at risk. No population and no place in the world would be safe so long as the underlying cause of immune system failure was unknown.

A decade after the first patients showed up in emergency rooms and clinics, and after several trial balloon names proved misleading, researchers were able to give the new disease a scientifically accurate name: acquired immune deficiency syndrome. The acronym — AIDS — stuck so well in people's minds that within months AIDS was recognized as a medical, social, economic and political priority at the local, national and international levels. The dots between diverse symptoms and illnesses were finally getting connected. Money, research, education, potential treatments, protocols, drug trials, organizations, celebrities and changed behaviors gathered around AIDS as around no other global crisis in recent memory.

## Emergence of a Critical Planetary Condition

AIDS threatens the lives of perhaps sixty million humans. By contrast, if mistreated or left untreated, the global pandemic I'm calling Critical Mass threatens Life as we know it and all of our lives now and for generations to come. So let's track the startling and instructive number of similarities there are between the AIDS crisis and this unimaginably worse one.

Warnings of a potential worldwide convergence of environmental, economic, social and political crises were issued as early as the 1930s by visionaries in many fields. However, symptoms only began to intensify enough to get attention in the major media on a regular basis in the 1970s.

The earliest symptoms of global Critical Mass ranged from increasing numbers of endangered species, the outsourcing of prosperous nation manufacturing jobs to poor nations' sweatshops, local and regional financial crises, dead lakes, polluted air and rivers, the loss of family farms and poorly protected toxic and hazardous waste sites, to increasing

"It is argued that biological immune systems share a number of similarities with ecological economic systems in terms of function. The similarities include the ability to recognize harmful invasions, design measures to control these invasions and destroy the invaders, and remember successful response strategies. Studying the similarities ... between immune systems and ecological systems can provide new in-sight on ecosystem management."[12]

numbers of oppressive dictatorships, energy shortages, persistent fam-
ines, intensifying ideological, religious and territorial conflicts and
widespread corporate environmental and civic irresponsibility.

None of these crises seemed on its own catastrophic. Just as some
people seemed to be more likely than others to succumb to the infections that characterize AIDS because their bodies had already been
weakened — by chronic illness or malnutrition, for example — some
places were more likely to succumb to the afflictions that characterize
Critical Mass. People in parts of the world — particularly south of the
equator — that had long been designated as The Third, undeveloped or
developing world, experienced the most symptoms and suffered them
hardest. Like gay men and drug addicts, they were widely if inaccurately
assumed to be responsible for their own suffering. Though it behooved
the prosperous nations to assist the poorer nations — in order to keep a
majority of them afloat and their resources cheap and available, as well
as for altruistic reasons — the poor lived worlds away. Their problems
were, finally, their problems.

By the 1980s, the symptoms of Critical Mass were recognized to be
spreading and dangerous, to be not worlds away but worldwide, largely
because that's when prosperous countries began to experience the same
symptoms that poorer countries had experienced for decades such as
failing ecosystems, crumbling infrastructure, disappearing species,
unmanageable immigration, health-threatening pollution, homeless-
ness, government ineptitude and a widening gap between the richest
and poorest.

Like the earliest presenting symptoms of AIDS, newly universal problems were in the late 20th century still deemed to be temporary, relatively
minor or to belong in separate and distinct categories: environmental,
economic, social or political. Experts, leaders, managers, agencies and
institutions charged with monitoring problems in each of these separate
categories were the ones ultimately responsible for fixing whatever was
broken. The rest of us could go about our business.

The enormity and coherence of the threat that the sum of the problems posed, the fact that they constituted a single syndrome with a
single underlying cause, was not understood. With the exception of a
few original thinkers — scientists, journalists, futurists and social critics

who were frustrated by their inability to attract attention and criticized for their gloomy prophecies — most of us missed the fact that problems were not just adding up but multiplying exponentially and would affect the rest of us sooner or later.

## Crisis Multiplication in Complex Systems

As is the case in an HIV-infected body, on an Earth beset with the equivalent of HIV/AIDS, the particular problem or set of problems at which we're looking at any point in time trails others behind it like the clouds of sand and dust that followed tractors plowing the overworked soils of Texas and Oklahoma in the US Dust Bowl of the 1930s and that follow the plows and vast herds of sheep across the plains of western China today. On a living planet there is no such thing as a single problem or a simple fix. And the problems we're facing can no more be organized into neat categories and solved separately than those dust clouds can be made to settle down to be swept into tidily separate piles.

A person infected with HIV may at first experience fairly minor symptoms like oral thrush, a persistent cold, numbness or tingling in the extremities, headaches or a minor skin rash. But that's never all, or the worst, that's going on in that person's body. In chillingly similar fashion, Critical Mass may appear first as a manageable environmental problem like drought, but closer inspection reveals that the seemingly solo and solvable problem has created two others — say, farm foreclosures and dried up wells — that create or merge with even more problems, like farming-related business closings, water rationing that affects manufacturing, factories laying off workers, employees unable to pay their bills, plagues of locusts and lifeless soils. In short order the first problem is dragging a dozen others behind it. While they multiply, each of the problems also amplifies and is amplified by one or more of the others, just as bronchitis amplifies a cold and is amplified by pneumonia in its turn.

This is the way both HIV/AIDS and Critical Mass work. One times two doesn't equal the tidy two our minds and simple math know well. With these two diseases — as with all complex systems from bacteria to brains to the biosphere, and from neighborhoods to nations — one times two equals something closer to twelve.

Why?

Because it is the nature of complex systems that every thing or participant in the system is connected directly or indirectly to every other thing or participant, and therefore each thing or participant is capable of influencing or being influenced by the others. The original Greek word for system means to set up or establish something *along with* one or more other things. The point is that nothing in a complex system comes or goes, shrinks or grows without affecting something else or in some cases everything else in the system.

> System: A group of interacting, interrelated and/or interdependent elements forming a complex whole.[13]

There are non-living complex systems like governments, corporations, factories, public utilities, cities, air traffic control programs and economies; we organize and manage them, more or less ably, to serve our purposes. The longer they exist, the more likely it is that even such non-living systems acquire some of the spontaneous characteristics of living systems and something like lives and minds of their own. But they are still products of our imaginations, systems we've designed and created. We have some degree of control over them (for instance, over whether they persist or we "kill" them) and some degree of understanding about how they work.

On the other hand, complex living systems — natural systems — organize and manage themselves. When humans try to reorganize or manage natural systems without knowing much about how they work, as we've been doing for several millennia, we throw off carefully evolved internal processes. We cause changes that ripple through the natural systems and then come back to us again in ways we didn't anticipate and aren't ready for.

Humans get wrong-footed by unanticipated crises in natural systems because we've lost sight of the fact that the non-living systems we've created and the natural ones we didn't create share the same planet. We are all part of the same larger system — Life — which is part of the largest system that's of immediate concern to us: Earth. And on Earth, Life rules, we don't. Why? Because, though complex systems that we create effect how life works, our systems exist within and ultimately depend on Life, not the other way around.

This is an inarguable, inescapable fact, one we simply must internalize. **Life rules. We don't.**

The upshot of this is that crises within non-living systems affect not only other non-living systems but also all the living systems with which they share this planet. And crises that occur in living systems, whether they are human-made or natural, affect non-living systems like the ones we've created.

For example: British Petroleum's (BP's) unprecedented Gulf of Mexico oil rig leak damaged the Gulf's marine and coastal ecosystems and they in turn damaged coastal communities' economies, BP's continued existence, political careers and perhaps the regulation of further deep-water oil drilling necessary to keep affordable fossil fuels flowing into and through the already vulnerable US economy.

In complexes of complex systems, the feedback loops are without end, the crises multiply endlessly and sometimes exponentially. That's what we're experiencing now with the convergence, multiplication and interaction of economic, environmental, social and political crises in the syndrome I call Critical Mass.

CHAPTER 2

# Symptoms of Critical Mass — Making the Connections

L IKE THE OPPORTUNISTIC INFECTIONS AND DISEASES that afflict every part of an AIDS patient's body, the conditions, signs and symptoms of Critical Mass are interacting with, mutually reinforcing and playing off each other in ways that are not easy to predict and that change constantly.

Nonetheless, it is possible to get an inkling of how future symptoms may interact by discovering some of the interactions and connections among the symptoms we are already experiencing. The regularly updated *Merck Manual of Diagnosis and Therapy*,[1] widely used by physicians and others in the medical community to diagnose and describe illness, disease and injury and explore treatment options, lists a dozen conditions that are attributable to or complicated by HIV and twice that number of indicator conditions, illnesses or symptoms, any combination of which suggests that a person might be infected. It is important for us to understand how the hodgepodge of environmental, economic, social and political symptoms that we are grappling with now can constitute a disease syndrome. We must begin to make the connections between symptoms of Critical Mass that we have been viewing as if they were distinct and for the most part separate.

What follows is a sort of mini-*Merck Manual* of Critical Mass symptoms that is intended to show some of the ways our present crises interact to form this planetary syndrome.[2]

## Food

Food is, obviously, a necessity. If we do not have enough food that is sufficiently nutritious, we weaken, sicken and die, whether from starvation or from our resulting vulnerability to infection. When food — its quality, quantity, preservation, production, distribution or cost — is a problem, so is everything else. We can't work, maintain our health, learn, play, respond effectively to our circumstances, reproduce or take care of our families if we don't have enough to eat.

Of the world's seven billion people, one third are well-fed, one third are underfed and one third — a couple of billion people! — hover between malnutrition and starvation.[3]

Though rates of hunger are rising in prosperous countries now, too, the number of hungry people in India increased by 65 million — more than the population of France — between 1990 and 2005, to over 400 million.[4] The UN Food and Agriculture Organization estimated in 2010 that nearly 600 million in Asia and the Pacific Islands, 250 million in Sub-Saharan Africa and 55 million in Latin America are undernourished.[5] That's a tremendous number of people who are unable to participate happily, consistently or competently in their lives, families, communities and economies, a lot of people who need publicly funded aid services and extra medical care. That's a lot of people who are hungry because they are poor and who remain poor in part because they are hungry.

There may be over two billion more human inhabitants of Earth by 2050 if symptoms of Critical Mass haven't dramatically trimmed our populations by then. The 50–60% increase in food production needed to feed them will require that we are able to increase supplies of water, arable land and energy to grow, harvest, process and distribute the food. This requirement collides head on with widely predicted water, arable land and petroleum shortages. We are already unable to feed everyone on Earth enough, let alone well.

Oil has been the key to producing food on a global scale in a global economy. Our present industrial-scale food production system is dependent on the availability of cheap oil — which in its various derivative forms is a major component of fertilizers, pesticides, herbicides and plastic packaging — and on cheap oil, natural gas and coal which directly or indirectly fuel the operation of farm equipment and the processing, transportation and storage of food. As the price of petroleum rises due to inevitably increasing shortages and expensive, often military competition for what remains (see the peak oil discussion in the next chapter), the quality, quantity, preservation, production, distribution and cost of food will *all* become problematic.

> "If land erosion continues, if developing or restoring land proves too expensive, if another doubling of yield is too difficult or environmentally hazardous, if birth rates do not come down promptly ... food could become suddenly limited not only locally but globally."[6]

Food riots, hoarding, rationing and toxin lacing, insufficient inspection and monitoring and curbs on food exports are rapidly becoming more common, if not the norm. Every human and business link in the chain from seed producers, farmers, trucking companies and agricultural equipment manufacturers to food processing companies, advertisers, supermarket chains and us — the end-point consumers — is threatened by potential shortfalls in food production.

We are already experiencing diminished grain stockpiles and price spikes for both grains and staple foods. Corn and vegetable oils may be channeled off into biofuel production, reducing their availability and raising their prices. Supplies of fish and seafood are already threatened by overfishing and by destruction of marine nurseries on coastal shelves and coral reefs caused by dredging, pollution, warmer ocean temperatures, intense storms and oil spills.

In a 2008 open letter to US President-Elect Barack Obama, Michael Pollan, author of *The Omnivore's Dilemma*, noted that "the way we feed ourselves contributes more greenhouse gases to the atmosphere than anything else we do — as much as 37 percent, according to one study ... The 20th-century industrialization of agriculture has increased the amount of greenhouse gases emitted by the food system by an order of magnitude, transforming a system that ... [uses] 10 calories of fossil-fuel energy to produce a single calorie of modern supermarket food."[7] Fossil-fueled methods of food production are also polluting and degrading soils, compromising ecosystems and polluting water supplies. Ironically, the way we've gone about trying to raise enough food is affecting whether we will be able to continue to raise enough food.

The Sahel region of Central Africa — where, according to April 2012 UNICEF and Oxfam reports, 15 million people, among them 1.4 million children, are at risk of dying of malnutrition — and Haiti — where now, as before the 2010 earthquake, the hungry mass-produce and actually eat mud pies — are what Critical Mass looks like when insufficient food is its most blatant symptom.

## Water

Growing plants and raising livestock for food require freshwater. Growing food for a global market as we do now uses two thirds of all the water that's available to us on Earth. It takes upwards of 2,500 gallons of water to produce a pound of beef or bring a bushel of corn to harvest by current agribusiness methods. And water is involved in every post-harvest aspect of food processing, too. There might only be a quarter pound of beef in a fast food burger, but over 1,300 gallons of water went into producing the whole sandwich, 635 gallons went into the burger alone. A loaf of store-bought bread? 150 gallons. Sixteen ounce soda? 33 gallons. Eight ounces of coffee? 37 gallons of water. Your latte bought on the run? Triple or quadruple that 37 gallons.[8]

Manufacturing and all forms of energy production are also heavily dependent on water. They consume the majority of the remaining one third of total available freshwater.

Prosperity and progress such as would be necessary to return the global economy to a modicum of health carry a high water price tag. People in the US use, on average, 100 gallons of water per day. Residents of the world's poorest nations use fewer than five. Lack of water guarantees both personal and economic poverty; personal and economic poverty guarantee lack of water. In the most densely populated (and hungriest) countries in the world — in Africa, India, Eastern and Southwestern Asia — it is prohibitively expensive to bring water from where it is to where people need it. Women in some villages in Africa and India commit as many as eight hours a day to walking to where the water is and carrying it back. The economies of those countries, as well as good jobs, living wages and quality of life are stymied by the lack of sufficient freshwater.

For those of us who have plenty of water this is inconceivable. But the truth is, less than 3% of the Earth's water is fresh, and it is not equitably distributed around the planet. So much of that freshwater is still locked up in glaciers, polar ice sheets and ancient underground aquifers (only some of which will refill), that only 1% of the Earth's freshwater is actually and readily available.[9]

There's no more water coming from anywhere else. What exists on Earth now is all there's ever going to be. Wasting as much of it as we do means we don't get to use a lot of what there is. And neither do all the other-than-human living things and living systems that need it, too. Consider, for example, that open canals deliver water across Arizona's deserts, with untold gallons evaporating along the way; urban water systems leak 25% of the water they carry; acres of rain run off the roofs of buildings and parking lots into storm drains and ditches. Glacial and polar ice meltwater flows into rivers or into the sea without ever being available to natural and human communities. And we're draining aquifers so fast that the land and buildings above them are sinking.

> "We are now looking at the potential wholesale evacuation of cities as aquifers are depleted and wells go dry. ... With the vast majority of the 2.4 billion people to be added to the world by 2050 coming in countries where water tables are already falling, water refugees are likely to become commonplace."[10]

As Earth's climate destabilizes (see next chapter), distribution of rainfall around the world is altered. As lakes drain or expand and soils dry out or drown, the weather systems above them and the climate itself become more unstable.

Worldwide demand for freshwater will exceed supply by 50% as soon as 2025.[11] And water, like food, is necessary to sustain life. Yet because water has become scarce in many places, it has become profitable to own, withhold and sell. Privatization of urban and regional water supplies has made water too expensive for many of the people who need it most and has increased poverty and illness, placing a drain on public monies, social services, aid organizations and economies. In fact, financially strapped local governments can temporarily ward off bankruptcy by selling water rights.

The feedback loops between sufficient, clean, freshwater and almost every other symptom of Critical Mass are dazzlingly complicated.

## Pollution

What remains of freshwater in most countries rarely gets the treatment needed to make it safe to drink. Poor nations cannot in the present economy afford to construct viable, universally available sanitation and pollution treatment systems, and their leaders typically do not choose to invest in constructing them. Nations that do not have universal sanitation and water purification systems cannot advance economically. Water pollution-related diseases drain health care systems and cause more deaths than HIV/AIDS, malaria, war and accidents combined.[12]

Waters polluted by agricultural and industrial runoff and human waste eventually flow, as freshwater does, into underground water tables or into rivers and on to the sea. They pollute the waters on which the roots of plants depend, sicken and kill aquatic plants and animals and trigger explosions of marine algae that suck up oxygen, asphyxiate marine life and create dead zones at the mouths of the world's rivers. By January 2011 researchers had identified 530 dead zones and 228 other delta and continental shelf sites worldwide that were approaching that designation.[13]

But water pollution is just one of the pollution-related symptoms of Critical Mass that triggers or amplifies others. Treating Earth as a sink and sewer represents as serious a crisis as unchecked consumption. By way of analogy, think what difference it makes for a person with HIV to add substance abuse — street drugs or alcohol — to the mix of opportunistic conditions by which their bodies are already assailed.

Rates of pollution-induced asthma and lung cancer and the incidence of code orange days (signifying unhealthy air) are on the rise in most major urban areas, the result of unregulated or insufficiently regulated manufacturing processes. In Beijing, residents have names for the flavor of the air they taste as well as breathe. Residents of Mexico City, Bombay and Los Angeles could well come up with names of their own. Brown clouds of industrial-strength dust and soot trail hundreds of miles out to sea from China's major cities and the Indian subcontinent, blocking out as much as 20% of the sun's light, and in once pristine Himalayan valleys, the summer sky is the saffron color of Buddhist monks' robes. Mercury from unfiltered urban smoke stacks settles out of clouds downwind, poisoning fish and the local economies based on them which have no control over the larger economies that are producing the mercury.

The jet stream flowing over the US carries mercury-laden droplets as far north as the Arctic Circle. They precipitate as rain over the Arctic Sea. The insoluble mercury enters a marine food chain at the top of which are seals, bears, walruses and fish. The Inuit mothers who eat this meat have learned that it makes their breast milk toxic.

Pollution also results from the way we use and the amount we use of Earth's minerals and metals. Heavy metals like lead, cadmium and arsenic and "persistent organic pollutants" (POPs) like PCBs and dioxin linger in soil and water for what amounts to forever. Petroleum-based synthetics — like plastics, fertilizers, industrial chemicals and pharmaceuticals — and fossil-fueled methods of manufacturing, farming, distribution and transportation increase the quantity of consumer goods and foods as well as the quality of human health. They also pollute water, farmland, food and our bodies, and they change the chemical makeup of the atmosphere which influences weather systems and, over time, the climate.

Solid waste — garbage, rubbish, refuse, trash, e-waste (electronic equipment and its parts) — is achieving critical mass in every major city in the world to the extent that bags of it sometimes accumulate for weeks at a time on streets and sidewalks (as, for example, in Naples, Italy in 2007) and dumps like Fresh Kills outside New York City achieve the height of small mountains. Populous islands and many cities ship their trash to places with more space and a willingness to be paid to receive it. Oahu, Hawaii, for example, ships barges of trash to rural Klickitat County in southern Washington State. But on a finite planet there are only a finite number of places to put infinitely expanding tons of trash. And people live in many of them.

Pollution from toxins, many of them petroleum derived, provides an additional challenge to public funds and institutions that clean up and monitor hazardous waste sites, as well as to health care providers, other-than-human species (both wild and domestic) and ecosystems like wetlands and marine nurseries that are poisoned by them.

Discarded plastics create swirling, floating islands the size of Texas in the Atlantic and Pacific Oceans. Fish, marine mammals and aquatic birds ingest them and die. (In the future, we may wish we had recycled and reused these plastics when the petroleum derivatives that are needed to make them become unaffordable.)

## Hyper-Urbanization, Joblessness, Poverty, Dislocation and Disease

These five symptoms of Critical Mass, along with the previous three, are inseparably connected to each other. While fossil fuels were cheap and abundant, food, work, water and other resources could easily and inexpensively be moved around in the global economy from one location, region or continent to another. The bulk of such goods and resources has always gone to the world's large cities where they are most in demand and, at least until now, many people could afford them. Jobs and people in need of them have followed resources and the money that can be made processing them, to the extent that half of the world's people now live in cities. So many people have left towns and villages, following jobs into the world's cities, that they have formed a labor pool so vast and desperate that employers can pay them a pittance and fire them at will.

Mike Davis reported in his 2006 book *Planet of Slums* that Dakha, the capital of Bangladesh, Kinshasa in the Democratic Republic of Congo and Lagos, Nigeria, for example, are each 40 times larger than they were in 1950. But they do not have 40 times the public funds, private financial or natural resources or assets necessary to support that population growth. He noted the *Financial Times* report that in the 1980s alone, China added more city dwellers than did all of Europe, including Russia, during the entire 19th century. In the next few decades, the number of cities with populations above 15 million (hyper-cities) will explode, and nearly all of them will be located in countries that cannot afford to support them. In a 2003 report, *The Challenge of the Slums*, the UN Human Settlements Program predicted that by 2030 Bombay could reach 33 million, Shanghai and Lagos close to 30. Tokyo already has a population of almost 35 million, roughly the population of California. The capital city of an island nation, Tokyo is almost completely dependent on

imports, which means it is almost completely dependent on the continued availability of the cheap fossil fuels necessary to produce and deliver
those imports.

Tokyo is not alone. Hyper-cities cannot and do not support themselves. Their economies and residents are entirely dependent on other
places to supply them with everything they need from food, fibers and
clothing to building materials, metals, medicines and energy. And since
many of the world's cities are growing exponentially, they are dependent
on the willingness and ability of other places — aptly called "supply
regions" and for the most part located in the developing world — to provide them with ever-increasing amounts of such manufactured goods,
agricultural products and resources. Or they are resigned to not having
enough of what they need and to the continued growth of slums and
the consequences of people in dire poverty living in uneasy adjacency
with each other and with people of means. Cities as we know them are
what Buddhists call *hungry ghosts* — entities that are incapable of ever
having enough, ever being satisfied. They are complex systems we have
created that, under present economic arrangements, cannot help but
live beyond their own and Earth's means.

And because jobs continue to go where the money and resources are
— from China now to Bangladesh, for example — they keep on moving as the money and resources move. And when they move they leave
behind millions of workers, many of whom moved from their native
villages and towns to the cities precisely to get those jobs.

Over one third of working-age people worldwide are unemployed
or underemployed. Among young males aged 24 to 30 the rate of
unemployment in much of the world hovers around 50% with little
indication of relief in the short term. While estimates range from 50%
in Sub-Saharan and 30% in Northern Africa, 10% to 23% in southern
and eastern Europe and the Middle Eastern countries to "only" 8% to
12% in Latin America, the number has grown too fast, changed too
often to track accurately in the present global recession.[14] And it is not
surprising that the number of people living in poverty (as a reflection
of the number of unemployed, underemployed and underpaid) is also
rising in all but the few countries that are, for now, still experiencing
economic growth, like China, India and Brazil. Even such generalized

statistics as these begin to explain why mass migration and the dislocation of whole populations are symptoms of Critical Mass.

> More than a billion people live on less than a dollar a day and in parts of Sub-Saharan Africa whole families "make do" with less than a dollar a day. Almost half the world's population — 3 billion people — live on less than US$2.50 a day. And 80% of the world's people live on less than US$10 a day.[15]

If poverty is the future of a majority in the world's hyper-cities, disease, pestilence and plagues are their constant companions. AIDS, influenza, measles, malaria and tuberculosis are all on the rise. As many as two billion people were infected with tuberculosis in 2011 and many active cases, particularly in the developing world, were caused by strains of the disease that are drug-resistant and untreatable.[16]

When concentrations of uprooted, desperate people converge with disease, shortages of necessities like housing, food, water, medical care and social services, Critical Mass reaches fatal proportions.

## Species Extinctions and Ecosystem Collapse

Reports from the Convention on Biological Diversity and the Union of Concerned Scientists suggest that that between 10 and 20% of all species will be driven to extinction in the next 20 to 50 years. If present trends persist, an estimated 34,000 plant species and 5,200 animal species — including 1 in 8 of the world's bird species — faces extinction. The current and impending rate of human-caused extinctions is conservatively estimated to be 100 to 1,000 times the background [natural] extinction rate depending on the species.[17] This so-called "Sixth Great Extinction" translates into about three species lost per hour. By 2100, half of all species may be gone because we've eradicated them or have taken over, poisoned or destroyed their habitats.[18]

What difference does this make? Doesn't it leave more of the resources other species consume for us? Since humans are part of this complex system called Life, we are directly affected by damage done to any part of it. The greater the damage, the greater the impact on us. The fewer the kinds of other-than-human living things and ecosystem communities that survive Critical Mass, the fewer of us will. When enough species die off in any ecosystem — or are killed off or replaced by a single dominant species like us — the whole ecosystem, like an AIDS victim's immune system, is vulnerable to failure. Like the AIDS victim, the ecosystem dies. And that matters because every ecosystem performs services — like water purification and circulation, soil-making and maintenance and balancing the mix of gases in the atmosphere — that support Life and human lives as well. We are all in this together.

## Conflict, War, Chaos and Terrorism

Conflict rarely arises when there's enough to go around for everyone and a majority of us have access to it. On the other hand, it nearly always arises when there is not enough to go around or one person or group claims more than their share. Even the few archeological sites around the world that suggest prehistoric episodes of large-scale human violence can be connected to periods of naturally induced Critical Mass. Mass human graves are found to have been dug in times of dramatic, rapid climate change or when earthquake or volcanic activity caused sudden shortages of food, space, familiar ecosystems and/or water.

It can be reasonably argued that the history of organized warfare is really the history of episodes of regional Critical Mass.

Ironically, the extended conflicts and wars that arise from shortages of necessary resources cause shortages of them in return. It's the persistence of such complex feedback loops that has made "war-torn" a regrettably well-earned description of large regions in the Middle East, Africa and the Indian subcontinent that were, not coincidentally, the locations of the first civilizations and the first true wars. Civilization has never been a peaceful socio-political phenomenon, and civilization's armies are excellent consumers and destroyers of resources.

Oil and natural gas are already primary causes of expensive diplomatic and military conflict and will continue to be. We will enter a particularly threatening period in the next few decades as former oil exporters like Mexico and Russia become oil protectionists, holding on to whatever they have, and then oil importers. They will vie with the US (where deepwater offshore drilling may become too economically, politically and environmentally costly), China, India, Japan, Taiwan, Malaysia,

South and North Korea and Indonesia for control of remaining oil fields and the oil they produce. Saber rattling is already, or still, under way over the South China Sea, Arctic and Persian Gulf fields.

In his book *Resource Wars*, Michael Klare warns of potential conflicts over the freshwaters of the Nile, Jordan, Tigris-Euphrates and Indus River Basins and the river waters flowing out of the Himalayas both to the north and the south.[19] Competition is already increasing in the South Pacific, Southeast Asia and Central and Western Africa for control over global trade in timber, metals and minerals.

If the global economy weakens further or just proves to be unpredictable for a time, competition and conflict over every kind of necessity will wear down national economies, communities and individuals and the natural communities and ecosystems in which they are located. Canadian environmental policy consultant Roy Woodbridge predicts in his book of the same name that scarcities will be the trigger of *The Next World War*.[20] That would be one of the most catastrophic consequences of reaching global Critical Mass and would, according to the laws of complex systems, exacerbate all of the others.

## Treating Symptoms

Through the 1980s and 1990s, non-governmental organizations (NGOs), interest groups, researchers, funds, advocates, celebrities, policy makers and local, regional and federal agencies gathered around each of the exponentially multiplying symptoms of Critical Mass, just as local medical communities gathered around each of the symptoms of AIDS, with the aim of treating or proposing how to treat them. The results of human ingenuity, initiative and the effort and speed with which NGOs in particular could organize and act were often impressive.

Some species received protection — particularly those like tigers, gorillas, whales and wolves — called flagship species because they were popular with the public, easily romanticized, and symbolic of a particular ecosystem, history or culture. Training in information and service sector jobs was offered to many unemployed former factory workers in flourishing economies. Rivers, lakes and the skies over some major cities were cleaned up. Acid rain became less acid in the US (though more acid in the newly industrialized nations). The holes in the ozone layer began to close. Some waste sites were closed, others cordoned off, new ones somewhat more tightly regulated and, after long court battles, reparations were made to some of those who had lost their health, lives or homes to the presence of pollution and toxins.

Participating in the healing process offered benefits in addition to the mitigation of symptoms. For most people, doing something useful alleviates despair, strengthens and integrates healing skills and gathers participants in common cause. Doing something constructive enhances mutual respect, improves our ability to cooperate and collaborate and helps beleaguered peoples, communities, species and ecosystems to regain some measure of health.

Also in the 1980s and 1990s, a surprising number of dictatorships were overthrown in violent or bloodless coups as the governments of more countries became at least nominally democratic. Private and public monies supported a flurry of alternative energy research projects. Food from the grain-rich West was sent to starving people half a world away. Some conflicts were fought to unsatisfactory conclusions, some were given up; others festered somewhere below the level of outright war or were negotiated to uneasy peace. Laws were written and regulations more or less enforced, depending on how much financial threat a particular trespass posed to an economy, corporate sector or political clientele.

But treatment of symptoms separately and often by fiat was not rewarded with a dramatic reduction in problems or diminishment of the general malaise any more than treatment of the early symptoms of AIDS prevented death or forestalled the spread of the disease. Treatment of symptoms alone — whether of AIDS or of Critical Mass — is essentially palliative. It relieves some suffering but not the cause of suffering. And treating only some of the symptoms of a syndrome, or treating them without taking into account how they may interact with each other and what has caused them, is ultimately ineffective. It does not cure the disease.

Consequently, symptoms in every category of our planetary malady have persisted and continue to worsen like the symptoms of the early victims of AIDS.

As well, problems continued to emerge in new places, reemerged in places where they were thought to have been solved, worsened in places where they'd proven intractable and spawned or were joined by

"I find to my personal horror that I have not been immune to naïveté about exponential functions. ... While I have been aware that the interlinked problems of loss of biological diversity, tropical deforestation, forest dieback in the Northern Hemisphere and climate change are growing exponentially, it is only this very year that I think I have truly internalized how rapid their accelerating threat really is."[21]

new problems that had their own symptoms. Crisis wound around crisis until the sum of them eerily echoed the snarl of infections and illnesses that wore down the first victims of AIDS along with caregivers and public health agencies. Decades passed in which the longing for worldwide cures to worldwide problems went unrequited.

As fireworks ushered in the new millennium, whole cities, peoples, species, ecosystems, cultures and economies suffered more severe symptoms of the undiagnosed global mystery disease. Richly diverse, carefully adapted ways of being in the world that had taken Life untold millennia to establish were said at one time or another to be at risk. Deaths mounted — of individuals, villages, industries, cultures, creatures, strains of plants and gene lines — often without satisfactory explanation. Armed conflict, genocide, terrorism and increasingly violent weather claimed the limbs and lives of millions. By some accounts over 230 million people died in wars and conflicts alone, many if not most of those arising out of competition over human and natural resources.[22] Many rainforest tribal groups — 87 tribes in Brazil alone according to researchers at the Rainforest Information Centre — were decimated by disease or assimilated and their lands co-opted to support the global economic participation of the nations within which they were located. With them went hundreds of species of frogs, climbing vines and insects.[23] Lists of former villages and small towns in Eastern Europe, Ireland, the American plains states, rural China and drought-plagued Australia and central Africa and lists of extinguished tree, flower, frog and beetle species flowed out of the world's universities like ticker tape onto the floors of pre-digital stock markets. This is exactly the way deaths had mounted inexplicably and inexorably in the decade before the diverse symptoms of AIDS were recognized to be manifestations of a single illness.

## Finally Catching On: Reason for Hope

We are now, at the start of the 21st century, at the same point in the evolution of Earth's immune system disease as we were in the early 1980s in the evolution of HIV/AIDS. Some few environmental, economic, social and political analysts have recognized that the knot of stubborn worldwide crises that are competing with each other for attention, funds and solutions is in fact a syndrome. And they too have discerned that syndrome's underlying and unifying pathology: The function of Earth's natural communities and ecosystems — in the terms we're using here, its immune system — is being compromised.

Like the diverse parts of the AIDS patient's immune system, every challenged, besieged place on Earth has lost in some measure the ability to protect itself from and minimize infection, to the extent that every part of the Earth's immune system is being weakened. The self-healing methods that Life and humans evolved over stretches of time that make the ages of nations seem inconsequential have been seriously compromised.

Some of the people who have seen into the future that this realization portends hesitate to report what they've seen. As evident as the truth of it is to them, they will not talk about it until they can prove it. Most members of the various affected scientific communities are careful not to incautiously support big new ideas or ideas that cross disciplines. They know they need

"We are not only extinguishing present forms of life, we are eliminating the very conditions for the renewal of life in some of its more elaborate forms." [24]

to be able to demonstrate links, causation and increments. Some few climate scientists, seeing before us what they believe to be a mega-weather Armageddon, are less cautious though not necessarily less correct. Members of the medical community who predicted similarly that AIDS would be a world changer were often said to be alarmists. They were not.

There are also ranks of nay-sayers, doubters, deniers and creditable honest scientists prepared to challenge, in the media and online, details of the data regarding particular economic, environmental, social and political problems. And there are bought-and-paid-for — bespoke

— scientists on both sides of every set of data about every one of the issues we're confronting.

But despite fiercely held opinions and variations in single-symptom statistics, a majority of scientists, futurists, systems analysts and millions of lay people around the world who are suffering the converging symptoms are certain that the critical condition we're calling Critical Mass is worsening. They know empirically (by means of observation and experience) and intuitively (in that way we often know things without having to fit them to abstract theories) that we are dealing with one very big, burgeoning problem rather than myriad unrelated and variable lesser ones. And they accept anecdotal support, of which there is an abundance, for their intuitive leap.

Some of the first in whose minds all the pieces of this crisis came together are, several decades later, frantic. Like the first members of the medical community who made the symptom/syndrome connection about HIV/AIDS and imagined where it might lead, they believe that if we don't do something about this planetary pandemic now, we will be among the victims of a great extinction of our own causing. From their perspective, we're behaving as if the only absolute proof that Earth has the equivalent of AIDS would be an autopsy!

In the several decades they have attempted to warn us in books, papers, conferences, websites and films, increasing numbers of those who have seen this crisis coming have become resigned. They have reduced their expectations of a cure. They have almost come to terms with the idea that even if it isn't quite too late yet, we are apparently unlikely to recognize how big this problem is and do the necessary big things about it before it is too late. Too late for what? To preserve what we think of as civilization on a recognizable, human-friendly, Life-enabling planet.

But while so-called doomsayers have reason to doubt we will save ourselves from the worst Critical Mass can do, they also have reason to hope that we might. It is still possible for us to fix a great deal of what has gone wrong everywhere at once and to avoid the worst of Critical Mass. If we choose to.

Our AIDS/Critical Mass analogy can help us understand why cautious optimism is warranted.

## Discovering the Cause

In 1983, researchers at Paris's Louis Pasteur Institute isolated the virus that caused AIDS. Though it went by other names for several years, the human immunodeficiency virus (HIV) was discovered to be the villain in the piece. It invaded the human immune system and undermined its function, leaving those who were infected susceptible to all manner of opportunistic conditions their bodies would otherwise have warded off or minimized.

Researchers were slow to discover what caused AIDS because one of the virus's techniques is stealth. When people are infected with HIV they experience mild flu-like symptoms after which the virus goes into hiding for as long as 20 years, multiplying secretly and ceaselessly. During that long latent period patients experience so few symptoms that they usually don't realize they are seriously, perhaps fatally, ill. Meanwhile HIV is aggressively colonizing the unsuspecting victim's immune system, commandeering its cells for its own purposes.

If the virus is detected during this latent period and an effective protocol is administered, the worst ravages of AIDS can usually be avoided and death can be postponed for many decades. What's a *protocol*? It's the medical equivalent of a detailed plan or blueprint. Based on studies of prototypes that have worked to heal a patient or cure a disease, a protocol synthesizes and outlines a course of treatments that can be adapted to particular circumstances and patients. Like an architect's rendering of a building that is adjusted and fine-tuned all the way up to the building's completion, a protocol is an established, time-tested set of guidelines for mitigation and cure. At the same time, it's a work in progress, always open to new discoveries, improved techniques and better ideas.

The protocol for AIDS, for example, includes a mix of immune system boosters — a cocktail of medicines — and a set of dietary and behavioral prohibitions and recommendations specific to patients' overall medical history and physical condition and the severity and range of their symptoms. Several decades in the making, the AIDS protocol continues to evolve. When the protocol is successful and a patient's symptoms no longer multiply or worsen, the patient is generally said to have HIV rather than AIDS. This verbal shorthand has led to a common belief that a patient diagnosed with HIV does not actually have AIDS.

This is not the case, however. HIV and AIDS do not name different diseases. They name the early chronic and late acute stages of the very same disease. For if the virus is not detected and its expansion is not minimized or stopped during that latent period by application of the protocol, HIV comes out of hiding, goes into high gear and manifests as full-blown AIDS. By then the victim's immune system has been disabled and decades of life are reduced to years.

We may still be in the latent period in the evolution of Critical Mass. It may not yet be too late for us to do something about it.

I do not mean to minimize the enormity of the task. More than 30 years of dedicated effort have failed to produce a cure or vaccine for AIDS. We cannot afford 30 or even 10 more years of ignorance or denial where Critical Mass is concerned. Billions of human lives and the possibility of a humane future — the human future — are at stake. But in one regard in particular Critical Mass is not like AIDS. It won't take decades of trial and error for us to discover and implement a protective and healing protocol.

Though most of us haven't yet understood how badly we need them or how best to use them, the elements of a protocol for treating Earth's AIDS and the techniques, teachings, teachers and many of the technologies we need to fulfill that protocol — the equivalent of a blueprint for survival — already exist. We only need to realize what they're good for.

All that stood between the medical community and a protocol of effective treatments for mitigating the symptoms of AIDS was knowledge of what caused it. All that stands between us and a protocol of effective treatments for mitigating the symptoms of Critical Mass is knowledge of what has caused it.

CHAPTER 3

# Discovering the Common Cause

THE MEDICAL COMMUNITY went down several wrong streets on its way to nailing human immunodeficiency virus as the underlying cause of AIDS. Lymph system disorders, a herpes-like virus, various recreational drugs and inherent immune system weakness were among the possibilities investigated. None explained all of the conditions AIDS patients experienced or the ones that were often the immediate cause of death: a generalized debilitation and wasting away and one or another form of respiratory failure, often a fungus-induced form of pneumonia, *Pneumocystis jiroveci* pneumonia. Treating misdiagnosed causes did not relieve symptoms for very long or reduce patients' susceptibility to new ones.

Similarly a variety of causes have been proposed for the economic, environmental, social and political crises that presently plague us. Among them have been:

> *overpopulation,* the dominance of the human presence on
> Earth, sheer numbers of heavy resource consumers
> *insufficiently regulated technologies* capable of damaging nat-
> ural and human systems and communities
> *unregulated capitalism,* the capacity of our focus on vari-
> ous forms of money and wealth to facilitate both excessive

resource consumption and inequitable distribution of resources

*extraction and combustion of fossil fuels,* leading to ecological distress, atmospheric and climate instability, pollution, dislocation of human populations, resource wars and eco-system collapses

*hyper-urbanization,* concentrations of humans that lead to ecosystem collapse, poverty, disease, crime and degradation of supply regions

*industrialization,* unprecedented large-scale extraction, man-ufacturing and distribution of goods that disrupts and degrades natural and human systems

*the rise of China* as a superpower with the capacity to push the world's human and natural communities to a tipping point.

Persuasive as each of these factors has been as a potential root cause of Critical Mass, two others are getting the most attention and stirring the most heated arguments: *peak oil* and *climate change.* They get the lion's share of media coverage (there is a vast amount of print and online lit-erature surrounding both), and they are the focus of fierce national and international political wrangling, for good reason: We depend on oil for our lifestyles and on the climate not changing for our very lives. And the two are inextricably connected to each other and to the eventual severity or mitigation of Critical Mass.

Peak oil and climate change are the elephants in the room of life as usual. Each and together, they are said to be the probable cause of a dramatic shift from life as we've known it to something unrecognizable and potentially barbaric. Significantly, each has its instructive analog in the way HIV/AIDS cripples the human immune system.

## Peak Oil = AIDS Wasting Disease

Peak oil — a term coined in 2000 by British petroleum geologist Colin Campbell and popularized by energy analysts and writers like Richard Heinberg, Kenneth Deffeyes, Paul Roberts, Jan Lundberg and Michael Ruppert — names the point at which we produce in a particular country or worldwide the most oil we will ever be able to produce. Since there's no more oil coming from some place else (like water it represents a one-time and therefore finite deposit in Earth's accounts), what we have of it is all there is. Passing peak means two things.

First, it means passing the halfway mark in the amount of oil in either a particular field or in all the presently operating fields, after which there will never be as much oil as there was.

Second, it takes into account the reports of petroleum geologists who suggest that all potential new sources of oil:

1. are in fields located in places that are very or even prohibitively expensive to drill, in other words the oil's neither cheap nor easy to get
2. are in forms like tar sand that require the use of other limited resources like natural gas and water to extract and distribute
3. cannot be extracted without the likelihood of causing chronic environmental disruption or catastrophic long-term destruction of natural and human communities
4. require more oil energy to extract than the amount of oil energy they will deliver
5. tend to hit their peak and go into decline much more rapidly than present and past fields
6. will provide at best only a few years' worth of the oil the global economy requires.

Passing peak also means passing the point where we can expect new reserves of oil to make up for the ones we've lost and are losing. After we pass peak, all oil is tough oil.

As investigative journalist Michael Ruppert comments in his book and documentary *Confronting Collapse*, "The rush to drill off America's coasts is a rush to find small swimming pools, hot tubs and even bathtubs of oil. It may be necessary to do that but not with the expectation of a return to lower prices and the same consumption patterns of years gone by."[1]

The Deepwater Horizon oil rig in the western Gulf of Mexico, the tar sands fields of central Canada and the warships of several nations that are staging mock battles and preparing to defend territorial boundaries around the perimeter of the Arctic Ocean are indicators of our already

> "Just as the human body adapts itself to the regular intake of 'hard' drugs, its systems coming to depend on them to such an extent that the user goes through a period of acute distress if they are suddenly withdrawn, so the use of 'hard' fossil energy alters the economic metabolism and is so highly addictive that in a crisis a user-community or country will be prepared to export almost any portion of its annual income to buy its regular fix."[2]

having passed the point of finding additional affordable, environmentally safe new reserves. The pipes and drills of the sunken Deepwater Horizon oil rig go down expensively, dangerously and, as it happened, disastrously through nearly a mile of water and several formerly species-rich marine ecosystems to a total depth of over three miles. The tar sands operations are causing a series of interrelated crises. They are:

- devastating thousands of square miles of Canadian prairie and First Nations' lands
- consuming millions of gallons of freshwater
- sidelining natural gas that would otherwise be put directly to use by Canadians and Alaskans
- creating a widening political divide in the US on one side of which stand those for whom jobs and monetarily cheap oil are the priorities while on the other those like Bill McKibben and James Hansen, for whom the priorities are climate change mitigation and ecosystem maintenance, gather in fierce protest

And on the continental shelf that rings the Arctic and in deep sea fields under the Arctic Sea lie fields of oil and natural gas to which Canada, the US, Russia, Denmark and Norway are all laying claims that China, Japan and the European Union hope to deny.

None of these represent a practical or sustainable solution to the problem of peak oil.

### Peak, Plateau, Precipice, Depletion

These terms refer to stages of decline in the supply of oil. The first period after peak and before depletion, which is the still distant point at which we will have run out of retrievable oil, is called the *plateau*. Given technological, financial and geological uncertainties, which vary from field to field, there's almost no way to be sure how far into the future a single field or the sum of the world's fields can carry us.

> "There is a growing insufficiency [of oil] and it's going to undermine civilization as we know it. Not tomorrow, not in the next year or two, but in the next five to ten years."[3]

Some experts say we may have 20 years of plateau. Some say we may have the rest of this century to squeeze, wring, dig and suck out what's left in the ground. That is if we can afford to commit oil we already have to getting oil we still want, and to make the necessary investments of money, military engagement and freshwater. Increasing numbers of analysts, including many of those who work for major oil companies, estimate that we could arrive at the *precipice*, the point at which available supplies of oil fall off faster than we or our economies can adapt to, in as few as ten years.

## When Is Peak?

Estimates of the date we did hit or will hit peak oil range from 2005 to 2044.[4] Since estimates are scientifically informed best guesses, certainty is out of the question. Uncertainty is amplified by the general unwillingness of oil companies to accurately report, to the extent they know, what's left in their fields. We won't be entirely sure that we've hit peak in worldwide production and potential viable new reserves until we've passed it and are suffering the consequences of not ever again being able to get as much as we need to preserve our accustomed lifestyle and economic growth.

Arguably we are already suffering the consequences, given that Deepwater Horizon, the Canadian tar sands and the pending seizure of the Arctic by rim nations are not the only indicators of mounting desperation and competition. Plans proceed apace to drill ultra-deepwater oil and gas wells "off the coasts of Ghana and Nigeria, the sulfur-laden depths of the Black Sea, and the tar sands of Venezuela's Orinoco [River] Basin." *Newsweek* journalist Mac Margolis explained why we would tempt fate to deliver us more spills, murdered landscapes and disasters.

"Blistering growth in emerging nations has turned the power grid upside down. India and China will consume 28 percent of global energy by 2030 [the US already consumes 25 percent of what's available], triple the juice they required in 1990. China is set to overtake the US in energy consumption by 2014.... The International Energy Agency reckons the world will need 65 million additional barrels a day in 2030."5 Production had already fallen behind demand by several million barrels in 2007. Given how long it will take to prepare to function with little or no oil, the 40-year difference between the 2005 and 2044 predictions isn't significant anyway.

Among the known peak oil facts are these: US oil fields peaked around 1970. The US now produces only one third of its own oil, and most of that is in the endangered Gulf of Mexico coastal and deepwater fields. It imports the majority of its oil from Canadian tar sand operators. The rest has to come from the conflict-riddled nations in the Middle East, Africa, Central Asia and the Caspian Sea region, hardly easy territories in which to do business. Britain's North Sea fields peaked in the early 2000s, China's biggest fields have peaked, Saudi Arabia's fields are at or approaching peak and several former oil exporters, like Indonesia, are now importers. Hoping for 2044 is really optimistic.

If we put all the estimates and compilations of data and petroleum geologists' charts and peak oil experts' predictions together, we end up more realistically with peak oil occurring somewhere between 2007 and 2013. Most major oil company executives don't argue with the latter of these two dates.

2007. 2013. Peak oil is either here or just around the corner. And hopes that natural gas and/or coal are substitutes are understandable but misguided. These, too, are *fossil* fuels; that is, finite. What at present seems to be an abundance of shale gas — in the US, for example — is the result of the infamous extreme-retrieval technique, *fracking*, that offers a quick but very short term supply fix. In January 2012, the US Geological Survey trimmed its estimates of the amount of available gas in the country's largest natural gas field, the Marcellus, by 66%, concluding that at present rates of drilling the US could plan on 6 rather than 17 years of supply. And neither natural gas nor coal is a conveniently gasoline-like liquid.6

## A Sea of Red Herrings

There will be red herrings — events that camouflage the peak by causing temporary shortages and/or price increases. They will allow us to imagine there is no pending or passed peak and to believe for a while that, since prices will come down again at least part way, we can return to business as usual, just as people with AIDS believe during the latent period in their disease that they're just as healthy as they always were.

Among the red herrings that may confuse us and distract us from the harsh reality of running out of what our economy runs on will be:

- producers playing with prices or withholding or refusing to increase supply, which will automatically cause prices to rise
- refineries under repair or unable to keep up with demand
- violent storms, equipment failures, acts of sabotage or incompetence that damage or destroy petroleum infrastructure
- investors buying oil futures and engaging in related forms of speculation
- oil companies getting richer while they can and gas station owners behaving unscrupulously
- competition arising from new automobile markets and expanded manufacturing in Asia and India, putting pressure on demand and, therefore, on prices
- governments imposing increased gas taxes

But the ultimate cause of rising prices and increasing shortages — hitting peak oil — won't make the front pages. It's too difficult a pill to swallow, too bitter a medicine for elected officials in oil-consuming nations to force their people to swallow. And the range of red herrings will seem to make peak oil nay-sayers' case: Prices wouldn't drop again if we had hit peak oil already, would they? (The willingness of merchants to sell their inventories at rock bottom prices in order to corner and keep the market, so long as there is one, puts the lie to that logic.)

But the salient points are that, despite denial and wishful thinking:

1) on this finite planet there is a finite amount of oil

2) indications are strong that we're getting to the portions of that oil that are difficult, expensive and dangerous to extract

3) after we pass peak in all the Earth's fields there is a plateau beyond which the available oil will not keep up with our demand for it, and we will be less and less able to pay for it

The global economic system, which is abjectly dependent on cheap, abundant oil is beginning to go hungry. In its efforts to get every last affordable, though less energizing drop, it will put at risk natural and human communities, destroying some with abandon, weakening and destabilizing others and dramatically altering the climate to which all living things are accustomed. And the prevailing economic system will exercise itself mightily to find alternatives that will keep it going and growing, wearing itself out and pushing us toward peaks in natural gas and high quality coal in the process.

"The general picture is inescapable," wrote peak oil expert Richard Heinberg. "We are today living at the end of the period of the greatest material abundance in human history — an abundance based on temporary sources of cheap energy that made all else possible. Now that the most important of those sources are entering their inevitable sunset phase, we are at the beginning of a period of overall societal contraction,"[8] not unlike that which the AIDS-assailed human body experiences when it enters upon wasting disease.

"This much is certain: no initiative put in place starting today can have a substantial effect on the peak production year. No Caspian Sea exploration, no drilling in the South China Sea, no SUV replacements, no renewable energy projects can be brought on at a sufficient rate ..."[7]

## Peak Oil as an Economic Wasting Disease

The global economy runs on oil and its fossil fuel relatives, coal and natural gas. Oil is the economy's primary food. When oil is combined with raw materials and labor to support a manufacturing process it is even called a *feedstock*. Oil is not energy, but like food in a healthy body, it produces energy. It does the global economy's heavy lifting and moving the way muscles do ours. Many kinds of economies can run on non-petroleum energy sources. The global economy in its current form and the national economies that participate in it cannot.

Many of the goods the global economy produces are also *made* of oil and its derivatives in much the same way that our bodies are constructed out of the elements in ours (and our mothers') food. Petroleum-based synthetics, plastics, pharmaceuticals and composites have replaced or enhanced many natural resources like wood, metals, plant fibers, rubber and plant medicinals with which we used to make the items that furnish our lives, transport, clothe, heal and house us. Our well-oiled economy helped us deplete Earth's abundant supplies of those natural resources. Consequently we cannot rely on them to stand in for oil when we have run through our once-abundant supply of it, too.

When people with AIDS don't take in enough food or their bodies don't process it well, they begin to waste, emaciate and weaken. *AIDS wasting* is defined as the loss of more than 10% of body weight along with more than 30 days of diarrhea, weakness and fever. Wasting victims lose fat first and then muscle or lean body mass. Lost muscle contributes to lost stamina, activity and vitality. AIDS patients' bodies convert protein into high levels of sugars and fats that burn quickly, deploying heat around the body in an effort to destroy infection. Several factors contribute to AIDS wasting disease, chief among them low food intake, poor nutrient absorption and altered metabolism. Each of these factors has its peak oil correlate.

In wasting terms, the global economy stands to lose a whole lot more than just 10% of its weight if it runs out of affordable oil. There are no other energy "foods" that will do all that oil has done as cheaply and conveniently as oil has done it, and none that will appease the economy's appetite or keep it fit. It will lose fat first, in the form of luxuries, wealth, amenities, growth and savings. But it will also lose muscle. The economy's capacity to do the necessary work — food production, construction, and manufacturing, for example — and to provide customary mobility for goods and people will decline radically as we move further out onto the plateau and closer to the precipice. The economy's metabolism — its literal high energy — will slow to a crawl. In an effort to keep itself heated up, it may burn quickly and for less than vital purposes the oil that might be used over time to maintain a modicum of life quality for future generations. The way the economy abuses and wastes oil and derivatives is similar to the way nausea and chronic diarrhea abuse and waste the nutrition and calories in an AIDS patient's food.

This global economic correlate of gastrointestinal dysfunction will contribute to both economic exhaustion and to the other most often cited cause of Critical Mass: a feverishly heated, occasionally chilled, malfunctioning and potentially collapsing climate.

## Climate Instability = Earth's Respiratory Disease

While peak oil is still not a common subject for the mass media, best selling books, talk shows, late night comedy or public dispute, climate change is. In the limited space available here, I cannot hope to sway climate change deniers. (I admit to siding with the believers.)

Simple explanations are not possible because there are no straight lines in the operations of complex living systems. Where climate is concerned, causes and effects are subject to the snarling, doubling back, mutual reinforcement, amplification and multiplication that are characteristic of all complex systems. We will hardly ever, if ever, be able to say that human activity A caused weather event B or shift in climate pattern C. Because climate is a complex system that is part of and an expression of the complex living system of Earth, we will only be able to infer that A sets of activities have influenced or can logically be linked to B, C, and D sets of climate variations which have also through time both influenced and been influenced by L, M and Q sets of measurable and observable changes in weather and climate patterns.

However, doctors can infer or deduce that when a patient with umpteen other symptoms of the acquired immune deficiency syndrome begins to show signs of susceptibility to respiratory ailments, those ailments are likely to be related to the same condition that's causing the other symptoms. They are not surprised when *Pneumocystis jiroveci* pneumonia presents itself, and they can be reasonably certain AIDS is its cause. Similarly, when so many things are going wrong everywhere at once in the world, it should come as no surprise that those "so many things" might include the climate, which is part of the system those things influence. The interaction of Life with the Earth's weather is as old as Life on Earth. Changes in the way Life works have always changed the weather and vice versa.

The results of burning fossil fuels and living large will not be limited to global warming alone because the climate does not shift, even when the causes are entirely natural, from one state to another everywhere at the same time. The Earth's climate is a complex system made of complex subsystems, each of which will go through its phase changes in its own way and sequence. There may be spells of cooling on the way to the predicted Hot Times ahead, or protracted warming may lead to the

> "Global warming is not equivalent to climate change. Significant, societally important climate change, due to both natural and human climate forcings, can occur without any global warming or cooling."[9]

collapse of the North Atlantic conveyor current and trigger another ice age. Meanwhile it will be cool or hot in places where it never used to be.

And what lies ahead will probably not be quite as simple as the name climate change suggests. Climate change implies a one-shot deal: a spell of chaos and then a return to stability. It allows us to imagine that the Earth will switch from climate A to climate B in some sort of time frame we can conceive of, and all that's really debatable is whether climate B will be better or worse for us than climate A. Once it's under way (which most close observers and even a number of climate warming deniers suggest that it already is) we cannot know how long the change process will last. Even if the climate hits a dreaded tipping point, due to natural or human causes or both, and becomes unrecognizable to us in a matter of years or decades, many generations will pass away before what it changes to has lasted long enough to feel familiar or be remotely predictable.

What it will feel like, what it already feels like, is unpredictable — unstable.

Here as in so many aspects of its process and progress, Earth's immune system illness bears a disheartening resemblance to the human version. Respiratory disease, the most frequently identified immediate cause of death from AIDS, names a wide range of systemic conditions. It allows for transitions from one condition to another and between stages within a condition, for example, from the common cold to bronchitis to pneumonia.

Because it also names a wide range of systemic conditions, I suggest that *climate instability* may be the most serviceable name for what's going on with the Earth in terms of weather at the local, regional and global levels. It names and embraces the full range of climate experiences that complex systems logic dictates may lie ahead of us. Or be upon us. 2010 may have been the climate's tipping point.

## A Tale of Two Respiratory Systems

The *human respiratory* system — comprised of closely interacting parts like the nasal cavity, lungs, diaphragm, trachea and alveoli — works in tandem with the circulatory system as a gas and moisture exchange system. In essence the lungs gather energy-producing oxygen from inhaled air and deliver it to a dense network of outgoing capillaries that distribute the oxygen throughout the body. At the same time a branching network of incoming capillaries delivers carbon dioxide ($CO_2$), a toxic waste gas that is collected in the blood, to the lungs to be exhaled. Oxygen in, $CO_2$ out; energy in, poison out. Breathing keeps the amount of the two gases in a range the body can handle. It also maintains the body's acid/alkaline balance (excess $CO_2$ acidifies the blood) and filters the air.

Respiratory illnesses — like AIDS-related pneumonia and tuberculosis — throw the respiratory system out of whack. The gas exchange process breaks down, the blood and body are starved of oxygen and $CO_2$ accumulates in the blood causing it to become excessively acidic. Oxygen starvation and $CO_2$ poisoning are symptom multipliers. Gradually, every part of the body is affected to the extent that multiple organ failure can occur.

The *Earth's respiratory system* is a gas and moisture exchange system, too. It is comprised of closely interacting participants, including:

- photosynthesizers — like forests, grasslands, mats or islands of seaweed and algae, oceanic "clouds" of phytoplankton and some bacteria — that inhale $CO_2$ and exhale oxygen
- their animal counterparts that inhale oxygen and exhale $CO_2$
- glaciers, oceans and other bodies of water that supply moisture (the Earth's circulatory equivalent of blood) to the system or withhold it
- land masses, the system's physical infrastructure, which perform services including $CO_2$ and methane sequestration, heat and water storage and distribution, wind and shade management

When its constituent parts are functioning properly and in harmony with each other, Earth's respiratory system successfully manages the

"Human institutions and planetary systems operate on very different time schedules. Large planetary systems, with huge amounts of inertia, maintain their equilibrium for centuries, frequently for millennia. But when they do begin to move toward a new state, their momentum may be unstoppable until they settle into a new equilibrium — one that will probably make conditions on the planet far less hospitable to organized civilization."[10]

atmosphere's accounts of gases and moisture, helps to regulate Earth's temperature, maintains the planet's acid/alkaline ratio, filters particulates from the air and pumps currents of air and water reliably around the Earth the way the human diaphragm pumps air and moisture reliably in and out of the lungs.

When something destabilizes the Earth's respiratory system, the world's weather — its climate — becomes unstable. For as long as the system is out of whack due to natural or human-induced causes, weather crises multiply and mutually reinforce each other in ways that are unpredictable. Oxygen, $CO_2$ and other atmospheric gases may go out of balance. Moisture congests in some places and is denied to others. Acidification and pollution increase. Wind and circulation patterns shift. Wind and ocean current speeds increase or decrease, or both, in different places. Temperatures and the amount of weather-making energy in the atmosphere fluctuate.

These and other symptoms of climate instability affect every part of the Earth, though not all in the same way, to the extent that existing natural and human communities — Earth's immune system — may cease to function in ways we think of as normal, or at all. For a very long time. If we add to this pathology our relentless push toward peak oil and growth economies, then planetary immune system compromise is guaranteed.

## Empirical and Anecdotal Evidence for Climate Instability

Climate instability and global warming doubters often use as support for their arguments statistics regarding single events or phenomena, like a year's thickening of a portion of Arctic or Antarctic ice or the reduced rate of melting of one glacier, and trends that parallel and amplify but do not cancel out or contradict trends that indicate instability.

But the Geneva-based World Meteorological Organization offered mounting evidence in several 2010 reports and studies that we may be at a tipping point with the Earth's climate. Among the early 21st century symptoms of instability are:

- severe and protracted droughts in typically wet places as well as typically dry ones that are shrinking reservoirs and drying lake beds
- National Oceanic and Atmospheric Administration (NOAA) reported the hottest 12-month stretch on record — April 2011 to April 2012 (First quarter of 2012 broke the record for high temperatures by 1.4 degrees Fahrenheit. Typically NOAA records are broken by only one- or two-tenths of a degree.)
- deluges that call to mind the Biblical Noah's famous flood
- severe wind, sand, dust and fire storms
- deserts burying small cities
- US Department of Agriculture officially moved plant hardiness zones in the US northward in 2011, reflecting consistently warmer temperatures in every zone since 1990
- plant and tree species migrating northward, following increasing warmth or moving to higher elevations where temperatures are cooler to escape heat
- warmth-loving fish species, marine mammals, insects, disease-causing pathogens and animals spreading northward
- destructive storm systems that follow on one another's heels and occur in places they had not
- killer summers so hot that many children, elderly and infirm people who do not have air conditioning die
- extreme cold in places unprepared for it
- snow storms and blizzards in low latitudes unused to them
- dramatic day-to-day changes in local temperatures
- unpredictable start and finish dates for seasons
- ocean acidification that kills larval fish and inhibits the formation of corals and of shells on crustaceans like crabs, oysters, clams and tiny

calcareous plankton, one of the primary sources of food for marine
mammals and fish

- methane belches and sink holes in millions of acres of melting tundra
and taiga
- die-off of northern evergreen tree species and Indonesian corals
- glaciers reduced by more than 50% in the past half century and con-
comitant reduced spring meltwater to fill rivers and reservoirs
- summer temperatures inside the Arctic Circle 5°F warmer than in the
1970s, winter temps even warmer
- Antarctic ice shelves calving icebergs the size of small countries
- surface water temperatures in the North Atlantic remaining unusually
high through the autumn months[11]

## Natural Causes

Obviously the climate can create this sort of pandemonium without
any help from us. The world's weather changes in the natural course of
things. Ice ages come and go on a fairly predictable schedule: 100,000
years of extreme cold and drought are typically followed by around
10,000 years of warm and wet, punctuated with decades or centuries
of relative cold. The last ice age ended around 11,000 years ago, which
suggests we ought to be heading into another ice age about now. And we
might be if something weren't postponing its onset.

A number of natural factors have in the past contributed to the kind
of climate instability we're experiencing now:

1) the Earth's tilt and position relative to the sun

2) sunspots and solar flares

3) continental drift

4) asteroid collisions

5) massive volcanic eruptions that cloud the Earth for years

6) dramatic changes in the location of the polar jet stream, frontal
boundary air pressure gradients and the rising and sinking or relocation of ocean currents

7) systemic feedback loops among these natural and cosmic forces

Several of these natural causes may contribute to climate instability at the same time, the same way that several mutually reinforcing physical conditions can contribute to AIDS respiratory distress at the same time. With the exception of eruptions and planetary collisions with large objects, these events cause gradual changes in the world's weather, until or unless they hit a tipping point.

### What Humans Have Got to Do with It

We have nothing to do with the first five of these causes of climate instability, and there's nothing we can do to prevent or manage them. We may have a lot to do with the sixth. And any one or a combination of them can lead to the seventh, which would effectively shut down Earth's present respiratory system, the natural communities that have maintained it and natural and human communities that depend on it. Though many climate scientists' voices are becoming more shrill as they attempt to convey to a largely indifferent human species sooner-than-expected changes in the world's weather, the complete collapse of our present climate is probably not imminent. But the degree of our widespread ignorance about how climate works, how complex a system it is and how intertwined it is with every other human, other-than-human and living system on Earth would make it hard to know if we were there.

Whether or not most humans agree that human activity jump-started the present episode of instability, human activity is making it worse. We've added our activities, requirements and demands and the huge numbers there are of us into the mix of complex feedback loops. We are thwarting the natural course of things on Earth the way AIDS thwarts the natural course of things in a healthy human body.

Our ways of living, producing and consuming aggravate the Earth's meteorological systems the way smoking, taking street drugs, eating junk food or having the misfortune to live in a slum or poor village in Sub-Saharan Africa aggravates AIDS-related pneumonia.

How?

1) Our reliance on combusted fossil fuels and our large scale agricultural and livestock raising practices are altering the mix of gases and amount of humidity in the atmosphere and increasing the acidity

of the oceans. In particular we are loading the atmosphere with greenhouse gases like $CO_2$ to levels unprecedented in the past three million years (31.6 gigatonnes in 2011, 3 times the 1990 release).

2) We are adding pollutants, toxins, aerosols, dust, soot and other particulates to the atmosphere which alters regional amounts and patterns of precipitation, alters atmospheric chemistry, increases the toxicity and acidity of both rain and snow and influences cloud formation and movement.

3) We are removing natural systems like forests, wetlands and prairies that maintain climate stability and minimize the intensity of weather systems.

4) We are dominating Earth's land mass, using it in ways that amplify changes in atmospheric gases and moisture and dramatically alter local and regional temperatures, wind speed and direction. For example, large cities and sprawling suburbs create their own local climates, such as heat islands, by concentrating heat produced by engines, machines and utilities and using heat-retaining materials like tar and concrete. Industrial scale agricultural practices — intensive irrigation, monoculture (single-crop farming) and soil fallowing (leaving fields bare), for example — disrupt local and regional weather which influences overall climate patterns.

5) We're doing these things unnaturally fast without understanding their consequences or interactions with each other and with natural systems. To the degree we are even attempting to minimize our impact on the climate, we are concentrating almost entirely on just one of these human forms of climate impact: $CO_2$ reduction.

It is reasonable to believe — as those do who say the climate is not destabilized and if it is we are not the cause of the destabilization — that only *intense, prolonged, widespread* changes in the way Earth's complex living systems work could actually have a major impact on a system as vast and powerful as the whole planet's climate. I agree. And I add that burning long-sequestered fuels that are poisonous to living things and accumulate in the atmosphere, and living ever larger as the dominant species for over two centuries qualifies as *intense, prolonged and widespread.*

But is the influence human activity is having on the world's weather the fundamental cause of Critical Mass? Or is peak oil the cause? Or is one of the other suggested factors the actual cause of our present mega-crisis? Until we know that we can't get past it.

## So, What's Causing Critical Mass?

A syndrome is a complex system of symptoms that share a common cause. The only way to effectively treat a syndrome and all of its symptoms is to discover and treat that common cause. The common or root cause of a syndrome is the force or agent that explains the vulnerability of *all* of its victims to *all* of its symptoms.

In the case of Critical Mass, none of the commonly proffered agents nor any combination of them meets that criteria. Each of them contributes to the severity of Critical Mass and explains some of its symptoms. None accounts for it. Peak oil and climate instability are present and future phenomena. But Critical Mass has been in its latent, strength-gathering stage for decades.

I propose that peak oil and climate instability, along with the other factors listed at the beginning of this chapter and the grim litany at the beginning of Part I, are also symptoms of Critical Mass, not its root cause. That's why tackling them, to the extent we have, has not mitigated or cured us of Critical Mass.

So what *is* the root cause of the Critical Mass of environmental, economic, social and political crises we face today? What's the Critical Mass equivalent of HIV?

The way we live, produce and consume is challenging the way the Earth's natural communities work, compromising their ability to function as the planet's immune system. The way a people live, produce and consume is determined by the kind of economy they live in.

We live, produce and consume now under the influence of a global capitalist industrial economy. That economy is the root cause of what's going wrong everywhere at once.

### The global economy has gone viral.
### It is Earth's equivalent of HIV.

With this premise in mind we can now complete our answer to the question "Why is so much going wrong everywhere at once?"

We are living beyond Earth's means, inducing Critical Mass, a syndrome of crises that is undermining Earth's immune system of natural and human communities. The economy has gone viral and is behaving as if it were larger than Life. It's not. Life is the largest complex system — the largest economy — on Earth. Life rules, we don't.

None of the other proposed causes of Critical Mass accounts for all of the symptoms of Critical Mass as simply and decisively as HIV does for AIDS. Only the viral global economy does. Let's look again at that list of conventionally suggested causes from earlier in this chapter and see why they are not the root cause of Critical Mass:

> *Human populations* have grown exponentially in sync with a globalizing economy that promised, and for a while was able, to support them. No booming economy, no population boom.
>
> *Technology,* which was widely believed to be capable of bailing us out of whatever trouble we got ourselves into, has been funded by and put in service to the global economic activities that are causing and amplifying our present troubles.
>
> *Unregulated capitalism,* the globally dominant economic ideology, could only expand its influence and monetary assets to the ends of the Earth if there were an economic system powerful and universal enough to support and promote it.
>
> *Fossil fuels* could only be mined, processed and distributed around the world and the various kinds of damage they caused be hidden or their effects postponed by a well-coordinated globalized economy.
>
> *Peak oil, gas and coal* are a pending challenge precisely because the gluttonous, fossil fuel dependent global economy demands ever-increasing amounts of them to support its growth.
>
> *Hyper-urbanization* has only been possible because jobs the global economy rewards with any kind of pay at all can only be had in or on the industrial edges of cities where

the financial, physical and service resources people need are concentrated.

*Industrialization* on the scale in which we have engaged in it depends on the five previous conditions and on economic coordination, integration, standardization and management at the global level.

*The rise of China* to superpower status has depended on the continued expansion and growth of a global economy that has provided a world of resources and materials to its manufacturing sector, a world of desperate nations to rent additional land from, and a world of markets for its cheap products. No global economy, no Chinese miracle.

*Climate destabilization* is influenced by all of the above forces and is therefore attributable to the global economic system on which they depend.

The viral global economy is a human creation. This means that it is our actions, activities and appetites that are causing global Critical Mass. The members of a transnational elite whose power is unprecedented in history are the prime movers, shapers and primary beneficiaries of this pathological economy.

"Working only within the system will, in the end, not succeed when what is needed is transformative change of the system itself."[12]

But willingly or unwillingly, all of us are now complicit in its perpetuation. And what *this* means is that, like people infected with HIV, we cannot mitigate, recover from or prevent the recurrence of this Life-threatening planetary syndrome until we change our behaviors, particularly our relationships with the global economy and its managing elite.

The protocol for curing Critical Mass cannot be doing more of what caused it. That's a hard reality to swallow, but the central truth of syndromes is that the only way to mitigate or cure one is to disempower the thing that caused it. Before critical masses of us can disempower the economy within which we all live and from which many of us have and many more of us still hope to benefit, we must understand how it caused this planet-wide disease syndrome.

## HIV and the Viral Global Economy: Powerful Similarities

HIV is a package of genetic information, an RNA code for a particular type of virus.

**The global economy is a package of socio-economic information, a set of ideas about a particular type of economic system.**

HIV is held together by a protein wrapper that works like the coating on a pill to camouflage the virus, making it "taste better," or at least not taste bad, to the human bodies it aims to infect so that they don't reject it on first pass.

**A capitalist ideology of perpetual growth and progress and universal prosperity is the sugar coating that makes the viral global economy taste good and camouflages its intent. This ideology is an easy sell to communities and nations comparatively lacking in material well-being.**

Though it has some of the characteristics of living things, HIV cannot exist on its own. It's a parasite, a taker. It lives off its hosts' resources. In the process it weakens and sometimes kills them.

**Without human workers, consumers and believers, without Earth's raw materials, other-than-human species and ecological services, the global economy cannot exist, feed itself, expand or grow. It's a parasite — a taker — too.**

As a group, disease-causing agents like viruses have a name: they are called *pathogens.*

**As a group, the directors, managers, promoters and primary beneficiaries of the disease-causing global economy have a name: they are called *the Powers That Be,* or simply *the Powers.***

The secret of a virus's success is mobility. Viruses need reliable methods of transportation to move them from host to host. Many viruses are airborne. HIV is liquid-borne. It gets around in bodily fluids like semen, blood and breast milk and through contact between mucous-lined (moist) tissues.

**The global economy also relies on mobility. It spreads from community to community, nation to nation by means of liquid assets and fluid exchanges of money, credit, loans, "floats," entitlements, tax breaks and incentives and**

**through money-lined contacts between its participants, particularly the Powers.**

HIV targets, takes over and dominates the immune system which, when it is functioning properly, protects, defends and heals the body. By means of this domination of the immune system HIV dominates the whole body.

**The viral global economy targets, takes over and dominates the Earth's equivalent of an immune system — the natural and human communities that in the past have been able to protect, defend and heal themselves, their ecosystems and the biosphere. With this takeover of Earth's immune system, the global economy dominates the body of Life on Earth, the biosphere.**

HIV invades immune system cells, disables their protective and healing capabilities and reprograms them to make millions of copies of itself. After it has used up a cell's resources, its copies disperse to other parts of the body and other hosts. Captured cells and whole organ systems are destroyed in the process.

**The global economy persuades, buys, cajoles, coerces and invades human and natural communities. It undermines their ability to provide for and protect themselves and reprograms them to support its growth and expansion instead. When it has depleted local resources, it moves on, leaving communities and nations in ruins.**

The human immunodeficiency virus makes the body vulnerable to all manner of infection and disease.

**The viral global economy makes every place on Earth vulnerable to the environmental, economic, social and political symptoms that result from inducing global Critical Mass.**

LK p.59

Untitled

Thomas Piketty: Capitalism in Its Current Form Undermines Democracy
Wednesday, 28 May 2014 09:44 By Thomas Piketty, Harvard University Press
The distribution of wealth is one of today's most widely discussed and
controversial issues and its evolution over the long term data covering three
centuries and more than twenty countries [shows that] when the rate of return on
capital exceeds the rate of growth of output and income ... capitalism
automatically generates arbitrary and unsustainable inequalities that radically
undermine the meritocratic values on which democratic societies are based.
http://truth-out.org/progressivepicks/item/23976-thomas-piketty-capitalism-in-its-c
urrent-form-undermines-democracy
Thomas Piketty: "Capital in the 21st Century"
Sunday, May 25, 2014 |
http://www.cbc.ca/thesundayedition/shows/

# CHAPTER 4

# What's Wrong with a Global Economy?

I F LIFE COULD BE SAID TO HAVE A PRIMARY RULE OR PRIME DIRECTIVE, it would be this:

## Live within Earth's means.

Though we have grown confident in our ability to live beyond any limits Earth may impose, this directive to live within Earth's means is logical — or more to the point, it is ecological — and absolute. Live beyond Earth's means long enough and in due course you will run out of what you need to live and you *will* destroy the other-than-human species and natural communities on which you actually depend for your life.

How has Life met the requirements of its prime directive? Solutions to problems like finiteness, meteorite collisions, climate instability and other natural causes of global Critical Mass have emerged when the most adaptable living things in every ecosystem have found ways to cope with them. Once Life strikes on a particularly successful solution — a form or format, pattern of behavior or coping mechanism (like immune systems which arose in primitive form in insects perhaps 500 million years ago) — it keeps that solution in its repertoire of survival techniques. Many of the most successful of those survival techniques are more than

"A bad solution acts within the larger pattern the way a disease ... acts in the body. A good solution acts with the larger pattern the way a healthy organ acts within the body."[1]

two billion years old. Humans, by contrast, go back only two and a half million years; humans that were physically like us only 40,000 years. We could still reasonably be said to be a species on trial. Life can do without us.

Life's exhaustively tested survival techniques represent a sort of protocol, a set of widely adaptable rules that guide the behaviors and relationships of all living things so that sufficient numbers of sufficiently diverse species can live well, but also well within Earth's means.

When we talk about living within our means — a habit many of us have failed to learn — we're talking about economics. Since Life's aim is to live within Earth's means, Life's survival protocol can be understood as an economic protocol. *Earth's* means — the quantity and kinds of resources Earth has and makes available or holds in its planetary accounts — determine how and how well living things can live. So Life's survival protocol can be even better understood as an Earthonomic survival protocol. The rules that comprise it are rules for surviving ecologically in an Earth-based economy. Or, since "ecological" has lost a lot of its punch, having been co-opted to describe and market activities and

Other-than-human species provide for themselves and each other in ways that are truly sustainable and relatively equitable, and they organize themselves and relate to each other in ways that are organically democratic, or biocratic.[2]

products that are not in the least ecological, perhaps I should say the rules that comprise Life's survival protocol are rules for surviving and even thriving *Earthologically* on this finite planet by living, as other-than-human species do, within Earth's means. Those rules, the basic elements of Life's Economic Survival Protocol, are the subject of Part II. For our purposes in Part I, this short version will do:

The species that last for a long time are the ones that obey these rules. Successful species tinker with the rules, revise and even bend them creatively, testing Life's limits in order to expand their own options. But they do not break the rules. Why? Because the penalties for breaking Life's rules are harsh. Extinction is one of them.

We stand alone as a species determined to break those rules. We have succeeded over the past 6,000 years — since the adoption of large scale agriculture and the establishment of the first walled cities, warring empires and civilizations — in creating an economic system that does not mimic Life's sustaining behaviors but instead mimics the behaviors of one of Earth's most virulent diseases. Life rules. We don't.

How the viral global economy breaks Life's rules and has pushed us to Critical Mass is the subject of the rest of this chapter.

Forgetting that Life does indeed rule has led us into four categories of error.

## 1. We Do Not Provide for Ourselves.

For the first time in human history, the majority of us do not provide for ourselves. The economy provides for us. Under the influence of this economy, we use money — or more often its funny-money equivalents like credit and debit cards, bank and home equity loans, quick cash and collateral in the form, for example, of real estate, stocks and bonds — to acquire the things we need and, if we're lucky, the things we want. But we do not actually supply ourselves with many or any of those items which used to be called *provisions*. Nor do we provide ourselves with most of the services that sustain us. And more seriously, we don't yet *plan* to provision ourselves or realize we may be required to. This is particularly ironic given that "provide" originates in Latin words that mean "to look forward," and by extension, "to plan for" and that we are, so far as we know, the only species that's capable of planning.

If we *don't* have the money to buy things — whether they are important, like adequate housing, food, clothing, transportation and health care, or merely pleasing, like toys, entertainment, vacations

"Mother Nature doesn't care about poetry or art or whether you go to church. You can't negotiate with her, and you can't spin her and you can't evade her rules. All you can do is fit in as a species. And when a species doesn't learn to fit in with Mother Nature, it gets kicked out. Every day you look in the mirror now, you're seeing an endangered species."[3]

and jewelry — the global economy doesn't provide us with them either. Making sure that all or most of us are well or at least sufficiently provided for now and in the future is not the global economy's aim any more than providing well for the body it preys on is HIV's aim. Their own survival and perpetual expansion are ambitions that the viral global economy and HIV share.

Most of us have little or no control over the manner in which or the degree to which the global economy provides for us. We are not self-reliant in that regard either. We are dependents. Most of us who live in prosperous nations have become as innocently dependent on the willingness and ability of the economy to provide for us as small children are dependent on the willingness and ability of their parents to provide for them. Like children, we have persisted in trusting the economy even when it has repeatedly disappointed us or even physically and psychologically abused us. In this we are both innocent and naïve.

"The real casualties of economic collapse will not be the people who have modest needs and the ability to grow, make, cook, mend, discuss and think about the future. The real casualties will be those who depend entirely on the economic and political system for their 'needs', especially those who have high-consumption lifestyles."[4]

We are, or have been, workers, though many of us now just wish we were. We are and have been suppliants, asking and hoping for fair wages and benefits and financial assistance in bad times. We are, and are encouraged to be, consumers, to shop and spend without ceasing. Some of us are voters, and some even movers and shakers. But the majority of us are not self-providers.

This distinction should not be lost on us. Its implications are stark. If the global economy experiences serious, long-term instabilities, or if it declines or collapses entirely — which it is poised to do — *we will not be able* easily or any time soon to:

- feed, shelter, heat, cool, clothe or doctor ourselves
- get enough freshwater to the places where we need it
- provide any basic utilities or services

- maintain our global digital and information networks
- transport ourselves or anything else very far

As consumers rather than providers, most of us have very little idea where the things we consume come from, who actually provides them and who or what is harmed in the process. During the global economy's long latent period — especially since the end of World War II, seven decades during which the economy promised the best of all possible worlds to all people and seemed capable of delivering on its promise — some of us and other living things were harmed while others of us consumed extravagantly and obliviously. Now nearly all of us as well as most other living things are being harmed.

How? Not least by the fact that we have no control over the work we do and whether it provides us with what we need. Work and the amount of money we earn for it are dependent on the whim of the global economy. The global economy only pays for the work it wants done, when it has enough funny-money to pay for it and where that work can be done most profitably for the corporations, major stockholders and other organizations that hire it, or more specifically, for the directors and managers of those corporations and organizations.

Whether that work produces what we, our families and our communities need is not the global economy's concern. Whether that work protects or compromises the health of natural communities and living systems is not really its concern. Whether the jobs we do endure or pay a living wage (a wage sufficient to purchase what we no longer provide for ourselves) is not its concern. When the economy fails or ceases to provide work, living wages and provisions, providing them becomes the concern of governments, at least of well-intentioned ones. But even the most well-intentioned governments can do only as much for their people as the global economy, its businesses and corporations and the flow of money will allow.

Symptoms of having hit Critical Mass like foreclosures, double-digit, long-term unemployment, cancelled pensions, shrunken retirement and savings accounts, a destabilized European Economic Community, post-Katrina New Orleans, mounting desperation, suicides, revolutions, protests and violent, persistent uprisings are consequences of counting on a global economy to provide for us.

## 2. The Global Economy Does Not Provide for Us in a Way That Can Be Sustained Long-Term.

According to Life's rules, an activity or behavior can be considered sustainable when it can meet the needs of the present generation of humans and other living things without compromising the ability of future generations to meet their needs. This is logical as well as Earthological: A species cannot persist over the long term if one generation systematically and routinely spends down what the next generation needs to live on, let alone if several generations do this.

Nothing about the activities of the viral global economy is sustainable. If the global economy could be said to have a prime directive, it would be the opposite of sustainable:

### Live as far beyond Earth's means as you can, for as long as you can.

By the reckoning of many resource and environmental analysts, we exceeded Earth's means of sustaining this economy — we overshot Earth's *carrying capacity* — a couple decades ago. What is carrying capacity? Ecologists define it as the maximum number of a species or collection of species that an ecosystem or environment can support long-term without suffering damage in excess of what the system itself can repair.

Let's bring carrying capacity one step closer to home so that we don't miss the point: The weight of the heaviest pack that you can carry on your back without falling down is your personal carrying capacity. If you can shoulder 60 pounds without crumpling, you haven't exceeded your carrying capacity. If 61 pounds drops you to your knees, then anything that weighs more than 60 pounds exceeds your carrying capacity. In Earthological terms 60 pounds is your "maximum supportable load."

"The capitalist world-economy rests upon the ceaseless expansion of material production and consumption, which is fundamentally incompatible with the requirements of ecological sustainability. Depletion of material resources and pollution of the earth's ecological system have now risen to the point that the ecological system is on the verge of collapse and the future survival of humanity and human civilization is at stake."[5]

Anything more is unsustainable. In these terms, Earth's carrying capacity — its maximum supportable load and measure of sustainability — is the number of us and other living things it can support long-term without, in effect, being driven to its knees.

According to Nicole Achs Freeling of the Global Footprint Network, what that means in economic terms is that we've "moved into the ecological equivalent of annual deficit spending, utilizing resources faster than the planet can regenerate them in any calendar year."[6] In other words, as a species we're doing to the planet what we've done to our financial system: postponing inevitable decline and bankruptcy and persisting in the habit of living beyond our means by borrowing from the future, hiding in the falsehood that we can actually pay back what we've borrowed or that we even intend to. The parallel HIV delusion would be that an infected person could continue to engage in unprotected sex with other infected people and do street drugs with shared needles and not transition into full-blown, fatal AIDS.

The global economy does not factor Earth's carrying capacity into its reckonings any more than HIV factors in the limited ability of a human body to support it. Ironically the very funny-money that has of late supported the global economy has made it next to impossible for that economy to support us sustainably.

## What Does Funny-Money Have to Do with It?

We live now in what ecological economist Herman Daly calls a *paper economy*. This was not always the case.

Until the establishment of nautical and overland trading routes, exchanges of goods and services were really local and relatively simple forms of barter. Barter or swapping is the exchange of one commodity for another. It was the method of exchange for tens of thousands of years for prehistoric individuals, clans, tribes and villages. Commodity for commodity exchanges can be symbolized as *C-C*. They represent the first step on the journey, mapped in the sidebar, to a funny-money paper economy.

Barter was as ill-suited to history's first civilizations as coins and cash are to a global economy. Civilizations are

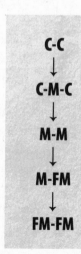

C-C
↓
C-M-C
↓
M-M
↓
M-FM
↓
FM-FM

expansive city-based societies for which the (unstated) economic goal is to produce more than people need so that a few people — the ones who run and manage the civilization — can have as much as they want. This allows them to hold onto the power to run and manage the civilization. Consequently civilizations have always required more stuff and more kinds of stuff than their territories can produce.

Complex, long distance, multi-party exchanges such as those that arose among early civilizations in the Middle East, and then between Southern Europe, the Middle East and Asia, required a more sophisticated system than barter. Coins came first, then legal tender, early equivalents of promissory notes and other units of exchange that could be agreed upon by all their users wherever they were. In other words, civilizations came up with money, a word that derives from *Moneta,* the name of a cult that worshipped the Roman goddess Juno in whose temple coins were minted.

Money changed everything. The money that was received as the price of sale of a commodity by Seller A could be used to purchase another commodity somewhere else from Seller B. The new economic arrangement was commodity for money for commodity: *C-M-C.* Commodities (resources or human-made products that had a definable value) were still involved. Money was merely another means of moving them around from places where they were to places where they were needed or wanted. In the famous Triangle Trade of the 17th and 18th centuries, for example, money greased the skids under shipments of slaves from Africa to the Americas; shipments of gold, sugar, tobacco, cotton, timber and rice from the Americas to Europe; and shipments of textiles and manufactured goods from Europe back to Africa.

For several thousand years money continued to be backed in this way by commodities, things as real as gold, silver, tobacco, sugar, copper, cattle, wheat, rice and human slaves. A hundred paper dollars or British pounds, for example, were actually backed up by what was commonly accepted to be a hundred dollars-worth or pounds-worth of gold, timber, slaves or whatever the chosen standard or agreed value in an exchange was. You couldn't have greater wealth in money than you had in, say, gold or cotton. Put another way, the supply of money was limited by the supply of real physical, material things. Paper money represented something real.

But it has been a long while since there were enough cattle, bars of gold or tons of rice or any other commodity to equal in value the many trillions of dollars, yuan, yen, pesos, pounds, rubles and euros floating around in the 21st century econosphere. The global economy's appetite for money exceeded decades ago both Earth's capacity to provide enough resources and its own capacity to produce enough real goods to satisfy that appetite. Money had to be reinvented. It had to be separated from real goods and resources so that the amount of it that was available for getting and spending would not be limited by the finiteness of Earthy things. Post-World War II negotiations at Bretton Woods initiated the process by pegging other currencies to the US dollar which was still pegged to gold. US President Richard Nixon completed the process in 1971. He unhooked the dollar from the gold standard when the costs of fighting the Vietnam War made it necessary to print more money than the US had gold to back it. The dollar, backed by nothing real, became the global standard.

And, voilà! Money in one form could be exchanged for money in other forms: *M-M*. Money became valued and was profitable for its own sake. However, as money has exceeded Earth's means to back it up, it has gotten progressively more virtual, phonier and funnier. Herman Daly and others call the money floating around in our paper economy quasi, faux or "as if" money.

Recently, categories of faux money, such as credit cards, credit-default swaps, algorithmic and flash trades, derivatives, hedges, collateralized debt obligations, structured investment vehicles and commodity futures have multiplied nearly as fast and as often as viruses into financial entities that look nearly as strange as viruses if you look at them closely. Take flash trading, for example. Insider Peter Green, a broker, trader, Founding Partner and CEO of the Kyte Group (talk about high finance) describes it this way: "Flash trading by definition is a form of high frequency trading. But the controversy about this particular type of trading (and this is peculiar to the US stock markets, and not all of the stock exchanges in the US) is where the exchanges effectively created a club of favored high frequency traders who were getting to see orders in a very short period of time — but still a period of time — before the rest of the market (who weren't members of that club) would get to see them. And because high frequency traders have algorithms that can make a thousand different decisions in a split second, by giving them even a fraction of a second to see an order before the rest of the market could see them, it gives them an unfair advantage. And so flash trading ... really got the goat of the politicians and the media in the States because this type of trading is not on a level playing field."[7] That's putting it mildly. Flash trading is funny-money moving at light speed.

But as we've been learning, painfully, none of these forms of funny-money stands for anything real. Funny-money is literally immaterial. The pattern of exchange now, completing our journey from barter to paper, is money for funny-money *(M-FM)* or even funny-money for other funny-money *(FM-FM)* with commodities *(C)* tossed into the equation occasionally and moved around according to who's got enough funny-money to purchase them.

Funny-money is backed, when it is backed by anything now, by other funny-money, by information about funny-money and by the idea and expectation of value, rather than the actual value of material goods, genuine provisions. It is, in other words, faith-based. In fact, faith or belief in the limitlessness of funny-money drove the boom that went bust in 2008 when faith ran up against reality. And declining faith in funny-money is presently challenging the faith some of us have in the global economy and its national subsidiaries.

Obviously one problem with funny-money is that it *isn't* limitless. We can't really afford for it to be. Why? The more of it there is, the less it's worth and the funnier it gets. As weakening national economies print more money and issue more credit in order to prop themselves

"Outsiders to the world of money who start to take an interest in it soon notice that most of the things that alarm and outrage the wider public are taken by insiders to be perfectly routine and unremarkable. Consider the sums that bankers get paid, or the disruptive impact of hot money zipping around the world at the click of a mouse, tearing up industries and whole economies at will. To moneymen, those are just givens of the way the world works, and have to be accepted, in the absence of a credible plan to go off to found a new system on another planet."[8]

up, money ceases to be worth much more than the paper it's printed on. In 2008, for example, Zimbabweans paid ten million of their dollars for a loaf of bread.[9] Money had completely broken faith with them.

But a bigger problem with funny-money is that, despite its insubstantiality, it comes between us and substantial things, the real goods, resources and ecosystem services that we actually need to live. Like a mirage — the shimmering lake we think we see ahead of us on the highway or out in the desert — funny-money prevents us from seeing what's really in front of us. Or isn't. "It is an abstraction," wrote Charles Eisenstein in *Sacred Economics*. "It exists in a realm far removed from materiality. In that realm it is exempt from nature's most important laws."[11] It prevents most of us from knowing or even realizing we need to know whether there are enough real goods, resources and healthy ecosystems left to support us. It prevents us from knowing or choosing to learn what we need to know to provide for ourselves in ways that are sustainable.

"Money now plays the central role in late industrial society that religion played in the late Middle Ages.... Today's army of accountants, bankers, tax-people, insurance and stock brokers, foreign exchange dealers and countless other specialists in money is the modern counterpart of the medieval army of priests, monks, nuns, abbots and abbesses ... and other specialists in religious procedures and practices."[10]

Funny-money allows us to feel independent of the people and to remain ignorant about the places and the other-than-human species that actually provide for us. It has, until now, allowed us to produce and distribute goods on a scale completely divorced from what Earth and Life can support. Much in the way that tools and machines make us feel stronger and faster than we really are, funny-money makes us feel more secure and self-reliant than we really are.

To be self-reliant is to be able to meet your basic needs yourself, not individually of course, but as part of a socio-economic group of some size, preferably of a not over-large size. Because funny-money *seems* to make us self-reliant (if we have enough of it we can buy what we need with it) we are considered in conventional economic theory to have personal economies. All the other individuals, families and institutional and corporate entities around the world that live by spending funny-money can be said to have their own economies, too. And most of us behave as if we do. We've lived for several millennia in money-based economies and a century or two in really funny-money ones. So we've gotten used to thinking that the basic units of economic activity are the individual, the family and the business or corporation, and that city, state and national economies are made up of lots of these personal, family and corporate economies. This way of thinking made it difficult for us to recognize how much was going wrong everywhere at once before it actually had gone wrong. Why?

We are about to discover, in what may come to be thought of as Phase II of our present global economic crisis, that all of those little, theoretically separate and independent funny-money economies and the funny-money national economies and global economy of which they are a part are *not* independent. They are completely dependent, not only on each other but also on the real goods, resources, other-than-human species, ecosystems and ecosystem services that only Life and Earth can provide.

If we exceed Earth's ability to provide these things — if, for example, the soils, crops, water, breathable air, marine nurseries, pollinators, major predators, forests or familiar weather give out — it doesn't matter how much funny-money we've got. But funny-money has made it easy for us to forget that. And our present desperate focus on getting more of it makes us continue to forget.

## Carrying Capacity, the Viral Economy and Reaching Critical Mass

We didn't realize until fairly recently that we could exceed Earth's carrying capacity. We didn't know until the 16th century that the Earth was round and that we couldn't sail on virtually forever finding more Earth beyond its ever-distant edge. But when the European explorers wound up back where they started without falling off the Earth, they reported ecstatically and also accurately that there was more than enough of everything on Earth to support everyone, to even spoil with luxuries — gold and silver, timber and tobacco, tea and coffee, spices, rum and furs, for example — the monarchs, banks and trading companies that funded their expeditions. "Vast" was the mantra of the Age of Exploration and "without limit" was its implication. But vast is a relative term — and on Earth, after all, there are limits. We're finally reaching them.

How did a species as intelligent as we're supposed to be let that happen? How did we miss the fact of finiteness? Our ability to invent tools and technologies of extraction and plunder got ahead of our understanding of how Life on Earth works. Every place on Earth seemed to open onto another place on Earth that was full of resources we could use if we just figured out how, so we assumed Earth was an open, unbounded and infinitely bountiful system, a bottomless cornucopia. We were ignorant until recently of the existence and nature of closed systems. And it turns out that — except for cosmic materials like space dust and the odd meteorite, atmospheric imports like sunlight and radiation and atmospheric exports like heat — *Earth is a closed system.*

What that means is that what Earth was made of in the billions of years before we arrived, which has been reconstituted, reused, renewed and recycled again and again by Life, is all we've ever had to work with. We've added the things we've made to Earth's original troves. We've made new products and substances, including toxins and pollutants, but we've made them out of materials that were already here, often in quantities that were vast but not infinite.

"First, no territory can support an indefinite increase in either its number of creatures or in consumption per creature, let alone both; second, all mainstream policies of all governments assume that, on the contrary, it can. Together these facts add up to the great global threat."[12]

Exceeding carrying capacity to the point of reaching Critical Mass is inevitable in a materially closed system if living things consume and multiply without ceasing. In a closed system if the consumers continue to increase, expand and consume raw materials, then sooner or later there will be too many consumers with nowhere to expand to, few basic raw materials left to consume and — since living things cannot consume without producing waste of some kind — more waste than the system and its inhabitants can process or contain.

A useful analogy is found in something as mundane as an egg. An egg contains all that's needed to support the life and growth of the fetal creature it protects. At some point in its development the fledgling bird or tadpole, turtle or wasp consumes all the food in the egg, gets too big for it, breaks the egg open — hatches — and is born into the larger world. We've treated Earth as if it were our collective egg, as if there were a larger world we could be born into after we consume this one.

As we'll see in Chapter 7, Life learned this lesson the hard way. Most of us, however, haven't learned it yet. That's understandable. For the past 6,000 years — the millennia characterized by the rise (and fall) of empires, civilizations, kingdoms, dynasties and nation-states — whenever we used up the resources that were available to us locally or regionally, we moved someplace else, expanded into some resource-rich New World or conquered an old one. Or we devised a tool, technique or technology — a new method of extraction, transportation, coercion, or processing, for example — that enabled us to import (to take by force or trade for) what we lacked or desired from someplace else.

We're stealing our present pleasures from tomorrow's children.

In the past century we acquired the ability to take what we want from the future, too. We are presently using up resources — from oil and freshwater to soils and seafood — that would otherwise be available to our children and grandchildren, other species, natural communities and ecosystems. William Catton, author of the groundbreaking book *Overshoot,* put it plainly. "Posterity doesn't vote and doesn't exert much influence in the marketplace. So the living go on stealing from their descendants,"[13] and also from the other living things and systems that would otherwise have been able to support them. NASA climate scientist James Hansen proposes in 2009's *Storms of My Grandchildren* that we are even stealing from our descendants the possibility of a habitable climate.[14]

The scientific and technological breakthroughs of the past several centuries have led us to believe that we can continue to steal (we like to think of it as borrowing) from the future, that we can expand and consume and find ways to import carrying capacity without end, limit or serious mishap.

But we can't. In a closed system, carrying capacity is an absolute limiting factor. An economy is only sustainable — can only meet the needs of the present generation of both humans and other living things without compromising the ability of future generations to meet their needs — when it takes that limiting factor into account.

The upshot of all this is that much of what we import now from other places in Earth's closed system — minerals, fossil fuels, metals, timber and the manufactured goods they go into — is not in infinite supply and will not be consistently or permanently available to a ceaselessly expanding global economy, no matter how technologically clever we become. What was here in the beginning is still all that's here. There's just this one egg and no larger egg or world to hatch out into. And the load that the global economy is imposing on our Earth-egg is unsupportable.

## Getting a Picture of Load

What does *unsupportable load* look like? Imagine an undisturbed thousand-acre evergreen and mixed hardwood forest. (I chose this particular ecosystem and story because I watched the process happen around my farmstead and the Northwoods in Maine in the 1990s. Stock the story with animals and plants native to where you live and change the ending to a new hydroelectric dam or a foreign-owned soybean or eucalyptus plantation or a newly demarcated economic free zone of factories and distribution centers, it's still the same story. It's still overload.) In it there are beaver bogs and stream-fed ponds and a lake that are home to dozens of species of fish, frogs and turtles, dragonflies and water sliders and other insects, freshwater clams and sponges. In spring and fall the lake and ponds are crowded with migrating waterfowl.

The forest is sung to sleep by spring peepers and whistling bats, haunted by owls, awakened by brilliantly-colored song birds, traversed by deer and bear, moose and mink, fox and quail, snakes and geckos

**A Very Plain Truth**

"Every environment can support only a certain level of load placed upon it by its inhabitants. The load consists of the resources the inhabitants consume as well as the wastes they expel. When the load exceeds what the environment can tolerate, the environment begins to break down. ...

"The natural consequence of carrying capacity overload is population crash."[15]

and snails and such other wild things of all shapes and sizes as have never seen or been hedged in or harmed by humans. Berry brambles and flowering trees rim the forest. Fungi and ferns, lichens and worms and mosses turn its fallen trees into rich soil that gives life to the next generations of understory shrubs and ferns and trees. It's the sort of forest in which over thousands of years every living thing learned its limits and works with Life — the sort of forest that isn't all about us.

Now picture that fabulous forest after it has been discovered by hunters who clear patches of it periodically with fire in order to encourage young shoots that attract deer. Imagine that after the hunters come loggers and then small-farmers with flocks and herds and fields of corn. Then come large-scale potato, hog and dairy farms, a sawmill and pulp mill or builders of dams. And finally, by the early 21st century, imagine that occupying the place where the forest stood there now stand a shopping mall, industrial and office parks and a handful of residential developments each offering a hundred or so new homes, some of them surrounding the dammed lake which now covers three times its original land area and is filled with jet skis and motor boats.

There's not much room left for woods, hard or soft, or for beaver or bears, frogs or dragonflies, or even for hunters and farmers. And the services those woods once delivered — air filtration, water cycle and weather management, and soil maintenance — are no longer deliverable. More disastrously, the thousand acres can no longer restore or heal themselves, and neither can we easily, if ever, completely restore or heal them.

Carrying capacity teaches us to leave something of undiminished value behind in the accounts of not only our children and grandchildren but also in Life's and Earth's accounts. When we do that we are living sustainably, that is, within Earth's means.

Obviously we aren't doing that. So-called primitive humans did that, instinctively at first and then as part of their Earth-spirit religions. Until modern civilizations conquered and partially assimilated all the Earth's indigenous peoples, they continued to live for the most part sustainably. But no civilization in history has ever lived within Earth's means. In fact, civilizations (their name derived from *civis*, the Latin word for citizen) have always lived beyond their means. They have exceeded first their regional means. Then, as the spread of human populations and advancements in technology permitted, they have exceeded their continental means. Now global capitalist industrial civilization, perhaps the last civilization, is rapidly and relentlessly exceeding the whole Earth's means.

Activist/philosopher Derrick Jensen has put it plainly enough. "Civilization is not and never can be sustainable. This is especially true for industrial civilization."[16] Moreover, "Industrial Civilization depends on economic growth and the unsustainable use of natural resources," explained Earth Blogger Keith Farnish. With Jensen and others, Farnish proposed that "The only way to prevent global ecological collapse and thus ensure the survival of humanity is to rid the world of Industrial Civilization."[17] Cities — and their civilizations — are always, proudly and unashamedly, about and for people. People in cities try to make their way against the odds of finiteness. City-based civilizations are

## Living Beyond Tomorrow's Means: Our Ecological Footprints

William E. Rees of the University of British Columbia, Mathis Wackernagel of the public policy think tank Redefining Progress and their colleagues and students around the world have devised a tool, the Ecological Footprint, that can help us determine whether as individuals, households, cities or nations we are living sustainably within or unsustainably beyond Earth's means.

Measured in acres or hectares, the Ecological Footprint reveals how much land and water is required to produce the resources we consume and to absorb our wastes. It also reveals the extent to which we are dominating the biosphere at the expense of other-than-human species and all future beings. Though this was not its explicit intent, the Ecological Footprint is ultimately a revealing measure of the global economy's abiding and deepening trespasses and inequities.

If every human's *Ecological Footprint* were 3 acres or less, Earth could sustain 7 billion of us indefinitely. Three acres is the sustainable ☞

footprint, until or unless increased population, increased consumption, destructive technologies or changed environmental conditions reduce it. China's and Egypt's per person footprints are presently just over four acres; India's, Mexico's and most of Africa's are less than two acres. But despite the fact that in 2009 two thirds of humans left sustainable footprints, the per capita human Ecological Footprint was still, on average, 6.5 acres and growing. We'd already overshot what would be a sustainable human footprint by almost 75%.

How can this be? While two thirds of us — the so-called poor — are living within Earth's means, the most prosperous one third of us are living way *beyond* Earth's means. And it's not just the fault of the global elite class. The average per person footprint in the US is just over 22 acres — over seven times what's sustainable! It's 19 acres in Australia, 14 in Canada and 10 in Northern Europe and Japan.[18] The reality is that in this viral global economy, only the poorest live within Earth's means and tens of millions of them hope fervently to join the prosperous over-consumers who live beyond them. The failure of the 2009 Copenhagen climate meetings to make real headway was owed exactly to this discrepancy between poor peoples and nations hoping to develop American-style economies and prosperous nations hoping to hold on to theirs.

Ecological Footprint sizes can be compared more revealingly in terms of how many Earths it would take to sustain a particular lifestyle. Even a relatively frugal, middle-class American lifestyle, for example, if all 7 billion humans could achieve it would require seven to ten Earths to support it! If we all lived as the rich do we would consume as many as 100 planet's worth of resources and environmental services. If we all lived like the world's very wealthiest? Several solar system's worth.

Even given the number of people whose lifestyles use the planet's resources and environmental services at a rate well within that which Earth can provide, as a species we live in the global economy as if we had available to us — every year — the resources and environmental services of one and a half Earths.[19]

necessarily dedicated to ignoring finiteness and defying limits. But on a finite planet, limits cannot be defied forever.

Symptoms of Critical Mass like dead soils and seas, dysfunctional and diseased ecosystems, spreading deserts, volatile weather and the social, economic and environmental devastation of most of the continent of Africa are among the consequences of our attempting to defy limits and ignore this one of Life's rules:

**Leave something behind, something of undiminished Earth- and Life-sustaining value.**

## 3. The Global Economy Is Not Equitable.

Like all of civilization's economies before it, the global economy tends to pit us against each other — neighbor against neighbor, business against business, nation against nation — in friendly or fierce competition for its rewards and remuneration. Competition is thought to make us stronger, and if it is not extreme competition, sometimes it does. It also creates false oppositions, among them the idea that for someone to win or do well economically, someone else must lose and do poorly. We hold onto two contradictory ideas about Earth:

1) that it can provide for all of us abundantly forever
2) that there is not enough to go around and we have to fight for it

The first is cockeyed optimism; the second has its origin in our prehistoric past when we lived closer to the reality of finiteness. The sort of rabid competition we engage in now presumes that a few people doing very well and many not doing at all well are necessary preconditions to some people doing reasonably well.

It's difficult to imagine that a herd, pride, hive or pack could do very well over the long haul if a few of its members thrived and a fair number survived, but most were hungry or starving. Except in the direst circumstances, that's *not* how the distribution of food and other necessities works in herds, prides, hives and packs.

Many of us are willing to help even strangers in difficult economic times. Ethics, morals and religious teachings have increased our capacities for empathy and altruism. But the idea that our own and our species'

"The basic Law of Economics is that resources are distributed so as to maintain the integrity and stability of the social and ecological systems within which they are distributed, which also means helping to maintain the integrity and stability of the [biosphere — the larger life] of which these systems are a part."[20]

very survival depends upon our actually supporting an *each other* that extends beyond our families and friends and includes other kinds of living things is not natural to us. Rather it is widely considered by economic and political theorists, many business people and those for whom the global economy produces wealth to be impractical and uneconomical.

The idea that the well-being of every kind of living thing influences and is important to our well-being is derided by the present economy's beneficiaries as naïve and sentimental. For them, the idea that everyone's well-being is necessary to any kind of sound, sustainable economy is heretical. The consequence of this reasoning is growing and unsustainable inequity.

The world's rich nations, for example, are home to less than 15% of the world's population, but they account for over 80% of the world's income.[21] The per-person purchasing power in North America in 2008 was nearly $45,000, and in Northern Europe and Japan, close to $35,000. By contrast, over 40% of the world's population lived on less than two dollars a day and 20% of its people on less than a dollar a day.[22] Present economic woes are whittling away at all of those figures, including the most meager.

Disparities in resource consumption within and between nations are no less inequitable than the financial inequities. In 2010, for example, the United States' per capita consumption of oil, measured in barrels, was 57.2. The Russian Federation equivalent was 36.8, Germany and France's around 31 barrels, the United Kingdom's 26.6. But in China the barrels per capita number — which in reality indicates how many of the goods and services that fossil fuel energy currently provides are available to an individual — is only 10.2, Mexico's 12.1, Brazil 9.3 and India 2.9.[23] Similar international disparities would be found for access to freshwater, fresh food, social services and public transportation and education.

A feature of all the world's civilizations, inequity also characterizes the relationship between humans and other living things. Competition

"Ours is the only species in all the long period of life on earth that has ever spread around the entire world, occupying every continent and nearly every island, effectively subjugating all the animals and plants and natural systems it has encountered and over a relatively short period of time establishing itself in vast numbers as the single most dominant species of all."[24]

for natural resources and environmental services between humans and other-than-human species is fiercer than the competition between groups of humans.

In human v. other-than-human competition, humans win hands down. For example, human economic activity has changed half of the Earth's land surface so dramatically and in such a short period of time that most other-than-human species and natural communities cannot adapt. Our increasing and ceaseless consumption of basic life-supporting resources like nitrogen, plant energy and fibers, good agricultural land, freshwater, forests and space leaves very little for the five to perhaps 30 million other species that also depend on those and other natural resources. These are species on whose long-term well-being we've forgotten we depend.

Life doesn't allow any single species or even a handful of them to take the lions' share of Earth's resources. Even lions don't really take what we mean by "the lion's share." They take what they need and leave the rest for other carnivores. Life won't allow us to keep breaking this rule either. Symptoms of Critical Mass, such as the collapsing economy, mass migrations and the world's slums, are the consequence of our thinking we could break Life's equitability rule with impunity.

## 4. The Global Economy Is Neither Democratic nor Biocratic.

We'll see in Part II that Life tends to work in fluid and rapidly adaptable organizational systems like circles and networks in which all members participate fully. It nests smaller, more active and vulnerable living systems within cooperatives: larger interdependent protective systems that are responsive to their ever-changing needs, habits and circumstances.

Life's systems are remarkably, organically, democratic. Or, since *demos* is a word that means people and leaves Life and other-than-human living things out of its politics, and *bios* is a word that means "life," Life may more accurately be said to be remarkably biocratic, inclusive of other-than-human beings and humans as co-participants in the business of Life-making.

The global economy is not democratic. That it has been deemed a rigged casino is indicative of this fact.

### *Pyramid Plot: Civilization's Other Dark Side*

It is not only natural communities, ecosystems and resources that the viral global economy has commandeered to its purposes. Ever since the establishment of the first cities, large scale social, political and economic systems have mimicked not Life's fluid and adaptable forms but a rigid geometric form: the pyramid, the shape of the tombs of the Egyptian pharaohs who ruled their kingdoms through layers of priests and administrators from the top down. Discovery of the pyramid, a sort of human-made sacred mountain, allowed Egyptian architects to build taller, larger stone structures than had ever been built before because the weight of the stones was distributed over a wide square base.

As a model for social structures, the pyramid allowed rulers of every kind to rise economically higher than they ever had before because they could draw taxes and work from a wider base of humans, and extract resources from a wider land base than ever before. A pharaoh could amass much more wealth and power than a chieftain or tribal leader because hundreds of thousands of laborers contributed to his treasury rather than only dozens, and his well-weaponed armies could conquer much larger territories than any band of club-wielding or spear-bearing warriors.

Today there is "a citizenship of the globalizers and the globalized; a citizenship with the capacity of playing the market and a citizenship with no capacity; a citizenship that possesses, knows, and has power, and another citizenship that does not possess, does not know and has no power."[25]

While pyramid-shaped social systems lift up those who occupy the top (the now-infamous 1%), some mid-level administrators and managers and those whom these fortunate few patronize and favor, the crushing weight of the pyramid falls away from those who lead, manage and benefit from it onto the humans who labor to support it and the land on which it sits.

As the eventual collapse of most pyramid-shaped societies suggests — historian Joseph Tainter lists as many as 18 — they are so busy dominating that they are slow to respond to challenges and change. The excesses, inequities and perpetual appetites of their economies routinely run them up against regional Critical Mass, but they are slow to recognize and slower to do anything about it.

Historian Ronald Wright noted, with a nod to the present dominant industrial civilization, that such societies are "most unstable at their peak, when they have reached maximum demand on the ecology. Unless a new source of wealth or energy appears, they have no room left to raise production or absorb the shock of natural fluctuations. The only way onward is to keep wringing new loans from nature and humanity." This leads inevitably to collapse, Wright adds, which "results in a society's extinction or near extinction, during which very large numbers of people die or scatter."[26]

How can it be that we have not learned this obvious lesson from history? How can it have happened that a highly intelligent species, one that regularly congratulates itself on its intelligence and highly developed consciousness and conscience, has brought the planet to this pass?

CHAPTER 5

# How Did the Economy Get to Be Too Big *Not* to Fail?

THERE'S A PRETTY SIMPLE ANSWER to that titular question. Like the economy of every major civilization, empire, dynasty, monarchy, dictatorship and centralized bureaucracy in history, the viral global economy is managed and directed from the top down and the center out by a relatively privileged elite class that gets the most benefit from it. And for them, enough is never enough. If humans are the dominant species, then the members of that elite, often called the *Powers That Be* or just *the Powers*, are the dominant humans.

Most leaders of nations, corporations, organizations and institutions are relatively powerful: They have more power to get things done in the world than the rest of us do. Only a few consciously or intentionally misuse or abuse power for their own gain. The Powers are those who do. Sometimes we know who they are; their corruption and self-interest are that obvious. Often we do not know who they are. They hide in plain sight until some particularly egregious act or particularly brave and insightful person — a whistle-blower — reveals them to us.

In particular, the Powers are at the helms of the world's major transnational corporations and of the institutions and organizations that coordinate and facilitate the activities of those corporations, usually behind closed doors, away from public scrutiny and accountability. The several annual global economic summits — held in places like Davos and Geneva in Switzerland and Dubai City, Dubai — involve the leaders of the seven, ten or twenty most powerful nations and corporations, the number depending upon what group is organizing the summit. Lesser nations, the ordinary, powerless peoples of nations and the employees of corporations are not invited.

Estimates vary of how many belong to that self-protective and well-protected global elite class that maintains the global economy through both legitimate and illegitimate means. David Rothkopf reckoned in his book *Superclass* that the most powerful of the Powers "number six thousand on a planet of six billion. They run our governments, our largest corporations, the powerhouses of international finance, the media ... and, from the shadows, the world's most dangerous criminal and terrorist organizations. They are at the helm of every major enterprise on the planet and they control its greatest wealth."[1]

The price of admission to the Powers or, conversely, the benefit of being admitted, ranges from a few hundred million dollars for the lesser Powers (of which something like $30 million should be "liquid," available for spending or investing) to several billions for much of the superclass. The average net worth of the wealthiest Forbes 400, for example, is $3.9 billion.

American social critic Samuel Huntington arrived at a more inclusive number — 30 million — by adding in lesser Powers. This still amounts to less than .005% of the human population. However the figures are figured, fewer than 1% of us sit atop the pyramid-shaped global economic system under the influence of which the rest of us are also living beyond Earth's means, though without getting most of the short- or long-term benefits of doing so.

"There is a new class — endowed with vast personal income, freed from the corporation, who set out to take over the state and run it — not for any ideological project but simply in a way that would bring them, individually and as a group, the most money, the least disturbed power, and the greatest chance of rescue should something go wrong."[2]

## *Evading Critical Mass*

The human immunodeficiency virus does not attack its own kind. HIV is not susceptible to AIDS. Similarly, the Powers are not susceptible to Critical Mass. Or at least they are not as susceptible to the early stages as the rest of us. Whatever their individual worth and the scope of their individual power, what the corporate, financial and global economic Powers have in common is the ability to purchase relative immunity to the consequences of reaching Critical Mass until such time as Life as we know it succumbs. Though they lost a lot in the 2009 recession, they still have a very lot more than the rest of us. And most of them still have their power.

Precisely *because* they are not much bothered by our having reached global Critical Mass, most of the Powers are still remarkably ignorant of and indifferent to its impact on the majority of the humans and other living things in the economic layers of the pyramid below them. The economy that, under their management, has induced Critical Mass and is impoverishing many of us is still enriching and empowering them beyond any former potentates' imaginings. They are not likely to voluntarily dismantle that economy, let it languish or ask the rest of us to help them to manage it more sustainably or equitably.

And since this elite group is scattered over the globe in corporate offices and headquarters, in penthouses and gated compounds, we are not likely to be able to topple them en masse as we could a consolidated, centrally-located power. Nor are we likely to be able to persuade them to make the economy work for us too, which on a finite planet would require that they allow it to work less well for them.

Some of the heads of nations and corporations are feeling the breath of angry mobs — Occupiers, revolutionaries, insurgents, opposition

"From an evolutionary perspective, current global economics violates the fundamental principles by which all mature living systems are organized. Global economics is a hierarchical system where one level survives at the expense of another level. This top-down approach is never seen in healthy biological systems. In mature natural systems there are no authoritarian governments."[3]

forces — on their necks. The leaders of some democratic nations have taken or promised to take the legal lash to those Powers who have shown themselves to be particularly deceptive, greedy or corrupt, but to little overall effect.

### Avoiding Democracy

Wealth, aloofness, indifference, lack of loyalty to nations and even to the businesses and institutions that made them rich, are characteristics the Powers share. "Above all, like anybody else — in fact, *more* than anybody else, given the obsessive, often narcissistic energy required of moguls, politicians and would-be messiahs," *Salon* senior writer Laura Miller charges, "these people are self-interested."[4]

To this condemnation Samuel Huntington added his own. The members of this geographically scattered, culturally diverse global elite, he said, "view national boundaries as obstacles that thankfully are vanishing, and see national governments as residues from the past whose only useful function is to facilitate the elite's global operations." This has had the effect of "merging national economies into a single global whole, and rapidly eroding the authority and functions of national governments."[5]

In his book *The Elite Consensus,* public interest writer George Draffan concludes that "Governments have become 'mere salesmen' promoting multinational corporations, which are the 'muscle' and 'brains' of the global economy."[6] It is not difficult to see how this has happened if we take into consideration the stark fact that of the 100 largest economies in the world, 51 are corporations.

"The men [sic] who run global corporations are the first in history with the organizations, technology, money, and ideology to make a credible try at managing the world as an integrated economic unit."[7]

There are, of course, exceptions to this characterization of governments, the heads of governments and corporations and the relationships between them. But clearly there have not been enough exceptions for the pyramid system of social, political and economic organization to have been left behind, overturned or undermined. It's true that pyramid shaped socio-political systems can be efficient at coordinating tasks and components, like military operations and soldiers or plantations and slaves, for example. But armies and slave plantations are decidedly undemocratic institutions. And pyramidal systems can only be efficient until or unless they become too large. When they become too large they also become too complex even for centralized authorities, administrators and experts to manage effectively.

Pyramidal socio-political systems can also be benevolent. But benevolence extended by the few to the many is neither genuinely democratic nor very often equitable. Benevolence can be measured, moderated or withdrawn. Pyramidal socio-political systems on the scale of many nations and the present global economy are far too large to be able to respond quickly and effectively to the challenges posed by self-induced Critical Mass and are far too self-serving to prevent them.

But given how many self-described democratic nations there are in the world today, how is it that this kind of top-down control, economic injustice and clearly unsustainable economic activity persist? How can the system have avoided being moderated by the spread of democracy? And why are the Powers still in power? Because we've given them the tools they need to hold onto it.

## Power Tools

How did corporations and a scarcely coherent, scattered group of highly competitive and self-interested individuals acquire so much power? They have taken or been given a handful of useful power tools.

### Corporate Personhood

In January 1885, Santa Clara County, California sued the Southern Pacific Railroad Company before the US Supreme Court in an effort to obtain pending and past-due real estate taxes on land the railroad mortgaged from the county. The railroad didn't think it should have to pay the taxes.

In *Unequal Protection*, Thom Hartmann explained why. "The main tool the railroad's lawyers tried to use was the fact that corporations had historically been referred to under law not as corporations but as artificial persons. Based on this, they argued, corporations should be considered actual persons under the Fourteenth Amendment" — the post-Civil War amendment that granted personhood and some of its rights and benefits to African Americans — "and [should] enjoy the protections of the Constitution just like living, breathing, human persons."[8] Humans get tax breaks on mortgages. So, the railroad's lawyers reasoned, should the railroad. Failing to pay taxes for six years was the railroad's way of protesting unfair taxation. It was their 19th century Tea Party.

It was also the railroad's way of trying to get the case for "corporate personhood" heard by the Supreme Court. Southern Pacific's attorneys aimed to further the efforts of several decades of lawyers to make "artificial persons" (legal entities created on paper) equivalent under the law to "natural persons" (us).

Obviously, given the size, wealth, transnational reach and number of actual persons involved in a corporation, there is no equivalency. It was precisely their wealth that by 1885 already allowed corporations like the Southern Pacific Railroad to hire battalions of attorneys to push lawsuits through the lower courts for years on end in order to get to the Supreme Court — something few individuals, except in huge, well-funded class actions, could afford to do. Even as artificial persons, corporations could buy a lot more law than mere people.

Those who were opposed to granting corporations personhood worried that, given rights like freedom of speech, freedom from search and seizure and the right to privacy, corporations could lobby legislators, finance political campaigns and block environmental and safety inspections. Furthermore, they might prevent audits of records and papers and overturn laws intended to protect individuals, communities, small businesses and the environment against corporate trespass. Corporations have done all these things.

Given the 2010 decision by the US Supreme Court to allow corporations to purchase campaign advertising and the game-changing effects of corporate campaign funding on the 2012 campaign season, they will continue to do all of these things. The implications for US politics and policy are stark and, because the "corporatist, capitalist, industrial global economy," as it is embracingly named by critics, is a global economy, those implications have a global reach. Think about this for a moment: A Chinese, Brazilian or Russian multinational corporation or consortium of them, or a US corporation that is invested more heavily in other countries than in the US, is chartered and has its corporate offices off-shore and pays no taxes in the US, could determine the outcome of future congressional and presidential elections. In *Miami Herald* columnist Leonard Pitt's terms, the next American president could be "sponsored, not elected."

But let's get back to the source of this historical act of judicial oligarchy. The decision in *Santa Clara County v. Southern Pacific* was pronounced in May 1886 by Chief Justice Morris Remick Waite. Thom Hartman explained that, before hearing attorneys' summary arguments and rendering the Court's decision, Justice Waite announced — *off the record* — that "The court does not wish to hear arguments on the question whether the provision in the Fourteenth Amendment to the Constitution ... applies to these corporations." In other words, he and the other judges had decided not to use the case as a test case for corporate personhood. But Chief Justice Waite didn't stop there. Apparently speaking on behalf of all the justices, he added a gratuitous aside: "We are of the opinion that it does."

The corporate personhood claim was never made in or heard by that court or any other. It was *never passed into law.* Nonetheless corporations have behaved and been treated legally as if it had been. Why? Justice Waite's off-the-record comment in its favor got written into the headnotes — the summary — of the report that recorded the case for posterity. It's not on the record but it's in there with the record. It may have been an accident or the result of a misunderstanding between the justice and the court recorder, or it may have been the result of the recorder's long, lucrative professional affiliation with railroads. However it happened, for over a century corporations have been able to get court decisions in their favor based on rights of personhood that they were never explicitly given but that they have not been explicitly denied either. The bottom line is that, legally, Walmart and Exxon Mobile, Monsanto, Procter & Gamble, Toyota and AIG are persons, entitled to the same rights as you and me.

In *Defying Corporations, Defining Democracy*, Dean Ritz summarized the impact of this transfer of rights and powers up the pyramid. "Corporations today act in the capacity of governments. Energy corporations determine our nation's energy policies. Automobile corporations determine our nation's transportation policies. Military manufacturing corporations determine our nation's defense policies. Corporate polluters and resource extraction corporations define our environmental policies. Transnational corporations determine our trading policies. And the wealthiest among us — with their wealth deeply rooted in corporations — determine our tax policies."9 And as US corporations have set up shop in other nations and corporations chartered in other nations have set up shop in the US, corporate personhood has almost become the international norm.

### The WTO v. National Sovereignty

But the transfer of power to the Powers and corporations didn't end in 1886. After World War II, leaders of the nations involved in the war met in Bretton Woods, New Hampshire, to find a way to stabilize economic relationships. They created several economic tools, such as the World Bank and the International Monetary Fund (IMF), and scheduled meetings of nations intended to hash out General Agreements on Trade and Tariffs (GATT). These were to be used to help rebuild the economies of the war's losers, expand the economies of its winners and, in an uncharacteristic show of generosity, to strengthen what were then called Third World economies. The underlying theory was that nations that are tied to each other economically won't have to attack each other to get what they need. (Western nations' relations with Middle Eastern oil-producing nations have disproved the theory.)

Too often the Bretton Woods institutional tools have been used to facilitate rich nations' use and consumption of poor nations' resources, and to winch more of the latter into the global economy, whether or

"The WTO was designed, in effect, to serve as a global governing body for transnational corporate interests. [It] has both legislative and judicial powers and a mandate to eliminate all barriers to international investment and competition. Under the WTO a group of unelected trade representatives acts a global parliament with the power to override economic and social [and environmental] policy decisions of nation states and democratic legislatures around the world."10

not the poor nations were willing or it was in their people's best interests. Touted as "economic globalization" by its beneficiaries, this process has been deemed "economic colonialism" by the leaders and peoples of many of the poorer and recently industrialized nations.

In 1995 the once occasional GATT meetings were institutionalized — legalized and also given muscle — in the form of the infamous World Trade Organization (WTO), a supranational organization that owes allegiance to no nation, government or people. The WTO has never decided in favor of an environmental law, regulation or policy. It has weakened the capacity of every nation to protect the jobs and wages of its people and the health of its agricultural, industrial, financial, public utility, technology and service sectors; to set prices for and limits on the sale of its raw materials, goods and services and to protect its balance of trade, health and occupational standards and environments.

Citizens of nations around the world are challenging their legislators to protect them from global economic trespass. The challenges are almost fruitless. As the WTO is presently mandated, its rule trumps the rule of nations. With its assistance, the viral global economy has, for now and in large measure, triumphed over the whole world.

## Tools of Disconnection

"HIV and the Viral Global Economy: Powerful Similarities" (see page 57) revealed that HIV invades and infects human bodies so successfully because it is wrapped in a protein covering that prevents the immune system from recognizing what it is and then, once inside, it captures and converts the system's cells to its own purpose. HIV's protein camouflage prevents the immune system from making the connection between it and the dysfunction and devastation it causes. The global economy works pretty much the same way. Propaganda, marketing, advertising, packaging and the capacity of corporate-owned media to engage in frequent repetition are strategies that effectively camouflage the aim and impact of the global economy on Earth's immune system.

In his book, *Time's Up*, Keith Farnish suggested that in order to stay in power and get maximum use of their power, the Powers and the agents of the economic system that supports them have learned how to employ a variety of what he calls Tools of Disconnection intended to keep us from making the connection between our present way of living and what it's doing to us and to Life as we know it. In this the Powers are like hypnotists, able to delude people into behaving as if they were chickens or sheep, or to persuade them the onion they're eating is actually an apple.

How do they do that? With input and guidance from Farnish's *Time's Up*, I suggest that this is how:

- The Powers reward us for being good consumers and praise us for continuing to shop and spend despite the damage shopping and spending are doing to our economic well-being and our environments.

- They make us feel good for doing trivial things that don't upset the status quo, like replacing all our light bulbs with compact fluorescent ones and recycling glass bottles. These are inarguably good things to do, but without massive systemic change they will do nothing to cure Earth or us of our present economically-induced disease.

- They give us selected freedoms like voting (though the Powers actually choose our candidates) and protesting (so long as we stay behind cordons and lines of police) so long as they own the media and can direct them not to cover the protests. Additionally, they withhold other freedoms that might limit their power, like providing the option on ballots of "none of the above."

- They make us think we have choices (for example of consumer goods and candidates for office) while making sure the choices we actually have support or at least do not thwart the prevailing economic and political systems and their own powers.

- They sell us a dream of a particular kind of "good life," one that's dependent on having and spending funny-money. With logos and neon, with billboards and painted buses and taxis, with pop-up ads, feel-good speeches, print and televised advertising they inculcate in us an idea of what's good that's entirely disconnected from what's possible on a finite planet and good for Life at large.

- They exploit our tendency to trust experts, authorities, specialists, leaders and bosses — and them. They say what we want to hear but do what they want to do.

- They lie to us about our actual circumstances and about what they're doing to address them.
- Perhaps most insidiously, they give us hope: hope that if we keep doing what we've been doing, if we keep doing what they have been encouraging us to do (only do it better and more than we have been) then all will be well. "The notion of limitless, linear growth is a chimera, a myth," wrote Green Party USA co-founder John Rensenbrink in *Against All Odds*. "Yet it has been this myth that has been used by the powers-that-be, whether thoughtlessly or irresponsibly, to cloak their drive for domination of nature and by implication, of all other people."[11] The Powers persuade us that doing more of the same things we've been doing we can preserve the status quo. Yet this is the biggest lie they tell us and only inspires false hope. Doing more of the things that haven't been working and expecting different results is one of the definitions of insanity.

In short, as Chris Hedges suggested in *Empire of Illusion,* they perpetuate the illusions that humans are larger than Life and that the present larger-than-Life economic system can and will take care of us. "The skillfully manufactured images and slogans that flood the airwaves and infect our political discourse mask reality. And we do not protest."[12]

### Democracies, the Powers and Global Economic Domination

Earlier I observed that "Only the poor live within Earth's means." Remarkably, the world's democracies do not. Ostensibly democratic activists and revolutions have dethroned monarchs and deposed autocrats and somewhat flattened the pyramid, but they have not renounced what business writer Marjorie Kelly called "the divine right of capital": money-power. Nor have they disempowered the Powers that inevitably come to wield it. The wealthiest 5% of ostensibly democratic nations hold over one half the collective wealth and enjoy the power that accrues to it, while the bottom 20% hold virtually no wealth and have little or no power.[13]

The leaders of democracies are elected but, because of the way in which campaign financing works and political campaigns are run, they are too often an elected elite. *Empire of Illusion's* Hedges rues that

"Democracy, a system ideally designed to challenge the status quo, has been corrupted and tamed to slavishly serve the status quo."[14]

It has been argued that digital and electronic technologies (cell phones and smart phones, laptops, the Internet, broadband, wireless and cable service, for example), for the most part invented by ostensibly democratic nations, are at least beginning to flatten the political pyramid a little by making it possible for people everywhere in the world to organize, make their opinions known, access more or less accurate information about local, regional and international circumstances and influence the decisions of leaders, Powers and governments. Digital technology, it is predicted, will empower the disempowered. In short, digital is said to equal democratic. The 2009 protests in Iran were considered exemplary of digital grassroots democratic organization.

There are two problems with that prediction. First, digital and electronic, information and entertainment technologies use huge quantities of electricity, more than the present grids in most countries will be able to support as millions of new users come online. Remember, all of this electricity is produced by the same fossil fuels that are changing the climate and are soon to be very expensive and less available. These technologies may have a half life of just decades.

But as former US Labor Secretary Robert Reich argues in his book *Supercapitalism*, "democracy and capitalism have been turned upside down.... Capitalism has invaded democracy."[15] This is the second problem with the "digital = democratic" prediction. A technology can only be considered to be democratic and supportive of authentic democracy if it is widely or universally available. In the present economy, available and affordable are not the same things. Cell phones may be dirt cheap and ubiquitous even in the world's poorer nations, but the broadband, cable, wireless and data services that are necessary to make them tools of vibrant democratic engagement are not.

Frank Bures revealed in a *Wired* magazine exposé that in Japan, for example, "broadband service averages 6 cents per 100 Kbps [kilobytes per second], with users typically paying 0.002 percent of their monthly salary for high-speed access. But in Kenya, that same hookup speed costs $86.11 — nearly twice the average monthly income." For those 100 Kbps Americans pay 49 cents, South Koreans 8 cents and Netherlanders

14 cents, while residents of Pakistan who are able pay over $100 — twice their average weekly pay.[16]

Capitalist democracies have not moderated the global economy's trespasses on most humans or on Earth's natural communities. On the contrary, they have intensified them. As novelist and nature writer Edward Hoagland has drolly noted, "Democracy seems no better suited than dictatorship to saving rainforests because money talks in both."[17] The economies of democracies are driven by consumption, literally. Upwards of 70% of the US economy, for example, now depends not on manufacturing but on consumer spending.[18] This is why, when people in the US stop shopping, economists worry that the bottom will fall out of their economy even though much of what they shop for is imported from China.

Western capitalist democracies have been proud of their position at the top of the socio-economic pyramid. Many of us who live in them have been, too. On this account democracy theorist C. Douglas Lummis, among others, calls them "imperial democracies."

Whether the Powers are elected or insist themselves into office, the calculus and consequences of the prevailing pyramid-shaped socio-economic system for human and natural communities has been the same: global economic, social and political domination threatens Earth's equivalent of an immune system and induces Critical Mass.

Like the human immunodeficiency virus, this domination system is as tenacious as it is inequitable, undemocratic and dangerous because its economic and socio-political aspects are mutually reinforcing. The global economy supports the socio-political pyramid and its Powers who support and spread the global economy in return. It's a continuous positive feedback loop with an obvious viral analogy: HIV establishes and maintains a biochemical domination system that, in turn, supports and spreads HIV. In the long term, the persistence of these cycles is devastating and potentially fatal for human bodies, human societies and Life as we know it. Ultimately, and perhaps very soon, even for the economy itself.

## Life's Backup Plan

More alarming than the characteristics that HIV and the viral global economy have in common is one characteristic they do not. Viruses like

HIV keep populations of species in check so that they cannot exceed Earth's means of supporting them and the other living things with which they share their communities. In particular HIV kept populations of primates and now keeps populations of humans in check. At the same time, viruses are kept in check by their hosts' immune systems. The global economy, on the other hand, has not been kept in check by its hosts, Earth's human and natural communities. It has overrun them.

But Life has a backup plan. If the hosts' immune systems fail to evolve protocols to protect them, populations of viruses are kept in check by the harsh reality that if they put their host species out of business they put themselves out of business at the same time. This is one of the ways Life eliminates species that overreach. Life has not yet checked or eliminated the global economy for one glaringly simple reason: The global economy is not a complex living system and therefore does not obey Life's rules. The global economy is a human creation. It is up to us to either limit or eliminate it. We have not. Such checks as have been placed on the economy have been like pebbles tossed in front of a flood. Such negative feedbacks as we have conceived have worked about as well as spitting into the wind. More often than checking its expansion and virulence, we have hoped that by spreading, feeding and speeding the global economy we could ease the suffering it has already caused. This is equivalent to spiking an AIDS patient's body with more HIV.

In 2008, economists and leaders of teetering economies played to this hope by promising to prop up the weakened global economy in order to make business-as-usual work better for more people. This approach is, to update one of William Catton's analogies, like a family

"Instead of planning for descent, many writers, journalists, and political leaders encourage a continuation of the established public mind-set on growth that was okay for the time of expanding resource use. For some it is failings in their education; for others it is over-focus on the short range. Over six billion people are in denial, and for leaders to speak of a non-growth period is viewed as political suicide. But the paradigm of growth is a shared global attitude that may switch all at once for all together when the truth becomes obvious through some galvanizing event."[19]

whose members are living far beyond their current income and heading for bankruptcy, urging the head of the household to solve their problems by getting better at using the ATM machine.

In disease terms there is, of course, that precedent we've invented for beating evolution to the punch: vaccination, the small practice dose that prepares the immune system for a full scale assault. But there's no such thing as a small dose of a global economy. Its very nature is to grow, consume, expand, possess and dominate and to become as big as it can, as big as all the Earth and larger than Life. And it doesn't just grow, expand and consume by the same amount every year. The economy often grows exponentially, that is, by an ever larger amount year after year. Exactly as viruses like HIV would do if Life hadn't evolved immune systems and we hadn't invented vaccines to stop them. And there's the fact that we're already suffering the symptoms of having reached Critical Mass. It's too late for vaccination. Strengthening the global economy is tantamount to giving an HIV injection to a person who already has AIDS.

## Too Big *Not* to Fail?

Global economic theory relies on one particularly counterintuitive notion: that huge transnational corporations and organizations are not vulnerable to the defects inherent in all forms of gigantism. Rather they are believed to be "too big to fail." Why? Letting these giants go under would be too much of a risk for the national economies, investors, stockholders, suppliers and other people and organizations they would weaken or take down with them. Some other economy, corporation, organization, country or consortium of them will — or must — as a matter of course, bail out vulnerable megacompanies and institutions. They must not be allowed to fail.

Bailout Theory, as it is called, is fatally flawed, however, when it comes to the global economy. Again, why? Because "Mother Nature does not do bailouts," says former US vice president and climate change spokesperson Al Gore. Just as there's no other Earth to turn to if we live for too long beyond this one's means, there's no larger economy to turn to

**A Galvanizing Event:**
"This looks like the most synchronized recession in world history: We are all going down together."[20]

if the viral global economy operates much longer beyond its means. And there are no unaffected national or regional (subsidiary) economies that are sufficiently big, rich or independent to bail the global economy out.

The global economy's wealthiest, most powerful and aggressive subsidiary economies are heavily invested in each other's bad paper, foreclosures, bankruptcies and other forms of debt, and in development, infrastructure, energy, military and expansion projects that are so big that no subsidiary economy can afford to undertake them alone. The global economy's poorest subsidiary economies already hang on by a thread that the richest, finding themselves somewhat less rich, may choose to cut. National economies are propping up each other's credit and financial institutions in such a way that each of them is vulnerable to the failure of any of the others. Only one additional opportunistic condition is required to bring down this jerry-rigged, multinational system of props: protracted widespread drought, cumulative weather emergencies, failed grain crops, another major resource war, recognition of peak oil, a rapid or prolonged sequence of serious seismic events or meltdown of the US, Chinese or European Union economies, for example.

But surely economic collapse isn't inevitable, is it? After all, we pulled out of the Great Depression of the 1930s. That was a worldwide phenomenon too and the decades following the crash brought the most prosperity to the most people in human history. The mid-20th century miracles of industrial productivity, the phenomenally productive agricultural Green Revolution, computer and electronic technologies and free-market economic policies accomplished a number of ambitious goals. They enriched and added to the list of rich (or at least prosperous, powerful, developed, industrialized) economies and developing, industrializing economies. They hauled many so-called poor (by industrialists' standards) economies into the modern era. In the process they created a conceptual divide that gave industrialized nations a dangerous sense of superiority and entitlement and global aspirations that carried stock markets around the world to such heights that at century's end one investment analyst predicted the Dow Jones Industrial Average, which had yet to exceed 14,000 points, could hit 36,000.[21]

Couldn't upgraded versions of the same sorts of activities and policies that bailed us out then (policies we liked to believe were bailing us out in

2010) actually bail us out now too? No. Why not? Several once-in-an-Earthtime conditions permitted the boom that followed that early 20th century bust. Among them were:

- a war-driven, full-employment economy based on the production and deployment of conventional (that is, non-nuclear, non-biological, non-mass destruction) weaponry
- cheap, abundant fossil fuels and natural resources
- free, reliable ecosystems services
- relatively predictable, mostly good weather
- widespread faith in "endless capital" and big government
- a human population of little more than two billion

None of these can save us now. Perpetual warfare bankrupts rather than bankrolls nations and threatens unprecedented amounts of death and destruction. Earth's cornucopia of resources and fossil fuels will not be refilled. (In April 2012 researchers at MIT joined the ranks of scholars and scientists who have revisited the groundbreaking 1972 Club of Rome report "The Limits to Growth" on the 40th anniversary of its publication and concurred with its prescient, scrupulously careful authors: we are *still* poised to shoot irrevocably past Earth's carrying capacity by 2030.) Ecosystem services like carbon sequestration, soil maintenance, flood control and water purification have been seriously taxed by global economic activity over the past half century. The climate has already become noticeably unstable. Capital is not infinitely expandable. Or as American sociologist Immanuel Wallerstein has written, "The endless accumulation of capital" is not possible. (The late 2010 drift of the American economy into the second stage of its Great Recession and serious volatility of the world's stock markets in the first quarter of 2012 were indicative.) And the capacity of governments to manage at the global or even national level the complex of symptoms that characterize Critical Mass is in doubt.

"Thus it is that we can say," Wallerstein concluded, "that the capitalist world-economy has now entered its terminal crisis, a crisis that may last up to fifty years.... As the world-economy enters into a new period of expansion it will exacerbate the very conditions which have led it to this terminal crisis."[22]

"Collapse, if and when it comes again, will this time be global," observed US anthropologist and historian Joseph Tainter. "No longer can any individual nation collapse. World civilization will disintegrate as a whole."23

"For every animal, object, institution, or system, there is an optimal limit beyond which it ought not to grow. Beyond this optimal size, all other elements of an animal, object, institution or system will be affected adversely."24

In short, the booming, credit-driven economy that those once-in-an-Earthtime conditions permitted is the biggest economy there is and ever has been. There's no bigger economy for it to turn to for help. It's too big *not* to fail.

Bottom Line: For the global economy to cease to pose a threat to most of us and the Earth's immune system of natural communities, it would have to become something it cannot become: *not global.*

CHAPTER 6

# The Prognosis for Global Solutions Is Poor

S o here we are, between the proverbial rock and a hard place. The economy on which we have come to depend for nearly all the goods, services and provisions we require and many we simply want has turned on itself and us. This syndrome of economic, environmental, social and political crises has become ever more critical in the years during which this book has been written. As competition for resources becomes fiercer and jobs and living wages become scarcer, Earth's immune system of natural and human communities, which had been only compromised in function, becomes more susceptible to failure every day. That failure could come suddenly (like the sudden submission of the human body to one AIDS symptom too many, or to the finally fatal assault of HIV itself) or it could come slowly, by fits and starts, as HIV/AIDS seems to do when it's diagnosed early and the whole, difficult course of the syndrome is recognized.

But there seems to be little probability of avoiding the dramatic decline or total collapse of the global economic system if we continue to try to do business as usual (or business only slightly

"We are nearing the end of our fiscal and monetary ability to bail out the system. We are steadily becoming vulnerable to disaster on an epic scale."[1]

tweaked) and to live lives at cross-purposes to Life. Nothing about our lives or Life as we know it is invulnerable.

Nonetheless, every effort of the Powers and also of the world's best intentioned leaders is dedicated to strengthening the global economy. Emerging economies like China, Brazil, India and Indonesia, and even the economies of some African nations, that showed signs of "recovery" in 2010 and seemed poised to challenge, supersede or at least influence the game plans of spendthrift, aging and late-stage economies, are in 2012 experiencing slowed growth. The commitment of the leaders of both kinds of economy — the stagnant-but-hopeful and the less-stagnant and also hopeful — to more of the same and business as usual commits their people to living ever further beyond Earth's capacity to sustain them and Life as we know it.

These actions may succeed in propping up the system for a while. There may be a bit more lift left in funny-money, and there's surely enough ink and temptation to print more. But because the Powers, both greater and lesser, aging and emerging, have not understood that almost everything that's gone wrong everywhere at once can be attributed to the activities of the viral global economy, neither they nor the ablest and most earnest of our leaders seem to understand that attempting to restore it to health will not help. It will result only in worsening Earth's equivalent of HIV/AIDS and all its symptoms, including economic destabilization. Or as Michael Ruppert quipped in *Confronting Collapse*, "To put it simply, recovery is what will kill us."[2]

Because most of us have not understood these things either, we are cheering their efforts to do more of what brought us to this condition in the first place. That's the rock.

## The Hard Place

What we need to do to restore health and proper function to Earth's besieged natural and human communities is a political non-starter. Drastic change is a hard sell. There's almost no market for "new" or "different" that doesn't promise bigger, more or some other variation on "improved." And there's no public support at all for economic stimulus packages that don't promise a return to what we in the prosperous nations have come to think of as normal — and what the rest of the

"If an activist president set out with good intentions to rewire the engine of [global] capitalism — to alter its operating values or reorganize the terms for employment and investment, for example, or tamper with other important features — the initiative would very likely be chewed to pieces by the politics. Given the standard legislative habits of modern government, not to mention the close attachments to the powerful interests defending the status quo, the results would be marginal adjustments and might even make things worse."[3]

world has learned to long for: perpetual growth, expansion, material progress and the promise of universal prosperity.

No Powers would benefit from and no well-intentioned leaders could get elected after telling their people how bad things really are or how much worse they could still get. Some of our more insightful, forward-looking and honest leaders and legislators may try to give us a hint, a bit of a heads up. But no one at the top of any of the socio-political pyramids is going to ask those who have done well, or at least well enough under the present system, to make the kinds of dramatic changes in their ways of providing for themselves and in their standards of living that would allow us as a species to mitigate and congenially survive Critical Mass. And it's a certainty no one at the top can require people to make those changes without employing draconian measures used by the worst dictators.

Like our leaders, most of us still behave, for the most part unconsciously, as if humans are larger or at least smarter than Life and, therefore, absolved of the rules that shape, inform and sustain it. Like them, most of us can't imagine an alternative to the global economy.

It's not hard to understand our leaders' ineptitude and recalcitrance. They are creatures of the system. It shapes, defines and rewards them. It put them where they are. They believe in it, or at least they must try to because it's what they know. As former dean of Yale's School of Forestry and Environmental Studies James Gustave Speth observed, present leaders "are hooked on growth — for its revenues, for its constituencies, and for its influence abroad."[4]

Our leaders are obliged to work with and within the existing system. It may not be bigger than Life, but it is bigger than they are. The best they can do is fit in and try to make the system work as well as it can for as many of us — or at least as many of their paying constituents — as it can, for as long as it can. Given the viral and self-destructive nature of that system, this is a futile task, like trying to make HIV work for the body.

Many of those who have gotten the most benefit from the global economy, and therefore have the most faith in it, have so far been spared the worst of its viral symptoms. In all likelihood, and understandably, these beneficiaries will continue, at least for a while, to hope that someone can work an economic miracle. Though even conservative and conventional economists are speaking in terms of a five or six year downturn, most of the members of the world's middle and upper classes and their leaders and representatives still hope for a quick turn around. The media and many analysts and leaders feed that hope and amplify even the slightest indication of its being met.

Even the five or six more years recession or persistently jobless and partial recovery predicted by groups like the Conference Board that support economic expansion, will have a lasting impact on existing systems. Just as many parts of a body damaged by HIV/AIDS do not fully recover even when the mitigation protocol is administered and the virus held in check, many families, human communities, businesses, manufacturing sectors, cities, national economies, governments and distribution systems will not recover even if the global economy temporarily regains strength. And those who lose their jobs will need in the interim to figure out a way to occupy their time and contribute to their own maintenance and survival. Most of their jobs will not be coming back — at least not to them.

## In a Perfect World ...

For our purposes — that is, for the purpose of human survival on a habitable, familiar planet — it's sometimes helpful to imagine what a perfect world might look like, even though there is no such thing. Imagining it can help us think about what we might do to achieve something like it.

I offer here a few of the characteristics that some of the more environmentally-minded proponents of global solutions to global problems ascribe to the more perfect world of their imagining.

If there *were* a perfect world according to my terms in these pages, it would be such a coherently Earthological, Earthonomical world that our place in it might actually be comprehended and managed all of a piece. We might know how Life on Earth works almost as well as we begin to know how our bodies work. We might actually "mobilize to save civilization" as Earth Policy Institute founder Lester Brown suggested in *Plan B 4.0*, the fourth book in a six book series.

"Mobilizing to save civilization means fundamentally restructuring the global economy in order to stabilize climate, eradicate poverty, stabilize population, restore the economy's natural support systems, and, above all restore hope. We have the technologies, economic instruments, and financial resources to do this. The United States, the wealthiest society that has ever existed, has the resources to lead this effort."[5]

There are symptoms of Earth's HIV/AIDS syndrome that many analysts believe can only be addressed effectively if they are analyzed and addressed at the level of the whole planet, in effect, by mobilizing globally. In his book *High Noon*,[6] Jean-Francois Rischard, a former World Bank vice-president, suggests that climate instability, biodiversity and ecosystem losses, fisheries depletion, deforestation, water deficits, ocean pollution, jobs migration, poverty, hunger and pandemic disease, for example, require cooperation on a planetary scale. Many ecologists, environmentalists, ecological economists, climate and marine scientists, futurists, agriculturalists and others who are considered to be economic realists and pragmatists agree. Like most of us, they don't see how these challenges can be met on anything but a global scale using global networks and tools.

And in a perfect world this would be feasible. National governments and the leaders of peoples would actually try to work together to fashion constructive global systems and viable global solutions. And many, particularly those leading and working through non-governmental organizations, are trying heroically and against the odds to do exactly that. Political leaders, on the other hand, may more often need to be prodded into action by a combination of coordinated worldwide protests, election boycotts, letter-writing campaigns, "none-of-the-above" candidate write-ins, e-mobilizations, flash-mobbing and workers' strikes. But in a perfect world they could conceivably be prodded into taking appropriate actions, after they agreed on what those actions should be.

In that Earthologically perfect world a critical mass of the world's leaders might recognize that dealing with our planetary crisis requires that the WTO and others of the supranational organizations that have managed to push both the global economy and the planet into debt and default be decommissioned. In their absence we could, as Lester R. Brown suggested in 2003's *Plan B*, "build an economy that does not destroy its natural support systems, a global community where the basic needs of all the earth's people are satisfied, and a world that will allow us to think of ourselves as civilized. This is entirely doable."[7]

The supranational organizations' financial assets, budgets and huge databases could be folded into the UN's accounts, their data shared out among its various agencies. New Earth-friendly — Earthological — agencies could be created to serve Life's purposes as well as ours, and the UN's own Earth Charter might guide all nations' activities. The members of that once venerable organization would, in a perfect world, help it to function as it was intended to. They could recognize the sovereignty of nations but also facilitate coalition building among them, more effectively and officially mediate disagreements between them, maximize international diplomacy, help to negotiate and keep the peace between nations in conflict and, where possible, protect the rights and well-being of the world's people. Representatives to the UN might be held accountable in ways that the directors of supranational organizations — however well-intentioned and trained they may be — currently are not. Yes, this vision presupposes a fairly universal and functional commitment to the common good, but in a perfect world, most or at least many of the leaders of nations would have that commitment.

With their sovereignty restored in such a perfecting world, a critical mass of nations would use remaining fossil fuels and funny-money to help their people, cities, towns and communities to avoid completely spending down fossil fuels and real money, and to repair the damage that both have done to human and ecosystem health and to the Earth's climate. Nations would use that money, for example, to facilitate a rapid transition to extreme energy efficiency and alternative, inexhaustible, non-polluting, carbon-free forms of energy. They might also determine the best and highest uses of remaining fossil fuels and coordinate the creation and monitoring of reserves.

Wealthy nations might use their money (if it's still worth something) to help willing poorer nations — and, of course, in a perfect world many or all nations would be willing — to convert their export economies to healthy, equitable, non-growth economies of the sort ecological economist Herman Daly and others call "steady-state."

> In a perfect world, prosperous nations would transition to self-sustaining, Life-friendly, no-growth economies.

In order to be both fair and exemplary, more prosperous nations in a perfect world would simultaneously convert their own economies to self-sustaining, Life-friendly, steady state — that is, Earthonomical — economies.

Prosperous nations would stop using less prosperous nations as supply regions. And they would not only stop using less prosperous regions as trash and hazardous waste sites, but they would also cease producing both trash — stuff thrown away in dumps, landfills and oceans — and hazardous waste.

In a perfect world, a critical mass of nations might adopt the Green GDP (Gross Domestic Product) or one of the other economic measures of well-being as their measure of prosperity and mandate transparent, true cost accounting. Their economies would for the first time "tell the ecological truth." "Economic prosperity is achieved in part," Lester Brown has written, "by running up ecological deficits, costs that do not show up on the books, but costs that someone will eventually pay ..."[8] with precious remaining funny-money, degraded ecosystems, polluted air, diminished human health and volatile weather, for example. Alternatively, the Green GDP and honest markets would factor in expenses that are presently hidden and kept off the books, like:

- environmental damage caused by using fossil fuels and the cost of repairing that damage
- systemically induced damage to human health and the resulting increase in the cost of health care
- job and income lost as a result of outsourcing

- the value to the human economy of services that only healthy ecosystems can provide

In a perfect world, nations would not depend on the invisible hand of markets to create the right economic environment for sustainable practices. They'd create the right economic environment for markets to do that. "Markets are not just open fields to which you simply add water and then sit back in a lawn chair, watch whatever randomly sprouts, and assume that the best outcome will always result. No," three-time Pulitzer winner Tom Friedman argued, "markets are like gardens. You have to intelligently design and fertilize them — with the right taxes, regulations, incentives, and disincentives — so they yield the good, healthy crops necessary for you to thrive."[10]

"Finding ways to halt ecological decline while still meeting the provisioning requirements of human societies must be made a political priority in every country in the world."[9]

Accordingly, in this version of a perfect world, nations would tax what they don't want (pollution, carbon emissions, mass firings, wastefulness and waste, for example) and subsidize what they do want (energy efficiency, forest, wetland, savannah and soil restoration, alternative energy, climate mitigation, sustainable food production systems, efficient electricity grids, equitable health care systems, effective education, transportation systems and water conservation, for example). And deficit reduction policies would fall on everyone equally.

They might, as British futurist and economic and financial advisor James Robertson has suggested, "shift public spending away from big public and private sector organizations that provide top-down public services, and onto providing an unconditional citizen's income to all citizens — to reflect our rightful share in the value of common resources, and to enable us to look after ourselves and one another better than so many of us can today."[11]

Nations in our imagined perfect world would deny corporations the rights of actual persons and would allow and encourage communities and nations in which corporations are chartered to hold them accountable fiscally and environmentally. Nations would export only what they have more than enough of, and only when exporting would not compromise their natural and human communities now or in the future. Prosperous nations would strive to require as few imports as possible. And, as Lester Brown and Roy Woodbridge have proposed, the community of nations in a perfect world might declare the equivalent of a world war on ecological decline and the conditions that it contributes to, including economic inequity, poverty and hunger.

In a perfect world, at least from Earthological, Earthonomical and ethical perspectives, there would be no haves and have-nots. There would be no jockeying by the latter group for favor with transnational corporations, the World Bank and the IMF in order to attain coveted better status in a global economy which can grant that status only temporarily and at great cost. There would be no attempt by unaccountable supranational organizations and institutions to force nations and peoples into supporting a viral global economy instead of their own.

## Perfectly Green and Trustworthy

In a perfect world, the resources that all the world's people and other-than-human species depend upon would be recognized to be what international policy advisor James Bernard Quilligan and others call a *global commons*. And those commons would be managed according to terms mutually established in commons trusts. Included in the commons would be, for example: clean air and water; tolerable weather and a Life-supportive atmosphere; healthy oceans, soils and forests; the rights to issue money and determine its value according to needs and circumstances, to save seeds and use local land to raise food for local consumption; universal literacy and numeracy; access to health care, land, housing, information and the basic tools of communication.

"Management of global resources requires global instruments. ... [The] idea of a climate trust fund might be a powerful initiative at the global level. What could indeed be effective is a global trust fund with the mandate of managing the atmosphere for future generations and of investing its revenues in social programs and environmental projects worldwide, according to the equal rights principle."[12]

"Commons trusts," wrote Quilligan, "are institutions, usually involving both physical and financial assets, which preserve and manage resources inherited from past generations on behalf of present and future generations." Such trusts would be "the only fiduciary institutions accountable for the long-term preservation and sustenance of a common resource," putting private concerns out of the business of pillaging resources and thwarting ecological services that are necessary for the continuation of Life as we know it.[13]

## Ten Key Green Party Values

1) Grassroots Democracy: Every human being deserves a say in the decisions that affect their lives; no one should be subject to the will of another. Therefore we will work to increase public participation at every level of government and to ensure that our public representatives are fully accountable to the people who elect them. We will also work to create new types of political organizations that expand the process of participatory democracy by directly including citizens in the decision making process.

2) Ecological Wisdom: Human societies must operate with the understanding that we are part of nature, not separate from nature. We must maintain an ecological balance and live within the ecological and resource limits of our communities and our planet. We support a sustainable society that utilizes resources in such a way that future generations will benefit and not suffer from the practices of our generation. To this end we must have agricultural practices that replenish the soil; move to an energy efficient economy and live in ways that respect the integrity of natural systems.

3) Social Justice and Equal Opportunity: All persons should have the right and opportunity to benefit equally from the resources afforded us by society and the environment. We must consciously confront in ourselves, our organizations and society at large, barriers such as racism and class oppression, sexism and heterosexism, ☞

ageism and disability which act to deny fair treatment and equal justice under the law.

4) Nonviolence: It is essential that we develop effective alternatives to our current patterns of violence at all levels, from the family and the streets, to nations and the world. We will work to demilitarize our society and eliminate weapons of mass destruction, without being naïve about the intentions of other governments. We recognize the need for self-defense and the defense of others who are in helpless situations. We promote nonviolent methods to oppose practices and policies with which we disagree and will guide our actions toward lasting personal, community and global peace.

5) Decentralization: Centralization of wealth and power contributes to social and economic injustice, environmental destruction and militarization. Therefore, we support a restructuring of social, political and economic institutions away from a system that is controlled by and mostly benefits the powerful few, to a democratic, less bureaucratic system. Decision making should, as much as possible, remain at the individual and local level, while assuring that civil rights are protected for all citizens.

6) Community Economics: We recognize it is essential to create a vibrant and sustainable economic system, one that can create jobs and provide a decent standard of living for all people while maintaining a healthy ecological balance. A successful economic system will offer meaningful work with dignity, while paying a living wage which reflects the real value of a person's work. Local communities must look to economic development that assures protection of the environment and workers' rights, broad citizen participation in planning and enhancement of our quality of life. We support independently owned and operated companies which are socially responsible, as well as cooperatives and public enterprises that spread out resources and control to more people through democratic participation.

7) Gender Equality: We have inherited a social system based on male domination of politics and economics. We call for the replacement ☞

of the cultural ethics of domination and control, with more cooperative ways of interacting which respect differences of opinion and
gender. Human values such as equity between the sexes, interper-
sonal responsibility and honesty must be developed with moral
conscience. We should remember that the process that determines
our decisions and actions is just as important as achieving the outcome we want.

8) Respect for Diversity: We believe it is important to value cultural,
ethnic, racial, sexual, religious and spiritual diversity and to promote
the development of respectful relationships across these lines. We
believe the many diverse elements of society should be reflected
in our organizations and decision making bodies, and we support
the leadership of people who have been traditionally closed out of
leadership roles. We acknowledge and encourage respect for other
life forms and the preservation of biodiversity.

9) Personal and Global Responsibility: We encourage individuals to
act to improve their personal well-being, and at the same time to
enhance ecological balance and social harmony. We seek to join
with people and organizations around the world to foster peace,
economic justice and the health of the planet.

10) Future Focus and Sustainability: Our actions and policies should be
motivated by long-term goals. We seek to protect valuable natural
resources, safely disposing of or "unmaking" all waste we create, while
developing a sustainable economics that does not depend on con-
tinual expansion for survival. We must counterbalance the drive for
short-term profits by assuring that economic development, new technologies and fiscal policies are responsible to future generations who
will inherit the results of our actions. Our overall goal is not merely to
survive, but to share lives that are truly worth living. We believe the
quality of our individual lives is enriched by the quality of all of our
lives. We encourage everyone to see the dignity and intrinsic worth
in all of life, and to take the time to understand and appreciate themselves, their community and the magnificent beauty of this world.[14]

Political parties in such an Earthological, ethical, common-goods world might write into their platforms versions of the ten core values of the Green Party USA. By doing so they would recognize these values as fundamental to the health of all human and natural communities, as largely beyond partisan debate and as the basis on which we could build viable communities, a functioning community of nations and an Earthological political culture. Leaders of nations and their people might view partnership as a deeply Green and more powerful survival tool than conflict, and regard provisioning the world as a more practical ambition than plundering it.

## What's the Prognosis for a Perfected World?

Those who promote these and similar visions of an Earthological, Earthonomical, equitable global future are really hoping for a widespread transformation in the way the Powers, the leaders of nations and the peoples of nations think and behave. They have pointed the way — for several decades in magazine articles, books, blogs, reports and lectures and at conferences and summits around the world — to transformation that might help us to create something closer to a perfect world.

And in a perfect world this kind of transformation of the consciousness, consciences and worldview of a critical mass of leaders would happen right now when we desperately need it to. And we would be inspired and helped by them to transform our own consciousness, consciences and worldviews too.

For this to happen from the top down, globally, a critical mass of leaders and Powers would have to become what's usually called "enlightened" and acquire attitudes and behaviors that are usually associated with spiritual teachers and the founders of religions. We ought not to

"As we enter the time of planetary initiation and find our historic moorings gone, social reflection may enable us to reach beneath the surface chaos and discover potentials for collective knowing and communication that were always present but required demanding circumstances to draw them forth.... [W]e could simply get it into our collective mind to do things differently."[15]

hold our breaths. Most spiritual teachers have not been heads or leaders of governments. They have, instead, been imprisoned, beaten, tortured and executed, or at best ignored, repudiated, condemned, patronized or scorned by the prevailing leaders and Powers.

Dramatic changes in human consciousness and in the way our brains and minds (and therefore our lives) work have occurred several times in the past. They have most often been triggered by naturally-occurring episodes of Critical Mass. (This is the subject of Chapter 14.) And it has taken many generations, even many millennia, for them to take hold in enough humans to influence the behavior of whole societies and cultures. They have occurred in an evolutionary time frame, not a human-life-span time frame such as we need now.

It is significant that changes in consciousness and worldview have come in response to crises, not in time to avert them. It is also significant that most such changes in collective consciousness have been caused by changes in the behavior and relationships of a critical mass of humans that conferred a survival advantage and therefore became contagious and desirable.

Transformation of some humans' worldviews away from the pyramidal vision of economies and societies toward ways of seeing and being that are Earthological, Earthonomical and equitable is arguably already under way. However, in the seats of power and hearts of the Powers who manage the global economy — not so much.

*New Yorker* financial writer James Surowiecki reminded us soberingly that "both history and theory suggest that tough economic times," such as those that are upon us, "make people less interested in sharing burdens, not more. One recent study found that people who had been treated unfairly," whose numbers now are legion, "became more selfish," not less

"[M]any of those who call for such a great awakening vaguely envision it as a kind of miraculous revolution, a crisis-induced change of heart that will bring us all together through a new vision of our essential unity within the greater earth community. Such sentimental hopes for global transformation are indeed charming, but hardly realistic.... To be sustainable, the transformation we seek must come about as a result of evolution, not revolution."[16]

selfish as they would need to be to support the sorts of global policies that would create the perfect — that is a humane, sustainable — world.[17]

Ironically, in either a perfect world in which the pathological economy has been thoughtfully disciplined and redesigned, or the imperfect one in which that economy suffers repeated tremors and ultimately collapses, many of our global problems would begin to solve themselves.

Since jobs would stay at home, people could stay in their home countries and home places. Corporate and business taxes would stay at home and could support those jobs and people. To the extent that despoiled soils and harsh weather would allow, the world's so-called supply regions could supply food and basic goods for their own people because there would be no global export market and no multinational corporations to which they'd be forced by their governments to lease their land and labor instead. The customary receivers of those supplies would have no choice but to learn how to provision themselves. Given that there'd be more physical work to do, less processed food to eat and less long distance travel by people, pests and contagious diseases, physical skill levels and health might well improve across the board.

In the perfected or wounded world, factory fishing fleets that troll the world's oceans depleting fish stocks and nurseries would be idled. We'd be making less or none of what pollutes the oceans, air, soils and water. Threatened species and ecosystems would begin to heal because there would no longer be a single-species globalized economy or heavy equipment, toxic emissions, wastes and fumes to abuse them. Cultures and languages threatened by the present hegemony of the English language, and by US media and passive entertainment, would revive. We would not be pushing the climate further and faster toward tilt. And funny-money would no longer be the key to success and survival and the source of intolerable inequities.

Good soil and water would matter more than good incomes and investments; good relationships rather than weapons or wealth would be key to one's receiving good treatment. That *would* be perfect.

## But in the Real World ...

It may seem pragmatic for global problems to be fixed globally, and it would be very convenient if they could be. But in the real world that has

"So, international policies are needed if we are to deal with a potentially game-ending global issue like climate change, yet there is now convincing evidence that national and supranational institutions are incapable of producing effective climate policies.... It's not enough that national governments can't get together to solve climate change. They can't solve economic meltdown, peak oil, water scarcity, soil erosion, or overpopulation either."[18]

never been the case. Global problems have been tinkered with, sometimes ameliorated and often put off. But when crises have become as intractable, complex, widespread and beyond the reach of funny-money as this one is, conflict and war have been, if not our solutions of choice, then at least our fallback positions.

Communities and nations have coordinated the use of technologies that benefited all of them — highway, air transportation, emergency response, telephone, communications and banking systems, for example — but have kept to themselves those technologies that give them a competitive edge and capacity to defend themselves. Communities of nations have taken up positions or weapons against other communities of nations, but there has never been "a" community of nations such as there would need to be to mitigate and effectively cure Critical Mass from the top down and center out — globally.

There are several reasons why the diverse and worsening crises that constitute Critical Mass cannot actually be effectively dealt with from the top down and center out — globally. One of the most glaring is that sufficient fossil fuels and funny-money to implement global solutions may not much longer exist. Stefan Theil reported in *Newsweek* in February 2010 that if the debt of the governments of prosperous nations (the ones that are supposed to pay for the transition to sustainability and a survivable climate) were to be accounted for rather than hidden or moved off their books, it would reach 500% of their Gross Domestic Product, their actual financial assets.[19]

Agreement about how to use what remains of fossil fuels and funny-money will never be widespread, let alone universal. In 2003's *Plan B*, Lester Brown recommended "a massive mobilization to deflate the global economic bubble *before it reaches the bursting point* ." (italics added) He meant: before funny-money could evaporate into thin air taking expensive global healing options with it. By the time Brown's *Plan B 4.0* was published in 2009, "before" had already yielded to "after," rendering the United States, while still reputedly the wealthiest society, one of the most indebted societies that has ever existed, and making any mobilization effort considerably less doable. And that was before the European fiscal crisis-cum-catastrophe and the embarrassingly myopic, vicious and dysfunctional 2011–2012 US campaign season rendered all intelligent political discussion moot and the dream of democracy a hallucination.

The most disheartening reason that global solutions so often fail is that there are a lot of places for which there may not *be* a solution, or at least not a very palatable one. Whole swaths of the Earth have always been too hot, cold, dry or flood-prone for continuous or dense human habitation. In many cases our activities have made them even less habitable. Only abundant funny-money, cheap, abundant fossil fuels and the utilities they supported and imports they supplied have made it possible for any of us, let alone millions of us, to live in such places. In their absence fewer of us will be *able* to live in such places, and more of us will need to try to find somewhere else to live. Given that there's nowhere habitable now that we don't already occupy or that some of us haven't already staked a claim to, clashes between occupants and immigrants are already intensifying. Addressing this insoluble global problem as individuals, communities and societies will be one of the biggest challenges to our humanity and our survival as a species, as well as to the prospect of our perfectibility.

Global problems are, finally, too complex to be solved with the one-size-fits-all solutions that are characteristic of global attempts at problem solving. Geneva, London, Brussels, Paris, New York, Washington, Beijing, Tokyo, Mumbai and other centers of global power and policy making are simply too far away from the problems they're trying to solve to know how to solve them well. Our inherent inability to think well globally is what got us into this mess.

## What We Can and Can't Know

With time, attention and training we are capable of understanding in some measure the workings of local and regional ecosystems and of the natural communities that create and maintain them. We can inventory local and regional assets and resources, including human resources — our invaluable cache of skills, talents, training, energy and expertise. We can create computer models to help us gauge how our activities might affect our immediate environments and existing ecosystems and stick to activities that would not harm them. We can learn how to enhance local and regional natural capital as well as how to conserve it and make good decisions about what we can ecologically afford to trade or sell to surrounding communities. In short, we can learn how to work with what we are — or can become — familiar with. We've been doing that for a couple million years or more and we have knowledge and technologies now that make doing it easier.

We are *not* capable of knowing or doing any of these things Earthologically at the level of the whole world. Our brains are simply not up to the task. Some of our hearts may be able to love that large, but none of us can think that large. And though computers can handle, integrate and hold a world of information about the world, they are not clever enough to tell us what to do with that information worldwide and Earthologically because we are not clever enough to program them for that task.

We are told that we may be close to the much anticipated singularity, a sort of cyber-space critical-mass moment at which our computers and information systems will have become intelligent, able to think without us and think better and faster than we can (like those algorithmic brokerage computers that can trade stocks faster than we can read what they're trading). It would be foolish, however, to expect such non-biological,

"Properly speaking, global thinking is not possible. Those who have 'thought globally' (and among them the most successful have been imperial governments and multinational corporations) have done so by means of simplifications too extreme and oppressive to merit the name of thought.

"Global thinking can only be statistical. Its shallowness is exposed by the least intention to do something. Unless one is willing to be destructive on a very large scale, one cannot do something except locally, in a small place."[20]

non-living entities to deeply understand what it means to care about the well-being or continued existence of biological entities, including us, that comprise Life on Earth. In any case, any contribution that intelligent machines or machine-body mergers might make is likely to be forestalled by the end of the oil needed to energize them and the deepening of the crises we've caused by thinking we are more clever than we are.

Despite his former association with the World Bank, *High Noon* author Jean-Francois Rischard agrees that it may be naïve to believe "that the current international setup has any chance of delivering global solutions in time" to solve what he describes as converging crises of complexity and governance.[21] The World Bank's own internal Evaluation Group acknowledged in April 2009 that in the ten previous years fully "one third of the health, nutrition and population programs ... produced unsatisfactory results, with weak monitoring and overly complex projects contributing to the problem."[22]

Consider these few examples of why bigger governments and globalized non-governmental institutions have failed to solve our increasingly bigger problems:

> *Disease Management*: Some global attempts to solve global problems will simply not prove effective. A World Health Organization report found, for example, that while the nearly $200 billion spent since 1990 on disease prevention, mitigation and cure in Third World countries has reduced the numbers of new cases of yellow fever, malaria and AIDS, "it's tough to gauge the effectiveness of pricey programs led by the United Nations and its partners, and in some cases, big spending may even be counterproductive." Researchers "concluded that some U.N. programs hurt health care in Africa by disrupting basic services and leading some nations to cut their [own] health spending."[23]

> *Ozone Depletion*: Some one-size-fits-all attempts to solve global problems will create other problems as serious as the ones they were intended to solve. The Montreal Protocol, signed by 189 countries between 1987 and 2007, was

meant to curb the release of ozone-depleting chemicals like chlorofluorocarbons (CFCs) into the atmosphere. As with most solutions directed at specific symptoms rather than their root cause, it had an unintended consequence. The protocol permitted the companies around the world that manufactured or used CFCs to decide what to replace them with. Having primarily their bottom lines in mind, those companies chose the cheapest possible alternatives to CFCs. The cheap substitutes do leave the ozone layer alone. However, it turns out that no research predicted the fact that those substitutes are climate destabilizing greenhouse gases that are up to 10,000 times more potent than $CO_2$.[24]

*Carbon Trading*: Some global attempts to solve global problems are con games rather than cure-alls. The cap-and-trade plan for curbing carbon emissions is already proving to be one of these. Carbon trading has become the fastest-growing commodities market in the world, to the tune of $300 billion in 2009, predicted to rise to $2 to $3 trillion if the US enters the market. It's likely to become the next global investment bubble and to make the usual suspects richer. It is indicative that the companies getting the most financial benefit from the cap-and-trading scheme so far — JP Morgan Chase, Goldman Sachs, Barclays, Citibank, Cargill, BHP Billiton (the world's largest mining firm) and the companies hired to monitor carbon emissions — are mostly the world's largest multinational corporations and financial firms.

But carbon trading fails to verifiably curb carbon emissions. Why?

The world's major carbon emitters, like power generating utilities, steel and cement manufacturers, purchase credits from low emitters or low emission projects (wind farms, solar plantations or revamped charcoal kilns that emit less carbon) that are planned to come on line sometime in the future. In other words, the major carbon emitters are under no compulsion to reduce emissions, and the projects that are supposed to counterbalance their emissions may or may not ever come on line or may not actually be low-emissions projects when they do. And the UN has no clout, no authority to penalize either the major emitters or the failed projects.

"The market is, in essence, an elaborate shell game," wrote Mark Shapiro of the Center for Investigative Reporting in Berkeley, California, "a disappearing act that nicely serves the immediate interests of the world's governments," and the major players in the global economy, "but fails to meet the challenges of our looming environmental crisis."[25]

Efforts will continue to be made, some of them heroically and with integrity, to solve global problems globally, nationally and internationally. It is what we think we know how to do, what we still think we *should* do. And some of those efforts — the true greening of some corporate production and distribution systems and product lines, for example — will accomplish more good than harm. But for one simple reason they will not cure us of Critical Mass: They will still be directed toward supporting and restoring health to the viral global economy that induced this planetary disease in the first place because they are dependent on the funny-money that economy produces. And that economy is:

1. the cause of our present crises
2. no longer in a position to either reliably support global solutions or provide sufficient funny-money

In summary: The prognosis for global solutions to our global problems is poor. As the largest complex system on the planet, only Life is qualified and equipped to deliver global solutions. The true and only source of our wealth and well-being is one that we and our economy are not, after all, larger than. And after all, every human economy is dependent on Life's support.

Life rules. We don't.

## Why Life Rules

Obviously, Life rules *because* it is the largest complex system, the largest *economic* system, on Earth. But it got to *be* the largest and also the longest lasting complex economic system on Earth by learning how to deal with Critical Mass and avoid causing it.

Ours is by no means the first episode of global Critical Mass. The episodes most of us know about — like the asteroid collision that put an end to the dinosaurs — humans had nothing to do with. We weren't even around for them. In the past half-billion years as many as twenty episodes of Critical Mass have been caused by atmospheric or climate change, planet-shaping seismic and tectonic plate events, asteroid collision or catastrophic volcanic eruptions that sent up clouds of ash so thick and persistent that they threw much of the Earth into the dark, triggering years-long winters that killed much of the plant life on which animal life directly or indirectly depended. Each such cosmically or geologically induced episode of Critical Mass caused a mass extinction (the demise of whole ecosystems and many kinds of life) and dramatically altered the mix of players in Earth's immune system of natural communities.

"Five of these [events] — the so-called Big Five — were so devastating that they are usually put in their own category," explained Elizabeth Kolbert, a climate and environment writer for *The New Yorker* magazine. "The first took place during the late Ordovician period, nearly four hundred and fifty million years ago, when life was still confined mainly to water. Geological records indicate that more than eighty percent of marine species died out."[26] The third brought an end to the Permian period, around 250 million years ago. As many as 95% of all species vanished in an event of unknown cause that's appropriately called "the great dying."

The fifth great extinction, which occurred 65 million years ago at the end of the Cretaceous period, is the most famous. That's the one that put the dinosaurs and something like 75% of all other species out of business practically overnight. The scientific consensus is that an asteroid as large as six miles across crashed into Mexico's Yucatan peninsula turning Earth's atmosphere into "a hell furnace," according to the American Museum of Natural History's Michael Novacek. "Temperatures in the upper atmosphere might have hovered around 700°C (1,300°F) for several hours.... The thermal pulse would have been global, at a power level more intense than an oven set at 'broil.'"[27] Scientists are not certain why anything at all survived or why some sub-species within a family of species survived and others didn't.

But "extinction also leads to opportunity," said Novacek. "A computer simulation analysis showed that under certain conditions 80 percent of the original phylogenetic structure — the larger branches of the tree of life, or clades — can survive a 95 percent loss of their species and become evolutionarily fecund once more."[28] Happily, among the 25% of species that survived the explosive end of the Cretaceous were the tiny mammals from which all other forms of mammalian life, including us, evolved.

Significantly, while it was learning to survive episodes of Critical Mass that it couldn't avoid, Life — back then, the whole-Earth community of *other-than-human* living things — was also learning how to improve the odds of survival by not causing additional episodes of Critical Mass.

We can learn how to mitigate the current symptoms of Critical Mass, how to survive it and how to avoid causing it again from the ultimate Critical Mass survivor: Life itself.

**We can obey Life's rules,
adopt lifeways that mimic Life's ways
and by that means live within Earth's means.**

# Part II

## How Life Deals with Critical Mass

"In *The Interpreters,* a book written at the height of the Irish Revolution by the Irish author known as AE, there is a passage in which a group of prisoners, a disparate lot, sit around discussing what the ideal new world would look like. One of them, a philosopher, advances the now-familiar vision of a unitary world order with a global, scientific, cosmopolitan culture. Another, the poet Lavelle, argues fervently against this conception, trying to show that the more the world develops in its technological superstructure, the farther it gets from its natural roots. 'If all wisdom is acquired from without,' he says, 'it might be politic for us to make our culture cosmopolitan. But I believe our best wisdom does not come from without, but arises in the soul and is an emanation of the Earth spirit, a voice speaking directly to us dwellers in this land.'

"It is not difficult to imagine the alternative to the peril the industrio-scientific, [global economic] paradigm has placed us in. It is simply to become 'dwellers in the land....'

"But to become dwellers in the land, to relearn the laws of Gaia, to come to know the earth fully and honestly, the crucial and perhaps only and all-encompassing task is to understand place, the immediate and specific place where we live."[1]

## Chapter 7

# Life's Steep Economic Learning Curve

Like us, Life learned its limits the hard way.[1] Life almost put itself out of business three times before it learned to live within Earth's means. We can learn a lot from Life's near-fatal experiences with self-induced Critical Mass, despite the fact that the entities that did the inducing and almost paid for it with extinction were Earth's first and (possibly) most primitive life form: bacteria.

Why take our cues from bacteria? For starters, somehow, without benefit of consciousness, conscience or computers, bacteria found their way out of all three crises and figured out how not to repeat the behaviors that caused them. And what they figured out has formed the basis of Life's repertoire of survival techniques ever since. Life locked in, or genetically encoded, bacteria's solutions to the problem of self-induced Critical Mass. Those solutions must have been good ones.

Granted, bacteria are about the most minimal kinds of living entities we can imagine. Single-celled species with

> "One legitimate answer to the question 'What is life?' is 'Bacteria.' Any organism, if not itself a live bacterium, is then a descendant — one way or another — of a bacterium or, more likely, mergers of several kinds of bacteria... Bacteria may be life's tiniest life forms, but they took giant steps in evolution."[2]

nothing more than an infinitesimally thin membrane standing between them and hard knocks, bacteria nonetheless are the life form from which all other life forms, including humans, derive. We wouldn't be if they hadn't been. So when we talk about Life lasting — about its phenomenal endurance — and when we consider accordingly what we would need to do to bring our lifeways into harmony with Life's ways, we're really talking about variations on the theme of bacteria. To a certain extent, mimicking the way Life works means mimicking the ways bacteria — and all the successful life forms they gave rise to — work.

"Ancient bacteria invented technologies of energy production, transportation and communications, including a World Wide Web still in existence today, during their competitive phase and then used those very technologies to bind themselves into the cooperative ventures that made our own existence possible."[3]

We are understandably leery of bacteria. Some of them make us sick, some can even kill us. Leaving aside the rogue members of the species, however, billions of other kinds of bacteria are good for us. They create and maintain not only the worlds we live in but our own bodies. It is estimated that humans are home to somewhere between 500 and 1,000 different kinds of bacteria, each of which provides a service we can't live without. For example, every one of the approximately five trillion cells in our bodies contains a thousand or more mitochondria, descendants of ancient bacteria that made themselves useful by producing energy inside cells. However, for a very long time the single-celled organisms that learned how to survive and also how to avoid causing global Critical Mass were very *good* at causing it.[4]

Obviously bacteria could not *choose* to stop causing Critical Mass. It just happens that the only kinds of bacteria that survived long enough to get around to participating in larger organisms like us were the ones that *did* stop causing it. Prompted by a conscious desire to survive, we could choose to learn how they did that and then do the same.

## Earth's First Global Economic Catastrophes

Four billion years ago bacteria were the only living things. They had a world full of raw materials to work with and no competitors except each other, nothing to stop them from multiplying exponentially and spreading everywhere. Each bacterium was an entity unto itself in heated competition with each other bacterium, but together they were the dominant species and their economy was genuinely global. Sound familiar?

Since Earth was not at all like it is now, primal bacteria had to provide for themselves in very different ways than present strains of bacteria do. For eons of time they had no hosts to prey on, nor any means of or instinct for preying. And, like us, bacteria were and are unable to produce their food or life energy internally. They depend on external sources of nutrition to make the energy they run on. Ancient bacteria fed on chemical nutrients and organic compounds they absorbed from Earth's still forming seas and crust, and from its volatile original atmosphere of greenhouse gases like hydrogen, methane, ammonia and $CO_2$. They literally soaked up their environments.

They made the sugars that powered their activities by fermenting some of those organic compounds (it was their equivalent of burning fossil fuels), and their bodies were constructed out of carbon they mined from atmospheric $CO_2$. Happily, the planet's churning, lightening-charged surface manufactured a constant supply of vital organic compounds. And since it also burped greenhouse gases continuously, there was plenty of $CO_2$ for them to work with.

For a while.

## Critical Mass # 1: An Energy Crisis

Bacteria are, of course, microscopic. But over a hundred million years or so a planet full of them ran through a lot of organic compounds — just as, in only 250 years, we've run through a lot of fossil fuels. Inconveniently for the bacteria, while their populations and appetite were growing exponentially, the planet's crust was cooling and becoming more stable. It no longer replenished as reliably as it had the foods and fuels that supported the bacterial way of living. Unable to predict pending shortages, bacteria continued to multiply, spread and consume with abandon. And so as early as 3.9 billion years ago, Earth's first dominant species was already encountering its version of a peak oil problem.

They might have passed peak and overshot their fuel supply, but they didn't.

Just in the nick of time — though after a trial and error process that took both the lives of inconceivable numbers of the tiny things and what would seem to us forever — some plucky bacteria discovered photosynthesis. They switched their economy from reliance on an exhaustible source of energy (fermentation that depended on a finite fuel supply) to reliance on an inexhaustible, widely available source of energy: sunlight. They went solar, just as humans could plan to do. In their case, bacteria used sunlight to process $CO_2$ and hydrogen to make the sugars that powered their activities. By that means they took themselves off the short list for extinction and got past Critical Mass.

For a while.

## Critical Mass #2: A Climate Crisis

Although photosynthesis solved Life's first *energy supply* crisis, it set Life up for an *energy related* crisis. But bacteria didn't see it coming. Still unable to predict the consequences of their actions, in essence they globalized their economy again. What was wrong with that? With the adoption of photosynthesis as a means of food production, bacteria all over the world were now using carbon for both body-building and sugar-making. But by 2.5 billion years ago the Earth's crust had long since stopped spewing copious fresh supplies of $CO_2$. Diminishing supplies ran on a collision course with increasing consumption. It's not difficult to predict the result. Despite fierce competition for the remaining $CO_2$ and survival of only the fittest and most fortuitously located members of the species, by around 2.3 billion years ago bacteria had drawn down enough atmospheric $CO_2$ to trigger Earth's second episode of Critical Mass.

"These processes would have been slow on our time-scale, but before many tenths of an eon had elapsed, the composition of the atmosphere would have changed considerably as the carbon dioxide content was gradually depleted. If the planet [had previously been] kept warm ... by the blanket effect of carbon dioxide gases ... a runaway worldwide fall in temperature would be inevitable."[5]

How?

Humans are learning now that if you add too much $CO_2$ to the atmosphere, the climate gets warmer. Our globally ambitious microscopic predecessors discovered that if you take too much $CO_2$ *out* of the atmosphere, the climate gets cooler. Without that dense layer of $CO_2$ to contain it, virtually all the sun's warmth radiated back out into space. Earth froze and so did a lot of bacteria. The planet's first ice age would have reduced their soft-bodied populations to shattered, scattered remnants.

## Critical Mass #3: A Pollution Crisis

That second lesson about the inherent vulnerability of global economies was lost on Life, too. Carbon wasn't the only element for which Earth's dominant species had an insatiable appetite. Bacteria consumed hydrogen as if *it* couldn't run out either. There was no reason not to. After all, they had been able to depend on abundant atmospheric hydrogen for eons. Now it was dwindling along with atmospheric $CO_2$. But bacteria got lucky before they ran out. The planet was still full of resources, if not exactly the ones bacteria were used to. When the ice melted again they were blessed with the equivalent of a permanent line of credit. There was water — hydrogen dioxide, $H_2O$ — everywhere.

At first bacteria didn't know how to use water-based hydrogen. It took them millions of years and the learning curve was steep, but finally some resourceful bacteria discovered — again by a long process of trial and error involving a high body count — that by making a few adjustments to their form and function they could tap into that virtually infinite supply of $H_2O$, separate the hydrogen from the oxygen, fuel up on the first and discard the second through their cell membranes as waste. A third bacterial economy went global.

What went wrong *that* time? Why isn't bacteria still the only life form on Earth? By around two billion years ago they had almost polluted themselves into extinction. We can relate to that crisis, too. Since there were no other species around that could clean up or recycle their waste oxygen, the atmosphere loaded up with it, going from less than one part in 100 billion to one part in five, and sometimes even one part in less than five.

For us and other more modern life forms, a 20% oxygen atmosphere is life-sustaining or at least survivable. For those early bacteria, it was a death sentence. Oxygen is an electron thief and highly flammable. In concentrations over 20%, which back then it periodically reached, it tears compounds apart to get at their electrons and sets soft tissue on fire. Earth's hyper-oxygenated atmosphere turned "vibrant living cells" into what Brian Swimme and Thomas Berry describe as "a disconnected and chemically meaningless scrap heap."6

For the third time the planet's first life form almost became the planet's last life form. Almost two billion years after its first failure and 300 million years after its second, a global economy that was managed by a dominant species failed, taking most of that species with it. Swimme and Berry explained how Life pulled back from the brink of extinction *that* time. "Instead of failing, life mutated. A [new kind of] bacterium appeared ... that could deal with this oxygen, this powerful element that was tormenting all life. The [new] bacterium not only survived, it invented respiration, the power to deal with oxygen."7 But this is not all that those ancient bacteria did.

## Life's First Earthological Economies

Sorely tested by Critical Mass and pushed by then into the most extreme forms of competition (including cannibalism), bacteria made several dramatic changes in their ways of living. What they did next set the pattern for Life: In effect, they gave up economic globalization. They downsized, diversified and got organized. They created Life's first Earthogical (long-term sustainable) economies. In the process they evolved a set of rules, an economic and remarkably democratic survival protocol that helped them to avoid causing Critical Mass again and to survive it when it occurred due to circumstances beyond their control. It is this protocol that facilitated the gradual organization of the whole-Earth network of natural communities that — until humans intervened — managed the planet's equivalent of a high-functioning immune system.

"Life hangs on to what works. At the same time, it explores and tinkers."8

Life has found an inconceivable number of ways to tweak and tinker with this protocol. Evolutionary biologist Elisabet Sahtouris calls it "improvising."

The truth of the matter is that status quo produces nothing new or improved. Life has a genius for new and improved, for making something brand new out of what's already on hand. Koalas, kudzu and coral reefs were not the result of tentativeness or repetition.

In complex systems theorist Stuart Kauffman's terms, Life may like order but it is "partially lawless," and the partially lawless — verging on chaotic — part is the creative, innovative, improvisational part. Tinkering, tweaking and bending the rules bring new life forms and improved lifeways into being. But the chaos that would result from ceaseless tinkering and innovation is inevitably destructive.

> "This world of wild exploration is one which tinkers itself into existence. But life's tinkering has a direction. It tinkers toward order — toward systems that are more complex and more effective. The process used is exploratory and messy, but the movement is toward order."[9]

So Life has tinkered with its original protocol, the one that bacteria eventually arrived at, but it has not rejected it or seriously changed its basic tenets. Why? Chaos must be balanced by order. The protocol imposes — or builds in — the necessary order. Sticking to the protocol has allowed Life to operate within Earth's means, to improvise exuberantly without incurring unacceptable risk. In other words, obeying the short list of rules that comprise this protocol (see the end of this chapter) is what has allowed Life to last, despite the occasional round of self-induced or unavoidable chaos. Life has learned how to keep chaos — the creative principle — in balance with order — the rule-obeying principle.

> "There's an internally recognized beauty of motion and balance on this planet [when it's healthy]. You see in this beauty a dynamic stabilizing effect essential to all life. Its aim is simple: to maintain and produce coordinated patterns of greater and greater diversity. Life improves the closed system's capacity to sustain life. Life — all life — is in the service of life. Necessary nutrients are made available to life by life in greater and greater richness as the diversity of life increases. The entire landscape comes alive with relationships and relationships within relationships."[10]

Life can teach us how to do the same thing.

Volumes would be required to convey all of this protocol's subtleties and possibilities. We have not even learned all of them yet. We may never learn them all or understand them fully. But the basics are fairly easy to understand and sufficient to point us in the same direction they pointed Critically-Massed primal bacteria: away from both economic globalization and pyramidal socio-political structures.

## Life's Economic Survival Protocol
## A Ten Commandments of Sustainability

1) Life's successful (long-lasting and sustainable) economies waste nothing and produce no waste they cannot consume or sequester.
2) They run directly or indirectly on inexhaustible forms of energy, the foremost of which is solar.
3) Life's successful economies are relatively equitable, common good economies.
4) Life's basic units of economic activity are locally self-reliant, interdependent, mixed-species communities.
5) Locally self-reliant natural communities organize, regulate and govern themselves within limits set by their environments and by the needs of the larger communities of which they are a part.
6) They exchange information and pool intelligence in real time.
7) They distribute leadership according to task.
8) In hard times, Life's successful — long-term sustainable — communities cut back.
9) Natural communities operate in ways that are inherently — organically — democratic.
10) Natural communities seek stability rather than perpetual growth and expansion.

CHAPTER 8

# Life Is Earthonomical, Naturally

L IFE'S SUCCESSFUL ECONOMIES are Earthogical economies — they are sustainable over the long term — in part because they are waste-free, primarily solar, common good economies.

## Waste-Free Economics

Life is not wasteful. It does not make things it isn't going to use. Put another way, everything Life makes gets used, whether for its original purpose or another, perhaps lesser one. Plants, for example, put out masses of seeds. For a variety of reasons many of those seeds don't produce viable seedlings. But the excess seeds and failed seedlings are not wasted. They are food for insects or birds or they decompose, feeding soil microbes and returning their nutrients and tissues to the soil as food and building material for subsequent generations of plants.

Life does not treat even used things as waste. Everything is food for or good for something else. Manure, minerals,

"In a continuous cycle, plants and animals exchange the chemicals necessary for energy and [body] building materials. One creature's 'exhale' becomes another creature's 'inhale.' And each generation of living things depends on the chemicals released by the generations that have preceded it."[1]

bodies, water, leaves, trees, atmospheric gases like nitrogen, oxygen and carbon dioxide, sea shells, salt: If Life produced it, Life takes back what's left of it or what it has turned into, refreshes it if possible and uses it again.

The Earthologic of recycling and reuse are as old as that first bacterially-induced episode of Critical Mass. One of bacteria's first responses to shortages of geologically produced nutrients was to ingest and digest (recycle) the nutrient-loaded bodies of their dead kin. Since physical resources are finite, the more times and ways they can be used and the more living things that can get some use out of them the better. If you can't create more of a resource, the next best thing is to figure out how not to use up the supply you've got. Finding ways to keep using things is the better part of Life's Earthonomic wisdom. Waste not, want not.

Another benefit of not making waste is that most of the time no one kind of waste alone accumulates to the point of becoming pollution. At present, Life's economies are not producing anything that they can't either recycle in real time or sequester — as plants sequester $CO_2$ — until it can be recycled. For the most part Life has either found ways to limit potential pollutants, or one or more life forms have learned how to put them to good use. This highly efficient and economical waste management system persists in established natural economies until some force like climate change or a viral global economy intervenes and disrupts it.

## Solar Economics

The economies of virtually all natural communities, whether they are long lasting, successful economies or tryouts that fail, are powered by sunlight. With very few exceptions — the array of weird creatures that live around gas-spewing vents in the oceans' floors, for example[2] — natural economies run on solar energy. But even those strange, lightless communities depend indirectly on temperature variations, currents and other conditions that are maintained by solar-driven communities. "Life," says microbiologist Lynn Margulis, "is a solar phenomenon."

Life's economies access solar energy in several ways. The food web is one of them. Plants obtain energy directly from sunlight by means of photosynthesis (which means "working with light"). They use that energy to produce carbohydrates that fuel their growth and reproduction. Animals obtain solar-fueled carb energy indirectly by eating plant material and converting plant nutrients into proteins and fats, or by eating other animals that eat plants. Sunshine powers a moveable feast as solar energy is distributed from plants out through Life's food web. Fungi, insects, bacteria, viruses and other microscopic life forms also obtain solar energy indirectly as they feast on the nutrients in plants or animals. They too transfer solar energy around the web.

An estimated 10% of energy gets lost at each remove away from plants, much in the same way that electrical energy gets lost as it travels through the millions of miles of wires that carry it from generating stations into buildings. Unlike fossil-fueled electricity, however, sunlight is for all intents and purposes inexhaustible. Solar energy is continuously replaced (though at varying levels of intensity) and distributed worldwide.

Life uses solar energy in real time to power its activities. But sunlight is not a 24/7 resource, and it is not entirely predictable. The day-night and seasonal cycles, clouds and physical features like mountains and trees that cast shadows all influence the availability and intensity of sunlight. Life has adapted to those constraints. Plants and other photosynthesizers store solar-powered carbohydrates in their cells and tissues. Earth's forests, jungles, grasslands and algal mats (floating islands of algae) function as a vast reservoir of stored solar energy that can be called upon even when sunlight is reduced or absent.

There's no peak solar event anywhere on the horizon.

## Common Good Economics

Life treats resources as a common wealth and Earth as a common inheritance. What's in Earth's accounts in any given place belongs not just to a few species or a few members of a species, but to all of us. Why? If even a few participants in a natural economy are deprived of the resources they need, they decline or die off. That affects the economy as a whole just as the failure of a sector like steel or textile production affects an entire human economy. If a majority of species is deprived of the resources they need to survive — as they are now being deprived by our single-species global economy — Life is compromised.

Widespread prosperity, or even sufficiency, makes natural econo-mies strong and that makes Life (the whole-Earth network of natural economies) strong. Competition and predation prevent any one spe-cies from dominating a resource. But Life also locked in behaviors that resemble sharing because they guarantee commitment to the common good, which increases the likelihood that a natural economy will be sustainable.

How do Life's common good economics work?

Well, for example: The feeding habits, migration patterns, teeth and body shapes of different species of grazing animals allow them to share the same browsing range without any species regularly depleting the others' food supply. A half-dozen species of animals or more, some of them predators, may share a savannah water hole at the same time, as if a sort of truce were declared when a scarce and necessary resource is involved. Scores of species share a single rainforest tree or coral colony, billions of microbes share the same square foot of soil.

Squirrels don't hoard their wealth of acorns in secret stashes so that the one with the biggest stash wins and gets to rule over squirreldom. They bury acorns all over the place where they become new oak trees or food for other squirrels, mice, birds and chipmunks. The burying process itself serves the common good: It both loosens the soil, mak-ing it permeable for roots and habitable for the thousands of life forms that work and live in it, and burying aerates the soil, which lets in and distributes water as well as air.

Like reliance on solar energy and waste not-want not, equitabil-ity — what we might call economic justice — is not altruistic. It is Earthological. It's another way Life gets the maximum possible use out of the finite resources it has at its disposal without depleting those resources. And that's, simply, Earthonomical.

"The argument here is not that [individual members of a species] sacrifice themselves for the group. All group-oriented behavior ... serves the individuals who perform it.... But even so, group-oriented behavior improves the quality of the social environment not just for the individuals who show it, but for every one else as well...."[3]

## We Already Know These Rules

Recycling, adding solar power to the energy mix and spreading the wealth around, by means, for example, of charitable giving, tax deductions and social support programs, are not new ideas for us any more than they are for Life, though we have not locked them in as firmly as Life has. We break those rules more often and more exuberantly than we obey them. They are not in the Powers' or their global economy's best interests. Nonetheless, even the staunchest supporters of the global economy and some of its most fortunate corporate and individual beneficiaries are adding recycling and solar to their lists of priorities when they are profitable. And some recognize the need to make the economy more equitable, if for no other reason than to reduce the severity of social unrest, potential violence or revolution that the collapse of the global economy will inevitably trigger.

But the global economy could not cure us of Critical Mass even if it were to bounce back, get greener, reduce waste and wastefulness, add some solar to the energy mix and spread some of the wealth and assets around.

Again, why?

It would still be a global economy. Obeying three of Life's economic rules without obeying the other six would be about as effective a fix for what's going wrong nearly everywhere at once as giving an HIV patient a bronchial dilator for her pneumonia and a protein supplement for her wasting disease without restoring her immune system to full function and her to full health. Better than nothing, but not enough; a postponement, not a cure.

The continuation of Life as we know it hangs on the remaining rules in Life's Economic Survival Protocol. They reflect lessons that bacteria

"The natural world is full of models for a more sustainable economic system — prairies, coral reefs, oak-hickory forests, old-growth redwood and Douglas-fir forests, and more. These mature ecosystems do everything we want to do. They self-organize into a diverse, integrated community of organisms with a common purpose — to maintain their presence in one place, make the most of what is available, and endure over the long haul."[4]

learned the hard way and Life hasn't forgotten. They are the rules that have made Life so successful and allowed Life as we know it to endure.

The keys to our surviving Critical Mass are economic downsizing and diversification (Chapter 11) and biocracy, a kind of economic and ecological democracy, that is organic — encoded in other-than-human species and their interactions (Chapter 12).

CHAPTER 9

# Life's Earthonomical Communities — Prototypes for Deep Green

B ACTERIA DID NOT CHOOSE TO DOWNSIZE, Critical Mass downsized them. Individual bacteria that couldn't make the adjustment to their new circumstances — an oxygen-rich atmosphere, for example — died. Critical Mass will most likely downsize us too. It has downsized human populations many times before by means of ice ages, floods and geophysical catastrophes. Genetic data indicates that as recently as 75,000 years ago, several years of volcanic winter, resulting from a massive eruption in Indonesia (called the Toba mega-volcanic event) that produced lingering clouds of ash, devastating acid rains and a mini-ice age, may have reduced Earth's human population by 60%.[1] None of our wondrous technologies even now make us invulnerable to the worst that Critical Mass can do.

Downsizing could be a relatively humane and constructive process, however, if we were to mimic the ways bacteria responded to being downsized. They did not do what we are currently trying to do (more of the same things that caused global Critical Mass). Instead they participated actively in their downsizing and learned how to make it work to their advantage. In the process they acquired habits and skills and evolved behaviors that are exemplary for us and might, when (or if) we adopt them, be called *Deep Green*.

## Taking It from the Bottom

It is customary to treat bacteria as a lump, a single species. Lynn Margulis and her son, science writer Dorian Sagan, agreed that "If the standard definition of species, a group of organisms that interbreed only among themselves, is applied to bacteria, then all bacteria belong worldwide to a single species."[2] They added, however, that as long as three billion years ago, there already were several different strains of bacteria. Why might that be?

Though Life's ways are ecological rather than logical from an intellectual perspective, there is an intellectually logical explanation for Life's early foray into variety. When Earth's surface stopped seething it settled into continents, familiar landshapes, oceans, seas, rivers and smaller bodies of freshwater. It presented remnant populations of bacteria with what must have been a bewildering array of physically very different environments. Some of those environments were harsh beyond our imagining. All of them were slowly but constantly changing under the influence of wind, water, geological forces, the comings and goings of ice and the chemical activities of the bacteria themselves. Faced with diverse environments, bacteria diversified their economies. They adapted forms, methods of mobility, diets, metabolisms, lifeways and ways of using solar energy that allowed them to survive the wide range of unique physical conditions in which they found themselves.

Bacteria tinkered with and tweaked their form and function so often and so creatively in order to fit into their changing environments that whole realms of entirely new kinds of living things gradually emerged. While survival of the fittest may have worked for individuals, survival of the fittingest (those that fit themselves into and worked with their environments) worked for these new entities.

By 1.6 billion years ago, clouds of microscopic plankton, the primary source of nutrition for all marine animals, drifted on the world's ocean currents and foraged for nutrients on the continental shelves. By 600 million years ago the first simple forms of animals had appeared. By 570 million years ago they were joined by fungi and plants and around 400 million years ago by insects. These species also diversified themselves and their economies continuously. They adapted to every microclimate and geographic neighborhood on Earth, giving rise through time to every kind of organ and organism we know of and many we do not.

Life is still tinkering and tweaking, of course. New entities and beings are still arising, though our activities make it difficult for all but the smallest and toughest — like HIV — to survive. And established species are still diversifying their economies, in no small measure because our dominance and depredations and our insistence on running against Life's Earthonomic grain have required them to.

The immediate advantage of diversification for bacteria was survival. The long-term advantage of diversification to Life was that it put an end to single-species domination which in turn put an end to the possibility that any species could expand its economy to the point of inducing Life-threatening global Critical Mass. Life's economies ever after would be smaller scale (downsized) economies.

But downsizing and diversification conferred yet another benefit on Life. Every different kind of living thing discovered, refined and passed on a unique way of surviving in its particular environment and unique ways of adapting to change. The more different kinds of living things there were, the more survival techniques Life had in its repertoire. Diversification guaranteed that when Critical Mass occurred naturally — during an ice age, for example — some species might fail but others would persist. Life would continue.

> "It might be useful to think of the role of diversity as one of insurance against discontinuities....
>
> "The more diversity a system displays, the more ... challenges it is capable of dealing with."[3]

Diversity by itself was not a sufficient survival strategy, however. Each species had a specialty: It was particularly good at one way or set of ways of surviving. But as we're learning painfully, specialists are ill equipped to deal with multiplying and multifaceted crises and with problems outside the range of their expertise. That takes teamwork, the integration and coordination of multiple, diverse forms, abilities, techniques, perspectives and kinds of information and intelligence. *Teamwork* — more specifically teamwork that led to the creation of remarkably democratic mixed-species communities — was one of Life's next and most effective Earthonomical solutions to the problem of self-induced Critical Mass.

Most human endeavors benefit greatly from teamwork too, of course, and in the past several decades many corporations and organizational consultants have worked to maximize the benefits of teamwork. But one of the reasons we've hit Critical Mass now is that for the last several thousand years, monetary economies have not depended directly on teams or teamwork, on democracy or, for that matter, on the communities that comprised them.

Why?

In part it's because funny-money has obscured the reality of finiteness and our dependence on healthy environments and natural communities. But in large part it's because, while we are capable of choosing to work with Life and like Life does, we're also capable of choosing not to. We're a young species, and the first self-conscious one. We are, in a way, doubly self-conscious. We are aware of ourselves as selves but we're also a bit stuck in and stuck on our selves. We won't evolve or mature naturally under Life's tutelage in the direction of teamwork and community as other-than-human species have, as hominids and so-called primitive humans did and as new species eventually do. *Each one of us* will have to choose to evolve in that direction. Why would we, why should we?

## Why Community?

Life's basic unit of economic activity is not the individual, though Life has a penchant for individuality. Life exists because of the interactions of incredibly different, individual living things each of which has an inherent interest in self-preservation and in creating circumstances that give it a good shot at survival and reproduction. Though we use the word as a noun, a thing, in its essence Life is a verb. It is what living things do. In particular it is what they do *together* — in communities.

Every individual living thing — apparently even the lowly bacterium — is, like us, driven to work out its own existence and make the most of its opportunities. Each is inherently interested in its own survival and in producing more of its kind. Each is unique. Each embodies a combination of traits, talents, techniques or twists of form or function that give it identity, possibility and intrinsic value as one of Life's experiments with new life. Accordingly, each living thing and living system establishes or grows a boundary around itself that defines and preserves its identity, its "self." Cells have membranes or walls, we have skins, animals have territories, forests have edges. But no individual, no matter what kind of boundary it maintains, can live on its own.

Living things, wrote philosopher Christian de Quincey, are "not so much 'individuals' as *interviduals*."[4] The boundaries that living things and systems create around themselves are not hard and fast. They are permeable and flexible. They are intended to let out and keep out what might be harmful but also to let in and share what's useful or beneficial. Life's boundaries anticipate collaboration and facilitate interchange. They permit living things from the smallest to the largest to engage — without risk to their integrity or individuality — in what Elisabet Sahtouris has described as "constant negotiations" with their environments and with the other living things around them. Cells exchange electrochemical information through their walls and membranes. Skin sweats, exudes pheromones, blocks pathogens and admits sunlight. Animal territories overlap like waves on a beach, and the borderlands between ecosystems like fields and forests are crossed and recrossed by species that get benefits from both environments.

Life's basic unit of economic activity is also not the family or single-species group. Animal families, single-species animal groups like herds, prides, pods, hives, schools, flocks and packs — and plant groups like stands, groves and clumps — are stronger, smarter and better protected than any of the individuals in them would be on their own; they are better able to access partners for procreation. But no family or single-species group, no matter how strong or well protected, can live on its own. Prides of lions can't live without herds of impala to prey on; impala can't live without clumps of grasses to graze and grasses can't thrive without strains of bacteria like *Clostridium* to fix nitrogen in the soil. Conversely, bacteria can't live without the manure of herd animals like impala to feed them; herds of impala can't thrive without predators like lions to trim their weakest members and so forth. For this reason

## Life's basic unit of economic activity is the mixed-species community.

We apply the term "community" to almost any collection of people who share an interest, demographic or purpose, whether or not they are residents of a particular place or have even met. There are virtual and online communities, workplace, ethnic, religious and professional communities. Membership in these communities is discretionary or conferred, and active participation is rarely obligatory.

*Natural communities*, however, are not just located *on* but embedded *in* very particular places. Members of natural communities reside permanently or seasonally in those places. They are more familiar with each other and their environments, their lives are more fully integrated and intertwined, than most of us can imagine being. And they are active participants in their communities the way that our hands, feet and eyes are active participants in — members of — our bodies. Members of natural communities are also partners in a common cause: the well-being and survival of their communities.

### Natural communities are communities of place, partnership and purpose.

If we choose to assuage the symptoms of Critical Mass and cure ourselves of it, so will our future economic communities be, Earthonomically, communities of place, partnership and purpose. As you read the rest of this chapter, you might want to imagine what its implications are for you and the sort of community you and those around you might decide or need to create in order to cope with the symptoms of Critical Mass.

## Communities of Place

No money, funny or otherwise, stands between other-than-human species and the resources they require. The economies of natural communities are resource-based and, by extension, *place-based*.

With the exception of solar energy, other-than-human species cannot deliberately import and export resources like we do, and many of them do not travel far or at all. Consequently, the resources on which natural communities base their economies have to be readily accessible or regularly available in the place where the communities are located. The plants, animals, insects, fungi and microbial life that create a natural community and manage its economy cannot count on imports of energy, soil, mineral dust, seeds, pollen or manure. Planetary phenomena like wind, ocean currents, floods, rain, landslides, glaciations,

"In real life, there must be many taboos written into the genetic coding ... to ensure that exotic outlaw species do not evolve into rampantly criminal syndicates.... Perhaps [the biosphere's] continuing orderly existence over so long a period can be attributed to another Gaian regulatory process which makes sure that cheats can never become dominant."[5]

volcanic eruptions, earthquakes and animal migrations may improve a community's resource base by bringing it imports. But such random phenomena can also degrade or take away resources on which a community has come to depend. Since neither gains nor losses are predictable, natural communities rely on and learn to work within the limits of the solar energy and resources that are available to them locally, most of the time. Hence, their economies are *locally self-reliant* economies.

Places afford the species that inhabit them particular kinds of resources in amounts that vary from one season and climate cycle to the next. Though abundance of resources is not uncommon, it cannot be counted on. Making do is closer to the truth of Life. Life would have exceeded Earth's means long ago if it hadn't built into genetic codes universal mechanisms of *frugality*, a predisposition to leave enough of necessary resources for later, for other members of one's species, for future generations and for the other species in their communities.

Or, looked at from the other side, Life wouldn't have lasted if it hadn't encoded a predisposition to not take more than what's needed and to minimize how much is needed. Since natural communities can't borrow, buy or import more supplies to replace what they use and cannot even temporarily substitute virtual wealth (the equivalent of living on credit or printing more money or incurring debt) for real wealth, they can't consume their way into a semblance of Earthonomic health. On this account, natural economies are *subsistence economies*.

If the word subsistence conjures up images of drudgery, destitution and unfulfilled desires, it's because we have been persuaded that where material goods are concerned, enough is never enough. The global economy, its Powers and the consumer culture that supports them constantly advertise the idea that we should want and can always have more. The viral economy needs us to want and try to acquire more; otherwise it cannot grow without ceasing. In natural economies, however, growth for its own sake is a sign of disease, and perpetual growth is fatal. To subsist is a good thing.

The word subsist derives from ancient roots that mean "to support" and "to stand." Successful natural communities support themselves sufficiently well that they can stand — can survive and even thrive — for extended periods of time against the odds of unpredictable or limited resources and environmental change. This is why we can call them successful communities. Except in periods of unavoidable crisis, successful natural communities are not impoverished. They avoid generalized or persistent want and hardship, but they do that by not using more resources than their environment can replenish in real time, by not exceeding the carrying capacity of the places they live in.

Except when the combination of food scarcity and high population triggers extreme competition, other-than-human species do not consume to excess. Lions that participate in a savannah community don't take every impala they can get their claws on; they take enough to fill their bellies for the present and leave the residue for other carnivores. Impala don't chew all the available grasses down to the ground; they fill their bellies sufficiently for the present and move on. Grasses don't suck up every drop of moisture the savannah's seasonal rains provide; they take only as much as they need to support their passage through cycles of growth, seed-making and hibernation. And soil bacteria don't hoard the nitrogen they withdraw from the atmosphere. They share it with plants through their roots and store the excess for periods of increased demand.

By such means the participants in natural economies subsist. Together.

## From Competition and Chaos to Cooperation and Conserve-atism

The nasty, brutish and very short lives of the archaic bacteria were characterized more by competition than cooperation. Cooperation was a learned behavior. The learning curve was steep and took a very long time. Cooperation has continued to be a learned behavior for other-than-human species every time natural or, more recently, human-induced disasters have brought down whole ecosystems and left empty spaces in their place.

Complex living systems go through stages of development, maturity and dissolution that roughly replicate the stages single-celled entities went through and are very much like the stages of development, maturity and dissolution through which human bodies and human societies pass in the natural course of things. Ecologists call the process *succession* because one stage of development succeeds (evolves out of or follows) a previous stage.

In the case of natural communities, an expansive, consumptive and competitive juvenile or rapid growth stage comes first. New and revised species, first arrivals in an open space, are highly innovative and willing risk-takers. They compete as fiercely for space and resources, both among each other and with other species, as rival adolescent cliques, gangs or the Dutch, French and British who fought over territories and resources in Africa and the Americas and Boomers and Sooners who competed for freeholds during the 19th-century land rushes in Oklahoma. No surprise that the first species on site are called *pioneers*, a word that describes those who venture into unclaimed or empty territory to settle it. No surprise either that for a time chaos reins.

This stage is characterized as much by diversification as by multiplication. Kinds of species increase exponentially along with populations within each species. There is, after all, all that "empty space" to work with and all the resources that have been left behind for species that can diversify fast enough to figure out how to use them and multiply fast enough to get them before they run out.

But growth can't be a permanent condition in living systems on a finite planet any more than it can in the human body. Perpetual growth of species and populations is as unsustainable as unchecked HIV. So what comes after the growth stage, what Life came up with as the antidote to protracted adolescence and chaos, is conservation, maturity, order. The species that settle down, settle in, grow up, form relatively stable relationships, get organized and trade consumption for what we might call *conserve-atism* are the ones that last.

How do they do that?

## Communities of Partnership

Diversity is a form of specialization and while specialization expands Life's range of options, it limits the specialists' options. For those ancient bacteria, trying to out compete each other and survive by their diverse, individual skills — like swimming, breathing oxygen, eating their distant kin or changing color to avoid baking under the hot sun — left them in the same situation we're in because we imagine we're economically independent. It left them vulnerable.

*Interdependence* and mutual support in due course became a much more viable, life-sustaining arrangement than going it alone and extreme competition, just as local proved to be more successful and sustainable than global had been. How did interdependence come about?

"Partnership — the tendency to associate, establish links, live inside one another, and cooperate ... is one of the hallmarks of life."[6]

To overcome their individual limitations, different strains of bacteria that may once have been incompatible or even fiercely competitive found ways to partner. They cohabited, cooperated, collaborated — or all three — merging their special forms and functions in order to accomplish survival tasks they couldn't accomplish alone. They learned how to share resources, to live and work with each other. Living things have partnered and benefited from related forms of interdependence ever since.

The distinction between dependence and interdependence is important. Dependence is usually a one-way reliance. The relationship it establishes is one of benefactor/beneficiary. Though benefactors get something out of the relationship, they do not need it to the extent the beneficiaries do. Dependence makes one party in the relationship in some way subordinate to and insufficient without the other, just as children are subordinate to and not self-sufficient without their parents and we have become subordinate to and dependent on the global economy.

Interdependence, however, is a reciprocal relationship. The parties are interdependent *with* each other. The brilliant late biologist and living systems theorist Paul A. Weiss wrote that "The salient feature of participants in complex living systems is their enmeshment in a network of interdependence. They are not a package of independent items, as unrelated to each other as the content of a soldier's emergency kit, but each makes indispensable contributions to the existence of the others, just as its own existence and operation, in turn, depend inseparably upon theirs."[7] Each party maintains its essential identity, a skill, characteristic or behavior it contributes to the mutuality. Each has equal standing in and is equally necessary to the success of the relationship. Since bacteria first discovered the benefits of partnership and allowing for the necessity for competition (to keep species and their members sharp), mutual support has been the hallmark of successful economic relationships.

Since Life is ceaselessly innovative it has encoded several kinds of Earthonomic partnerships, each of which has as many permutations as there are species partnering. *Symbiosis* comes from Greek words that mean simply "living with." Ecologists use the term to name close interdependent relationships between individuals from two or more different species. Some symbiotic relationships are parasitic. In those instances, one of the partners gains while the other loses. The symbiotic relationship between viruses like HIV and humans is parasitic.

It's ironic that while one of the partners in a parasitic relationship suffers, the larger living systems in which both partners participate benefit. Why?

Parasitic relationships keep species populations in balance. This is one example of the common good trumping the good of individuals or species.

More often, however, the term symbiosis is used to describe relationships in which the partner species cohabit — live intimately with each

"Once upon a time, before there were multi-celled organisms, the distant ancestor of the [mitochondrion that processes energy in your cells] was a free-living, self-sufficient cell; and the distant ancestor of the cells the mitochondria now inhabit — your nucleated cells — was also a free-living, self-sufficient cell. Then the two free-living cells merged; the mitochondrion specialized in processing energy, and the larger cell handled other matters, such as locomotion. The two lived happily ever after in blissful division of labor."[8]

other or even inside one another — and also collaborate and support each other in important ways. These are touching relationships in both senses of the word: the partners live so intimately that they physically touch each other and their interactions are so sympathetic and mutual as to seem tender. Since many of the species we know came into being only because partners in symbiotic relationships began to function as one, Lynn Margulis described Earth as a "symbiotic planet."

Though in humans, symbiosis looks like compassion or a romantic strategy, it isn't. It's a fair-trade survival strategy. Life partners provide a variety of services to each other ranging from nutrition, shelter and transportation to pollination and protection. In some cases partners' lives may become so intertwined that, even though their partnership does not produce an entirely new species, the partners cannot live without each other. Many grazing animals, for example, cannot convert tough plant cellulose into energy producing carbohydrates without the help of several varieties of microorganisms that live in their guts. The two vastly different species have evolved a sweat equity sort of arrangement in which the grazers benefit from the digestive services provided by the microorganisms and the microorganisms get free room and board: warm, comparatively safe shelter and a steady supply of nutrients that are available in the grazers' guts. Both grazers and microorganisms benefit from their interdependence.

Other symbiotic relationships are somewhat less intimate and obligatory, more like coalitions or synergies, occasions in which two or more species work together in such a way that each supports or enhances the life quality or survival or reproductive rate of the other. The partners in synergistic coalitions facilitate or improve each other's lives. The goby fish, for example, cleans parasites from the teeth of the Nassau grouper fish. What does the goby get in exchange for aligning with the grouper? Hanging around sharp toothed groupers gets gobies top-of-the-line protection from predators. To take another example, there's the odd pairing of rhinos and oxpecker birds. In exchange for acting as eyes and an early warning system for near-sighted rhinoceroses, the far-sighted birds get to harvest ticks and lice from the rhino's hides.[9] The partnership between bees, bats and other pollinators and the flowering plants they pollinate is even looser, but no less necessary or mutual.

## The High Order Earthologic of Partnership

Most of Life's solutions to challenges like Critical Mass solve more than one problem and meet more than one species' needs at a time. In his essay "Solving for Pattern," philosopher/farmer/poet Wendell Berry suggested that all effective solutions to problems, whether they are Life's solutions or ours, address multiple problems at the same time because the problem solver is seeking to solve the problem in a way that honors and preserves the larger patterns and systems on which the solution will have an impact.[10]

Within this context, even competition among members of a species can be seen as the solution to more than one problem. It solves the problem of overpopulation — reduced resources and habitat, for example — by limiting numbers, and it solves the problem of potential degradation of gene lines and weakening of the species by weeding out the weaker, less well adapted, less fit members of a species. And, as Edward Goldsmith observed, "competition has a role to play in the behavior of living things, in particular in a pioneer ecosystem, in which it serves to eliminate randomness and hence to increase the viability of natural systems, helping to maintain the ecosystem's critical order. Competition also serves in such conditions to space out living things which must, among other things, favor the development of increasing diversity which [supports] a greater range of environmental challenges."[11] Competition within and between species also serves as a sort of exercise regimen that, if it is appropriately balanced with cooperation, strengthens the gene lines of all the competitors.

Manure is another example of a solution that solves more than one problem at a time, maintaining larger patterns of Life simultaneously. Manure might have been a solution to the problem of getting toxic wastes out of bodies that created more problems than it solved. It might have created a problem of pollution, exactly as bacteria's wastes did until partnership turned one bacteria's waste into another's feast. Instead, manure also solves the problems of plant nutrition and depleted soil nutrients by returning to the soil and the roots of plants things they can use, and addresses the problem of dispersing heavy seeds by shipping in bowels seeds too heavy for wind to carry. Manure lands where seeds need to be (in the soil) and provides them with their first shot of food (the very manure that transported them).

Life repeated the pervasive and persistent pattern of the egg by using manure in this way. Like an egg, dung is both a container for new life (seeds) and also their initial food supply. Of course the seed also repeats the egg pattern: It carries the germ of the new plant and the sugars that jump-start the plant's growth. This is a *very* high level of Earthologic.

Life's partnerships are another example of Berry's "solving for pattern." They are practical well beyond their capacity to increase the survival rates of the partners. For example, around the time that the continents were forming, four different types of bacteria — each with a useful survival skill, each trying to survive and prosper — merged to create a new life form with a higher probability of survival than any of them had on their own: green algae.[12] Green algae's longevity and universality suggest that, despite the fact that they traded independence for mutual obligation, each of the four participating strains of bacteria has prospered. Their Earthonomical partnership and collaboration has worked well for them.

But more importantly, it has worked for Life and for us, too. How? Because green algae are phenomenal photosynthesizers, they have played a significant role in the management of Earth's temperature and maintenance of its water supply. Before our fossil fueled economy interfered with the process, the algae sequestered enough $CO_2$ to help prevent the planet from overheating and its large bodies of water from evaporating as a result. Green algae are a perfect example of Life's apparent aim — to last — having been written into even the smallest of living things.

Life's Earthonomic partnerships are not entered into loosely. They are not limited liability partnerships. They are, instead, general partnerships. Every partner is fully liable, responsible for its partners' well-being as well as its own. But like sharing, partnership is not altruistic, it's Earthological. Life has built it in. Why? Successful partnerships make for successful species; successful species create and maintain successful communities.

"Networks are the only form of organization used by living systems on this planet. These networks result from self-organization, where individuals or spe-cies recognize their interdependence and organize in ways that support the diversity and viability of all."[13]

Successful communities live within Earth's means and do not induce Critical Mass. That's Earthonomical, and that's good for Life in general.

## Communities of Communities[14]

In fact, Earthonomic interdependence and partnership were so good for Life that Life locked them in at the intercommunity level too. Natural communities are not much more independent of each other than individuals in partnerships are. Though the economic relationships between natural communities are looser than the partnerships between species, they also range from fairly intimate (equivalent to symbiosis) to more casual (equivalent to the goby fish and groupers).

In general:

*Natural communities have close, functional or symbiotic, economic relationships with neighboring communities.*

The margins of these communities overlap like the edges of neighborhoods in a city. Clusters of adjacent communities share the same environment and weather, the same families of plants and animals and even some individual plants and animals. They all have a stake in access to and conservation of local resources and maintenance of life-sustaining environments. They have a vested interest in the common good.

*Natural communities have looser — or synergistic, economic relationships with communities farther away.*

With these other communities they share and cooperatively maintain a large territory called an *ecoregion* or *bioregion*. The Great Plains, Great Barrier Reef, Amazon rainforest, Siberian tundra and Gulf of Mexico are bioregions. Each bioregion is home to many community clusters, just like a large city is home to many clusters of neighborhoods. Among the things the clusters of communities in a bioregion have in common — the physical features that connect them economically — may be large geographical features like mountains or a watershed, climate, water distribution systems like evaporation and transpiration, a similar range of plant, insect and animal species, migratory species and soil types.

Although the communities at one side of a bioregion are not intimately involved in the economies of communities at the opposite side, they are still affected by changing conditions everywhere in the system. For example, if wildfire destroys the forest at the head of a watershed, denuded topsoil washes off into streams, making them shallower and warmer. The waterlogged soil becomes silt that flows into tributaries and the river they feed. In flood season, silt finds its way to the mouth of the river where it fills in wetlands, buries mangrove swamps and creates a delta. Every community along the entire length of the watershed is indirectly affected by the wildfire that directly destroyed only the forest community at the headwaters. Ironically, the disappearance of the wetlands at the river's mouth would reduce evaporation, which in turn might well deprive the headlands of the rainfall they'd need for the forest to regenerate.

Because all of the communities in a bioregion rely on the well-being of the whole bioregion and many animals roam widely throughout its extent, all or a portion of its resources may fall within the range of "local." Natural communities are therefore more accurately described as *locally and regionally* self-reliant.

## The economic relationships between and among communities at the level of the biosphere are sympathetic and circumstantial.

For example, natural communities in the Amazon River basin have nothing obvious to do with natural communities in the Nile or Yellow River basins. Only dramatic and widespread environmental events like volcanic eruptions, climate instability or a viral global economy affect all their economies at the same time. In fact, because all of the Earth's continents were once part of a single enormous continent called Pangaea, some natural communities (like the boreal forests of the far north, for example) have more in common with their boreal forest counterparts on the other side of the world than they do with adjacent communities. Their economies are similar despite the oceans and miles that separate them.

Natural communities on opposite sides of the Earth have nothing to do with each other functionally. Nonetheless, the diverse ecosystems in which they participate often facilitate each other's existence in surprising ways. Andreas Suchantke wrote, for example, that "The Amazon rainforest would have been facing a natural doom if its annual deficit in [rain-leached soil nutrients] had not always been made up, and from a very unexpected quarter. The Passat, the wind that blows off the Atlantic from the northeast, brings with it mineral dust from the Sahara. The Earth's 'death pole' [its desert tropical zone] is quite literally a key element in keeping the 'vegetative pole' alive. This is a truly astonishing example of ecological interdependence. Here two of Earth's large-scale ecosystems, geographically separate and widely differing in function, are seen to be so attuned to each other that their behavior can only be compared to that of organs within an organism."[15]

In any case, even such far-flung bioregional communities as the Amazon and Nile basins have a shared interest in the health of the planetary environment that they all have in common, and they have a vested interest in maintaining it.

## The Economics of Ecosystems

Perhaps the most significant economic partnership is the one formed by natural communities with the places in which they arise, the geographical locations in which they make their lives and livings. The economic give-and-take between a natural community and its environment — the way it uses its environment and, conversely, the way its environment variously limits, shapes and facilitates it — results in what we call an *ecosystem.*

The official definition of ecosystem is "an ecological community together with its environment, functioning as a unit."[16] What allows a natural community and its physical environment to function as a unit? The way resident species learn to make decent livings in and from that environment. The way they learn to work with it — yielding to it when necessary, making it yield to them when possible — without undermining its capacity to continue to provide them with decent livings. In other words, ecosystems are economic systems. And successful ecosystems are the consequence of carefully negotiated, adaptable economic partnerships between natural communities and their environments.

**communities + environments = ecosystems**

Let's put this another way, a way that may better help us understand what we need to do, too.

Barring unavoidable crises, when natural communities organize, regulate and govern themselves (that is, when they manage their affairs in such a way that they live within the means of their environments to support them), they and their ecosystems are bound to be successful. When the majority of Earth's natural communities are doing that, Life's bound to be successful, too.

This is why it is possible to compare Earth's natural communities to the human immune system. Each of them and all of them at the same time (the diverse organs and communities of cells that constitute the immune system, such as white blood cells, lymph nodes, skin and blood among others) strive to maintain the health of the body. In similar fashion, one location at a time and all at the same time, the whole-Earth ecosystem of diverse natural communities maintains the health of the biosphere (Life itself).

Several pages earlier I wrote that "every partner is fully liable, responsible for its partners' well-being as well as its own." In ecosystem terms it would be more accurate to say that *every partner contributes to the well-being of the other partners by regulating and governing its own economic activities in ways that maintain the health of the environment on which it too depends.* When species take care of their environments, they take care of each other by extension.

To a large extent the physical characteristics of an environment do determine the type and size of natural community that can inhabit and make a living in it over the long term. Is it hot or cold, dry or wet, high or low elevation, level or mountainous, rocky, sandy, mucky, salty, windy, acidic or alkaline, land-based or aquatic, located near the equator

In mechanics a feedback device that restrains an engine or motor, preventing it from surging out of control, is called a *governor*. It is in this sense that the members of natural communities — by cooperating, partnering, sharing, conserving, cycling and recycling — can be said to govern themselves and that natural communities can be said to be *self-governing*. They exercise self-control.

or the poles or in between? You won't find lush rainforest communities trying to make a living on Saharan sands or on the permafrost tundra.

But ecosystems are full partnerships. Natural communities are not passive recipients of prevailing environmental conditions, and so the reverse is also true. To a large extent natural communities create and recreate their environments. They adapt to the given environment, but through time they also adapt that environment to meet their needs. They improve and manage the place they live in as they manage and govern their ways of living in it Earthonomically.

And governing in this case does not mean pushing expansion, population growth and consumption. Governing in natural systems means limiting, regulating, restraining, harmonizing, coordinating and integrating. Governing means keeping obstreperous young species in check while liberating them just enough so that their creativity and innovativeness aren't completely squelched. For members of self-governing natural communities, responsibility is encoded along with freedom.

The dense mass of plants and 200-foot high, solar collector canopy of trees that for millions of years has managed the Amazon rainforest on behalf of more animal and insect species than we can imagine were responsible for making the nutrient poor soils, complex river systems and precipitation cycles of northern South America work for the whole forest. But they made these things work for the forest the way Asian rice farmers made the seasonally wet, hilly Southeast Asian environment work for them. Native rice farmers didn't level the hills or build complex irrigation systems to keep rice lands wet in the dry season. They didn't feel free to take what they could get from the land. They worked gently, responsibly with their environment, terracing the hills to hold the soil and walling the terraces to contain the rainwater. Similarly, the rainforest community governed its activities so that it could maintain the condition of its soils and rivers while coaxing life sustenance out of them, and in that way it left the precipitation cycles undisturbed.

Very different kinds of natural communities have devised ways of storing the sun's warmth and encouraging the wind-scoured, shallow-soiled, water-logged and bitterly cold tundra to support them, to function with them as a unit and to govern themselves while freely enjoying the benefits the tundra provides.

"Life actually makes and forms and changes the environment to which it adapts," Lynn Margulis said. "Then that 'environment' feeds back on the life that is changing and acting and growing in it. There are constant cyclical interactions."[17] Those cyclical interactions comprise the "constant negotiations" Elisabet Sahtouris has observed.

Successful natural communities, those that obey Life's economic rules, those whose negotiations with their environments do not overshoot their environments' carrying capacities, those who govern themselves and manage their economies for the common good, strive to maintain healthy ecosystems that, in return, can sustain them. Communities that don't function Earthonomically destroy their ecosystems and themselves in the process. This is simply Earthological.

## The Upside of Downtimes[18]

Subsistence and recycling are two of the methods Life has used to conserve resources. There's another. It reflects Life's willingness to yield to certain built-in environmental constraints — to limits. Life conceded to the inevitability of the day/night and seasonal cycles and found a way to turn them to its advantage: conserving resources and energy by giving them time to be replenished or replaced. In other words, there is no natural equivalent of the global economy's 24/7-365 production-consumption frenzy. Some portion of the planet is always in the equivalent of an *economic downtime*.

Earth's rotation guarantees that half the planet is always in the dark, turned away from the sun, and most of the species that live in that darkened half are asleep or resting. The ones that aren't, the nocturnal species,

"Life loves loops. Most biological processes, even those with very complicated pathways, wind up back where they started. The circulation of the blood ... migrations ... the cycle of birth and death and [of the seasons] — all have the habit of looping back for a new start.

"Loops tame uncontrolled events. One-way processes, given sufficient energy and materials, tend to 'run away,' to go faster and faster unless they are inhibited or restrained."[19]

sleep or rest during the daylight hours. At all times, half a planet's worth of other-than-human species is not aggressively producing or consuming, but storing, restoring and conserving energy and resources instead.

The tilt of the Earth's axis and its orbit around the sun create the equivalent of a fiscal year in which Life has no choice but to balance its accounts. Periodic long nights, cold temperatures and/or reduced precipitation and times of less or no sunlight force annual economic slowdowns. For half the year, the North Pole points away from the sun, bringing summer to the southern hemisphere. For the other half, it points toward the sun and summer arrives in the northern hemisphere. Maximum growth, expansion and consumption — in other words, maximum economic activity — never occur at the same time in both hemispheres. One of them is always in the equivalent of a several months long snooze, storing up energy and water, shoring up supplies of nutrients and raw materials, holding them for future use or putting them back into circulation. This amounts to an obligatory resource savings and investment plan that is distinguished by the fact that the savings for the most part stay in the local ecosystem and investments benefit the local community.

Animal migrations and deciduous trees' shedding of leaves in autumn are examples of the means by which species and communities have learned to yield to the requirements of their environments. Succulents, among the plant family, have adapted to dry and desert climates by growing protective gray fuzz, developing leathery surfaces that hold water in, keeping leaves small and reducing their size and expanse when water is particularly scarce. Pasturelands and schools of feed fish are replenished when grazing animals and large fish follow the seasons north and south; and fallen leaves build soil to support spring growth spurts.

When our activities don't thwart them, these periodic, predictable downtimes lock in long periods of conservation, rest and restoration that allow natural communities to accumulate what we might call *life savings*, to allow their resources to renew themselves and regain value. In the equatorial band where there is no dark season, killing cold or blanketing, Life has responded to the absence of restorative downtime with rainforest ecosystems in which constant growth is supported by constant Life-refueling decomposition: no downtimes but no bank-rupted accounts either.

## Communities of Purpose

Clearly, maintaining the health of its environment is a natural com-munity's highest purpose just as maintaining the health of the body in order to avoid illness is an immune system's highest purpose. One reason natural communities are able to fulfill that purpose as often as they do is that all of their able members and member species contribute in some way to the creation, survival and success of the community, just as all of the able cells and cell communities in the immune system contribute to the proper function and health of the body.

Other-than-human species and individual members of those species can't choose their life's purpose as we can, but they can serve a purpose nonetheless. We fill necessary roles in our various kinds of communities just because of our particular combinations of intelligence, skills and experience or simply because of our age, size, shape, physical makeup, monetary assets or social standing. It is in this sense that the members of natural communities can be said to have a purpose and that the commu-nities they create together are *communities of purpose*. This is how they become — like hands, feet and other body members — true members of their community: They are each and all responsible for one or more tasks that contribute to its continued existence and well-being.

We've seen that pioneer species like lichens, for example, create out of Earth's rock-bound crust the soil that sustains plants. For their part, plants capture and sequester excess $CO_2$, helping to maintain an atmosphere within which all of Earth's species can live. Birds and small mammals distribute seeds. Predators as small as pigmy owls and as big as lions limit populations of rodents that might otherwise deplete whole generations of those seeds and of browsers that might otherwise deplete the local and regional plant storehouses of solar energy. Predators also help to remove aging and ill members of a prey species, which helps to keep that species viable and vital. Fungi, carrion beetles, yeasts, earth-worms, sowbugs, nematodes, mites, springtails and bacteria are among the organisms that decompose plant and animal tissue and release their nutrients back into the soil.

In other words, natural communities are full employment communities. All species and their members have jobs. Ecologists call them *niches*. When all the niches are filled, that highest Earthonomic purpose of the community — protecting and maintaining its environment for the long haul — is served. The dark side of the full employment equation is that when any of the participating species die off or are removed, other species must fill their niches or else the community and, by extension, its ecosystem are weakened, just as we are weakened if aspects of our immune systems are compromised and not healed.

Life has minimized the likelihood of significant niches going unoccupied by building in *redundancy*. Since every species meets more than one of its community's needs, there are always several species that share responsibility for a task. Unless humans intervene, there's always more than one marine species filtering water, more than one kind of plant moving nutrients through the system, more than one ecosystem processing methane or sequestering $CO_2$. In human terms, species and communities wear many hats, and many species and communities wear the same hats.

Locally and regionally self-reliant communities depend as much on the diverse skills, activities and intelligences of their resident species and on the capacity of those species to bring those skills to bear on the common good as they depend on locally available physical resources.

How's that for democratic?

CHAPTER 10

# Life Is Organically Democratic

SHARING, EQUITABILITY, COOPERATION, partnership, coalition, commitment to the common good, full employment, full participation, self-regulation, self-government — these are among the characteristics of Earthonomical natural communities that have allowed their participating members to live within Earth's means. They are also among the characteristics we commonly ascribe to democracy at its best. But democracy is a human invention. Right?

Wrong. The word "democracy" was first used to name certain widely empowering human political arrangements, but the arrangements it names have their origin in Life itself.

Life has managed to live within Earth's means by locking in relationships, behaviors and methods of organizing that are arguably more democratic than any we have adopted so far. In fact, democracy has been a crucial component in Life's

"A kluge is a clumsy or inelegant — yet surprisingly effective solution to a problem.... Nature is prone to making kluges because it doesn't 'care' whether its products are perfect or elegant. If something works, it spreads. If it doesn't work, it dies out. Genes that lead to successful outcomes tend to propagate; genes that can't cut it tend to fade away; all else is metaphor. Adequacy, not beauty, is the name of the game."[1]

Economic Survival Protocol for dealing with Critical Mass ever since bacteria discovered the advantages of downsizing, diversity, downtimes and community.

Democracy is entrenched in our collective consciousness as a high ideal, but it is still a relatively new tool in our political repertoire. For most of us democracy is still a stretch. We have to choose it as our guiding principle and work hard at it. Competition, self-interest, self-preservation and ego are still our go-to instincts just as they are for individual members of other-than-human species.

But for Life, democracy is almost as old as the hills, certainly as old as the first bacteria that settled in the hills. It is not a matter of principle, morality or ethics any more than partnership is an expression of affection or sharing a form of altruism.

For Life, democracy is not a matter of choice. It was simply the first method of organization that achieved Life's aim — to last — by facilitating its prime directive: to live within Earth's means. The survival of the whole Life experiment on Earth trumped the survival of any one species. Democracy is what other-than-human species learned to do together in order to survive and thrive — and what each new species has eventually learned to do in order to be among the survivors. Since it worked, Life kept it. Democracy got built into Life's operating system early on.

By now it's organic.

## Finding Democracy in Unexpected Places

It has long been assumed that most animal societies are organized as we are with Powers and cowerers, doers and done to, top dogs and underdogs, alpha males and dominance everywhere you look. That view is changing. A growing number of biologists, ecologists and systems theorists are discovering that many species of animals also exhibit democratic behaviors. It may be that, along with survival, democracy is a default setting for relationships within as well as between species.

### *Democracy All the Way Up ...*

Larissa Conradt, an evolutionary biologist at the University of Sussex, UK, has written that "In social species many decisions need to be made jointly with other group members because the group will split apart

unless a consensus is reached. Consider, for example, a group of primates deciding which direction to travel after a rest period, a flock of
birds deciding when to leave a foraging patch, or a swarm of bees choosing a new nest site. Unless all members decide on the same action, some
will be left behind and will forfeit the advantages of group living."[2] And
if too many were to be left behind or wander off in other directions,
the group would fall apart leaving the members in a state of chaos and
confusion and at a survival disadvantage.

It is the greatest good for the greatest number that has brought Life
along from age to age since bacteria learned that lesson. And the greatest
good for the greatest number apparently dictates that "group decision-
making is a commonplace occurrence in the lives of social animals."[3]

In studies of the behavior of red deer that she conducted with her
colleague Tim Roper, Conradt found that when it comes to making decisions about moving on from a resting place, feeding ground
or watering hole, it's not the sexually dominant alpha male or even a
group of sexually-dominant males that make the decision when to go
or even, necessarily, where. In so far as sex, disciplining younger males
and defending the herd from attacks by competitor males are concerned,
alphas take the lead. But time has taught red deer the hard way that even
the most experienced, strong, clever alpha might decide to move the
herd (as some of the Powers in recent years have unilaterally decided to
move us) based on nothing more than a sudden urge or misinterpreted
sign of danger, even though many members of the herd are still thirsty,
tired or hungry.

Barring clear and present danger, members of red deer herds, gorilla
bands, African buffalo herds and other close-knit animal societies vote
their readiness to depart by standing up and pointing themselves in the
direction they want to go. When a significant majority have stood or
pointed themselves in the chosen direction, the group moves on together
in the direction they've chosen together. In a statement that until recently
the scientific community would have considered unorthodox or heretical, Roper and Conradt concluded that "Democratic behavior is not
unique to humans."[4]

Dolphins cooperate when hunting and catching fish; they wait until
a majority of them awakens from a drifting snooze and signals readiness

before they continue their migration. Anna Dornhaus of the University of Arizona and Nigel R. Franks at the University of Bristol in the UK have found that some varieties of bees and ants engage in information pooling and consensus decision making. "Democracy is not something that humanity invented," Dornhaus has concluded.[5]

The sort of generosity characteristic of high-functioning democracy may not indicate the same form of moral compass humans are supposed to be guided by and may not be unfailing in other-than-human species, but it is prevalent. Primatologist Frans de Waal reported an experiment that has been done with Capuchin monkeys. "The experiment consists of two monkeys in two cages facing one another but separated by a partition so neither can see the other. Adjacent to these two cages is a third cage in which a third monkey can observe both of the other two. The experimenter feeds one of these two apples, bananas and so forth. The second monkey receives scraps. At some point, the observer monkey, well fed itself, is given extra food. What does this animal do?" Not what many of the world's Powers have become accustomed to doing when they've been "well fed." The observer monkey "gives the extra food to the monkey who received the scraps. These monkeys have evolved a sense of fairness," surely characteristic of democracy at its best.[6]

Thom Hartmann has written of this new understanding of animal behavior that "Without exception the natural state of group-living animals is to cooperate, not dominate. Democracy, it turns out, is hard-wired into the DNA of species from ants to zebras. And it includes all of the hominids from the great apes to *Homo sapiens*."[7]

## ... and All the Way Down

Examples of democratic activity and even activism can be found at levels as far down life's food chain as *Homo sapiens* is up, as far down, in fact, as bacteria. Philosopher Werner Krieglstein and biologist Mahlon Hoagland offer a particularly impressive example, in this instance, of situational democracy.

"In recent years," wrote Krieglstein, "scientists have documented a remarkable sequence of behavior that might well be suited to serve as a metaphor if not as a lived example for how we human beings can and should behave in times of need." In times, for example, of global Critical

Mass. "Scientists observed this single cell organism cooperating in a quite extraordinary fashion when the food supply was running short."

Facing a life threatening famine, single-celled amoeba called *dictyostelium* gather from every direction and every part of famine territory by the thousands and turn themselves collectively into a new creature: slime mold. Having one thing in mind — species survival — they sacrifice independence and sometimes their own lives. They opt for radical interdependence and symbiosis, for organically democratic behavior. "They group together, forming a community, to achieve goals they could not achieve by themselves."[8]

Scientist Hoagland explained how this works: Recognizing pending catastrophe, "a single amoeba, apparently self-appointed, begins to emit a chemical signal. Near-by neighbors, irresistibly drawn to the signal 'ooze' over and attach themselves to the signaler. Each new member of the cluster amplifies the signal by releasing its own signal. More amoeba arrive." It's like a grassroots flash mob at this point in the process.

"Then a startling transformation occurs: The aggregate shapes itself into a slug and begins to migrate to a new location, leaving a trail of slime behind it. As the slug moves the cells differentiate into three distinct types."[9] The spontaneous flash mob becomes a purposeful community as each takes up a task vital to the group's survival.

They form a creature that looks like a tiny futuristic floor lamp with a base, a post and a round, covered bulb. The base roots the slime mold in its new food-rich environment. The post raises the bulb high so that its equivalent of light will cover as large an area as possible. And what's the equivalent of light in this amoebic democracy analogy? Spores, like tiny eggs. Dispersed like photons in their new space when the bulb "turns on" and emits them, they become new single-celled amoebae. The cycle of amoebic life begins anew. Individuals do their own thing until collective, democratic action is required to deal with another shared crisis.

Naturalist and science writer Steve Talbott has tracked democracy to an even more infinitesimal level. "There's an amazing coordination within the living cell, which is no less meaningfully patterned than a democratic society." It would seem that democracy as "an endless and confounding pattern of mutual interaction" goes to levels as small as our technologies allow us to see.[10]

## Getting It Together

We saw in the previous four chapters several of the ways in which Life has used democratic behaviors and relationships — behaviors and relationships like equitability, cooperation and sharing that many of us still consider to be discretionary and uneconomical — to its Earthonomic advantage. There are two more ways Life manifests a predisposition for democracy that have significance for us. The first is implicit: By means of complex feedback systems, cooperation and collaboration, natural communities *regulate and govern themselves* — which is more than can be said for modern liberal democracies in thrall to the global economy. And natural communities also *organize themselves*. More accurately, their participants organize them, grassroots style. The sophistication, stability, adaptability and longevity of natural communities and communities of natural communities *emerges* from the interactions of the participants. Participants or "agents residing on one scale," summed up science writer Stephen Johnson, "start producing behavior that lies one scale above them: ants create ant colonies," dolphins create pods, amoeba create slime mold, and people create tribes, neighborhoods, and communities.[11]

Doing collaboration and cooperation — doing democracy — creates stable, high-functioning community, And stable, high-functioning communities are sustainable in ways that top-down, pyramidal social structures are not.

## Back to Bacteria, Briefly

We've seen that our bacterial ancestors were faced with circumstances a lot like ours: a changing planetary environment, increasingly harsh living conditions, reduced resources, swelling, restive populations and a failing global economy. In short, self-induced global Critical Mass. If they wanted to survive let alone thrive, they had to do something dramatically different than what they had been doing.

But two billion years ago there was no one to tell them what to do. There was no single-celled equivalent of a monarch, president, prime minister, premier or any other kind of Power to proclaim that they must downsize, diversify, go local and learn how to provide for themselves economically. No congress or parliament determined for them how they should go about that task or offered a stimulus package or bailout plan to sustain them while they figured it out. No laws were written to help bacteria define equitability and sharing; no partnership contracts, land use or waste management agreements were drawn up and agreed upon. No small group of bacterial intellectuals or revolutionaries gathered in the microbial equivalents of a Philadelphia tavern, Paris café or St. Petersburg cellar to hammer out a survival plan to deal with global economic collapse. There was no top from which direction could come down. Our tiny, desperate predecessors had no choice but to sort it out for themselves. And, since they couldn't sort it out effectively as individuals — one group's success meant another's failure and competition to the death — they had no choice but to do it together. And they did it without benefit of brains, history, consciousness or conscience.

To be fair to bacteria and honest about us, though these shortcomings seem like a curse, they might have been a blessing. Bacteria couldn't choose to operate democratically, but neither could they choose to ignore Life's rules that locked in democracy. We can and do.

From the point at which bacteria and other single-celled entities first partnered, collaborated and created sustainable microeconomies and neighborhoods, natural communities have been organized and when necessary reorganized from the bottom up, within the constraints placed on them by their environments. Put simply, locally self-reliant, Earthonomical natural communities were organized by the individuals and species that lived in them. Life's most successful survival technique — community making — began in grassroots fashion in every unique location on Earth with what would appear to be the least significant, least powerful, least intelligent life forms, the microbial equivalents of the proverbial "common people." We, the people, single-celled version.

Small is both logical and Earthological in part because small is fleeter and faster, more adaptively graceful and responsive than big. Whenever

"What ecosystems exemplify are beautifully unified democracies.... [Life] is not a mechanical, hierarchical system but an organic, self-organizing system."[12]

"The Gaia hypothesis implies that the stable state of our planet included [humans] as a part of, or partner in, a very democratic entity."[13]

naturally occurring Critical Mass or local crises like wildfire, volcanic eruptions or flooding have wiped out established communities or reduced their populations or their capacity to function economically, the smallest, simplest life forms have been the first on site to repair the damage and start life over. Microbes and lichens, tiny mosses and fungi and ferns have always created the small cooperatives, symbiotic and synergistic partnerships, neighborhoods and communities that laid the ground, literally, and prepared the way for other species to settle in vacated spaces and, in their turn, organize more complex communities and intercommunity coalitions.

This is such a common, continuous occurrence that we rarely think about how amazing and how utterly unlikely it is. Unlikely precisely because those creatures at the grassroots level that do the organizing, regulating and governing — the other-than-human entities that do the work that maintains Life as we know it — have no brains. How have they done what we seem unable to do?

They've made each other smart. Democratically.

## Acquired Intelligence

A natural community's ability to organize, regulate and govern itself effectively in tandem with surrounding communities and in harmony with the larger regional communities in which they participate depends on an uninterrupted flow of accurate information about its members' status and the status of their shared environment. An Earthological system — ecosystems are, of course, naturally Earthological — runs on what we call *intel*. Robert Wright concluded that "In societies, in organisms, in cells, the magic glue is information. Information is what synchronizes the parts of the whole and keeps them in touch with each other as they collectively resist disruption and decay."[14] Organizational consultant Margaret Wheatley puts it even more plainly: "Life uses information to organize matter into form, resulting in all the physical structures we see," from bodies to the biosphere.[15] Or as Stephen Johnson framed it, natural communities "get their smarts from below."[16]

For living systems, intelligence is to decision making what sunlight is to energy making. This too is Earthological. Since individuals, species, communities and communities of communities provide for themselves using what's available in their immediate environments, they need to know what the available resources are. They need to know what local resources are good for or what good can be made of them. They need to know in real time which resources are abundant and which are not, when to consume, when to build in downtimes, when to let a resource renew itself,

"What we need to talk about, what someone needs to talk about, particularly now, is our ever-deepening ignorance (of politics, of economics, of history, of current affairs, of pretty much everything important) and not just our ignorance but our complacency in the face of it."[17]

Since a community's well-being depends on the health and proper function of its diverse species, it needs to know the state of their health, too, and whether or not they are functioning properly. Communities need to know when they are threatened and by what as well as when a threat has passed. Life has learned to deal democratically with this necessity for accurate, timely, universally distributed information. Every member of a community is included in the information-gathering process. And every member is able and allowed to exchange, access and interpret that information for its own benefit and for the benefit of its species and community.

Yale democracy theorist Robert A. Dahl has put access to accurate information on his very short list of criteria for democracy. He also acknowledged, ruefully, that citizens of nations we call democracies rarely if ever have it. In truth, few of them demand it. Newspapers are going under at a great rate in part because so many of us are addicted now to "new" rather than "news" and to data rather than details. Few national governments are knowledgeable enough about conditions in distant and diverse locations within their borders to be able to provide us with useful economic and environmental information even if we do demand it. Relative ignorance is an abiding characteristic of huge, top down, pyramid-shaped socio-political and economic systems.[18]

The fact that few of us have understood why so much is going wrong in so many places is proof of our being variously uninformed, misinformed and disinformed. It's also proof of our having settled for a childlike dependence on others' intelligence. The fact that apparently few if any of the authorities or Powers at the top of the global economic system seem to have any coherent and consistent idea of what to do about our present crises or, conversely, that they have too many conflicting and complicated ideas about what to do, is reason for us to give up this form of dependence, too.

Unlike us, members of natural communities do not rely on an authority higher up to provide them with information about their circumstances or to digest that information and tell them what do with it. They can't afford to. Any single entity's or species' ignorance of its own and its community's immediate Earthonomic and environmental circumstances would result in death. Other-than-human species collect their own information. And they share it with each other.

How do they do that?

They send each other genetic, chemical, electrical or vocal signals, or relay what they know with body language or gestures. Bacteria, for example, routinely exchange genes — packets of chemical information — that enhance each other's rates of survival. Oak trees "read" chemicals (ecologist Eugene Odum called them "environmental hormones") that are broadcast on the wind by the leaves of other oaks that are under attack by insects. Female squirrels "count" acorns and use their tally to adjust the levels of pheromones they release upwards or downwards to attract appropriate numbers of males. Migrating herds smell water and point their bodies in the appropriate direction.

Colonies of ants coordinate the number of foragers they send out for food according, in part, to the amount of food that's currently available within marching distance. How do they know how much food there is? Foragers periodically regurgitate bits of recently digested food in the colony's tunnels or on their well-beaten paths. Fewer samples on the ground signifies that there's less food available. This means that fewer foragers wear themselves out in vain, and the colony does not overshoot its food supply, but trims reproductive rates and lets the food supply renew itself instead.[19]

Most of the species that comprise natural communities lack the equivalent of brains, and none possess what we consider to be high intelligence or self-awareness. But each of them is a storehouse of particular kinds of information about its environment and its own and its group circumstances. Given the diversity and number of its members, any natural

"It seems a principle of evolution, perhaps the *fundamental principle*, that the greater the capacity to receive, store, utilize, transform, and transmit information, the more diverse and complex the entity.... Once that capacity transcended organisms, there was immediate evolution of complex communities of organisms — hives, flocks, packs, colonies, herds and tribes."[20]

community possesses a breadth and depth of information about itself that we should envy — and figure out how to mimic. Since information is communicated between all members and circulates continuously around the community, it binds individuals and species together in a kind of mutual understanding. Knowledge transcends difference, turning it to advantage, creating the opportunity for the natural equivalent of consensus — or at least sufficient agreement for the natural equivalent of decisions to be made, behaviors coordinated and actions collectively taken.

Granted, with the exception of the higher animal forms, other-than-human species are guileless. Unlike humans they are (for the most part) incapable of lying, withholding, misinforming, underreporting or censoring.

Among honest creatures, shared information acquires some of the characteristics of intelligence. As energy circulating through a natural community supports life, information circulating through a natural community supports collective and more comprehensive intelligence. It confers on a community expanded learning and problem solving capabilities so that the community as a whole becomes a kind of brain that is mindful of how and what it is doing in real time and what may be demanded of it next.

Biologists Francesco Varela and Antonio Coutinho have suggested that "the [body's] immune system can best be understood as a kind of intelligence, a living, learning, self-regulated system — almost another mind. Its function does not depend on its firepower but on the quality of its connectedness," its communications.[21]

The same conclusion may be drawn about the whole-Earth network of natural communities that functions (barring our intervention) as Earth's immune system. After all, information circulates not just within but also among natural communities. Together they too constitute a kind of brain (it was Sir James Lovelock who named it Gaia) that is mindful of environmental and Earthonomic conditions everywhere on Earth and that remembers, as the immune system does, what works and what doesn't.

Information and the collective intelligence it facilitates are the only survival tools that Life globalizes, and it does so from the bottom up, network-wise, not from the top down, pyramid-wise. Because they are continuously informed and informative, natural communities have what James Surowiecki calls "the wisdom of crowds,"23 what democracy activist Tom Atlee calls "co-intelligence" and what *Wired* magazine editor Kevin Kelly has called "distributed intelligence." Communities and networks of communities are simply smarter than any individuals or single species can ever be.

> "A network has no 'top' or 'bottom.' Rather, it has a plurality of connections that increase the possible interactions between components of the network. There is no executive authority that oversees the system."22

One of the ways the global economy has compromised the health and proper function of Earth's immune system is that it has deprived natural communities of their native intelligence. It has opened gaps in their lines of communication, broken down ancient signal systems and sent them false chemical and genetic signals. It has effectively thwarted their organically democratic process.

In any case, information and intelligence are only as useful as what gets done with them. Natural communities and their members use the information they receive and the intelligence they acquire about their ever changing circumstances to help them respond quickly and effectively to those circumstances. They are responsive to information because it makes them response-able. For example, the oak trees that receive chemical reports of infection from surrounding trees are able to respond by producing their own chemicals to increase their immunity to that infection. And species that proactively downsize and diversify when their communities or ecosystems grow old and threaten to collapse are able to do that and know when to do it because they have accurate, timely information upon which they can make intelligent decisions.

Every member of a natural community is a potential first responder, and taken together, they are profoundly response-able.

## A Different Kind of Hierarchy

It is fashionable in some quarters to maintain that complex natural systems are organized and operate in ways that are opposite the ways most complex human systems work. Until fairly recently it was considered by many to be a scientific fact that natural systems were not hierarchic. It was obvious, even to non-scientists, that natural communities and ecosystems simply aren't "designed," aren't shaped like pyramids and don't function like a Forbes 500 company, the Roman Empire, the Chinese Communist Party or even the ostensibly democratic but still pyramid-shaped European Union and government of the United States of America.

But more recent research in ecology, evolution, epigenetics and complex systems reveals that natural systems from the smallest organ or ecosystem to the biosphere are hierarchies and derive the benefits of organizational coherence that accrue to hierarchical systems. But Life's hierarchies are of a wholly different order and serve completely different purpose than most human hierarchies.

### A Different Order

The larger communities emerge out of the activities of the smallest participants and communities. They exist *because* of and *are dependent on* the cooperation, collaboration, persistence and success of a sufficient number of the smaller communities of which they are comprised. Life as we know it depends on the success of a sufficient number of the natural communities and species that have comprised it for 100 million years. Take away the workers in our globalized capitalist economy and, apparently, for some period of time the top 1%, 10% or 20% and enough of the funny-based economic system can survive, even thrive, without them. Take away the microbes, lichens, phytoplankton, wetlands, prairies, forests — the workers in Life's economy — and Life as we know it is finished.

### With a Different Purpose

Since this natural hierarchy, a pyramid turned on its point, is dependent for its very existence on the success of its constituent communities (as they are dependent on the success of their participating species), its purpose is to serve the needs of its constituent communities. This is the essence and model of "all for one and one for all." It is democracy of the highest order.

And the advantage of this all-for-one/one-for-all, bottom up, organically democratic organizational structure is stability over the long term. To paraphrase pioneer systems theorist Donella Meadows:

> If the constituents and constituent communities (Life's subsystems) can largely organize, manage and govern (take care of) themselves and at the same time serve the needs of and cooperate in sustainably managing the larger systems of which they are a part
> While the larger systems coordinate and enhance the functioning of their constituent systems
> Then a stable, resilient and efficient as well as sustainable democratic structure results.[24]

For this to happen as it does in complex natural systems, Life has locked several different kinds of leadership.

## Leading the Way

There are no Powers in natural communities, no individuals that call the shots for all the diverse species that participate in them. There are not really any Powers within other-than-human species. There are dominant males and, sometimes, dominant females. But all their dominance gets them is the best or the most sexual partners. Dominance is usually won in mock battle and brings the dubious honor of having to engage in real battles to protect the pack, pride or herd from attack by other groups or another species. Unlike human males, the dominant members of other-than-human species are not protected by their dominance. They are exposed to danger by it.

Natural communities do have leaders, after a fashion. Or perhaps it would be more accurate to say there are leadership roles (or niches) that are filled by certain species. And they must be filled in order for the community to function properly.

One might be called the *entrepreneurship* role. Like futurists, activists, inventors, risk takers and other sorts of pioneers, some species and some members of a species simply "get there first." Yes, bacteria had to work together democratically to solve the problems with which their self-induced Critical Mass challenged them. But some of them solved those problems before or better than others did. And since bacteria exchange genes in order to share survival information, those entrepreneurial bacteria got to spread their winning ideas around quickly and widely. They led with the best survival techniques.

Another is the *servant leadership* role. Organizational consultant Robert Greenleaf laid out a vision of the servant leader based on exemplars like Moses, Jesus of Nazareth and the Buddha.[25] But, though servant leader species are similarly humble in demeanor, they are usually — unlike the founders of religions — great in number. Like the partnering bacteria that laid the way for every subsequent kind of living thing, servant leaders are the species that do the trial and error, prepare the way and lay the groundwork for other species or maintain the conditions that make the success of other species possible. They often come first in time, though not in a superior/inferior sense. Bottom feeders that clean the water for all the other species, the microscopic creatures, lichens and tiny ferns and mosses that create soil, the algae and phytoplankton that maintain the atmosphere that sustains Life: they are servant leader species. They do not take more from their ecosystems than they need and typically give as much or more to their communities than they take. They do not dominate a community or ecosystem; they enable it.

Environmentalists speak of *flagship* species, but they are not so much leaders as poster species for environmental causes. Elephants, tigers, the spotted owl, sea turtles, polar bears from a marketing perspective do not do something so much as they stand for something. They represent whole natural communities and ecosystems which we might not trouble ourselves to save but for our attachment to them. They capture and hold our attention and sympathy. For whatever cultural, historical or mediated reason, we care what happens to the flagship species.

The best known natural leadership role is filled by *keystone* species. From their position at the top of the food chain in an ecosystem, they take the lead in ecosystem regulation. To a certain extent their leadership role resembles that of the Powers: They are known for the degree of influence and control they exert despite their small numbers. And they are usually predators, like the big cats of the African savannah, the alligators of the Everglades, the wolves of the tundra and the Atlantic and Pacific blue fin tuna. But not all are predators. "A keystone species, black-tailed prairie dogs impact the prairie ecosystem in multiple ways: 1) Their burrows act as homes to other creatures, including burrowing owls, badgers, rabbits, black-footed ferrets, snakes, salamanders, and insects. 2) Their burrowing activity works to loosen and churn up the soil, increasing its ability to sustain plant life. 3) Their foraging and feeding practices enable a more nutritious, diverse and nitrogen-rich mixture of grasses and forbs (broad-leafed vegetation) to grow. 4) Black-tailed prairie dogs play an integral role in the prairie food chain; they are a critical food source for such animals as the endangered black-footed ferret, swift fox, coyotes, hawks, eagles and badgers."[26] For the American plains, prairie dogs are as much a leader species as the grass-managing grazers like bison and cattle.

Unlike the Powers, however, keystone species limit excess and expansiveness rather than encourage it; they keep populations of other species in check. Keystone species are named after the stone at the top of an arch in a wall that distributes the weight of the wall so that all the other stones work together to keep the arch open and the wall upright. Take them out of a community and it collapses as surely as the arch and wall do if you knock out the keystone.

There are four significant things to keep in mind about Life's leadership arrangements that may help us as we improve our own:

1. Though leaders and leader-species are not elected democratically, they lead because they competently or even brilliantly fill a niche and fulfill a roll that facilitates the survival of the community as a whole.
2. Leaders do not play favorites and they are not favored; they are functional.
3. Leaders with different skills and experience all lead at the same time. "Collective leadership is the norm in much of the animal world," wrote Ken Thompson in *Bioteams*.[27]
4. Because through time one kind of leadership may be more vital to a community's well-being than another, leaders share leadership in a

remarkably democratic arrangement the ancient Romans called pri-
mus inter pares, first among equals. Because the community needs
several kinds of leadership, there are several kinds of leaders. As the
needs of the community change different species rotate into leadership positions.

## In Short: Proactive, Response-able, Resourceful, Resilient

Size does matter. Big, top down, centralized systems cannot keep track
of the widely divergent conditions that prevail in every location within
their purview. They cannot respond quickly or effectively when crises
multiply or ratchet up in intensity, spread and become syndromes.
This is why the diverse kinds and communities of cells that manage the
immune system are distributed throughout the body, not centralized. It
is these immune system cell communities rather than the busy, preoc-
cupied brain at the top of the body that gather and share the information
that protects us from pathogens. They interpret information and coordinate and deliver appropriate responses.

Like the cell communities that comprise the immune system, the
scattered, locally self-reliant, interdependent, organically democratic
natural communities that comprise the biosphere are constantly aware
of changes in their economies and environments that call for changes
in their behavior. They are small enough to be able, most of the time,
to respond to those changes. They are smart
enough and well enough informed to be able
to respond intelligently and appropriately. And
they are adaptable enough, most of the time,
to bounce back, retain or recover healthy function and maintain their basic identity when a
change has been effectively dealt with.

> "Resilience is the capacity of a system to absorb distur-
> bance and still retain its basic identity and function."[28]

Unlike the viral global economy and the
pyramid-shaped socio-political system that attempts to manage it,
organically democratic, Earthonomical natural communities are *proac-
tive, response-able, resourceful* and *resilient*. That's why such communities
were able (until we got in their way) to manage the equivalent of a high-
functioning immune system that does not induce Critical Mass and is
able to recover from it.

## Harsh Realities and Silver Linings

Nothing on Earth is either perfect or permanent. No matter how democratic, smart, cooperative and/or mutual their organizational structures and relationships are, the lives of natural communities are punctuated by episodes of both unavoidable and creative destruction.

In the first category there are wildfires, protracted droughts and devastating floods, earthquakes, volcanic eruptions, ice ages and the ends of ice ages and other causes of local or global Critical Mass to be coped with, survived or done-in by. And there are glitches. Innovative, improvisational processes like Life's are fraught with them. Some natural communities never really hit their stride, never get the hang of Earthonomics. Sometimes a combination of species fails to establish effective partnerships and collaborations and never becomes a well-organized, well-run community. Sometimes niches don't get filled or refilled, or new species arrive on site before an environment is suited to them and sufficient resources are available to sustain them. Sometimes a new or deranged native species becomes a deadly opportunist and savages other species or its environment.

The second category, creative destruction, encompasses an aspect of Life's recycling rule that microbiologist Mahlon Hoagland has called _turnover_. Whole ecosystems get turned over, recycled. They release stored energy and become food for or good for succeeding ecosystems. On a finite planet, living things and systems are rich storehouses of resources.

The harsh reality is that even successful communities, the ones that manage to avoid both glitches and natural catastrophes and learn how to conserve resources and energy, don't last forever. Sooner or later, if unavoidable crises don't do them in, time does. They wear out and wear down. The conserve-atism that allowed them to become stable, sustainable and mature finally works against them. Rather than allowing their constituent communities to regularly rejuvenate and reorganize themselves in response to changes in their circumstances, they lock in organizational structures and govern their constituent communities more restrictively. Like most of our present governments and systems of governance (both the ostensibly democratic and the obviously undemocratic ones) they get stuck in their ways.

As they lose boldness ecosystems also lose vitality and adaptability. As they lose adaptability they become less resilient. They store up and hoard energy rather than investing some of it in innovation. They use energy less efficiently. *Entropy* (the universal tendency for energy to dissipate and physical stuff to become less viable with use and through time) catches up with them. In short, they get old.

An aged ecosystem can meet its end suddenly or slowly. It can easily be pushed over a threshold and thrown out of balance. Then, like an octogenarian who falls and breaks a hip or gets pneumonia, it will decline and may collapse and die. Or one of an ecosystem's overworked or undernourished communities may begin to fail, causing death to cascade though interdependent communities much the way death cascades through an aged human body from one system to another. The whole-Earth community — Life — is not at risk when an ecosystem passes away, but whole regions of communities and other ecosystems may be.

Ah, but there is a silver lining. After systemic collapse there's a relatively empty space waiting to be reoccupied and a residue of resources and decaying matter available to support new life. Minerals, organic chemicals and energy that were locked up by the collapsed system are released, and the cycle of Life begins anew. The demise of one ecosystem leads to the birth of another. This may be the fate of the human species or at least of a lot of humans and human communities.

But there's still another silver lining: Life offers an alternative to the aging → decline → death → birth cycle, a radically democratic alternative from which we can learn.

**Rebellions, secessions, resistances and revolutions
are Life's solutions to species and community
survival in the face of systemic failure.**

We think of democracy as a stable form of government and consider any action taken to overthrow, undermine, change or challenge that government as heretical, unpatriotic, treasonous, undemocratic. But many governments we call democratic were envisioned and initiated by rebels in periods of rejection of the status quo and prevailing system. In periods, that is, of anarchy. The new political systems became orderly only when the rebels had gained the capacity to self-organize and self-govern democratically.

When ecosystems get locked in, they become the equivalent of dictatorial. They make it difficult for the species and natural communities that comprise them to protect, defend, provide for, adapt and heal themselves. Some of those species and communities go down with the system. Those that are able to challenge, withdraw support from the system and reorganize or transform themselves survive. In effect, they quit the oppressive and potentially failing system as surely as American colonials quit Britain, citizens of former Soviet states quit Russia and Tibetans are attempting to quit China.

It is vital for us in our present circumstances to understand this one of Life's survival methods: The species and communities that survive systemic collapse are the ones that:

- Withdraw support from an old, destructive or maladaptive system proactively, *before* it takes them down
- Adapt their function, their ways of providing for themselves, and their form, structures and requirements.

They give themselves an opportunity to co-create the sustainable communities and ecosystems that will carry them into the future in that place.

## In Hard Times

We are living in hard times. We may soon be living in the hardest times modern humans have ever known. Let's take one more, quick look at what Life's four-billion years of experience teaches us to expect and to do in a period of global Critical Mass.

Brief hard times, such as those that follow a fire, flood or ice storm, for example, are usually local or regional. They may cause the affected communities a few seasons or years of hardship, but the communities retain their basic identities and integrity and bounce back fairly quickly to something very like their previous conditions. Hardwood forests, tall grass prairies and coastal wetlands come back as something like their former selves. (At least they did before our activities undermined their natural resilience, completely took over their space and commandeered their resources.) In brief hard times, communities don't change the way

"In the Everglades, resilience is reflected by the marshland's capacity to absorb the repeated disturbances of flood, drought, and fire. [Excessive quantities of] nutrients introduced into the system by agriculture, however, reduced the resilience of the sawgrass regime. Now in many parts of the Everglades, opportunistic phosphorous-loving cattail is displacing sawgrass (and the habitat it provided for many species of water birds). The system is no longer absorbing disturbances as it was once able to do, and has shifted into a new (cattail) regime."[29]

their economies work dramatically or at all. They muddle through until the resources that they depend on are restored. We call our equivalent economic challenges recessions. And some of us think we are now in the muddling through phase and don't need to change what we're doing.

But long or dramatically hard times, periods that are fraught with multiple and converging crises, force natural communities and Life itself to retrench. Whether it comes on suddenly, as after a sky-darkening volcanic eruption triggers global Critical Mass, or slowly, as when the cumulative depredations of a viral economy induce it, protracted hardship causes the equivalent of a *Great Depression*. This, I have been suggesting, is what we're facing now.

Depending on its cause and the way it plays out, some species, communities and ecosystems are always better equipped to survive a Great Depression than others. Bacteria, viruses, rats and cockroaches come to mind. But in general, when Life faces long hard times, some species of plants die. Others die back in numbers and breadth of distribution or go into dormancy. In any case there are fewer species and individuals trying to live on a reduced base of soil, water and space. Remaining plants put out few or no seeds or fruits and grow very little or not at all. They retreat into their roots like bears into caves in the winter. They live very frugally on stored reserves of solar energy as bears live on reserves of fat. They adapt to diminished carrying capacity.

Animal populations reduce their consumption drastically by a variety of means. The old die at an earlier than normal age. The hearty reduce their consumption. The space between reproductive cycles lengthens when females are perpetually hungry, so there are fewer births. Stressed females produce fewer viable offspring per birth and keep even fewer alive. Populations die back to the level that the available resources can support. Competition for resources increases but, except in humans, not to a genocidal level.

In worst cases, when a downturn in a natural or a human community is very long and severe, animals — including humans — have resorted to cannibalism, an extreme form of nutrient recycling even for other-than-human species. The fittest and also those that are best able to adapt to new conditions manage to survive. Among the most successful adaptive strategies are the ones that save not just strong, aggressive, competitive individuals and species but also larger numbers of genetically diverse individuals and species. Because communities fare better than solitaries, members of strong communities fare better over the long term than isolated strong individuals do, and longer than communities that resort to dog-eat-dog behaviors. Opportunists may do well in the short term but they always run up against the limits of their excesses. Organically democratic, subsistent, self-reliant, mixed-species communities are sustainable, suited to the long haul.[30]

Many natural communities don't bounce back at all after a long hard time because too many of their members and species die or the post-depression environment is too different from what it was before to support them. Different combinations of species eventually take over places that are left vacant and create very different kinds of economies based on the new environmental conditions.

Life's most drastic forms of frugality do have about them, in Thomas Hobbes' terms, a "nasty and brutish" aspect. But they are not cruel or unconscionable. They are Earthological. Regional and global Critical Mass leave only the strongest and the most innovative, resilient, cooperative, creative and adaptable individuals and species standing. They *force* natural communities to downsize, diversify and live within Earth's newly reduced means. Together.

## Not Earthonomical by Accident

Each one and all of them at the same time, natural communities maintain the health of Earth's immune system because the majority of them live within Earth's means most of the time. Downsizing, diversity, avoidance of wastefulness and pollution, local self-reliance, equitability, subsistence, reliance on inexhaustible sources of energy, partnerships and other forms of interdependence. Earthonomical behaviors like these have allowed Life to avoid causing Critical Mass for two billion years. These behaviors did not become the key characteristics of Life's successful economies by accident any more than growth, consumption, expansion and waste accidentally became the key characteristics of the viral global economy. The success of natural communities results from the remarkably democratic ways that other-than-human species have learned to organize themselves, relate to each other and coordinate their Earthonomic activities. By contrast, profligacy, injustice and despoliation of the living systems on which we've forgotten that we depend have resulted from the undemocratic ways and societies in which most of us live.

There are patterns in the behaviors of other-than-human species that we can repeat and that we can teach our children so that they can repeat them too. These patterns constitute Life's Economic Survival Protocol which can help us to transform ourselves exactly as other living things — beginning with the smallest and most primal — have transformed themselves when Life demanded it.

## One More Lesson from Bacteria

Bonnie Bassler is a Princeton University microbiologist and MacArthur Foundation genius award recipient. Her specialty is microbial communications, the key to Life's organically democratic operations. She listens to bacteria. Why? Bacterial cells account for nine out of ten of the cells in our bodies. We are "at best," Bassler says, "only 10 percent human." And that statistic applies to Life at large. Life rules, but bacteria were the first lawmakers. "They make up 50 percent of the biomass of the earth and nearly 100 percent of its biodiversity."[31] What better species to teach us how Life works and why it works democratically?

"Bacteria survey their ranks, they count heads, and if the throng is sufficiently large and like-minded — if there is a quorum — they act." A quorum, a critical mass of diverse bacterial activists, voters, movers and shapers, willing participants and collaborators, "can band together and perform the work of giants."[32]

So can we.

## Democratic Earthonomical Communities v. the Pyramidal Global Economy: Striking Contrasts

| Community Economics | The Global Economy |
| --- | --- |
| Local economies | National and global economies |
| Self-reliant | Dependent |
| Mutually supportive | Self-interested |
| Embedded in place | Abusive/indifferent to place |
| Resource-based | Money-based |
| Subsistent | Consumptive |
| Periodic downtimes | Constant economic activity |
| Equitable | Inequitable |
| Solar | Fossil-fueled |
| Reuse, recycle, renew | Use up, discard, pollute |
| Waste nothing | Wasteful, polluting |
| Organized from the bottom up | Organized from the top down |
| Self-organized | Organized by a few |
| Adaptive | Inflexible |
| Self-governed | Professionally governed |
| Communitarian | Individualistic |
| Common good | Private gain |
| Primarily cooperative | Primarily competitive |
| Share vital information | Withhold vital information |
| Task-based leadership | Power-based leadership |
| Self-limiting | Unlimited |
| Proactive, response-able | Reactive, irresponsible |
| Resilient | Vulnerable |
| Sustainable | Unsustainable |

## We Can Do This

"Through the entire course of written history the shrewdest, the strongest, the best fed and most comfortably housed have gained wealth and power, kept them and added to them. This has been the central sociological principle followed by the wealth-owning, power-wielding oligarchs of one civilization after another. Nature has been polluted, despoiled, pillaged. Society has been exploited and plundered. Most civilizations, during most of their history, have been led and ruled by the rich and powerful, who have used their wealth and power to advance their own interests, with scant respect for the hewers of wood, the drawers of water and the tillers of the soil. Those at the imperial center have milked the periphery. Cooperation has been occasional and confined largely to pre-civilized communities. In all civilizations, exploitation has been the rule; the exploitation of nature, of workers and of the social fabric....

"[But] we humans could by-pass the restrictions and limitations imposed on human creative genius by the structure and function of civilization. ... Humanity could play a creative role in accordance with our capacities and our destiny as an integral part of the joint enterprise to which our sun furnishes light, warmth and vibrant energy — life itself. We have latent among us the talent and genius necessary to play such a part. Do we have the imagination, courage and daring to accept the challenge?"[33]

— Scott Nearing

"... In just about every town or city in our land you can find some groups or coalitions that, instead of merely shouting at politicians, have come together to find their way around, over or through the blockage that big money has put in the way of their democratic aspirations. Also, in the process of organizing, strategizing, and mobilizing, these groups are building relationships and community, creating something positive from a negative.

"This is the historic, truly democratic, grassroots populism of workaday folks who strive (and, more often than
not, succeed) to empower themselves to change economically as well as politically."[34]

— Jim Hightower

# Part III

## Deep Green Methods for Surviving the Global Economy

### The Heart of the Healing

If we wish to mitigate and survive Critical Mass, and avoid causing it again, and if we wish to restore health to Earth's besieged immune system, we will create clusters, coalitions and networks of regionally interdependent Earthological communities that provision themselves and each other using human and natural resources that are regionally available and forms of energy that are inexhaustible or renewable and, in large measure regionally produced and cooperatively managed.

If we are bold, we will persuade our leaders by any and all means available to us, short of doing them physical harm, to use a significant portion of our remaining fossil fuels and funny-money to pay for the transition from global and national to local and regional rather than spending precious funds of both to prop up a sure-to-fail, pathological economy. And then we will fire most of them and begin again by reorganizing and governing ourselves locally and regionally according to Life's organically democratic model. And we will choose leaders who would facilitate our Earthological and Earthonomic ambitions. We will engage in Six Degrees of Separation from the Global Economy: We will

1) drop out or drop back
2) downsize
3) diversify
4) decarbonize
5) dematerialize
6) democratize

And if we are wise, we will internalize such universally adaptable, Life-sustaining, Deep Green ideals as those summarized by Kirkpatrick Sale in

*Dwellers in the Land:* "ecological understanding, regional and communitarian consciousness, nature-based wisdom and spirituality, biocentric [Life-centered] sensibility, decentralist planning, participatory politics, mutual aid, and humility."[1] And, along with our deepest religious and spiritual traditions, we will teach them to every generation of children.

CHAPTER 11

# Mimicking Life's Economics — Improving the Odds and Our Lives

THIS CANNOT BE REPEATED TOO OFTEN: Life rules, we don't. We are not larger than Life, and we cannot live apart from Life though we have tried mightily to do just that. Life is the only context within which we can understand what we need to do both to survive and mitigate this Critical Mass we have caused and to avoid causing it again. Acceptance of the fact that Life rules and knowledge of and obedience to Life's Rules are as vital to our survival as a species as genetic encoding of those rules has been to other-than-human species. Mimicking Life is how we may yet, if slowly, fix what's going wrong everywhere at once.

Accordingly, we need a version of Life's Economic Survival Protocol — the Ten Commandments of real sustainability — that's revised to guide human communities in becoming Earthological. The list below roughly translates those rules into language that's appropriate for human community making.

As treating just some of the symptoms of Critical Mass may worsen others and won't cure us of the syndrome, we will need to implement all of the elements of the protocol, not just those that seem easy, familiar or profitable. It helps that each element in the protocol grows out of, supports or leads to another just as each element in the AIDS treatment protocol supports or is supported by the others.

# Elements of a Lifelike Economic Survival Protocol

- The basic units of sustainable human economic activity are locally and bioregionally self-reliant, interdependent, fully inclusive communities.

- Truly sustainable, Lifelike communities are communities of place, partnership and purpose like the natural communities in which they are located.

- Truly sustainable communities organize, regulate and govern themselves democratically within limits set by their environments and by the needs of the larger socio-economic commons and natural communities of which they are a part. Regional economic coalitions and networks are politically subsidiary to local and bioregional communities except when the activities of any of those communities threaten the well-being or sustainability of the coalitions and networks of which they are a part. Regional economic coalitions and networks are collectively operated by participating communities.

- Long-term sustainable communities are biocentric: They are embedded in and harmonized with the ecosystems of which they are a part; they are partners with or sponsors of natural communities with which they share those ecosystems.

- Their economies are resource-based rather than primarily monetary. Their size, scope, content and cycles of production are determined

    1) by the kinds and quantity of resources that are available to them in their bioregion or that can be made available without causing harm to surrounding natural communities and regional ecosystems

    2) by the kind and quality of regional ecosystem services that are available or can be encouraged without damaging those ecosystems.

- Truly sustainable communities export only what they have or can produce in abundance without compromising their future well-being or the well-being of the natural communities and ecosystems in which they participate and on which they are aware they depend. To the ☞

"Given that all sustainable natural systems, from developing embryos to physiologically functioning bodies, are characterized by diffuse regional regulation and local control, it would be wise for us to model our own institutions, from governments to corporations, on such adapted economies."[1]

extent possible, they import what they cannot provide for themselves only from communities that export according to the same Lifelike economic rules.

- They waste nothing (or as little as possible) and produce no waste they cannot find a use for or safely sequester.
- Their economies are, to the extent possible, pollution-free, relatively equitable, subsistence, common-good, full-employment economies.
- Truly sustainable communities prioritize energy efficiency and run primarily on inexhaustible and renewable sources of energy that are managed locally and regionally and synchronized, to the extent possible, with surrounding energy systems.
- They exchange survival information and pool intelligence, particularly ecological (or, more pointedly, Earthological) intelligence, in real time.

"I envision a decentralized economy in which even small localities would have more control of their economic life than is now possible, but in which relative self-sufficiency would be possible only [regionally. This] would not end the environmental crisis or the human one, but it would position humanity in such a way that intelligent responses would be possible. It is a mistake today to look for ideal solutions. There are none. But it is not a mistake to look for ways to avoid catastrophes or at least to minimize those that may already be inevitable and to prepare to rebuild in a sustainable way. My conviction is that the decentralization of the economy and the organization of the political world in terms of communities of communities offers these possibilities."[2]

## The Way Forward, In General

So what is the way out from between the rock and the hard place? The way out is the same way those ancient bacteria took when their single-species global economy crashed and took their old ways of living with it. The same way that successful species have taken every time Critical Mass has threatened to wipe them out as it is doing now.

What does mimicking Life's ways mean that we need to do?

### Acknowledge Life's Wisdom

We treat Life's Economic Survival Protocol as equivalent to another Ten Commandments, Eightfold Path or Five Pillars of Wisdom.

### Take Charge

We take charge of our own economic destinies in the very diverse places and ever-changing circumstances in which the crisis finds us. We recognize that government-issued money and funny-money may not much longer represent wealth or purchase provisions for us. We use what we have left of them to prepare to do without them.

We will need to do these things anyway as the current global recession lingers and, at some point, settles into prolonged depression. Even the widely predicted half decade of recession is a long time to go without enough money to pay for basic necessities, especially as social services are trimmed and cut and systemic supports fail.

The world's slum dwellers and the rural poor whom top down, Powers-driven societies have left in this untenable position for time immemorial have long since devised ways to survive, if not thrive, in such conditions. Newcomers to conventional and funny-money poverty

"No one fully understands how, or even if, sustainable development can be achieved; however there is a growing consensus that it must be accomplished at the local level if it is ever to be achieved on a global basis."[3]

"It is becoming apparent that almost every issue of sustainable development which emerges at the local level will be replicated, in one form or another, at the provincial, national and international levels."[4]

can likewise discover ways of working together to provide for themselves and each other at least some of what the economy doesn't, can't and won't provide during and after economic collapse. Some hearty, innovative number of us have always managed to survive even ice ages, volcanic winters and regional ecosystem collapses.

In any case, the effort to learn how to provision ourselves will not be wasted even if the global economy bounces back for a while. Any successful Earthonomic innovations we may come up with during this period will serve as models for our collective long-term effort to survive the eventual demise of the global economy. Life locks in Earthological survival methods that work. So have we in the past. So can we now.

## Move Into Harmony

As quickly as we are able, in all the particular and diverse places in which the crisis finds us, we bring our lifeways into harmony with Life's ways and try as hard as we can to honor Life's prime directive to live within Earth's means.

Given how deeply and widely the present system is entrenched and how utterly dependent on it we are, we will only be able to take incremental steps in Life's direction. But the faster we can take them and the more of us who do, the better for our longer term prospects and for the likelihood of the continuation of Life as we know it.

## Take Responsibility

We treat Life, including human life, as if it had been given a death sentence that only we, working together and with Life, can commute. We become (as Paul Hawken has suggested that we can in *Blessed Unrest*) the equivalents of the antibodies in our immune systems that, after much trial and error, are equipped precisely to deal with such threats in every unique part of Earth's body.

## Cut Back

We do what other-than-human species do when the support systems on which they've depended fail: we cut back. How do we do that? All of us, everywhere trim our populations, activities, consumption and expectations. Mitigating Critical Mass is a task that falls to each of us able adults alike but to none of us only as individuals. It is a vital and necessary task at which we can only succeed together. Together, as families, neighborhoods, towns and villages, communities and communities of communities, we make do. We learn to work within the limits of resources that are available to us locally and regionally and we stop abusing the environments and ecosystems that provide them.

We do these things not because some political party or ideologues or pundits or preachers tell us we should, but because our survival depends on it.

### Honor All Life

We take the lives of the other-than-human species on whom our survival depends as seriously as we take our own and our loved ones' lives. We learn intellectually, emotionally, spiritually and behaviorally to perceive and to treat human and natural communities as they are in reality: one community, the community of Life as a whole.

We take the common good — the well-being and survival of the diverse species we did not create and cannot recreate — even more seriously than we take our own. Not only because, within the tenets of the world's major religions, it would be the right thing to do, but because it is necessary.

### Engage in the Healing

We give the natural communities with which we cohabit a chance to heal and to teach us how healing works. We engage in what Tim Watson, a North Carolina architect, teacher and president of the EarthWalk Alliance calls *eco-restoration*. We become partners with natural communities in the maintenance of our local ecosystems. And by that means we will increase the possibility that, taken together — each community itself and as many as possible at the same time, engaged in the process of evolving a planetful of Earthogical human communities — we may help to heal Earth's failing immune system so that there will be a human future and it will be worth living.

### Downsize Economic and Energy Systems

More specifically, we begin to downsize, diversify and decentralize our economies and the energy systems that support them. We learn to organize, govern and regulate ourselves as Earthological communities, and we do all of this democratically because life teaches us that democratic methods of organization and democratic behaviors and relationships (which are already being taxed by scarcity, recession and uncertainty) are fundamental to our survival.

> Our aim as we undertake to mimic Life's economies is not fundamentalist survivalism — the battle to the death for the last of everything — but *functional survival* — a brave effort to make what's left on Earth work for as many of us and other living things as possible for as long as possible.

## A Good Name for It: Deep Green

Eco-philosopher Joanna Macy and *Yes!* magazine publisher David C. Korten call the social, political, cultural and economic transition in which we may engage "the Great Turning." In his book of that name, Korten described it as a turning away from Empire (from Powers-driven socio-political structures and economics) and toward democratically organized, sustainable, cooperative "Earth communities."

Master conserver and scholar of ecological history John Michael Greer offers another name for what will come after the collapse of the present industrial capitalist civilization: "the Ecotechnic Age." Systems and evolutionary theorist Ervin Laszlo envisions what he calls a "Holos" civilization based on our growing recognition of Life as a whole and unitary phenomenon "hallmarked by the kind of thinking that enables people to see not just the trees in front of them, but the forest that is their planetary habitat."[5] Climate and peak-oil activists encourage planning toward and designing what they call a "Post-Carbon Era."

In 2007, China's then-president, Hu Jintao, and Pan Yue, then deputy director of China's State Environmental Protection Administration, offered the term "ecological civilization" as "a future-oriented guiding principle, based" the *China Daily* reported, "on the perception of the extremely high price we have paid for our economic miracle.... We need to put our relationship with nature in a new perspective: consider nature as part of our life rather than as something we can exploit without restraint."[6] The following year Peking University's Beijing Forum took as its theme the idea that "the 21st century is the age of transition from traditional industrial civilization to ecological civilization."[7]

Precedent suggests that "ecological civilization" is an oxymoron. The things the two words name are mutually contradictory. Historically, civilizations are human centered, urbanized economic and political systems that by their very size, methods of structuring, means of providing for themselves and gargantuan appetites for resources of every kind, run against Life's grain. A civilization might be ecological if it were a coalition of self-reliant, place-based communities or societies united and harmonized by a similar ecological world-view. But then it wouldn't, in conventional terms, be a civilization. It would be an ecological, or better still, an Earthological society comprised of Earthonomically diverse communities.

Nevertheless, to be civilized, as when the word describes a collective manifestation of civility, remains a high human aspiration. To be civilized in this sense and also Earthological could only be good.

The late cultural historian and influential eco-philosopher Thomas Berry foresaw a future he called "the Ecozoic,"[8] an age or era in which humans will have learned to work *with* rather than against Life and to partner with other-than-human species in a co-creative, life-making, Life-sustaining process. Berry recognized that we would have to engage in this process not only *with* other species but, as he wrote in *The Great Work*, from "*within* the community of living systems" — as part of nature, neither superior to nor apart from it. Because Ecozoic places our lives firmly within the context of Life, it may be the most accurate, most Earthological, name for what we hope the Great Work will achieve.

Given that we can't really know what Life and human lives will look like in 25 years let alone in a century or two, naming the next new age may be futile. It may be more appropriate to name the kinds of behaviors we can engage in now that would produce a desirable next new age, the kinds of lifeways that would mimic Life's ways so that humans are still around and life is still worth living a century or two from now.

Eco = home, home planet, Earth

Zoic = life, living being

Ecozoic = supportive of life on Earth as we know it

Can there be an oxymoron that is much more moronic, more cognitively dissonant than "industrial ecosystem?" But being able to make ourselves feel good about doing things that aren't simply by manipulating the meanings of words is one of the characteristics that distinguishes us from other-than-human species. And so, "sustainable" and "organic" have for some time been used to describe behaviors and prod-

> **Dangerous Oxymoron: "Industrial Ecosystems"**
>
> "More significant, there will be new industrial ecosystems that incubate and propel growth.... Constructing entirely new ecosystems is another discipline at which the US excels."[9]

ucts that are neither, and "green" as an inspiring term for environmental activism has seen better days. Once a fresh, energizing meme and rallying cry for environmentalists, green has been put in service to the very global economy it was intended to challenge. Weakened by savvy corporate co-opting, green has been used to market everything from upscale housing developments, automobiles, big box retailers and resorts to household cleaning products, oil companies, cosmetics and imported coffees. In going from counterculture to cache, green has suffered the same fate as organic and sustainable: Few people know how to define or defend it. It has become cheap green, promising to cost very little in terms of personal sacrifice or systemic change.

But Green Parties around the world still hold and promote genuinely Lifelike values, and green still motivates those of us who recognize the converging threats to Life as we know it. Green captures the essence of the plant kingdom on which our lives and all other forms of life depend. We shouldn't give it up, yielding it to the plunderers and Powers. We should pump it up so that it encourages us to live in ways that are deeply green rather than shop in ways that are weakly green. "Deep Green" might be a good name for the cure for Critical Mass. To be Deeply Green would be Earthological, sustainable and embedded in rather than larger than Life. Lifeways that mimic Life's ways would be Deep — deeply — Green.[10]

But whatever name we eventually give the time that comes after Critical Mass, we will, whether by choice or because we are forced,

> *Deep Green* describes lifeways that mimic Life's ways.

downsize, diversify, decentralize, dematerialize and decarbonize. And if we wish to live in a world that is at all equitable and humane, we will democratize our relationships, methods of governance and behaviors.

And I repeat: We will do these things not only because they are virtuous or altruistic, not because it would be nice, but because it is necessary. Our survival as a species may depend on it; our quality of life *will* depend on it.

The analogy of HIV/AIDS with our viral economy breaks down exactly here, and it breaks in our favor. The immunodeficiency virus in the human body dies only when the patient dies. The viral global economy is dying — if by fits and starts — and taking many human and natural communities with it. But not all of them. And not all of us.

There is a rapidly vanishing window of opportunity within which we can still rescue and restore health to many of our communities (even the designated poorest ones) and to the natural communities on which they, our economies and futures depend. We are yet able to become successful antibodies and active, cooperative, co-creative participants in Earth's equivalent of an immune system.

## What's in the Pages Ahead and What Isn't

Happily, we will not have to invent Deep Green economics or design Deep Green communities from scratch. We have available an abundance of resources from books and conferences to courses, projects, demonstrations and teachers that can guide our efforts to create communities and societies that mimic Life's Economic Survival Protocol. And there are existing sets of operating principles and prototypes — working models of methods and techniques suggested by the protocol — that we can adapt to our specific circumstances and adjust as our circumstances change.

*Permaculture*, an ecological design concept originated by Australians Bill Mollison and David Holmgren, names a set of place-based agricultural, land use, structure design and resource and waste management practices that mimic Life so successfully they allow communities to provide for themselves as close to permanently as is possible on an ever changing, finite planet.

An Internet search of the following topics will lead to resources that support Deep Green practices: permaculture, biomimicry, urban and suburban agriculture, organic farming and gardening, ecological design, restoration ecology, cradle-to-cradle materials and waste management, human and natural resource assessment, deep ecology, relocalization, resilience thinking, sustainable communities, Local First, natural capitalism, Transition Towns, community survival strategies, green design and green business, urban villages, local self-reliance, bioregionalism, local currencies, community supported agriculture programs (CSAs), intentional communities, no-growth economics, barter and informal economies, alternative currency and metacurrency systems, community corporations, life cycle assessment, local media, ecological economics, true cost accounting, energy efficiency, post-carbon and regional energy systems. Each of these will link to a wide range of other practices and to explanations of how they work and can be integrated to mimic and support Life's Economic Survival Protocol.

The new releases and extensive backlists of leading sustainability publishers like New Society, Chelsea Green, Island Press, Rodale, South End, Green Books and Earthscan also point communities to the resources they need. And the WiserEarth and Global Commons websites, among others an Internet search turns up, provide information about organizations and groups around the world that are advocating for, researching, testing or engaging in many Lifelike, sustainable, grassroots projects and programs.[11]

All we have lacked, really, has been the context within which these prototypes and principles could be harmonized and integrated. My intent in this book has been to address that lack, to give more of us reason to seek out those prototypes, principles, techniques and teachers and to offer a fairly inarguable context within which we could understand how — and why — to use them: Life itself.

What I offer in the following pages, then, is a vision of a Deep Green future. It includes some of the implications for human communities of adopting Life's Economic Survival Protocol and, in text boxes, examples of projects in progress. This is necessarily an incomplete and preliminary vision. New experiments with Deep Green practices emerge regularly and some older ones fail or are revised. I offer this vision as a conversation starter to help more of us get our minds around what it would mean for us to bring our lifeways into harmony with Life's ways in order to live within Earth's means.

## Moving to Relocalize

Up until the last 60 years or so, we humans lived our lives on a much more local scale than we do now. For that reason the popular term for what we need to do now is *relocalize*.

"The idea," wrote Toronto-based Edmund Fowler, author of *Building Cities That Work*, "is to become aware of our personal abilities to meet our own needs and desires by cooperating with friends and neighbors in our own communities."[12] Fowler cited participants in the Transition Towns Initiative, a rapidly growing international grassroots relocalization movement catalyzed by Rob Hopkins, a British permaculture educator and author of *The Transition Handbook*. In early 2010, 35 towns in the UK, 60 in the US and over 500 around the world were already seeking to make the transition from dependence on the global economy and fossil fuels to competence as Deep Green communities.[13] Members of such forward-thinking communities are discovering and sharing steps they're taking to become self-reliant in food, energy and materials, effective resource managers and ecosystem partners and self-confident and politically competent in the process.

Richard Heinberg called such self-transforming communities "Community Economic Laboratories," or CELs, and proposed "the seeding of a loosely coordinated national network" of them. He uses the term laboratory because "the sorts of efforts and enterprises that will best serve communities under rapidly evolving economic circumstances may not be apparent or even knowable at the outset — we will have to experiment. In any case, the mission of each CEL would be to increase personal and community resilience."[14]

"Local self-reliance does not mean isolation. It means diversification of local economies to support local needs, encourage cohesiveness, reduce waste and enable more sustainable trade practices with other communities.... The goal of a self-reliant community is to enhance local wealth by developing the community's existing resource base."[15]

Since humans are consumers of every kind of natural resource, most human communities, no matter how frugal, subsistent and restrained in their consumption and use of resources, would not be able to provide themselves with everything they need in their immediate locations. But if we stop short of destroying the living systems on which our lives depend, many communities would be able to trade with others in the same or adjacent bioregions in order to obtain at least necessities, perhaps even sometimes to enjoy what social critic and homesteader Scott Nearing called "ample sufficiency."

Locally self-reliant human communities would more accurately be regionally self-reliant. For our purposes in these pages the two terms are interchangeable. Accordingly, if we wish to mitigate and survive Critical Mass and avoid causing it again, and if we wish to restore health to Earth's besieged immune system, we will create clusters, coalitions and networks of regionally interdependent Earthological communities that provision themselves and each other using human and natural resources that are regionally available and forms of energy that are inexhaustible or renewable and in large measure regionally produced and cooperatively managed.

Because they would be local-regional economies, the economies of Earthological communities would be as different from each other as the places — the climates, natural communities, ecosystems and cultures — they are located in and the human and natural resources available to them there. As different as the Great Plains are from the Amazon rainforest. As different as the communities of monkeys, sloths, birds, reptiles, insects and plants that populate the 150- to 200-foot-high Amazon rainforest tree canopy are from the communities of animals, insects and plants on the ground below.

## Communities of Place and Subsistence Economies

Though it will be difficult for us and will go against habits and expectations that are several generations old, we who have had eyes bigger than our stomachs and an economy that has tried to be bigger than Life can retrieve habits and expectations that are written into our genetic code as they are into the code that guides every other kind of living thing. We can stop looking all over the world for food, clothing, building materials and energy and cease putting all our energies into acquiring enough funny-money to get them.

Instead we can look around our neighborhood, town, city, local ecosystem and bioregion and figure out how to produce as many of the things themselves as we are able. As Lifelike, resource-based communities, we'll get away from funny-money and back to provisions and provisioning. As participants in subsistence rather than perpetual growth economies, we'll focus on producing enough of what we need for everyone, rather than a great deal we don't need for a few. And to the extent possible, we'll base the kinds and quantity of our provisions on what the places we live in (our local and regional ecosystems) can provide without causing harm to those ecosystems. That is, we will use what's renewable in sensible time frames; we will use sparingly if at all what cannot be renewed. Exactly as successful natural communities do.

Whatever necessities we cannot produce for ourselves locally — specialized medical equipment and pharmaceuticals, for example — we will continue to acquire from the existing economy when we can afford them, so long as it's still producing them and preferably only so long as our acquiring them doesn't compromise the places and people we acquire them from. We will not be able to be purists. It's impossible to produce plastics and most pharmaceuticals, for example, without using fossil fuels and petroleum derivatives, and it's impossible to use them without causing some degree of environmental harm and spending down a non-renewable resource. We may have to make difficult decisions together about what kinds of equipment and medicines and other petroleum-derived materials, synthetics and chemicals are really necessary. To the extent possible, as subsistent Deep Green communities we will do without what we don't need if producing or acquiring it

"The effort begins, I think, with the sort of inventory and accounting that ecologists have done for natural ecosystems, a kind of accounting seldom if ever done for human-dominated ecosystems. How do we start thinking about what is involved in setting up the books for ecological community accounting that will feature humans? I emphasize accounting because our goal is renewability, sustainability."[16]

would compromise the ecosystems on which we, our descendants and our economies rely.

## Gift Economies and Commons Economies

There are models for the kinds of economic principles and habits we might need to adopt if we want to avoid the rabid, violent competition that has been characteristic of hard times, downsized economies and economies localized by default because of scarcity or failed larger systems. Economies based on expanded understandings of gift and common goods economics are among them.

### Gift Economies

Prehistoric human economies, that is, pre-money economies, were combination gift and barter or trade economies. Members of communities often gave each other what they had more than enough of, and sometimes what they did not have enough of, if sharing would protect and strengthen the community. Some communities gifted other communities — with food, tools, minerals and water, for example — in times of need, knowing from experience that when they fell on hard times the favor would be returned. Most communities bartered or traded goods, such as tools, medicinals and services (such as team hunting) with other communities.

Gifting is a form of redistribution of wealth, assets and necessities. It is a kind of built-in sharing. Unfortunately, the global economy shuns the idea of redistribution. If it "gives" something to people, a business sector or nation, it expects something of equal or greater value in return. As Lewis Hyde observed in *The Gift: The Erotic Life of Property,* in a monetary, buy-own-sell economy, power and position are accorded to those who possess the most. In a gift economy, on the other hand, status is accorded to those who give the most; power is detached from possessions and attached, instead, to aspects of personal character like wisdom, useful knowledge, expertise, vision, honesty and generosity.

In gift economies, gifting is not a form of charity. Charity is one-way giving. The charitable donor, expecting nothing in return, is absolved of having any ongoing mutual relationship with the recipient. In truth, the charitable giver typically does not even know the recipient. And the recipient is presumed in some way to be dependent on rather than interdependent with the giver. Charity is not a bad practice; it's just not a good practice for building healthy relationships.

In some gift economies, like the tribal economies of the North America's Northwest, giving has been organized by ritual or established occasions, like the potlatch, that redistributes assets from the wealthier and more influential members of the nation to the less wealthy and influential. For other gift economies, giving is more spontaneous and multidirectional and, while not obligatory, is supported by tradition and community values to the extent that it is expected and assumed.

In gift economies, giving — or gifting — is typically not done in private. It's often a ceremonial process. Nor does giving make the giver superior to the recipient. Gifting is public and the recipients, who may or may not actually need the gift, do not lose honor or respect but are considered worthy of the gift simply because they are members of the community who are presumed to be equally capable of *paying it forward* (gifting something of value in return or to others in the community).

Open source websites and technologies (which enable all users to influence content, programming and design), Habitat for Humanity, Amish barn raisings, blood bank and organ donation systems, regifting networks and Freecycle are examples of gift economies operating inside of the present market economy.

---

## For Example: Gifts That Keep on Giving

### The Potlatch

"The potlatch is an example of a total system of giving. Read this too fast and you miss the meaning. Spelled out it means that each gift is part of a system of reciprocity in which the honor of giver and recipient are engaged. It is a total system in that every item of status or of spiritual or material possession is implicated for everyone in the whole community. The system is quite simple: just the rule that every gift has to be returned in some specified way sets up a perpetual cycle of exchanges within and between generations.... ☞

"The gift cycle ... supplies each individual with personal incentives for collaborating in the pattern of exchanges. Gifts are given in a context of public drama, with nothing secret about them.... Just by being visible," which exchanges in market economies typically are not, "the resultant distribution of goods and services is more readily subject to public scrutiny and judgments of fairness than are the results of market exchange. In operating a gift system a people are more aware of what they are doing" individually and collectively.[17]

## Scientific Gifts

"Lest we think that the principles of the gift economy will only work for simple, primitive or small enterprises, [Lewis] Hyde points out that the community of scientists follows the rules of the gift economy. The scientists with the most status are not those who possess the most knowledge; they are the ones who have contributed the most to their fields....

"At a symposium a scientist gives a paper. Scientists do not hope others give better papers so they can come away with more knowledge than they had to offer in exchange. Quite the reverse. Each scientist hopes his or her paper will provide a large and lasting value."[18]

Gift economies can have the effect of binding people together, creating trust and engendering the habits of generosity, equitability and reciprocity in ways that buying, selling and trading never can. Communities struggling to survive the failure of the global economy by creating self-reliant, Deep Green local economies could find some encoded or ritualized form of gifting a key to community building.

## The Global Commons

Life treats resources and ecosystem services as common wealth. There is no private ownership in natural communities. It is not conceivable that we humans will do away with private ownership, and it may not be desirable that we do so. Furthermore, in a globalized economy, too often Powers, leaders and legislators have turned public holdings, particularly

"A commons is a resource, [in the past] most often land, and refers both to the territory and to the ways people allocate the goods that come from that land. The commons provided food, fuel, water and medicinal plants for those who used it — it was the poorest people's life-support system."19

land and the resources on it, into profit makers and commodities for a few of us rather than managing them sustainably for the future use and benefit of all humans and other-than-human species. National parks and public lands in the US West, for example are routinely made available for free and with few if any environmental strings attached, to paper, timber, gas and oil companies and agribusinesses.

As an alternative, people outside of the private and public sectors are proposing the establishment of global commons for any resources to which all people and peoples ought to have access because:

1) those resources are necessary to sustain life and quality of life
2) they need to be managed locally, regionally and, to the extent this is ever possible, globally
3) they need to be sustained over a long term for the benefit of all the humans and other-than-human species that are deemed to have need of them

Political analyst and policy advisor James Bernard Quilligan wrote that the commons movement "represents a consciously organized third sector," a complement to the private and public sectors, "including citizens as co-managers and co-producers in the shared management and preservation of their own resources.

"Those commons are not just resources but the sets of relationships they create, including the communities that use them and the cultural and social practices and property regimes that manage them. They represent the common responsibility of and opportunity for people to protect and sustain their valuable common goods."20

Among those common goods, according to the Commons Governance Work Group that champions legitimizing them, are cultural traditions, civil rights, languages, information, airwaves, the right to issue money, social innovation, stores of human knowledge, intellectual property, the

Internet, fisheries, forests, land, ecosystems, seeds, minerals, water, inorganic energy and the atmosphere.[21]

Through the mechanisms of commons trusts and social charters, leaders of this movement seek to build into legal systems restraint and equity — habits sadly lacking in the viral global economy — in the use of common goods and resources, just as Life has built them into the practices of other species.

## Restraint, Simplicity and Downtimes

Ancient humans did not have to practice restraint. They had neither the technical capacity for nor the cultural habits of excess. Indigenous cultures, living closer to the lifeways of the ancients and much closer to the Earth and more deeply in place than we do, have traditionally passed the habit of restraint from one generation to the next. Why? For place-based cultures, restraint has a high spiritual value. It honors divine purposes as they are revealed in the way Life works. Restraint in consumption, behavior, lifeways and relationships also confers survival advantage to the tribe.

When the word is used to describe truly sustainable relationships with provisions and resources, "restrained" is equivalent to "frugal": careful with the fruits of the Earth and of one's labors. The ancients were and long-lasting indigenous cultures are habitually frugal.

Members of Life-mimicking Deep Green communities will have to choose restraint and practice it with devotion and choose to value frugality over profligacy. But restraint sounds to many of us like giving up our freedom. Restraints are what bind and restrict children, pets, the elderly, insane and imprisoned. And "frugal" sounds to the post-modern ear too much like what poor people have to be and only the super-virtuous choose to be. In *The New Good Life* best-selling author John Robbins pointed to a more positive, less punitive vision of frugality. Its aim, he wrote, is "to achieve an overflowing life, a generous life, an exciting life, a joyful life, while spending less" on every kind of material thing. "The rationale behind the new frugality is not to become a miser (the word "miser" comes from the same root as the word "miserable"). The goal is to live better for less."[22] And with less.

In fact, what restraint or frugality would require of us is that we live more simply. Deep Green Earthonomical communities will do all that they do in less complicated ways in part because they will not have sufficient energy and resources to allow them to complicate what they do and in part because their survival will depend on simplicity as surely as the survival of ancient and indigenous peoples did.

"Simplify, simplify, simplify," were Henry David Thoreau's three rules for living a life in harmony with Nature, that is, within our own and Earth's means. A whole body of literature and multiple subcultures have already formed around the practice that best-selling author Duane Elgin called "voluntary simplicity." His 1981 book of that name jumpstarted a movement. Wanda Urbanska, popular public television host and author of several books on simplicity including 2010's *The Heart of Simple Living*, explained that "Simple Living's four tenets are environmental stewardship, thoughtful consumption, community involvement and financial responsibility."[23] Though the scale of our simplification and restraint will have to be as grand and far reaching as the scale of our complexification and consumption have been, engaging in these four practices would lead us, Urbanska suggested, in the direction of living good lives rather than "goods lives."

Humans have balked at both voluntary and involuntary frugality ever since greed and wealth have been an option. On the other hand, we have also often found peace of mind, freed time and a sense of belonging, self-worth and accomplishment when we have taken frugality up with the same passion with which we sought wealth of the propertied, moneyed kind. The desire to survive may stir that passion in us when we fully realize that doing more of what we have been doing is fatal.

One of the ways we can practice restraint is to follow Life's pattern of *downtimes*. Deep Green communities might use day/night and seasonal cycles like pre-modern societies did, as opportunities:

• to refurbish and repair tools, equipment, buildings, infrastructures and community and intercommunity relationships

• to both help and allow bodies and ecosystems to renew themselves

• to refresh and expand the community's base of knowledge

• to reflect on successes and failures and decide what needs to be done differently

For post-funny-money economies these activities will be seen as investments in personal, family and community well-being rather than time off or income lost.

Ecological economist Herman Daly calls the process of building in downtimes "'fallowing,' letting land regenerate after a period of cultivation. Fallowing is investment in short-term non-production in order to maintain long-term yields." Daly applies the same idea to every renewable resource: "Leave it alone. Let it grow in order to slow or reduce the exploitation. This conforms perfectly to the economic definition of

---

## For Example: Simplicity Itself

"This calamity calls for a simple life: eating true food that has been grown by someone I know or someone who doesn't live too far away from me; better would be growing it myself; wearing the same things over and over again, making the old clothes new, wearing the old clothes as if they were new; living in a sturdy dwelling that doesn't cost too much as it accommodates the elements; walking more and driving less; finding delight in the thing right next to me; minimalizing conflict by accepting the person next to me, even if the person next to me is completely stupid. All of that I can do...."[24]

"Despite the usual consumerist excesses that one can find (mostly in the major cities), Sweden also has something that many other countries do not have: the concept of lagom.

"The word *lagom*, which has no direct equivalent in English, appears often in Swedish conversation. For many people [there] it captures something essential about Swedish culture as well. Lagom has to do with quantity, with the 'how muchness' of something. Lagom is neither too much nor too little; but neither is it just 'enough.' (There is a different word for that.) Meaning 'exactly the right amount,' it can be applied to anything: stuff, people, the size of a room, the food on your plate ... even the atmosphere at a party. If it were a place, it would live north of sufficiency, but south of excess. It is hard to say exactly how much it is but you know it when you experience it. When something is 'just right,' it is lagom."[25]

investment — a reduction in present consumption in order to increase a future capacity to consume."[26] Fallowing is exemplified in the ancient Hebrews' Jubilee (see page 256), a ritual practice more honored in the breach than in the observance.

## No-Growth/Degrowth Economics

Just how restrained must we become? How much do we need to simplify? To find that out, we have to get Earth-smart. We have to live *in* our places rather than *off* them. We have to embed ourselves in the places we live in as if our lives and livelihoods — and our children's and grandchildren's — depended on them, because they do.

And if we do that, if we really pay attention to what surrounding natural communities and the ecosystem they've created tell us, we will quickly realize that natural economies are restrained in the extreme. They do not grow. They change and adapt as circumstances change, but they discover their limits within what's available where they are, and they don't push those limits either by growing populations perpetually or increasing consumption perpetually, both of which we humans are doing.

And so the answer to "How restrained must we become?" is restrained enough that our economies don't grow. Restrained enough that degrowth replaces growth as our common aim.

*Degrowth* is an increasingly popular synonym for downsizing. Coined by economist Nicholas Georgescu-Rogen and popularized in the writings of several European critics of economic globalization, *degrowth* inspired thousands attending conferences in Paris (2008) and Barcelona (2010) to explore methods of downsizing economically while upsizing (Gunter Pauli's term) the amount of time available for family, creativity, art, culture, community and the things of the spirit. An International Conference on Degrowth in the Americas, Montreal (May 2012) drew participants from Anchorage to the Andes and Australia, while Venetians planned a September 2012 event also for the purpose of imagining and planning toward a post-growth, healing Earth. As the first of Six Degrees of Separation from the Global Economy, degrowth's popularity is evidently increasing. Happily the word along with the vision it conveys translates well into French — *decroissance*, Spanish — *decrecimiento*, Italian — *decrescita* and Portuguese — *diminuição*. In a world that moves memes as fast as it moves money it has been co-opted in one of these translations by speakers of other languages. More fierce than no-growth, degrowth presumes not just status quo, quit where we are, but shrinkage — downsizing.

"But that's not possible," say conventional, neoconservative and liberal economists, who are estranged bedfellows otherwise. "Capitalism demands growth," which is the antithesis of restraint.

Yes, it is possible. In a 2008 interview with Charles Siegel, Preservation Institute director and author of *The Politics of Simple Living*, the Nobel Prize-winning economist Robert Solow stated without hedging that "There is no reason at all that capitalism could not survive with slow or even no growth.... There is nothing intrinsic in the system that says it cannot exist happily in a stationary state."[27]

Post-Carbon Institute Senior Fellow Richard Heinberg agrees. "It is possible for economies to persist for centuries or millennia with no or minimal growth. That is how most economies operated until recent times. If billions of people through countless generations lived without economic growth, we can do so as well — now and far into the future." To do that, we need to learn the difference between maximizing and optimizing. To maximize is to make as big or large as possible; to optimize is to get the most or best use out of something. It's a waste not but also want not principle.

"The end of growth does not mean the end of the world," Heinberg has written. "Life in a non-growing economy can be fulfilling, interesting, and secure. The absence of growth does not imply a lack of change or improvement. Within a non-growing or equilibrium economy there can still be a continuous development of practical skills, artistic expression, and technology.... Within a non-growing economy it is possible to maximize benefits and reduce factors leading to decay, but doing so will require pursuing appropriate goals: Instead of *more*, we must strive for *better*; rather than promoting increased economic activity for its own sake, we must emphasize whatever increases quality of life without stoking consumption."[28]

Perhaps because the idea of no-growth is so terrifying to many economists and consumers accustomed to being promised perpetual economic growth, Herman Daly and other ecological economists give the name "steady state" to economies that live within Earth's means and do not compromise their ecosystems. Given the present unsteadiness of the global economy, steady state sounds like a condition devoutly to be wished for.

## Home Study and Home Coming

How do we know what no-growth looks like, what constitutes compromise of our ecosystems, the places we live in?

We work together to learn the nature of the places we live in as if we and all our ancestors had always lived there, always known the plants and animals, soils and seasons and limits. We learn what the landscapes, landshapes and wildlife were like before settlement by urban humans. We do what California native and landscape ecologist Eric Sanderson did when he moved to New York City. He realized he wouldn't know where he was until he learned what had occupied that land before humans did, went deep into the ecological history of the place and understood how Manhattan Island had gone from a forest of trees to a forest of skyscrapers.[29] Only we do together what he did alone. We become as familiar with and engaged in our particular ecosystems as we have been with athletic scores, the lives of celebrities, new car models and our investment portfolios.

We, all the members of our communities, will need to take stock of our surroundings regularly. We will do home study, by which I mean

### For Example: Depaving

"We need not only to stop new paving, but to begin depaving what should never have been paved in the first place.

"A major motorway was recently removed from the side of the Willamette River in Portland, Oregon, and replaced with a riverside walk and park. A marsh full of native plants and wildlife has been re-established where the airport runway of Crissy Field used to be in San Francisco's Presidio. In the suburbs of St. Paul, Minnesota, in an area called Phalen Village, a failed shopping center and its enormous parking lot have been bulldozed to restore a lake filled forty years ago."[30]

not keeping children home from school to study, but treating our home places as worthy of study at every age. We will go outside, into backyards, local parks, surrounding farmlands or forests, as regularly and faithfully as we might go to church, the game or the mall. We will do this in order to become what Wes Jackson, director of the Land Institute in Salinas, Kansas, calls "native to place." Jackson has even suggested that colleges should offer courses of study in "home-coming."

As students of our home places, we will gather and integrate economic and environmental information as other living things do, in real time, and share it generously. We will do a brisk traffic in diverse kinds of intelligence and ways of knowing with the aim of acquiring ecological — or Earthological — conscience. (Conscience comes from root words that mean "to know with.") Accordingly we will learn to know not only about the ecosystems we inhabit as if they were something apart from us and our lives but also to know with them because in truth we are a part of them and their lives. We are subsidiary to them, not they to us. We will look at Life, as best we can, through its wild inhabitants' eyes and lives because our lives depend on seeing, hearing, sniffing out — having in our minds too — all that's "out there" and how it works. We will put a high priority at all ages and in all aspects of our lives on what David Orr calls "ecological literacy" and Daniel Goleman and Ian McCallum call "ecological intelligence."

re = again

source (L. *surgere*) = to rise

resource = to rise again

In short, for Deep Green Earthological communities, Life becomes the primary school in which we are all perpetual students, every creature, every natural and human process is a teacher, and every place on Earth is a classroom.

## Resource-Based = Re-Sourceful

The viral global economy has depleted Earth's resource base and degraded its ecosystem support services in much the same way that HIV depletes and degrades the body's resources and organ system support services. Some natural resources — among them certain metals and minerals, water, arable land and forest resources — are in short supply worldwide.

Some resources have never been abundant, are only available seasonally or cyclically or were never widely or universally distributed. Physical processes like erosion and the activities of other-than-human species like lichens have made many of these resources available to us, but it takes thousands of years to make a couple of inches of good soil, grow a mature forest or establish a high-functioning wetland. And, like metals and fossil fuels, some climate-managing ecosystems like tropical rainforests may have been a one-shot deal.

Since its economies are entirely resource based, Life has learned to be *resourceful*. Other-than-human species and the communities they establish help and allow necessary provisions to rise again, to replenish and renew themselves. Forms of life that can live without scarce resources or those that support their restoration, replace forms of life that can't.

If we want to be one of the life forms that lasts we will need to be resourceful in these ways too. How do we do that?

We get good at retrieving from things humans have made — buildings, cars, machinery, roadways, TVs, computers, appliances — materials that Life can't replace at all or can't replace in a time frame that makes any sense for humans. We do that by *rematerializing* (reclaiming materials from things we've already made) and by *dematerializing* (learning to use less of every kind of material and to use materials as many times and ways as possible) as Life does.

We practice subtraction (see Chapter 13) in all categories of our lives except for the non-material ones, the ineffable categories of the spirit, mind and heart. In *Plan C*, Pat Murphy wrote that "The key action is to curtail.... To curtail means to cut back and to downsize," like Life does in hard times. "*Curtail* reflects the seriousness of the current situation

## To be resourceful is to:

| | | | |
|---|---|---|---|
| renew | replenish | refurbish | reinhabit |
| restore | restock | reconstitute | repair |
| refresh | recycle | refill | rebuild |
| reclaim | recirculate | regenerate | retrieve |
| refine | reuse | rehabilitate | revitalize |

more than the politically acceptable word *conserve* [which] ... can imply a relatively small reduction in consumption."[31] Accordingly, we use as few of the resources we share with other living things as possible and give natural communities — Life — enough time and space to renew and restore the resources it can.

We realize that dumpster divers and the trash pickers of the world's dumps, tips and landfills have the right idea. Apart from toxic and hazardous waste, there's the equivalent of resource gold "in them thar hills." Everything from scrap metal and wood, plastic containers and bags, construction waste, wire and tires, to convertible white waste (like refrigerators) and paper (which is suitable for mulch, insulation and earthworm bedding when it can't be reconstituted as paper). When we can't make more plastic, we find ways to reuse the century's worth of it we've already made. We relearn cobbling together scraps of the old into something useful or beautiful and like new. We repurpose things.

Many resource retrieval activities currently require the use of fossil-fueled equipment, large quantities of water and toxic chemicals. Since those are among the resources we're running short of, we will need to explore ways to expand our base of resources that use human ingenuity and human energy — both of which in a period of double-digit unemployment we have in abundance — and the energy and work habits of other-than-human species like microbes and draft animals.

Neither Pat Murphy's Plan C nor Life's Economic Survival Protocol needs to be a punishing exercise in self-denial, unless the viral economy collapses before we're prepared to outlive it, in which case curtailment will be abrupt and harsh. Both Plan C and Life's Deep Green protocol "accept the need to contract," as Murphy wrote, "while at the same time offering a new way of living in community where economic success is not the principle motivation of society. [They seek] to mitigate the worst of possible suffering from the inevitable decline of fossil fuels," and other symptoms of Critical Mass.[32] And they do that at the only socio-economic level where real mitigation, real curtailment, rematerialization, dematerialization and subtraction are possible: the local community.

Along with not being wasteful we will want also to not make waste. Making less waste, especially less toxic waste, would be an inevitable beneficial side effect of using fewer resources, using them multiple

## For Example: Waste Not, Want Not

If humans are truly going to prosper, we will have to learn to imitate nature's highly effective cradle-to-cradle system of nutrient flow and metabolism, in which the very concept of waste does not exist. To eliminate the concept of waste means to design things — products, packaging, and systems — from the very beginning on the understanding that waste does not exist. It means that the valuable nutrients contained in the materials shape and determine the design: form follows evolution, not just function.

"[T]here are two discrete metabolisms on the planet. The first is the biological metabolism, or the biosphere — the cycles of nature. The second is the technical metabolism — the cycles of industry, including the harvesting of technical materials from natural places. With the right design, all of the products and materials manufactured by industry will safely feed these two metabolisms, providing nourishment for something new."[33]

"Why not build cities out of garbage? [Architect Mitchell Joachim] notes that if you could somehow convert waste into construction material, you could make another Empire State building out of what New Yorkers throw away in two weeks. There's enough trash in the city's Fresh Kills landfill, he says, to 'remake Manhattan island seven times at full scale.'"[34]

times, producing for local consumption, transitioning away from fossil fuels and petroleum derivatives and, in general, downsizing, downscaling and relocalizing.

## Bringing Food Production Home

Regionally self-reliant Earthological communities will need to feed themselves affordably and with a continuous reduction in the use of fossil-fuel energy and derivatives and imported water. How can they do that?

Communities can, for example, support family-size organic farms and farms leaning towards organic production with tax incentives and

Vertical farming is taking off as an efficient way to grow food close to the people who will eat it

**Paul Marks**

URBAN warehouses, derelict buildings and high-rises are the last places you'd expect to find the seeds of a green revolution. But from Singapore to Scranton, Pennsylvania, "vertical farms" are promising a new, environmentally friendly way to feed the rapidly swelling populations of cities worldwide.

In March, the world's largest vertical farm is set to open up shop in Scranton. Built by Green Spirit Farms (GSF) of New Buffalo, Michigan, it will only be a single storey covering 3.25 hectares, but with racks stacked six high it will house 17 million plants. And it is just one of a growing number.

Vertical farms aim to avoid the problems inherent in growing food crops in drought-and-disease-prone fields many hundreds of kilometres from the population centres in which they will be consumed. Instead, Dickson Despommier – an ecologist at Columbia University in New York City who has championed vertical farms since 1999 – suggests that food should be grown year-round in high-rise urban buildings, reducing the need for the carbon-emitting transport of fruit and vegetables.

The plant racks in a vertical farm can be fed nutrients by water-conserving, soil-free hydroponic systems and lit by LEDs that mimic sunlight. And they need not be difficult to manage: control software can choreograph rotating racks of plants so each gets the same amount of light, and direct water pumps to ensure nutrients are evenly distributed.

The whole apparatus can be monitored from a farmer's smartphone (see "Farming from afar"), says GSF's R&D manager, Daniel Kluko. He says the new farm in Scranton will grow 14 lettuce crops per year, as well

## Farming from afar

With software to handle much of the day-to-day tending of crops, vertical farmers will probably look after multiple farms remotely, claims Daniel Kluko of Green Spirit Farms.

The app he and his colleagues are developing will allow farm managers to tweak nutrient levels and soil pH balance from a smartphone or tablet, and sound alarms if, say, a water pump fails on a vertical-growing system. "So if I'm over in London, where we're looking for a future vertical farm site to serve restaurants, I'll still be able to adjust the process in Michigan or Pennsylvania," says Kluko.

This will help drive down the labour costs of vertical farms, he says, so that they can compete with conventional ones.

GSF's first farm was inspired by the long-term drought that has been afflicting many parts of the US. "Water is a big issue," says Kluko. "We have designed our vertical farms to recycle it, and they use 98 per cent less water per item of produce than traditional farming." That's done in part by scavenging water from the grow room's atmosphere with a dehumidifier. It's a machine with a dual role, as excess humidity can lead to problems like leaf mould.

Most vertical farms rely on natural light as much as possible. In sunny, near-equatorial Singapore, entrepreneur Jack Ng's SkyGreens vertical farm needs no artificial lighting to promote growth. Instead, his four-storey glass-sided farm contains mobile racks of Chinese cabbage and lettuce that rotate slowly up to the sunnier heights of the building on a low-power elevator.

Conversely, in Japan, Kyoto-based Nuvege (pronounced "new veggie") runs a windowless indoor farm. In a cavernous facility reminiscent of an aircraft that varies in intensity through the day – moving from an artificial dawn through to noon and dusk. Mimicking these changes will save energy too. Such tricks already play a small part at GSF: infrared LEDs mimic 5 minutes of a fading sunset at the end of each day. "It puts peppers and tomatoes into their flowering period quicker," says Kluko.

Advances in vertical farms could trickle through from other sources, too. The US Defense Advanced Research Projects Agency is using an 18-storey vertical farm in College Station, Texas, to produce genetically modified plants that make proteins useful in vaccines. Adversity also plays its part: the tsunami-sparked nuclear accident in Fukushima, Japan, in 2011 is leading to innovation in vertical farming because much of the region's irradiated farmland can no longer be used.

"Fukushima has had a riveting effect on this field," says Despommier. "People were taking their food to the Geiger counter before the checkout counter." ∎

"OK GOOGLE. Start my car and switch on the heating." This voice command would have ben useful to many of those affected by last week's icy blast in the US and Canada. It might not be too far-fetched, now Google has partnered with four major car companies to bring its Android operating system to vehicles in 2014.

Hyundai, Audi, Honda, General Motors, Google and silicon chipmaker Nvidia are the first members of the Open Automotive Alliance, announced at the Consumer Electronics Show in Las Vegas last week. The partnership's proposed vehicles will be the first to have built-in 4G internet, and will offer diverse applications, from entertainment to navigation. The technology will also provide the first foothold of internet connectivity for the autonomous cars of the future.

details later this year. Microsoft has also teamed up with car firms to put connectivity in vehicles.

Audi's Brad Stertz says this integration could let you read a book on an Android device, then get into your car and have the car's computer take over. "You can bookmark your page, call up the reader app and pick up where you left off, but with the book being read to you while driving."

Bryan Reimer of AgeLab at the Massachusetts Institute of Technology, who studies the interplay between cars and humans, says giving vehicles such capabilities, particularly if they are voice-activated, could eliminate the use of phones while driving, making roads safer. It could also improve the application many drivers value the most – traffic avoidance. Google Maps already has a traffic

**"Say you're walking to your car, you can surf Google Glass for a destination and send it to your car"**

prediction system, which uses data pulled from Android phones in moving cars. But data from a built-in Android system connected to each car's instruments would make such predictions far more accurate.

Barry Ratzlaff of Hyundai says the company plans to take advantage of Google Maps and Google Now – the intelligent assistant that uses your data to make helpful predictions – in its future cars. "There's a lot of rich content that fits around maps, and a lot of it is relevant to the car," he says.

Hyundai cars are getting a preview of this kind of connectivity. The latest Genesis model, due to be revealed at the annual Detroit car show this week, integrates with other devices to fetch navigation directions before you set off.

The firm has also developed a car app designed to work with Google Glass. "Say you're walking to your car, you can surf Glass for a destination and send it to your car," says Ratzlaff. ∎

« hangar, Nuvege's LED lighting is tuned to two types of chlorophyll, one preferring red light and the other blue. "Tuned to these spectra, you can grow a plant no matter where it is," Despommier notes. Indeed, Nuvege produces 6 million lettuces a year in this way, for customers including Subway and Disneyland Tokyo.

In such arrangements, the electricity bills can add up quickly. Today's LEDs are only about 28 per cent efficient, which keeps the cost of produce high and prevents vertical farms from competing in regions where cheap vegetables are abundant. However, lighting engineers at Philips in the Netherlands have demonstrated LEDs with 68 per cent efficiency, which could dramatically cut costs.

And the latest research shows that plants do not need always-on

SUZANNE AND NICK GEARY/GETTY

# The connected car

Wish our car had Android

as spinach, kale, tomatoes, peppers, basil and strawberries. Its output will be almost 10 times greater than the firm's first vertical farm, which opened in New Buffalo in 2011.

Proponents see vertical farming as a way to feed a global population that is urbanising fast: 86 per cent of the people in the developed

> **"If farmers protect their indoor 'fields' from pests, vertical farming needs no herbicides or insecticides"**

world will live in cities by 2050, the United Nations predicts. It could make food supplies more secure as well, because production can continue even when extreme weather strikes. And as long as farmers are careful to protect their indoor "fields" from pests, vertical farming needs no herbicides or insecticides. They

**Farm of the future**

Lea me with a view

tax breaks, low interest loans and mortgages, community sponsored apprenticeship programs and permaculture projects, and coordinated farm-to-community distribution systems. They can create and buy stock in the businesses that Woody Tasch, author of *Slow Money*, calls Slow Food Enterprises (SFEs). "Nurture capitalism" (also his term) would support businesses, including farms and cooperatives that are involved directly or indirectly in "the work of building healthy food systems in any given region."[35]

Communities can establish more community supported agricultural systems (CSAs) and community gardens in order to grow and raise as much of our own food, medicinals and fibers as we can locally and regionally and to shorten the distance between food producers and food consumers. There may be as many as 20,000 community gardens and a quarter-million community gardeners in North America already, many of the gardens operated by senior or youth centers, schools, churches, food pantries, universities, libraries, public parks, residential neighborhoods and developments. They have a lot to teach us, and we have a lot to learn.

Contrary to popular opinion, in many parts of the world smaller farms and gardens located close to the people they feed and managed with little or no use of synthetic fertilizers, herbicides and pesticides can produce enough food to feed local and regional communities sufficiently, if not abundantly.

> "Every increase in local capacity to grow food, generate electricity, repair, build, and self-finance will strengthen the capacity to withstand disturbances of all kinds."[36]

"According to the most recent USDA Census of Agriculture," Bill McKibben wrote in his 2007 book *Deep Economy*, "smaller farms produce more food per acre, whether you measure in tons, calories or dollars. They use land, water, and oil much more efficiently; if they have animals, the manure is a gift, not a threat to public health." Sustainable farming practices are by no means successful only in the US. McKibben cited English agronomist Jules Pretty "who has studied two hundred 'sustainable agriculture' practices on about 29 million hectares."[37] These practices have led to "'an average 93 percent increase in per hectare food production.... With 4.5 million grain farmers, average yields rose 73 percent.'"[38]

The authors of *Natural Capitalism* observed that "Organic farming goes a long way toward providing better food from far smaller and more sustainable inputs.... Standard US agricultural practice today requires at least 45,000 square feet of land to feed a person on a high-meat diet, or about 10,000 for a vegetarian.... However, bio-intensive [organic] gardening can provide for a vegetarian's entire diet, plus the compost crops necessary to sustain the system indefinitely, on only 2,000 to 4,000 square feet, even starting with low-quality land."[39] Per unit of food produced, the authors add, such smaller-scale, organic methods use 88% less water and 99% less imported energy.[40]

Increasingly sophisticated and adaptable methods of urban farming, livestock raising, food distribution, composting and wastewater recycling as well as linkages between cities and surrounding farms and farmland have the potential to make many cities relatively if not fully food self-reliant.

Because soils and environmental conditions vary so much from bioregion to bioregion, we will need to establish and support local seed banks and exchanges, and nurseries that sell plants that are native or can do well in our environments without out-competing native and naturalized plants. Some neighborhoods will take down fences and nonedible hedges, create easements, agree to ignore property lines and plant

---

### What Local Governments Can Do to Support Local Food Production

- "Encourage the production and consumption of local food by supporting needed infrastructure like farmers' markets.
- "Retrofit waste management systems to collect food scraps for conversion into compost, biogas, and livestock feed — which can be made available to local growers.
- "Require that some minimum percentage of food purchases for schools, hospitals, military bases, prisons [and regionally chartered corporations and those receiving local financial incentives] is sourced within 100 miles of the institutions buying the food. ☞

- "Make food safety regulations appropriate to the scale of production and distribution, so that a small grower selling direct off the farm or at a farmers' market is not regulated as onerously as a multinational food manufacturer."[41]
- Establish local/regional systems of inspection and accreditation for suburban, backyard, urban, small farm, organic, livestock raising and community garden and food preservation operations to be carried out by trained volunteers, including students.
- Change zoning regulations to permit such food production systems within city limits.
- Encourage seasonal community celebrations of "Best Food Yard," "Best Garden" and "Best Farm" practices.
- Offer real estate tax breaks for food producers and incentives for gardeners who use recycled water.
- Coordinate yard-sharing and equipment-sharing systems that connect potential gardeners with others who are willing to share yard space and gardening equipment.

community gardens, orchards, vineyards, nut trees and berry patches in yards that feather one into another, effectively turning squared-off single suburban lots into productive suburban farmland and flowing pollinator-friendly ecosystems.

We won't all become providers of food but we should all become complicit with the providers of our food and fierce about how our food is produced.

In short, if we want to provide for ourselves sustainably we would do well to grow "food, not lawns," as community organizer Heather Flores suggested in her book by that name,[42] and to preserve and restore farmland, support regional farmers' markets and treat soil as our life's blood and small farmers as if we really need them. We will encourage members of our families to become farmers and other kinds of land lovers. We will do well not to count on having oranges in winter in Wisconsin, peaches in winter in Italy, New Zealand lamb in Britain or exotic foods from

# For example: Food for Thought

## Farmadelphia

"Metropolitan 'food-sheds' must be relocalized — for example, reducing East Coast cities' dependence on lettuce from California and clementines from Spain.... Philadelphia's local food system [for example] consists of two basic parts. The first part includes producers who operate a range of farms in different parts of the region, on inner city brownfield [vacant lot] sites, greenfields within and outside the city, and larger farms in the adjacent hinterlands of Lancaster, Berks, and Bucks counties in Pennsylvania, as well as southern New Jersey, and the Delmarva Peninsula. The second part is a set of organizations that foster distribution, marketing, and some processing of food grown in the city and region. This institutional infrastructure effectively ties together the local — or, more accurately, regional — food system."[43]

## Grounded Technology

"Urban farming is an excuse to geek out with some awesome tech. Innovations from NASA and garage tinkerers have made urban food growing radically more efficient and compact than the victory gardens of yore. 'Aeroponics' planters grow vegetables using mist, slashing water requirements; hackers are building home-suitable 'aquaponics' rigs that use fish to create a cradle-to-grave ecosystem, generating its own fertilizer (and delicious tilapia, too). Experts have found that cultivating a mere half-acre of urban land with such techniques can yield more than $50,000 worth of crops annually."[44]

## Self-Reliant Island Communities

"Cuba has thousands of *organopónicos* — urban gardens — more than two hundred in the Havana area alone. The Vivero Organopónico Alamar is especially beautiful: a few acres of vegetables attached to a shady yard packed with potted plants for sale, birds in wicker cages, a cafeteria, and a small market where a steady stream of local people buys tomatoes, lettuce, oregano, and potatoes for their supper. (Twenty-five ☞

crops were listed on the blackboard the day I visited.) Sixty-four people farm this tiny spread....

"The city grew three hundred thousand tons of food [in 2006] — nearly its entire vegetable supply, and more than a token amount of its rice and meat."[45]

### The New Chinese Menu

The city of Shenzhen, which before China's rapid industrial expansion was a relatively self-reliant cluster of self-reliant neighborhoods, is investing nearly nine billion yuan in 39 agricultural projects around the city. The intent is to establish a safe, sustainable agricultural base for the city and surrounding villages that will involve an agricultural high-tech park, agricultural processing and city-wide distribution, urban tree-planting and eco-agricultural tourism projects, and the expansion of the Buji Farm Produce Wholesale Market. The city is also investing 600 million yuan to support family and community farms located around the city, with hopes that they will provide 60% of the meat, vegetables and aquatic products in the Shenzhen market. There has also been an emerging trend of going green and organic as a response to pollution and pesticides used in farming practices. Vegetable suppliers are required to pass certain inspections held by the city's Agriculture Bureau before their produce can be sold as "organic."[46]

around the world ever. And we probably won't eat much seafood until or unless populations of marine species bounce back, or farm-raised fish unless it is raised regionally and ecologically.

## From Disappearing Jobs to Meaningful Work

There is no end of work to be done by members of Earthological communities because most of it cannot be done somewhere else. And it is by no means all white collar, intellectual or desk work. Every kind of physical as well as mental skill, expertise and talent will be necessary for provisioning, healing and maintaining such self-transforming communities.

British futurist and financial advisor James Robertson predicted that as economies relocalize so will work and employment. "Although recent high levels of unemployment in all the industrialized countries have brought pressure on many people to accept jobs which they find distasteful, they have also provided the occasion for increasing numbers of people to earn their living in self-employment or community enterprises or other forms of what I have called 'ownwork' — that is, work which people themselves regard as valuable," and necessary. He added that "not just the locality but also the household may once again become an important center for production and work, as it was before the Industrial Age drove work out of the home into factories and offices and other institutions like hospitals and schools....

"Increasing numbers of people are already spending more time on DIY (do-it-yourself) and other informal kinds of work for themselves, their families, and their friends and neighbors. Food growing is one example." As this sort of bartered and unpaid work, which is characteristic of informal economies even in good times, takes hold "and as arrangements for exchanging skills and services outside the formal labor market continue to spread, this will stimulate further growth of productive work in and around the home" and community.[47]

Many jobs that we've recently called menial are of vital importance to self-reliant communities. There will be no shortage of conventional and creative work for legal, medical, technical, education, financial and business professionals. But men and women will also be of inestimable value who can successfully monitor our fresh and rainwater supplies and food production systems, turn household waste into compost and wastewater into clean water, build soils, create sustainable food gardens and raise rabbits and chickens, sheep and bees in the suburbs and the city, heal with herbs, create Earthological work spaces, select and save seeds, take used cars or computers apart for parts or put them back together, retrofit a leaky house or tighten up apartment and office buildings, install solar and wind systems, recreate forests where little remains but stumps and ashes and salvage old fossil-fuel parts to make new electric equipment out of it.

In short, our human resources will be as valuable to us as our natural resources, and we will need to learn how to use them as carefully and wisely.

Most of us have more than one skill, strength, kind of intelligence, expertise or experience to offer an Earthological community that the community actually needs. The very diversity of our capabilities and interests can become, as it was for the ancient bacteria, an advantage to both our communities and us.

## Getting Down to Business

To facilitate all these moves towards relative self-sufficiency, we can support regional and community banks, businesses, schools, clinics, entertainments, transportation systems and utilities, and where they do not exist we can create them.

And as if it were a spiritual practice and to the extent it's possible, we can buy local. In the early months of what may be a longer economic slump than many like to imagine, innovative communities and community leaders are already encouraging residents to support local businesses and are running publicity campaigns like "Local First" to support them.

We can create community-owned investment and brokerage businesses that set up, market and manage regional venture capital and mutual investment funds. We can initiate stock exchanges that support

---

### For Example: Buy Local

"About 130 cities or regions [in the US] now host 'buy local' groups, representing about 30,000 businesses, up from 41 in 2006. The membership of South Carolina's Lowcountry Local First doubled in 2009, to 325 businesses. Local First in Grand Rapids, Michigan, has almost 600 members, up from 150 in 2007," just two signs of "the growing influence of the 'buy local' movement — a longtime New Urbanist dream that has finally started to become a reality in the past two years.

"Advocates say that locally owned stores spend proportionately more on payroll than chains and that buying local will save jobs. Plus, for every $100 spent at a locally owned store, $45 remains in the local economy, compared with about $13 per $100 spent at a big box, according to research by the nonprofit Institute for Local Self-Reliance and Austin (Texas) consulting firm Civic Economics."[48]

local and regional micro, small and medium sized enterprises. We can offer tax and start-up incentives to them rather than to unaccountable large, transnational corporations that have little or no stake in the long-term well-being of our human and natural communities. We can create for-benefit "B corporations" and low-profit, rather than only non-profit, limited liability corporations that permit making money within the context of serving the public good. We can revoke or refuse to accept the charters of corporations that don't invest in our communities more functionally and intimately than only by creating jobs. *Going Local* author and local business consultant Michael Shuman has seen that prosperity and sustainability follow "when ownership, production, and consumption become intimately connected with place."[49]

We can establish public markets that sell only locally and regionally produced foods and goods. Pike Place Market in Seattle, Washington, Westside Market in Cleveland, Ohio, Faneuil Hall Marketplace in Boston, Massachusetts, City Market in Roanoke, Virginia, and Reading Terminal Market in Philadelphia, Pennsylvania, for example, have all drawn new local businesses, increased business traffic and brought millions of dollars — of both funny-money and local money — to abandoned or decaying downtowns.

Shuman, whose book has become a sort of bible of community self-reliance and a catalyst for hundreds of experiments in relocalization and scores of books that expand on issues he raised, has acknowledged that "It's easy to dismiss the principle of self-reliance by pointing to the many products that communities really cannot manufacture on their own. The goal of a self-reliant community, however, is not to create a Robinson Crusoe economy in which no resources, people or goods enter or leave.

"It has become possible to dovetail new manufacturing into communities and to integrate production, education, food production, waste treatment, housing, and the environment into an ecological whole. Almost all the assembly and much of the fabrication that today is done in large plants and factories could be decentralized and transferred to small [work]shops.... Micro-manufacturing can mean cottage industries which would strengthen local economies but would not break up neighborhoods."[50]

A community aiming to be self-reliant should simply seek to increase control over its own economy as far as is practical," or, as is rapidly becoming the case, necessary.[51] Medieval guilds and markets may serve as a viable example.

Economist David Fleming drove home the point. "Localization stands, at best, at the limits of practical possibility, but it has the decisive argument in its favor that there will be no alternative." The political economy of the future will have no choice but to be "lean, flexible, locally self-reliant, ingenious, robust, intelligent and very different from our own."[52]

---

## For Example: It's Our Business

In 2007, the last absentee-owned supermarket in Walsh, Colorado, closed, leaving the town of 640 with no alternative but a store twenty miles away, a long-haul through snow drifts in winter. Deciding against a feasibility study that would have cost the town $30,000 and resulted in its being declared "infeasible," "the town called a meeting. There, people voted to reopen the store as a cooperative. More than 300 residents bought shares at $50 each; they raised $195,000." The store thrives, is "open seven days a week, employs 14, grossed $1 million in sales" in 2008 and has become the local hangout, equivalent to a community center where residents find out how their neighbors are, commit random acts of neighborly kindness, and create something like a community intelligence, a smarter, more resilient and vibrant Walsh, Colorado.[53]

In 1997, the owner of the local Ford dealership in the city of Umeå in northern Sweden, who also owned land in a part of the city that had been set aside as a "green" business zone, decided to turn his land into a model eco-business park. Ford Motor Company agreed enthusiastically, which freed the dealer to persuade local owners of a Statoil gas station and a McDonald's to join in the venture. "By April 2000, GreenZone was operational." They have developed a business park that "uses 100 percent renewable energy, reuses 100 percent of its storm water on site, and reuses or recycles 100 percent of its waste by-products. All the ☞

buildings, whose parts can be disassembled after their useful life, are made of either natural or recycled materials. The buildings are so energy efficient that both their overall energy use and their electricity consumption are 60 percent less than those of a conventional design. Needs for freshwater use throughout the site have been cut by 70 percent.... During the first year of operation in GreenZone, the Ford dealerships car sales shot up 150 percent from its previous yearly average, and its service business increased by 100 percent." Both McDonald's and Statoil enjoyed increased business in a positive feedback loop that supports all the businesses in the Zone.[54]

"A former Salvation Army Boys and Girls Club building in eastern Winston-Salem, North Carolina is getting new life from a small-business and community initiative announced in 2010. The Atkins Community Development Corporation, which is part of Winston-Salem State University bought the 40,000-square-foot building which will be renovated and developed to be an incubator for 'green,' or environmentally friendly businesses. The incubator could house up to 20 businesses.

"Other goals include a health clinic, training in green jobs, a community garden, music and language classes, and a computer lab," said Carol Davis, the executive director of the group. "We want it to be a community resource again for residents, students, businesses and churches," Davis said.

"We will work to incorporate renewable energy, such as solar panels, and we will emphasize energy conservation and recycling in our operations and in our educational outreach."[55]

## Timing Is Everything

Life's lessons about timing are crucial for our understanding of the urgency with which we need to begin to mimic Life's Economic Survival Protocol.

Critical Mass threatens to bring down all the props on which our present lifeways depend just as untreated or mistreated HIV threatens to bring down all the systems on which the lives of AIDS patients depend.

The economy itself, the fossil fuels that drive it and the ecosystems and climate that the use of those fossil fuels threatens, are all vulnerable. The system is headed for collapse, but we cannot know whether the collapse will unfold over several centuries or only several decades. That depends entirely on what the last straw is. It would be better for us if the economy failed first. That would leave us some affordably retrievable fossil fuels and a still tolerable climate in which to transform ourselves.

But whatever the immediate cause of the crash, Life teaches us that if a large or the largest system crashes, whether slowly or quickly, every local community within that system is at risk.

Life also teaches us that those species and local communities and coalitions of communities that see the crash coming and prepare themselves to depend less on the larger system for their survival have the best chance of surviving and responding appropriately to the stages of the crash as they unfold.

Waiting for the present global economic system to break down, the climate to become intolerable, a critical mass of ecosystems to fail, species to become extinct or fossils fuels to become so expensive or difficult to retrieve that they are no longer a viable source of energy is an option. But it shouldn't be. Timing is everything.

Getting the timing right is Life's equivalent of a political challenge. It is the organically democratic nature of natural communities — the inherently democratic relationships, behaviors and methods of organization and self-governance in which they engage — that allows them so often to get the timing right.

CHAPTER 12

# Mimicking Life's Politics — Organically Democratic Principles and Practices

NATURE, OR LIFE AS A WHOLE, is not a political phenomenon in any obvious sense. Derived from *polis*, the Greek word for "city," politics could be considered antithetical to Life because cities as they've existed so far have tended to destroy other-than-human life forms and natural systems. Historically, politics is about people. It favors people as if we were not a part of but were larger than Life. More accurately politics is about — and most politics favor — some people.

But other-than-human species operate in some ways that resemble political activity. Life has lasted as long as it has because other-than-human species, beginning with bacteria, worked out — and Life encoded — organizational systems, methods of self-governance and economic behaviors and relationships that allowed them to live together in a fairly orderly manner, given all the chaos (both creative and destructive) that haunts Life's hard-won, relative orderliness. That's what politics is supposed to do: Keep a lid on chaos. And to a certain extent politics and governments do that. They facilitate people living together in a surprisingly orderly manner, given that both creative and destructive chaos is always trying to erupt, even in human societies.

But Life's politics accomplish one other absolutely vital thing: They help other-than-human species live within Earth's means. Life's socio-political arrangements and relationships hold chaos and order in a creative tension that prevents other-than-human species from exceeding the limits of a finite planet and putting Life on Earth out of business.

Human politics and governments do not help us live within Earth's means. Both have been compromised by and have yielded to an undeniably chaotic force: the viral global economy. For while leaders and Powers try to manage the economy and like to think they can and do control it, it has long since gone beyond human control. No combination of political efforts (equivalent to the medical efforts that produced an effective cocktail of drugs to check HIV) has succeeded in checking the global economy's influence, aggressiveness and spread. In both its creative and destructive aspects it has proven to be more unmanageable than the virus I've compared it to.

Since much of the activity we group under the label "political" at every level of every society has been distorted by money and many politicians have become the playmates and servants of the Powers, politics has devolved into ancient, failed, chaos-fueling behaviors: bought-and-paid-for politicking; rabid factionalism and partisanship; me first, us versus them and "break out the big guns" attitudes.

The problem is that humans have thought of politics as having to do only with the ordering of human lives and relationships. As we accept that our well-being depends on the well-being of other-than-human species, the communities they create and ecosystems they maintain, if we are wise we will not only include them in our political considerations, we will make them — and the rules that permit them to benefit from both creative chaos and order — the context of our politics.

If chaos, in the form of economically-induced global Critical Mass, doesn't beat us to the punch, a new understanding and practice of politics

**chaordic [kay-ord'-ic]**
1. the behavior of any self-governing organism, organization or system which harmoniously blends characteristics of order and chaos.
2. patterned in a way dominated by neither chaos nor order.
3. characteristic of the fundamental organizing principles of evolution and nature.[1]

along Life's organically democratic lines may restore and maintain the creative tension between chaos and order that VISA International founder Dee Hock calls *chaordic*.

## Building Democracy In

Whatever the tenor of politics in future, any political activity that intends to facilitate long-term sustainability will need to mimic Life's organically democratic model. That will require that we make a shift from politicking and partisanship to participation and partnership.

Life's Economic Survival Protocol is not a restaurant menu. If we want to mitigate and survive Critical Mass, we don't get to choose the parts of the protocol we like and leave out the ones we don't. Economic relocalization and diversification, bioregional resource and ecosystem management, community self-reliance, becoming native to place, interdependence and subsistence, for example, are not discretionary. If sustainability is our aim, democracy is not discretionary either. Since it proved to be the best method Life found for facilitating all the other elements of the protocol, Life built democracy in. Living systems are radically, directly, organically democratic systems. So must ours be if we want to survive Critical Mass. Why?

- So that, like the natural communities with which we need to reconnect and partner, our communities can, in Kelly, Atlee and Surowiecki's terms (see Chapter 10), distribute intelligence and benefit from the wisdom of crowds.
- So that our communities can be smarter, stronger and more competent than any of us alone or any homogenous group could be.
- So that we can avoid or at least minimize the intracommunity and intercommunity conflict and competition that will otherwise strain resources and drain us of the collective creative energy and diverse skills we will need to become self-reliant.
- So that adversity does not diminish our humanity and violence does not mire us in chaos.
- So that all of the members of our communities can, if they choose to, acquire the practical skills of democracy and be able to model and teach them to each other and the next generations.

- So that we can *thinker* with our possibilities for a better, more Earthological future together as effectively as Life tinkers with new solutions to the challenges it faces. Thinkering — a combination of thinking and tinkering coined and prototyped by Dale Fahnstrom and Greg Prygrocki of the Illinois Institute of Technology's cutting edge graduate Institute of Design — is a method of putting our diversely-gifted heads, hands, backs and hearts together to innovate, solve problems and meet challenges together.
- So that we can coordinate our activities as the equivalents of effective antibodies, participants in a planetary immune system that's capable of counteracting the viral economy that has caused this round of Critical Mass.

The human immune system is comprised of communities of cells that are distributed throughout the body in the same way that our Earthological human-natural communities will be scattered throughout the biosphere, the body of Life on Earth. Those communities of cells — like the thymus, spleen, lymph nodes and fluid, bone marrow and groups of white blood cells — that constitute and manage the immune system are as different from each other as ecological communities in Saharan Africa will be from those in the rainforest of the Congo River Basin and on the Mongolian steppes.

What makes them a coherent system capable of supporting, protecting, defending and healing the body despite their differences is the constant exchange of accurate information about the condition of their part of the body, constant attention to the well-being of their part of the body, a shared goal (the vitality and health of the whole body) and unfailing intercommunity cooperation and collaboration that turns the scattered clusters of cell communities into a complex, high-functioning, highly intelligent, self-healing and self-perpetuating system.

Repeated in every kind and scale of living system, this is democracy at its best. It is democracy we can emulate in our Earthological communities. Lifelike democratic political structures and practices will enable us to partner with other communities, life-forms and living systems with the shared goal of restoring health to Earth's immune system and surviving Critical Mass.

## Reality Check

Mimicking Life's organically democratic methods will be a huge challenge. "It should come as no great surprise," wrote Elisabet Sahtouris, "that the freedom of conscious decision making gives us a good deal of anxiety. We look around us and see these other species functioning on the whole the way our bodies do, untroubled by questions of whether what they're doing is right or wrong, good or bad. Yet we are stuck with choice-making conscious minds that are an experimental substitute for the innate evolutionary knowing of other species, and we must use those minds as best we can to decide how to behave."[2]

As more goes wrong and goes more seriously wrong everywhere, our instinct will be to just take care of ourselves and our loved ones as best we can — and the rest be damned. It's what the survival instinct tells the members of all species to do, at least in the short term. But when that doesn't work as well as we need it to, when instinct wears off and the distinctly human gifts of consciousness and conscience — or just desperation — set in, some of us will try democracy. Why? Because Life has shown us that democratic relationships and behaviors are the most effective, long-term-survival relationships and behaviors. And we are smart enough to figure out collectively what that means for us. Twentieth-century US clergyman Harry Emerson Fosdick got it right. "Democracy is based upon the conviction that there are extraordinary possibilities in ordinary people."[3] That covers most of us.

Humans have been creating ways of living together since time immemorial. We know more about ourselves, our needs and what makes us tick and stick together than ever before. We know more about the strengths and weaknesses of different kinds of democracy than any of our predecessors and can gather from them their best practices to incorporate into our Lifelike democratic communities. We know more than we did even a few decades ago about how complex systems, including human social systems, work most effectively. We have thousands of experiments in community living to study. We cannot fail at this difficult undertaking unless we choose not to succeed.

Of course there's no guarantee that all members of self-reliant Earthological communities will automatically behave better towards each other and their surrounding natural communities than people do now. But, however we may define "bad behavior," behaving badly toward each other or egregiously breaking Life's Rules is readily apparent in small communities, and the capacity to do damage on a grand or global scale would be reduced. Our ability to identify and do something about bad behavior would be increased as would be the opportunity to mete out justice fairly and democratically.

The International Forum on Globalization acknowledged that downsizing "does not *guarantee* democracy or equality or human rights; it just makes them more likely. Smaller communities offer people greater access to the sources of power and greater opportunity for positive outcomes."[4] As when resources are abundant and widely accessible there are fewer violent conflicts; so also, suggest democracy theorists including C. Douglas Lummis, Benjamin Barber and Thom Hartmann, when opportunities to have one's opinion heard, discussed and considered are abundant and widely accessible, there is less disaffection and conflict.[5]

And for most of us it is a little harder to behave badly toward people with whom we interact on a regular basis and on whom we depend for our well-being and survival, people whom we often look in the eyes, than it is to behave badly toward people far away into whose eyes and lives we never have to look. Conversely, we more often behave well toward those with whom our lives are intimately bound up than toward those whom we do not and cannot know intimately.

## Governance v. Governments

Although at the local level Earthological communities will likely establish organizations that are akin to governments, we will more nearly be engaged in governance itself (the process and practice of governing ourselves) than in creating institutions. "Governance is organic and all but unorganizable from above," observed Toronto urban policy writer, Edmund Fowler. "Rather it is cooperative and self-organizing from below."[6]

If established governments don't work with us (which will more often than not be the case), we will have no choice but to self-govern and work around them, preferably under their radar. We can do this. We can do what those ancient bacteria did: We can bend the rules. We can obey sovereign laws that we cannot afford to break (ones that would get us jailed or executed, for example). At the same time we can unofficially draft and, when necessary redraft, guidelines (unofficial laws) to serve the economic needs of our natural and human communities. And we can obey those Life-serving unofficial laws as if they were official. In effect, we can secede functionally from sitting governments. In the US, for example, 250 community land trusts (CLTs) have been established (See the South Boston, Massachusetts example in Chapter 13), many under the guidance of the Institute of Community Economics, to facilitate long-term ownership, democratic self-governance and sustainable management of both natural and human communities in places as diverse ecologically and socially as Cincinnati, Ohio, and Burlington, Vermont. CLTs, a grassroots, often deeply green, response to the failure of government and politics are on the rise in England, Canada, Kenya, Australia and New Zealand.[7]

*Going Local* author Michael Shuman assured us that, although "A local government committed to community self-reliance can accelerate the rate of transformation," all of the steps to relocalization "can be taken by individuals and organizations acting unofficially. There is no law in the United States that prevents citizens, working together, from framing a set of principles, awarding seals, compiling a State of the City Report, starting locally owned businesses and banks, training community-minded entrepreneurs, waging an invest-local campaign, and issuing a community currency. For each and every one of these initiatives, the participation of local government is not necessary — even though it can add expertise, legitimacy, and funding."[8]

In addition to the obvious advantage of relocalization and quasi-secession (we don't have to wait for sitting governments to fix problems they can't fix and may not fix for our benefit anyway) there's an additional advantage: Such unofficial structures of governance as community associations don't fall under the rule or jurisdiction of supranational organizations. They cannot be prevented from or penalized for choosing to obey Life's rules instead of, for example, the WTO's.

From time to time the Earthonomic and environmental well-being — the common good — of all the human and natural communities in a region will require that individual communities yield to the counsel of the larger coalitions and networks in which they participate. But as

# For Example: Civic Self-Governance

Founded in 1959 by members of a suburban Philadelphia community, the Chestnut Hill Community Association (CHCA) has been a remarkably successful experiment in civic sector community government.

The authority of the CHCA originated and resides not in laws but in the freely given consent of the people who live or work in Chestnut Hill. The CHCA supports and was designed to supplement Philadelphia's city government, to address problems and challenges city government didn't or couldn't effectively address.

In the intervening years the Community Association has brought new health to the Chestnut Hill shopping area and local economy; organized special events for seniors, young people and school children that create a sense of community; founded a successful newspaper that informs and links all segments of the community; planted trees and gardens; redesigned traffic patterns and parking systems; worked to alleviate or solve human relations problems of all kinds including clashes between classes, races and generations; rescued and restored historic buildings; bought up properties in danger of decay and turned them into community assets; helped to police the community and to "keep alive a vision of community in which impossible dreams can become reality."

The association has included all members of the community and participating businesses, organizations and institutions in its vision and decision making processes; rotated and shared leadership according to the tasks at hand; developed community-wide financial support and a consensual taxation scheme that not only sustains the association's activities but helps community leaders discern levels of community support or non-support for those activities; fostered mutually supportive partnerships between community institutions like hospitals, schools and colleges and evolved constitutive legal documents — called "Agreements, Definitions and Commitments" — designed to be changed as the needs and circumstances of the community change. ☞

> "[The] system has been seen by many observers of democratic government as the best, maybe the only, hope through which local communities can insure their own survival."
>
> Lloyd Wells reported that when the Chestnut Hill Community Association had fallen prey to the same sorts of failures — diminished democratic vision and energy, resident passivity, personal ambition and fiscal corruption and irresponsibility — that plague many modern US communities, a fresh batch of "Hillers" and some of the old guard who were distressed with the loss of consensual process were shaking things up in Chestnut Hill again.[9]

many decisions as possible should be made by the people most directly affected by those decisions.

Regional coalitions and interregional networks of communities would be cooperatively or collaboratively governed by councils of representatives of the participating communities. Nonetheless, their authority should, in general, be subsidiary to the authority of local communities except when the decisions or actions of local communities threaten the well-being of the larger human and natural communities of which they are a part.

Though regional and interregional governing bodies would serve some sort of protective, legislative, judicial and coordinative functions as bioregions do for the ecosystems that comprise them, it might be that their most important function — the most important function that encompassing natural systems serve — would be to facilitate the constant exchange of accurate information among human communities, to act as genuine central intelligence agencies as the brain and immune system do for the body and the rainforest as a whole does for the vine-based communities that hang from its branches. The real time collection, synthesis, storage, sorting, interpretation and dissemination of accurate information might be the new and most vital role of interregional and international agencies, organizations and regulatory bodies in a Deep Green, sustainable future. Why? Having information about the status, successes and failures of other natural and human communities will be the key to the success of each community and of all of them together. In this Critically Massed period in which we face simultaneous economic and environmental collapse, there will not be time for individual communities to reinvent the wheel. The widespread exchange of information about what works and what doesn't, particularly among communities located in similar ecosystems, will effectively speed the evolution of Earthological human lifeways.

## An Evolutionary Model of Governance

We customarily use "democracy" as a noun, the name of a thing, in particular, the name of a form of government. But like Life, in essence democracy is a verb. It is a process. It is a ceaselessly dynamic, scrappy, creative, adaptive and ever-evolving process which, like any exercise repeated faithfully, makes its practitioners better at doing it. Accordingly, as members of Earthological communities we will not organize ourselves once, establish "a government" and "there, that's done." In response to what Critical Mass and Life throw at us, we will, like the diverse members of Earth's natural communities, need to organize, disorganize and reorganize as circumstances warrant. We will need to design political organizations that have the kind of flexibility that immune systems have built right into them. The kind of organizations we need should, in Dee Hock's terms, be "infinitely malleable yet extremely durable. [They] should be capable of constant, self-generated modification of form or function, without sacrificing [their] essential nature or embodied principles."[10] No permanent capitol buildings or unalterable constitutions should stand in the way of an organically democratic community's capacity to evolve.

## Who Governs?

If we are to mimic Life closely, as many of us who are willing and able will participate in organizing and governing aspects of our communities. Our lives will depend on it. But this does not mean that we will all have to be hands-on or full-time involved in governance, just as not all of us will farm or rehab buildings or run businesses full time. Some aspects of community governance and maintenance will require full-time attention and particular skills, knowledge or experience for which we will select qualified members of the community to lead and represent us.

Leaders and representatives need not be — in fact probably should not be — professional, tenured politicians. Natural communities build in redundancy: Several or even many species fulfill roles necessary to the community's well-being. Our communities should also build in redundancy by giving many skillful leaders the opportunity to contribute their gifts to the community and prospective leaders the opportunity to become skillful.

Leaders and representatives of Earthological communities will be chosen on the basis of their familiarity with their human and natural communities, with many of their members, and with Life's Rules — in short, for their eco-literacy and for their flexibility, fairness and fidelity — rather than for wealth, influence, power or political acumen.

## The Role of Parties and Politicians

Political parties are so much a part of the psychological and historical landscape of the US now that it's as difficult to imagine not having or needing them as it is to imagine not needing laws to keep us in line and prevent us from cheating each other. And because even the most Earthological and self-reliant communities will have to function for the foreseeable future within larger existing socio-political systems, it's impossible to imagine that some members of those communities and sometimes whole communities will not continue to try to use political parties and to leverage politicians to act on their behalf. The desire to make existing systems work better and work for more of us is as ingrained as the difficulty we have knowing when to stop doing what's not working.

Accordingly, self-governing Earthological communities may choose to participate in existing political institutions and parties and may determine to permit or encourage the formation of new ones. Larger communities and networks of communities — at the bioregional level, for example — might find that Earthologically attuned political parties provide a way for diverse opinions to be integrated and consolidated and to find coherent expression. However, Earthological communities would not necessarily need either politicians or parties and might find them to be digressive and divisive. The fewer intermediaries that come

"At the local level, it is often possible to achieve a degree of direct democracy that is both effective and participatory. There may or may not be a need for political parties at this level. The need for them is less since the people can develop direct access to a common dialog via community meetings and direct conversation with governing officials.... But it may be [even at the local level] that parties can show and promote alternative pathways for public choice."[11]

between members of a community and the implementation of decisions they have made together, the better.

Of course, not everyone will choose to participate actively or constructively in the governance of even their local communities. And there will be no perfect world in which everyone chooses partnership over partisanship and self-interest. But if politics is the art of the possible, organically democratic or Earthological politics is the art of creating the possibility of a livable future, community by community by community, as many communities as possible at the same time. We all have a vested interest in the success of that undertaking. Michael Shuman, a community organizer, author and activist with years of experience under his belt, admitted that "decisions at the local level are [not] always efficient, fair, democratic, sensitive, creative and disaster-proof. But the more responsibility that we can place for politics at the local level, the more likely people are to take their politics seriously and act responsibly."[12]

## Deep Green Dreaming

Having said that Earthological politics and governance will need to work very differently than politicking and governments presently do, I must repeat that the closest we come to a political philosophy and social movement capable of helping us to envision, create and manage ecological communities is through Green Parties and their widely accepted Ten Key Values.

Green Parties are making inroads in legislatures and parliaments around the world, but their impact is less than is needed to upend politics as usual or provide a sufficient antidote to the viral economy. Too often Green candidates must yield principles, policies and whole chunks of their platforms in order to forge relationships with other minority parties and fund candidates and campaigns.

The Green movement, on the other hand, if it were to become deeply, ferociously and persistently green — if, that is, it were to take Life as its model and Life's Economic Survival Protocol as its operating manual — might well, as Critical Mass worsens, be able to draw a critical mass of related single-issue organizations worldwide into a world-changing coalition powerful enough to change politics forever. This Deep Green would embrace all of its constituencies' issues not as separate issues to be dealt with separately, but as interrelated aspects of one overriding issue: mimicking Life in order to live within Earth's means.

A worldwide, self-conscious movement of the kind Paul Hawken and his WiserEarth colleagues are creating by cataloguing non-governmental environmental and social justice organizations in every country could make Green Parties the most influential political parties in the world.

## Deep Green, Radically Conserve-ative and Profoundly Liberating

In his last State of the Union message, US President Ronald Reagan said that "Preservation of our environment is not a liberal or conservative challenge, it's common sense."[13] In the American political landscape, classical environmentalism and present post-carbon, climate mitigation and localization movements are routinely stamped as liberal and, there-fore, Democratic, Progressive or Green causes. Typically it is Democrats, Progressives or Greens and the equivalent parties in other nations that are in the front lines on these issues. And there can be no doubt that having or taking the opportunity to protect and defend the futures of our human and natural communities would be as profoundly liberating as it will be profoundly challenging. But concern for the environment is not particular to any one party or ideology, as an Internet search on green Republicans or conservative environmentalists will attest.

In fact, it can reasonably be said that successful, Lifelike Earthological communities would be not only deeply green but also radically conserva-tive precisely because the natural communities they will strive to mimic are radically conservative. Though the first of those two loaded words is often used to mean extreme or extremely unconventional, *radical* comes

"Shann Turnbull writes that 'The challenge for a new way to govern is to determine the simple basic design rules to create organizations that manage complexity along the same principles evolved in nature. The reason for following the rules of nature to construct ecological organizations is that these rules have proved to be the most efficient and robust way to create and manage complexity.'"[14]

from the Latin word for "root." Its original meaning is "arising from or going to a root or source." The primary source of support for all life on Earth is Earth. Earth is the physical source of Life. Natural communities are so deeply rooted in their places on Earth and in Earth-stuff — physical resources — that they are poster children for "radical."

When it is detached from several centuries of political connotation, *conservative* means "tending to conserve or preserve, protect from loss or harm, and use carefully or sparingly, avoiding waste."[15] This is precisely what successful natural communities do. Their inherent conservatism is what makes them sustainable and allows them and the ecosystems with which they partner to last for astonishingly long periods of time. Conservative columnist and blogger Andrew Sullivan pointed out that "At the core of conservatism, after all, is the word 'conserve.' [Hence my use of a hyphen in *conserve-atism*.] The earth is something none of us can own or control. It is something far older than our limited minds can even imagine. Our task is therefore a modest one: of stewardship, the quintessential conservative occupation."[16] To which, David Jenkins, the Government Affairs Director for Republicans for Environmental Protection (REP) added that "The notion of stewardship is central to conservatism. Without a strong stewardship ethic — and the forward thinking outlook it requires — the logic behind many conservative ideas falls short."[17]

## Leadership

Happily some of us in every community have that stewardship ethic and capacity to think ahead and, also happily, those ethics and capacities prompt people to steward and think ahead not only for their surrounding natural communities but their human communities, too.

The prime movers of grassroots democratic relocalization efforts are often gifted, persuasive visionaries, the equivalent of the entrepreneurial or pioneering species that are first on site when a geographic space opens up for resettlement. The best of them are also servant leaders. They lead both from the front and the inside, from deep familiarity with a community and the nature of the challenges it faces, and with the whole community's interests at heart.

Sometimes the spur for self-organization and self-governance will come from a group of visionaries and activists. The Earthaven community in western North Carolina, for example, was founded by a group, including intentional community scholar Diana Leaf Christian, permaculturalist Chuck Marsh and Arjuna da Silva, that was interested in "learning about, living, and demonstrating holistic, sustainable culture." Since 1995, Earthaven has grown to over 60 full members — from young children to a great grandmother — and expects to grow to 150. They have built homes and co-housing units in 14 neighborhoods on 325 acres, created gardens, common buildings, community power and water systems and developed on-site businesses ranging from construction, woodworking and a sawmill to market gardening, herbal medicines and a nursery. As part of their engagement in community, members run workshops in self-reliance skills, herbalism, community-building and permaculture, and they invite apprentices to learn these Life-mimicking skills.[18]

Sometimes ordinary people gather themselves spontaneously to deal with a crisis they all have in common. Groups of displaced farmers in Brazil, for example, organized the Landless Workers Movement and succeeded in reclaiming twenty million acres of fallow agricultural land on which they have established a mutually supportive coalition of dozens of self-reliant, self-determining agrarian settlements. And when Argentina's national economy collapsed in 2001 under the weight of strategic adjustments imposed by the IMF and World Bank, millions of Argentineans spontaneously organized popular assemblies — 200 of them in Buenos Aires alone — to coordinate food production and distribution systems, health care clinics, day care, alternative transportation systems, regional assemblies, community-based workshops and manufacturing plants.

In a 2010 address to the UN General Assembly, Queen Elizabeth II said that "It has perhaps always been the case that the waging of peace

## Visionary Leaders

- Scientist Wangari Maathai inspired and led the Green Belt Movement, a community tree planting, environmental reclamation and community democracy movement in Kenya, an accomplishment for which she won a Nobel Peace Prize and many Kenyans won increased competence and confidence.

- Community activist Lloyd Wells spearheaded the Chestnut Hill Community Association, advised several communities in Maine and inspired formation of the Center for Consensual Democracy.

- Architect Paolo Lugari gathered artists, technicians, scientists, carpenters, gardeners, educators, students and inventors and put them together with members of the Guahibo people in Colombia to create the self-reliant Gaviotas community.

- Artist, philosopher and social innovator Oberto Airaudi guided the creation of the Damanhur federation of self-reliant communities and ecovillages in the Valchiusella Valley of Northern Italy. Each village has its own social and political structures, businesses and particular vision for the future.

- Architect Paolo Soleri envisioned and orchestrated the evolution of cities that are designed to work like as well as with living systems, beginning with the small prototype Arcosanti in Arizona. Soleri called this fusion of city planning, design, landscape and building *arcology*. Principles of arcology have been adopted by communities all over the world.

- Urban ecology visionary Richard Register, author of *Ecocities*, helped residents, designers and leaders in Berkeley, California, begin the process of reinventing their city as clusters of live/work neighborhoods with natural, agricultural and re-wilded areas between them.

- Activist-priest Don José María Arizmendiarrieta encouraged his parishioners in the Basque region of northwestern Spain to establish the Mondragón cooperatives, a now 60-year-old coalition of more than 170 worker-owned-and-operated service and production ☞

entities that serve over 100,000 people in several self-reliant villages.

- Physicist and prolific writer Vandana Shiva founded an NGO in India called Navdanya (nine seeds) that coordinates the efforts of 5,000 local communities and villages to provide for themselves ecologically using local resources.

- Permaculture educator and natural builder Rob Hopkins co-founded the Transition Network and helped his own community of Totnes in Devon, England come together to prepare for peak oil and climate instability by becoming locally and regionally self-reliant.

- Urban planner and architect Jaime Lerner inspired and coordinated an effort by the residents of Curitiba, Brazil to imagine the post-peak city they'd like to live in and then create it.

is the hardest form of leadership of all. I know of no single formula for success, but over the years I have observed that some attributes of good leadership are universal, and are often about finding ways of encouraging people to combine their efforts, their talents, their insights, their enthusiasm, and their inspiration, to work together."[19]

There is a bit of popular wisdom to the effect that if you want to really help an impoverished community survive and thrive you don't give its people fish, you teach them how to fish — and maybe help them get or teach them how to make appropriately scaled fishing gear; you don't just give its people food, you help them to rebuild soil, adopt sustainable agricultural practices and maybe give them seeds — and better still, help them learn how to save their own. This is what Lifelike leaders will do for their communities and how Earthological communities will lead other communities toward sustainability.

## Servant Leadership, Community, Full Liability and Love

I had the pleasure of visiting and corresponding, briefly, with organizational consultant Robert Greenleaf in his last years, a decade after the 1977 publication of his groundbreaking book on Servant Leadership. Greenleaf practiced what he preached, which was in essence that the relationship between members of human communities including their leaders is, like the relationship of members of natural communities, a general liability or full partnership and is best characterized as a service-oriented, care-full and loving relationship.

"Love is an indefinable term," he wrote, "and its manifestations are both subtle and infinite. But it begins, I believe, with one absolute condition: unlimited liability. As soon as one's liability for another is qualified *to any degree*, love is diminished.

"Institutions, as we know them, are designed to limit liability for those who serve through them. In the British tradition, corporations are not 'INC' but 'LTD' — limited. Most of the goods and services we now depend on will probably continue to be furnished by such limited liability institutions."

Greenleaf proposed an alternative vision of leadership and liability. "Any human service where one who is served should be loved in the process requires community, a face-to-face group in which the liability for each other and all for one, is unlimited, or as close to it as it is possible to get. Trust and respect are highest in this circumstance, and an accepted ethic that gives strength to all is reinforced.

"Where there is not community," he wrote in *Servant Leadership*, "trust, respect and ethical behavior are difficult for the young to learn and for the old to maintain. Living in community as one's basic involvement will generate an exportable surplus of love which the individual may carry into his many involvements with institutions which are not communities such as businesses and churches, governments and schools...."

Greenleaf concluded, "All that is needed to rebuild community as a viable life form for large numbers of people in our society is for enough servant-leaders to show the way, not by mass movements, but by each servant-leader demonstrating his own unlimited liability for a quite specific community-related group."[20]

I have more recently had the equal pleasure of corresponding with August Jaccaci, a futurist, grassroots democracy visionary, 2010 Vermont congressional candidate and Thomas Jefferson scholar who is, like Greenleaf, an organizational consultant and servant leadership visionary. Jaccaci has also come to the conclusion that love is the key to every advance in human evolution.

"The global economy is being reshaped around technologies that enhance real-time communication, connectivity and relationship," Jaccaci writes in *General Periodicity*, "The nature of those human relations is becoming ever more critical as their emotional and spiritual dynamics become the value determinants of individual and cultural well-being. The new coin of the world economic realm will be the creative synergy in those relations, in the integrations, in the sharings that increase knowledge, power, profit and health....

"What happens in a major stage of transformation and renaissance like ours now," he continued, "is that for a short period of time we play with all kinds of new potentials, and, briefly, anything is possible.... Discovering potentials is the work of the hour."

Jaccaci is unrelentingly, persuasively optimistic about the capacities of the human mind and heart to heal, help, grow and expand the reach of their compassion. "While the shift toward democracy is still emerging, a new form of political economic power is gathering at the level of the nation-state. The all-pervasive, over-arching power of life itself, which I call Biocracy, is appearing. As humanity comes to realize that ultimately all life and all species must thrive and prosper or eventually none will, the values of dominance and control are giving way to the values of resonance and reverence....

"Humanity is awakening to the realization that the universe is made of love, by love, for love," he says. "Love is the source, substance and future of all being. So if we would build a sustainable culture, let us build it on a web of love and it will be both ephemeral and timeless, momentary and enduring."[21]

The words of such expansive thinkers along with the teachings of the world's spiritual masters and Earth sages prompt me to suggest that democracy, such as Life built into its very fabric, may be what love looks like away from home.

## A Force More Fierce: Refusal, Resistance and (R)evolution

Coming into the second decade of the 21st century, nearly every symptom of Critical Mass is worsening more rapidly than I had imagined, and they are converging and amplifying each other exactly as I had imagined. I find myself paying more attention to the proposals of those who call upon us to be more fierce than we have lately been in defense of Life as we know it — and of ourselves, our communities, our descendants and their future. I am attending to the possibility of the kind of Life-saving love of which our spiritual leaders and many of our secular leaders speak.

The solutions I synthesize in the next chapter are constructive, collaborative, non-confrontational and nonviolent. But I would be remiss not to acknowledge, again, that while some of our leaders may yield some of their power, the Powers and most of our leaders will not yield easily or willingly their power, their vision of the future as more-of-the-same or this economy and their control over the systems that maintain it. They will not yield to the Green vision or Deep Green politics willingly. Nor will we, so long as we believe the global economy is a healing force rather than a viral one.

Even when critical masses of us realize that we need to change dramatically, the Powers will not, for the most part, facilitate our efforts to heal Earth's flagging immune system and save ourselves from the worst that Critical Mass can do.

The longer the present viral global economic system persists, the less money, stamina and health and the fewer resources we will have left with which to create any kind of desirable future when the system collapses, as it most certainly will. And as it does, conflict and violence at every level of society will increase. Along with the tools of disconnection of which Keith Farnish writes, governments will be forced to use the tools of repression in order to maintain control, order and something like the status quo.

We will not be able to love our way into what follows Critical Mass in the usual ways we understand love. Love may need an edge.

Life gives us our lives. To respond appropriately to that gift, we need to preserve, not challenge, Life's capacity to continue to give life and more life and more kinds of life to Earth and to us. Respond comes from a Latin word that means "to answer to or promise or pledge in return." I've said that the members of natural communities and the communities themselves (the successful ones at least) are highly response-able. But they cannot pledge anything and cannot *choose* to offer Earthonomical behaviors in return for the gift of life. Appropriate responses to the gift are encoded, built-in. And among those built-in responses are *rejection* of collapsing or corrupt systems, *resistance* to dominance by any one species or members of a species, and *(r)evolution*. These may need to be among our responses to the forces that threaten Life as we know it.

Resistance in the form of prolonged, large scale protests and acts of civil disobedience such as those which Gandhi practiced to bring an end to the British Raj in India. Resistance such as oppressive Venezuelan, Iranian, Egyptian and Syrian governments have not been able to ignore or stifle may become — will likely become — more common. Acts of resistance are examples of democracy in action too. And because they are among Life's democratic, or biocratic, methods of survival, they are organically democratic actions.

While the Powers will probably ignore our fledgling efforts to localize some aspects of governance and economic activity (especially if it removes from them some of the increasing burden of responsibility for fixing things they cannot fix), they will not react passively and peaceably to political secessions or expanded and intensified forms of resistance and protest. These present a challenge to authority and to the flow of tax monies and political legitimacy. The Powers will doubtless condemn as terrorism such acts of resistance on our own, our children's, grandchildren's and Life's behalf. They may well treat resistors as if they were terrorists. In their continued efforts to get away with breaking Life's laws, the Powers will accuse resistors of breaking their laws. Those of us who have not yet become fierce, who have stopped short of breaking sovereign laws, may have to be more fierce, including perhaps by breaking sovereign laws that facilitate the trespasses of the present system, perpetuate harms done to Earth's immune system and hamper Life-saving alternatives.

In other words, secessionists, resistors and protestors may not always be able to act passively and peaceably either. We in the United States have the Founding Fathers' example and Declaration of Independence to consider in this understanding of the courage that freedom entails. In the two and a half centuries since their acts of resistance, revolution and reconstitution and in the first years of the present decade ordinary people around the world — in the former Soviet Union, in South Sudan, in Northern Africa and South Africa and Southeastern Asia as well as on the streets of many American cities — have risen to the occasion of their oppression, the destruction of their homelands, the outsourcing of their jobs, the inequity of their national economies and the theft of their resources and rights. And they have sought, though they have not always received or yet achieved, organically democratic alternatives to Powers and pyramids.

An increasing number of influential philosophers, activists, writers and critics of the present system are advocating for revolution, for hobbling the system and bringing it down before it can take everything familiar down with it. They believe that infrastructure sabotage and activities both small and large in scale that undermine the system's capacity to function reliably may push many typically patient and passive people to take charge of their own lives while there's still a relatively tolerable climate, ecosystem services and resources to support them.

What I advocate here might best be called by the same name I give it when other-than-human species engage in it: (r)evolution. But in this we cannot entirely take our cues from Life. Some other-than-human species can choose to leave or withdraw support from larger living systems that are failing them; they cannot choose to sabotage or overturn those systems. We can. Our attempts to mimic Life's survival methods may be punctuated with acts of sabotage, rebellion, disobedience and even armed resistance. These acts may be necessary if we want to speed and support a (r)evolution and transformation equivalent in ambition to the one that put an end to prehistoric lifeways and brought us the Powers, civilizations and patterns of dominance that have evolved over three millennia into the viral global system that threatens us now.

Happily for us, the Great Turning from empire to Earth community, from power over to power to, and from the Powers to democratically empowered people, is as old as the first empires.

## From Juggernaut to Jubilee: A Metaphor for a Great Turning from Empire to Organic Democracy

Throughout human history, myths and metaphors have changed people's minds about how the world works and how we they might best work with and in it. Here are two that can help us make the mental shift from larger-than-Life hubris to Life-saving Earthologic.

There's a Hindu god called Vishnu who is known by several nicknames. One of them, Juggernaut — *Jagannātha* in the original Sanskrit —

means "Lord of the World." In our time he would have been one of the Superclass, the 1% of the Powers That Be. In his role as Juggernaut, the grinning Vishnu — wouldn't you grin if the world was *your* oyster? — traditionally lived in a temple made to look like a chariot, with huge stone wheels at each of the four corners. The chariot on which Juggernaut reclined regally represents the world, his world — Earth and every thing and everyone in it — being pulled under his ostensible protection safely through its rounds of the heavens.

Traditionally, once a year Hindus put a statue of Juggernaut on a heavy wooden wagon and make a procession through cities and towns in order that the people, especially the scattered poor, the ill, lame and elderly who could not get to the temple to see him, might worship and be blessed by the god. In the past as now, hundreds of willing pilgrims along with an elephant or two pulled the huge wagon on which the ponderous stone god sat while the worshipful ran alongside throwing gifts of food, flowers, money — what few material goods they had — and even themselves on the wagon. But in the distant past, Juggernaut's parade was a mixed blessing. People were knocked about, kicked aside and trod upon as the ecstatic procession rolled through the streets and towns where gongs and horns tolled its raucus approach. Heavy as it was, and heavier as it grew with the addition of each new tithe or body, Juggernaut's wagon was very hard to pull up hill and almost impossible to stop when it was going down hill.

And so it was that Juggernaut often bore quite *unsafely* down upon his followers. The stony-eyed, greedy-hearted god in his faux chariot rolled over, crushed or maimed some, sometimes many, of the worshipers, the pilgrims, the lame, ill, elderly and any beasts who simply got in the way. Adoring, entranced hordes were swept willy-nilly along by the increasingly frenzied parade of worshipers and speeding wagon. Certainly the unfailing generosity and awe of the faithful left some of them poorer than they already were. And although some of them deliberately martyred themselves under the wheels, for the rest, loving Juggernaut was a mixed blessing.

Little wonder that the word juggernaut has come into modern usage meaning any force, event or power that is so heavy and huge or relentless that it seems both inescapable and unstoppable. Lording it over the

Earth, riding high atop the prevailing pyramidal socio-economic system, the viral global economy is our 21st century Juggernaut.

Several centuries after Juggernaut's parades got under way in India, the Jewish people of the ancient Middle East had almost been crushed by one empire and exile, one plague and famine, one flood and enslavement, one Critical Mass after another. According to their Torah, they were given by the divinity they called Yahweh a surprisingly democratic solution of such repeated juggernauts: Jubilee.

The word for the celebratory event called Jubilee derived from the Hebrew word *yôbēl*, the name of the rams' horns that announced it. By pronouncement of Yahweh through his prophets — democratically predisposed visionaries to a one — every 50 years the *yôbēl* were to be blown throughout the land to signal that the Powers That Be and everyone else must free slaves, forgive debt, restore property and land to its former owners (the peoples and other living things from which it had been taken), leave some of the land untilled, fatted calves unkilled, fruit and nut trees unpicked and unfilled and the people unbowed. This meant that those Powers, lords of *their* worlds, would suffer a loss of tribute, income and, yes, power.

Jubilee years were intended by the wise of that Critically Massed time in the Middle East to let the Earth and every thing and everyone in it heal, to let Earth's strained accounts refill and other-than-human beings and us find their own way.

As you might imagine, there have been very few Jubilees. Since the Powers in even ostensibly democratic nations still aren't inclined to grant the rest of us Jubilee, we'll have to grant it to ourselves, blow our own horns throughout all the lands, jam a stick or two through empire's wheels, unseat Juggernaut and take over the wagon. Or, better still, turn our backs and make our own Lifelike lifeways — democratically.

CHAPTER 13

# Setting a Good Example

SOME GROUPS AND COMMUNITIES have already declared Jubilee — or to use this book's driving analogy, have already declared "Enough!" to Earth's AIDS — and have begun to discover their capacity to find ways to organize themselves to live within Earth's means. For many of these groundbreaking Earthological communities (though none yet have this name for what they are doing) a gifted visionary has sounded the *yôbēl*. Some have been inspired by a particular environmental, social or economic movement. Some are self-starters: a small group organizes in response to a particular local crisis, concern or challenge and, as bread rises in the presence of a few activated granules of leaven, gradually or sometimes not so gradually a community of place rises and organizes itself around the activating group and its vision. Other communities have seen Critical Mass coming and have consciously gathered their members together to envision ways of mitigating or preventing it. And still others have experienced a crisis of conscience rather than of circumstance and have decided to withdraw their support from a social, economic and political system that causes so much harm. Some Earthological communities — calling themselves *intentional communities* — are organized from scratch. Most, however — like the ones we'll look at here — have reorganized themselves in the places where their members already lived, within or under the radar of the established system in order to address challenges their governments are not addressing.

But as different as their beginnings have been, they have these characteristics in common:

- each community has arisen or reformed itself in a particular place, organically and democratically
- each has organized itself for the purpose of providing for itself to the extent possible in that place
- each has kept in mind both the well-being of that place and the place of humans in it

I offer only a handful of examples here. A few are fairly well-known. Others are not. A literature and something like a mythic aura gathers around such communities when they do become known because what they are doing — turning away from the viral economy, taking Earth and each other to heart and their lives into their own hands — is both bold and fraught and yet expressive of what Joanna Macy and Chris Johnstone call "active hope." I offer here only the briefest introduction to these experiments in organic democracy in the hope that you will want to learn more, go and do likewise. Information about them is readily available. Since they are always evolving, what you read of them here will already be old. What they are facing and accomplishing by the time you read these words will be new.

None of these Earthological communities have achieved perfection, whatever that might be. I doubt perfection is something they'd think to aim for. As the Zen teachings would remind us, they are not the moon but only fingers pointing at it. Some of us will diminish or dismiss them on that account and will use their imperfections, lapses, inconsistencies and occasional failures to excuse ourselves from even trying to do what they are doing. We would do well to remind ourselves that, since democracy is, like Life, a process (something that we do together) there is no state of perfection to be reached. There is only the doing.

Some of these communities are further along than others in their evolution or in the degree of self-reliance they have achieved. But from each and all of them we learn that the first steps we take — democratically — away from the global economy, political systems and Powers are also our first steps away from Critical Mass. Any steps taken in the cause of Jubilee are brave, and every step taken makes the next more likely.

## Kenya

In the decades following World War II, the global economy came out of its latent period and went viral. Like HIV/AIDS seeking new host bodies, it sought out new territories to claim in those parts of the world where there was still some combination of empty space, cheap labor, abundant natural resources, corruptible or greedy government and no regulatory agencies. Like many countries in Africa, South America and Asia in that period, Kenya was just such a place. Several of its diverse ecosystems were resource rich or suited to large-scale agriculture. Expanding prosperous-nation economies, newly-empowered transnational corporations and the government in Nairobi saw an opportunity to profit from Kenya's natural assets. In fewer than three decades an essentially rural nation comprised of nomadic tribes and subsistent farming villages, a nation that had hardly recovered from the first round of colonial plunder, was transformed into an exporter of timber and rare woods, coffee, tea, cement, fruits and vegetables. Rural and wild Kenya became a plantation and supply region for Nairobi, the African continent and the world, and native Kenyans became stoop laborers dependent on their new overlords.

The consequences of industrial-strength timber extraction, mining and commercial agriculture for rural Kenyans and for Kenya's ecosystems were dire:

- lost native species
- reduced biodiversity
- deforestation and desertification
- degraded and collapsing ecosystems
- the triumph of exotic and opportunistic plant species over native species
- played-out soils
- a thousand-fold increase in the need for expensive, sometimes toxic soil amendments, herbicides and pesticides
- increases in air and water pollution

- drought
- scarcity and then complete lack of firewood on which most villagers depended for fuel
- in the wake of these depredations a dramatic reduction in the ability of rural Kenyans to sustain themselves, causing disease, malnutrition, poverty, despair, resentment and unrest

In short, decades of severe regional Critical Mass

Native Kenyan, Wangari Maathai, watched these consequences unfold with the eyes of a scientist, a lover of Life and of Kenya and her people. But she didn't just watch. She recognized that while a pathological global political economy was the fundamental cause of the crisis, its immediate cause was the loss of those forests that had been cut over for market and to make additional arable land available for export crops. Take away trees, she saw, and the inevitable result was that soils and waters that once sustained natural and human communities no longer could. Kenyans needed to plant trees. They needed to reforest Kenya, village by village, landscape by landscape. Accordingly, in 1977, with the cooperation of the National Council of Women of Kenya, Maathai founded the Green Belt Movement (GBM) to catalyze and coordinate as many of Kenya's villagers, beginning with the women, as were ready to take a first steps toward self-reliance, self-determination and ecosystem restoration.

What has evolved in a very Lifelike fashion out of Maathai's initial vision and out of the movement it inspired is a network that connects farmers in hundreds of village communities who not only make a living from their work but enjoy the material benefits that the resulting verdant swath of young forests is providing. Soils are being renewed. Under and around the soil-enlivening trees, villagers grow crops — nutritious traditional plants that require little processing like cassava, sweet potatoes,

"The GBM is a grassroots Non-Governmental Organization that focuses on environmental conservation and development. It does this mainly through a nationwide grassroots tree-planting campaign that is its core activity.... It is wholly managed by Kenyans and deliberately prefers to rely on local capacity, knowledge, wisdom and expertise."[1]

yams, indigenous green vegetables and fruits — to feed themselves and to trade or sell at local markets. Grasses and wild understory plants supply browse for small livestock and fowl. Local watersheds are restored, and the water in streams and ponds is clean enough to drink and support fish farming. Air pollution is reduced. Villagers once again have shade in which to gather and work, and temperatures in and around the young forests are moderated. There is wood for cooking and building again.

Since the first trees were dug in and the first nursery started, upwards of 100,000 women and a growing number of men have planted over 40 million trees that provide not only food, shelter and personal income but funds that support schools and clinics, allow communities to purchase small-scale solar and wind technology power and pumps for wells and meet villagers' household needs.

In addition to these substantial material gains, Kenyan villagers who have chosen to participate in the Green Belt Movement have reaped the benefits of the practices of organic democracy — among them self-confidence, collaboration, cooperation and mutual support — and they have acquired the skills of self-organization, negotiation, deliberation, problem solving, shared decision making and leadership at the community and intercommunity levels.

But the peoples' adoption of democratic methods and principles did not stop with local self-determination and increasing economic self-sufficiency. "Though initially," Maathai admitted, "the Green Belt Movement's tree planting activities did not address issues of democracy and peace, it soon became clear that responsible governance of the environment was impossible without democratic space."[2] Consequently village compounds and squares, the circles of shade under growing trees and vacant urban lots that were turned into tree-dotted gardens or nurseries have become places in which democracy also grows. "The tree became a symbol for the democratic struggle in Kenya," Maathai wrote. "Citizens were mobilized to challenge widespread abuses of power, corruption, and environmental mismanagement.... In time, the tree became a symbol [also] for peace and conflict resolution."

Critical masses of Kenyan villagers and farmers, having discovered their capacity for democratic self-determination, became activists. They were willing, and — in part out of desperation and in part because of their increasing economic independence — they were able to challenge and make demands on local, provincial and national governments. As participants in the nationwide 2002 effort to restore democratic governance to Kenya, GBM activists helped elect the first democratic government in several generations. Wangari Maathai was elected to Parliament and appointed as a minister for the environment. In 2004 she won the Nobel Peace Prize. She not only believed but had acted on the fact that "Once empowered, people are capable of making conscious and informed decisions for self-determination."

US Green Party co-founder John Rensenbrink believes that Wangari Maathai, her colleagues and the Kenyan people who are carrying on the work of the GBM since Maathai died in 2011 have succeeded in dispelling several myths about democracy and the environment. One is the myth that "the 'masses' (a word the authors and advertisers of this myth often use to describe 'the people') are not only fickle but they don't really care about the environment. Maathai believes," and Kenyan villagers have proven, "just the opposite. More democracy is what is needed. Not only is more democracy needed, it is THE answer to a lot of problems produced by the current powers-that-be in governments North and South."3

Another myth is that "economic security is a fundamental requirement for peaceful behavior and that only by bringing economies more effectively into the global market ... will people find a level of economic security."4 Communities that are participating in the Green Belt Movement for economic self-reliance, democracy, sustainability and peace have made a case for the opposing position: it is by *reducing* their dependence on the global economy and learning how to live within Earth's means, provide for and govern themselves sustainably that people and peoples may find a level of economic security in the post-collapse world.

## India

Among the triggers for an organically democratic grassroots (r)evolution in India have been the wholesale and interconnected privatizations of land, water, native seed and genetic stock. These are literal not figurative corporate takeovers. For example, according to free trade and WTO arrangements, agrochemical corporations can purchase and patent the genetic "information" found in native seeds like the seed of India's neem tree (which in various forms is effective in the treatment of ulcers, diabetes and skin disorders, and as an insecticide, antiseptic, soil additive and spermicidal). And, following WTO Intellectual Property Rights law, the purchasing corporations can also "purchase" legislation that makes it illegal for farmers to plant or use neem seeds they themselves have raised and collected. Instead they must buy back the seed or buy the medicines, insecticides, antiseptics, soil builders and spermicidals the corporation manufactures using that genetic information — or face fines or lawsuits.

A consortium of corporations can purchase from a nation's Powers the option to use, say, 60% of a river's annual flow, build a dam and divert that much of the flow away from its natural course through farmland and villages to, for example, a new hydroelectric facility that produces electricity which it sells at a profit, though not to those from whom the water was taken (because they can't afford it).

The result in India, as elsewhere, of such rampant hijacking of the local and regional commonwealth of resources by transnational corporations like Monsanto, Cargill, Pepsi, Coca-Cola, Vivendi, Hyundai and Bechtel has been:

- loss of native plant species and of subsistence farmers' control over their methodologies, crops and water supply
- spreading poverty
- weakened ecosystems
- dispossession
- malnutrition
- mass suicides (182,936 in India between 1997 and 2007)[5]
- the reluctant relocation of millions of Indian villagers to the subcontinent's hyper-cities. Most of them cannot provide the same quality of life for their families in the city

Physicist, educator and prolific author Vandana Shiva, winner of the alternative Nobel Peace Prize, the Right Livelihood Award, in 1993, is

"Navdanya's report 'The GMO emperor has no clothes' provides empirical evidence about the performance of [Genetically Modified Organisms] in farmers' fields. The GMOs have failed to increase yields or reduce the use of pesticides. The prevalence of pests and weeds hasn't decreased either. GMOs have, in fact, increased chemical use and led to the emergence of super pests and super weeds. To impose a failed technology with extremely high social and ecological costs undemocratically on India in the name of "science" is anti-science and anti-democracy. It is anti-science because real science is based on the new disciplines of agro-ecology and epigenetics, not the obsolete idea of genetic determinism and genetic reductionism."[6]

the visionary servant leader who in India made connections between the environment, the commonwealth of resources, community stability, economic self-reliance, sustainability and democracy. She calls the thread that weaves them together *Earth Democracy*. Earth Democracy is "based on local democracy, with local communities — organized on principles of inclusion, diversity, and ecological and social responsibility — having the highest authority on decisions related to the environment and natural resources and to the sustenance and livelihoods of people.... Self-rule and self-governance is the foundation of Earth Democracy. [It assumes] the intrinsic worth of all species, all peoples, all cultures; a just and equal sharing of this earth's vital resources; and sharing decisions about their use." Shiva's democratic vision arises from her intimate awareness that, "Not only do the marginalized have knowledge; they are the only ones who do have knowledge about the roots and causes of their marginalization and poverty" and what to do about them.[7]

Informed by study and by the tens of thousands of villagers with whom she has worked for several decades, Shiva's vision is three-fold:

1) An NGO called Navdanya (which means "nine seeds") coordinates the efforts of local communities to provide for themselves Earthologically using local resources and organic farming methods. The nine seeds come from traditional, indigenous staple food plants: barley, millet, pigeon pea, mung bean, chick pea, rice, sesame,

black gram and horse gram, which are highly nutritious beans used in making dal. The communities cultivate and sustainably harvest indigenous crops while warding off encroachment by the agents and agencies of the GMO.

2) A set of three organically democratic principles — *bija swaraj* (biodiversity and seed democracy), *anna swaraj* (food democracy) and *jal swaraj* (water democracy) — mobilizes farmers and villagers in common cause.

3) A non-profit scientific research organization supports the mobilization and acts as a sort of common brain for as many as 5,000 scattered communities and two million farmers and villagers, both men and women.

"Navdanya wanted to build a program in which farmers and scientists related horizontally rather than vertically, in which conservation of biodiversity and production of food go hand in hand, and in which farmers' knowledge is strengthened, not robbed.... We committed ourselves to defend and reclaim our fundamental freedoms related to land, forests, biodiversity, food and water. That is how the movements for Earth Democracy were born."[8]

The Hindi word *swaraj* means, variously, sovereignty, self-rule and democracy. All three were what Mahatma Gandhi meant to convey with his concept *gram swaraj* — village democracy. Since Navdanya's founding in 1984, 2,400 villages in eight Indian states have engaged in *gram swaraj*.[10] The villagers' efforts to reclaim control over their own destinies and retrieve management of their land, water and ecosystems is co-ordinated by a sort of intercommunity brain, that third pillar of Earth Democracy in India, the Research Foundation for Science, Technology

---

### Deep Democracy

"*Swaraj* represents a genuine attempt to regain control of the 'self' — our self-respect, self-responsibility, and capacities for self-realization — from institutions of dehumanization. As Gandhi stated, "It is *swaraj* when we learn to rule ourselves."[9]

and Ecology (RFSTE). RFSTE supports villagers' and farmers' independence and also their interdependence by offering them:

- training in sustainable methods of organic farming and gardening
- making available to them the results of current research
- creating an open source space where their experience and anecdotal data can be collected, collated and exchanged providing intellectual credibility for them and for the elected village and inter-village councils that are called *panchayats*

"Instead of deriving strength from Big Money," Shiva wrote, "the RFSTE drew its strength from local communities and in turn gave them strength and their struggles support. And it has been effective. We stopped limestone mining in Doon Valley and had the valley declared a Green Zone. We have changed the forestry, aquaculture and agriculture paradigms from monoculture to diversity, and from commerce to sustenance and sustainability. We have challenged the dominant Intellectual Property Rights paradigm and won cases against Neem [seed] and Basmati [rice seed] biopiracy."[11] As was the case in the Green Belt Movement, the hidden gains for Navdanya participants are competence, confidence and the increasingly widespread discovery of the power inherent in working together democratically to evolve Lifelike Earthological economies.

## Colombia

One of the most remarkable experiments in organic democracy is occurring in the backyard of the Colombian drug cartels. Gaviotas, about which a book has been written and a film made, has been called a "village to reinvent the world."[12] Its vibrant, diverse population of imported and adoptive visionaries, artists, technicians, scientists, carpenters, gardeners, architects, students, inventors and social innovators and its more permanent population of several hundred indigenous Guahibo people and urban escapees have found ways to create something like a self-sufficient paradise, a new kind of rainforest and a successful, sustainable local Earthonomy on the thin-soiled, nutrient-poor, soggy, empty savannah — the *llanos* — of eastern Colombia at the westernmost edge of the Amazon jungle.

Visionary Paolo Lugari began the work of Earthological community building in Gaviotas — which is named after a local river gull — about the same time Wangari Maathai began planting trees, a movement and democracy in Kenya. The similarity between the two projects ends there, however. Gaviotas is not a movement but one low-density village, located virtually in the middle of nowhere. And its first real settlers were not the native Guahibos but an odd-lot of visionaries who were inspired by Lugari's dream of causing a self-reliant community to grow up where nothing but bitter weeds and brittle grasses grew. But what it lacks in numbers, the Gaviotas experiment makes up for in sheer chutzpah, creativity and the diversity and collegiality of its short- and long-term resident-participants. Green dreamers and schemers of all ages from all over South America and beyond have found their way or been summoned to Gaviotas to lend their genius, muscle or particular gift to the venture to create, not a utopia (which Lugari says really means "no place real") but a subsistent, thriving, self-reliant *topia* — a real place. And the skills and traditions of Guahibos and other native peoples, which were being lost as surely as their languages, are not being preserved so much as they are being reenergized.

Sixteen hours from the nearest major city, in the heart of territories commanded by Colombian drug lords and their well-armed guerrilla paramilitaries, Gaviotas' indigenous residents, urban imports and cultural and ethnic transplants have created a community and an economy that combines characteristics and strengths of all three groups. Aware of their naturally harsh and politically dangerous setting, Gaviotans laid aside all the differences between them before those differences could *come* between them. They have pooled their intelligence and material resources, lived and cooked, built, worked and eaten together. They grow nearly all their own food and have raised cattle. They have invented and built, "wind turbines that convert mild tropical breezes into energy, solar collectors that work in the rain, soil-free systems to raise edible and medicinal crops" as well as "ultra-efficient pumps to tap deep aquifers — pumps so easy to operate, they're hooked up to children's seesaws." And they have done all this using scrap, cheap, local, found and recycled materials.

Because they paid close, patient attention to the landscape and its natural communities and to each other, Gaviotas' environmentalists, farmers and biologists discovered that where nothing but a scrubby variety of tree called a *chaparro* had grown, they can grow a variety of formerly-native Caribbean pine that not only grows quickly and produces a resin that is used to make marketable paints, turpentine and a high-quality rosin suitable for lubricating violin bows, but also produces wood that can be used to make traditional musical instruments. And that same beneficent tree, of which they have planted several million, restores *llanos* soil. "The pine trees protect the soil from the harsh sun and the continuous dropping of needles results in the creation of a rich humus [covering.] This has improved the pH [of the soil] and this in turn has facilitated the germination of a natural undergrowth of plants and trees."

Some 20 new species, their seeds and spores born by wind, bees and birds from as far east as the 300-mile distant Orinoco River have taken root in the savannah around Gaviotas. In a place where there had been no forest the impossible happened: a new latter-day rainforest has begun to grow. This is not so much a restoration of original forest as it is a do-over, a human-assisted forest evolving in parallel course with natural forests. This remarkable example of humans working patiently with Life rather than aggressively against it is validated by the Gaviotans' recent decision to forego planting additional pines and instead to plan foreword toward the kinds of alternative value-added products that the new mixed forest has made possible.

## Social Capital Rocks

Gaviotas' chronicler Alan Weisman tells a story that conveys these social-capital benefits perfectly:

Dawn. The saucelitos, musical, golden-eyed thrushes that dwell in the shrubbery at Gaviotas, faithfully signaled 5:00 AM. Within a half hour, Gaviotans were parking their bikes by the dining commons and wandering up the paths with their coffee cups. But at 5:40, stragglers arrived to find the rest of the community, nearly 250 people, assembled in the garden in front of the [community kitchen]. Facing them were two rows of young men and women, at rigid attention. They wore short-sleeved ☞

khaki uniforms, black rubber irrigation boots, and khaki jungle caps with a red star at the forehead. Each carried a rubberized green backpack, a full cartridge belt, a canteen, and a semi-automatic rifle with an attached banana clip.

The Gaviotans looked at one another and shrugged. This had happened before. The guerrilla comandante, a blond man in his mid-thirties, addressed the group. "Which one of you is in charge?"

"We all are," replied several voices.

The comandante paced in front of them. He and his troops, he said, were the [Revolutionary Armed Forces of Colombia], as if everyone didn't know. They were here to discuss the current need for armed struggle.

"We don't fight," said one of the villagers.

"This is neutral ground," said another. Their voices were calm.

"There is no neutral ground in Colombia," said the comandante. "You're either with us or against us."

"We're with people. Not politics."

"We're fighting for the people's rights," the commander replied.

"If you believe in the rights of el pueblo [the people], then just let us go to work."

"And please take your guns. They're not allowed here."

Nobody moved except for small children, who approached the guerrilleros to inspect their weapons. No one stopped them. Finally, a woman asked, "Are you taking us hostage?"

The comandante relaxed and smiled. "Our orders are not to touch anybody here."

The Gaviotans exhaled. "Why?"

"Because what you're doing here is too valuable."[13]

Gaviotans have built "a solar kitchen that operates on a semi-industrial scale, using not imported oil but vegetable oil extracted from cotton seeds heated in vacuum tubes," a school, common buildings, workshops and a field hospital and clinic which, when the Colombian government at least temporarily closed it on technicalities (insufficient number of specialists and lack of an insurable group of 10,000 members), was converted into a solar water distillation and bottling manufactory, a workplace where *manu* really means "by hand." Since the new forest's root system has purified local groundwater which once was the cause of 70% of indigenous diseases and illnesses, the distilling and bottling facility, which provides rewarding and gainful employment to a score or so of villagers, has taken on a portion of the challenge of preventive health care. The bottled water costs one fifth what water brought in from the capital had cost. And as if this were not sufficiently Earthological and Earthonomical for a backwoods, shoe-string operation, Gaviotas is, by design, a near zero-emissions/zero-waste community. Even the wastewater from the production of resins and turpentine, which was discovered to contain 3% essential oils, is converted into organic cleaning products, and the plastic bags in which resin is collected are reconditioned and processed into plastic pipe!

The advantages of productive work, education, health care, shared food provision, housing, child and elder care are amplified in Gaviotas, as they are in the Green Belt Movement and Navdanya, by the ineffable benefits of shared engagement in a self-reliant, organically democratic community. Gaviotans enjoy camaraderie, competence, confidence, commitment to a common cause and the courage of their Earthological consciences and convictions.

In Kenya, India and Colombia hundreds of thousands of largely uneducated, ordinary men and women, without benefit of technological gadgetry or magic, large capital investments, pristine or even healthy ecosystems, government subsidy, free-flowing, cheap energy or the habits of democracy as we in the West understand them have seized the opportunity their servant leaders have given them to rediscover, reinvent and reorganize themselves in order to deal with the symptoms of Critical Mass by learning, together, to live within Earth's means using methods that obey Life's rules.

## Brazil

A million desperately poor, landless, jobless men and women comprising over 370,000 families have engaged in non-violent protest, organized 2,500 land occupations and mobilizations, and used peaceful persuasion to secure from their government their right to settle and organically farm more than 20 million acres of fallow agricultural land scattered throughout Brazil. They see their self-organizing activism as the key to the construction of a more broadly democratic political alternative in Brazil involving coalitions of self-reliant, self-determining agrarian settlements. Not only is the Landless Workers' Movement — the *Movimento dos Trabalhadores Rurais Sem-Terra* [MST] — "fighting for their own rights, they are transforming their society into a more just one. Their approach may offer the best" — and certainly the most democratic — "solution yet to Brazil's environmental problems in the Amazon and elsewhere."[14]

Poverty, lack of education and the violence and corruption that are characteristic of life in Brazil's urban slums, where many of the landless settlers and their families began their struggle, are stumbling blocks to the Lifelike kind of democracy and community that results in self-reliance and self-governance. Fed up with their circumstances and emboldened by the failures of their governments, applicants to MST's new agrarian settlements put their lives on the line in peaceful protests and immerse themselves in local and national political activism and group decision making. They *earn* "citizenship" in their community by participating in the struggle to acquire land and planning for its use and protection.

Angus Wright and Wendy Wolford, American sociologists who have studied the MST, report that life in these self-determining, self-reliant communities affords settlers unprecedented degrees of freedom *from* want, oppression, disempowerment and fear — and of freedom *to* work with the other members of their Earthological communities, who have proven their equal commitment to shape safer, more satisfying and sustainable futures. One of the first commitments community members typically make to the future is to build a school or designate some spaces in the community as classrooms so that they and their children can learn not only how to provide for themselves and care for their natural communities but also how, democratically, to reduce the oppressive and destructive capabilities of the Power's-driven pyramidal political system and its pathological economy.

"With their increasing participation in local, regional and national politics MST settlers are having a noticeable impact on 'politics as usual,'" Wright and Wolford wrote. They echoed Vandana Shiva and Wangari Maathai's pride in the power of people to affect change not only in their immediate lives but in the halls of power. "This is perhaps most evident," they add, "in the realm of accountability. The cornerstone to any democracy is accountability, the transparency and the sense of responsibility for action or inaction with which the government conducts its business. With its membership of over one million people and its high visibility, the MST is forcing the government to pay attention to its constituency — people who have traditionally lacked the political and economic influence in Brazil to get their own concerns on the agenda."[15]

This organically democratic movement and the self-reliant agrarian communities that have settled out of it will in the coming years prove to be either particularly vulnerable or particularly exemplary. Transnational agribusinesses are purchasing the support of Brazil's money-scrapped government in order acquire acreage — some of that same fallow land to which the MST wishes to stake claim — on which to grow soybeans for China and cane or other biomass fuels for everywhere in the world rather than food for Brazilians.

## Argentina

Argentina's recent history shows us what organic democracy can look like when a part of the pyramidal socio-political system collapses and communities take a shadow government option. It also offers an example of the present system's staying power and the reality that, for now, all organically democratic communities still operate not only in the system's shadow but often still under its thumb.

In 2001, an economic meltdown froze Argentineans' bank accounts, filled their leaders' offshore accounts, bankrupted businesses, closed factories and drove foreign currency out of the country. The crisis represented one of the most egregious examples of the global economy's abject failure to deliver on promises of widespread prosperity. Millions of enraged Argentineans "took to the streets throughout the country, banging pots and chanting 'They all must go!'"[16] During the three decades preceding the economic collapse, as many as 30,000 Argentineans who were openly opposed to government policy were "disappeared" and thousands of others were routinely jailed. For years preceding the collapse, one after another corrupt government along with international financial agencies like the IMF and World Bank promised that foreign investments in the country would cause wealth to not only trickle but flow down. But in 2001, Argentina finally became ungovernable by normal means. The president, Carlos Menem, resigned. Subsequent governments cobbled themselves together and fell into disarray with the regularity of sandcastles at a beach's edge, and Argentina crossed the threshold into the unknown.

What came next made what had come first seem, for a time, worth it. Argentineans took the opportunity that chaos offered them to engage in thousands of experiments with spontaneous, organically democratic self-organization and self-reliance. Ordinary people, as much asone third of the population from every walk of life and social class, filled the power vacuum, "spontaneously creating an astonishing array of grassroots democratic organizations. The most ubiquitous of these [were] the *asambleas populares* (popular assemblies). Every week people gathered in parks and plazas across the country — including over 200 neighborhoods in Buenos Aires alone — to address the problems facing their communities: food distribution, health care, day care, welfare, and transportation. People organized themselves effectively to the extent that observers saw in the organic upwelling of democratic activity 'a new form of political organization.'" Something very like an immune system. Neighborhood assemblies networked to create intercommunity regional assemblies, roundtables and commissions, exactly as the diverse agents in the immune system network to share the work of healing.

There was a thrilling outbreak of village, community and neighborhood gardens — nearly half a million of them covering over 10,000 urban and rural acres provided food for nearly 10% of the population, over 2.5 million people. Leif Utne reported that workers who had lost their jobs to factory closings took the factories over and "turned them around — testing out new modes of self-management and worker ownerships. Many people ... disengaged themselves from the formal *peso* economy by joining 'barter clubs' — neighborhood-based economic networks, often with their own currency, that let citizens trade goods and services without dealing with the banks." A critical mass of Argentineans "went local."

What happened? Why is this section written in the past tense? In effect, the popular assemblies and organizations they created kept Argentina afloat long enough for the Powers, competing political factions and international trade and banking organizations to reassert themselves. The domination system in Argentina was after all only ailing, not moribund. Infusions of cash and political support from outside the country propped up old Powers and pumped up new ones. Because the people's efforts to provide for and organize themselves had been essentially local and only loosely networked, because they had not thought to or had time to organize themselves all the way up and out to the national level, there remained a vacuum of leadership at the national level. Like Life, nations abhor vacuums and strive to fill them.

Argentinean human rights activist, Graceala Monteagudo explained "At no point in this process … were the assemblies able to organize themselves as an alternative to the centralized power of the government. Political forces operating within the assemblies, such as the progressive peronists and leftist political parties, made that impossible. By the time some of the trotskyist parties decided to destroy the assemblies, because they could not control them, the participation of the middle class had already declined. This occurred partly because of the brutal repression that met virtually every one of their protests, but also because many people became frustrated, having found no immediate solutions.

"Although the actions were huge, the movement did not recognize itself, nor was it conscious of its power. Although [later protests and actions] opposed the representational political system, opposed neoliberalism, and advocated for civil liberties, most of the participants were not aware of the significance of their actions. Furthermore, these people failed to recognize themselves as a powerful movement that could build an alternative" to the global economic model.[17] In Life's "political" systems this would be equivalent to the participants in an apparently defunct ecosystem failing to take into account the lay of the land, the prevailing winds and the residue of environmental toxins as they evolved their smaller-scale alternatives.

What the Argentine experiment teaches us is that while the nation-state system is in place it will be difficult for Earthological communities in nations that are, by that system's measurements, functioning not to heed or prepare to deal with it. We would do well to remember, however, that when the opportunity and necessity presented themselves, Argentineans knew what to do with it. Certainly, they are not likely to forget.

## Basque Region, Spain

In the 1940s, Basques in and around the Spanish city of Mondragón suffered regional Critical Mass caused by General Franco's political repression, economic recessions, a harsh, war-ravaged landscape and fierce competition. Under the servant leadership of activist-priest Don José María Arizmendiarrieta, hundreds and then thousands of them responded by building, and for the past six decades evolving, a "vital, successful and resilient network of more than 170 worker-owned-and-operated cooperatives serving well over 100,000 people."[18]

The Mondragón cooperatives include "a large worker-controlled bank, worker-self managed technical assistance and research-and-development organizations, a chain of department stores, high-tech firms, appliance manufacturers, foundries and machine shops." Mondragonians have built schools, hospitals, houses and community centers, "created secure and well-paid jobs, forged innovative and responsive democratic decision-making structures, and invented increasingly sophisticated forms of democratic participation, cooperation and community.

"Their aim has been the pursuit of what they call *equilibrio*. This means not just equilibrium or balance, but also harmony, poise, calmness, and composure. *Equilibrio* is a vital, [organically democratic] process that harmonizes and balances a diverse and growing community of interests: those of the individual and the co-op, the particular co-op and the co-op system, and the co-op system and the community and environment.... Ecology, conventionally defined as the relationship of living things to their environment, is understood [at Mondragón] to encompass social well-being as well as biological reality and their interaction."

In the 1990s, competition from the global economy pushed Mondragón to increase its production for export. In the early years of the

## Hard Times? Pull Together, Mondragón Style

"Here's how it played out when one of the Mondragón cooperatives fell on hard times. The worker/owners and the managers met to review their options. After three days of meetings, the worker/owners agreed that 20 percent of the workforce would leave their jobs for a year, during which they would continue to receive 80 percent of their pay and, if they wished, free training for other work. This group would be chosen by lottery, and if the company was still in trouble a year later, the first group would return to work and a second would take a year off. The result? The solution worked and the company thrives to this day."[19]

21st century, the failure of the global economy to reward that transition sufficiently is causing the Mondragón communities to reconsider that decision to try to compete on the profoundly unlevel global playing field.

## South Boston, Massachusetts

Minority residents of an impoverished, violence-riddled Boston neighborhood — 25,000 residents, 37% black, with an average per capita income of $8,600 — collectively addressed their frustration with the failure of City Hall, state and federal agencies to solve their complicated range of economic, social and racial problems for them by organizing themselves as the Dudley Street Neighborhood Initiative (DSNI).

In 1987, DSNI instituted a democratic community revitalization process with the intention of empowering "Dudley residents to organize, plan for, create and control a vibrant, high-quality and diverse neighborhood in collaboration with community partners."[20] The open and inclusive planning and deliberative process resulted in the creation of a shared vision and widespread resident participation. With funding from a variety of sources, participants in the DSNI have collaborated in the effort to transform hundreds of blocks — 177 acres — of hazardous waste sites, condemned buildings, vermin-infested, dilapidated housing, crack houses, closed business and over 300 of 1300 vacant lots into "an urban village: a diverse, economically viable, and neighborly community that combines affordable housing, shops, and a community center"

with pocket parks, urban organic farms and markets, environmental reclamation projects and community houses.

## Sweden

And finally, on a scale more akin to Gaviotas, Kangos — a village
located in the far north of Sweden in the wild open land of indigenous
reindeer herding peoples, the Sámi — has taken its future into its own
hands. It is one of 60 communities in Sweden, some with populations of
over 500,000, that have made "radical, across-the-board changes toward
the 'true north' of sustainability" and have done that by choice, hands-
on, democratically. Unlike our examples in Africa, India, Brazil and
Argentina, these communities, representing 20% of Swedish municipalities, have the government's blessing. Their equivalent of a shared brain
is an exemplary democratic national association of eco-municipalities,
SeKom.

To the extent it ever caught Juggernaut's eye — during a brief
period of iron mining and manufacturing — Kangos and its 330 or
so inhabitants have long since been forgotten by the global economy.
The consequence of Critical Mass for Kangos was literally being left
out in the cold. It's too snowy, too far away and too small for the global
economy to trouble with. Its natural beauty and seasonal festivals attract
hunters, fishers and tourists, but federal funny-money even in socialist
Sweden has a hard time traveling in any significant amount that far from
center. Young people left the community. School enrollment declined.
And word came from the top that the local school and post office would
be closed, which, as for small, isolated communities anywhere in the
world, seemed the kiss of death.

In their study of Earthological "Natural Step" community revitalization practices, community planners Sarah James and Torbjörn Lahti
described the organically democratic resuscitation of Kangos: "Inspired
by the 1992 Rio Summit, two Kangos villagers began group get-togeth-
ers that continued throughout the 1990s. Discussions focused on ways
to reduce use of resources, increase recycling, and convert to renewable
energy sources. Groups began to work cooperatively with local businesses toward these objectives and also," with other communities north
of the Arctic Circle, "toward a regional goal of greater county economic

and social self-sufficiency.... In the late 1990s these efforts blossomed into a full-scale initiative to chart a new course for the village's future."21

With guidance from sustainability visionaries and some funding from the European Union, Kangos reinvented itself. There are now over 40 locally-owned enterprises in Kangos, 60 children attend the school which the community runs and staffs and which is also a cultural center and ecological training facility. There is "a general store, daycare center, assisted living housing, a nursing home, a folklore museum, and church."

Among the community's other accomplishments have been the development of a multigenerational all-activity house; an animal husbandry program operated by both adults and children that preserves, for example, species of native endangered sheep and increases village food and fiber self-reliance; a long-term ecological fish management program; waste reduction, recycling, composting and sewage management programs and restoration of postal service through a cooperative arrangement with the national postal service. Like Gaviotas, Kangos may be in the middle of nowhere, but it has made itself a place and made a place for itself.

## Maybe We're Not SO Bad

Visitors who have spent any time at all in these organically democratic Earthological communities and others like them report with a kind of awe the joy and vitality they see in the eyes of community members. The confidence bordering on fearlessness. The ease with which they interact with and respect each other, a comradeliness that belies the endless, prickly challenge of daily negotiating, living and working constructively alongside others with whom, at the start, they may have agreed about almost nothing, often in circumstances so harsh they defy description. These most human of qualities can be observed in the very countenances of people who have practiced organically democratic relationship. As well many of them evince a pride of place that has nothing to do with ownership and everything to do with gratitude, affection and belonging. The dark presence of Critical Mass can bring the opportunity for light with it.

In affluent nations we have grown unaccustomed to believing that anyone would want to work as hard and change as much — "give up so much," is the way it's usually put — as the participants in these communities have. As for the rest, those who live in Earth's most put-upon places and have not yet discovered for themselves the opportunity Lifelike organic democracy represents, awe replaces disbelief at how very much ordinary, put-upon humans can actually do for themselves, with each other, despite the odds against it and ten thousand years of empire and of Juggernaut bearing down. They are amazed by the real possibility of achieving what 20th century social critic Scott Nearing called "ample sufficiency." Thrilled to imagine how much richer their lives would be if they too undertook to blow their horns and declare Jubilee.

For me awe results from being reminded that, yes, together, democratically, in the places where Life finds us and the circumstances in which it finds us, we can learn to honor and obey Life's rules, live within Earth's means and meet Critical Mass with a much more critical mass of our own. We still can marry our lives to the larger Life within which we live them. As they have changed themselves and their ways of being in the world and with each other, the people who have engaged in these Earthological, local miracles of self-reliance and democracy have shown us that it is still possible for us to cure the disease we've become.

At the end of his book about Gaviotas, Alan Weisman reported that as the millennium turned into the Age of Critical Mass, Gaviotans decided to sell their herd of cattle and to raise rabbits, chickens and fish instead. With an evident sense of pride in the collective wisdom of his fellow Gaviotans, Paolo Lugari told Weisman that this decision exemplified the community's recognition "that too much red meat is bad for us, that too many cow pastures are bad for the environment, and that too much *hamburgerización* is bad for the world."

## What Are the Odds and Obstacles?

Despite the thousands, perhaps millions of little Earthological miracles ordinary people are working around the world, the arguments against localization and self-reliance, downsizing and economic diversification are many. Among the most commonly offered are

• lack of money
• peak oil

- population
- the severely degraded state of many of the planet's ecosystems
- the inequitable distribution around the planet of natural resources
- our woeful ignorance about how Life works
- the lack of globally unifying, locally adaptable ecological and economical principles
- human nature itself: its often evident selfishness, mental and physical laziness, greed, herd mentality and resistance to change

As real as these obstacles are to doing what we need to do now, they pale against the alternative: not trying. We must diminish or remove several of those obstacles to manifesting Deep Green schemes and dreams and in the process begin to *become* deeply green.

CHAPTER 14

# How to Become Deeply Green

F EW OF US WHO FACE THE CHALLENGE of adopting the behaviors and creating the systems necessary for us to survive Critical Mass actually know what it was like to live without funny-money and fossil fuels. It's not surprising, therefore, that we have a hard time believing it's possible to function economically or live lives we'd consider worth living without sufficient amounts of either of them. But there is life beyond funny-money and fossil fuels. The quality of that life depends upon whether we prepare for the end of funny-money and fossil fuels or wait until they've run out.

## If Money Is a Problem, Create Your Own

Money and monetary systems as we know them are human inventions intended to serve human needs. It is funny-money, and the love of it, not money itself that runs against Life's grain. Money can just as easily

"The general picture is clear enough. A combination of peak oil, climate change, and the bursting of the mother of all economic bubbles will result in a collapse of the global economy, perhaps of civilization itself. If we are still to avert the worst of a crisis that could eventuate in untold death, destruction, and tragedy, we need to restructure the world's energy systems and money systems immediately."[1]

accurately represent Earth's accounts and the real value of natural and human goods and services as it can inaccurately represent them. Money, reconceived, can help us keep track of and appropriately value the resources on which our Earthological communities will of necessity base their economies if they are to operate in ways that are more Lifelike and sustainable. There's no money at all in Life's Economic Survival Protocol, so any kind of money and monetary systems we introduce into it need to help us honor its resource-based focus, not veer away from it. Money must help us pay attention to and be frugal with what's in Life's accounts as well as in our monetary accounts. Money can become a form of information (which is Life's currency of exchange) about the goods and services on which our lives actually depend.

One of the best ways to break the funny-money habit and facilitate the creation of resource-focused Earthlogical communities is to bring money closer to home where we and the resources are. Local and regional currencies and monetary systems can help us to do that by serving as complements or alternatives to the national currencies and monetary systems that led us astray and allowed us to induce Critical Mass without realizing it.

## The Potential of Local Currencies

"Basically," says Susan Witt, Executive Director of the E. F. Schumacher Society and the New Economics Institute in Great Barrington, Massachusetts, "we're looking to find the way in which wealth generated in the region can be kept in the region. [Many of] our local banks, which did a very good job of that in the past, have now been bought up by larger and larger holding companies. So the deposits, the earnings, of rural regions and inner cities become like the wealth generated in Third World areas: It tends to flow out into a few central, international, urban centers.

"A regional currency is ultimately the way that communities can regain independence [and foster interdependence] and begin to unplug from the federal [and global] system."[2]

Local money is not a new idea. Michael Shuman noted that "During the Great Depression," for example, "an estimated 300 communities [across the US] scraped by, using their own scrip. Philadelphia, Pennsylvania, and Wildwood, New Jersey, printed homegrown money to pay teachers and other municipal employees. The city of Tenino in Washington State put $6,500 worth of wooden tokens into circulation, and promised to buy the currency back. By the time the date for redemption arrived, tourists and collectors had pocketed most of the coins, which left Tenino with a profit."3 In the US, so long as a local currency does not pretend to replace or substitute for the national currency, printing local money is entirely legal.

Local money can minimize or even erase the wealth/poverty gap because its value is based on its movement through many hands and lives and its wide circulation in a community. It is worth nothing until it is exchanged for goods or services with someone else in the community. When hoarded it has no value whatsoever. As a money maker, local money is a failure; as a maker of economical community, it's a winner.

Many alternative currency systems are already in existence in communities around the world. They are supported by websites like openmoney that are devoted to telling interested communities how to create, use, account for and integrate local currencies.4 It's precisely these sorts of currency systems that we will depend on when the national and global systems fail us. Once upon a time, money didn't exist. The ancients invented it. We can reinvent it.

> "Economics is not really about things. It is about relationships. Money ... is a way of organizing our relationships with each other and only secondarily about things."5

LETS, founded by Canadian Michael Linton, is a premier example of a local monetary system that supports a local ecological community in its efforts to provide for itself over the long term without destroying surrounding natural communities. A LETS, or Local Exchange Trading System, facilitates a sophisticated form of barter. In essence a community does the following:

• It issues its own currency with its own name, shape and design. It may be paper bills, checks or tokens of some kind and is typically given a name that means something to the community, like the BerkShares used by communities in the Berkshire Mountains of Western Massachusetts, the Salt Spring Dollar produced on Salt Spring Island near Vancouver and the Totnes Pound, originated by Transition Town Totnes in the UK.

- It establishes a central location like a community bank, though it may be just a computer in someone's office or storefront, where exchanges of the currency for goods and services are accounted for and balanced.

Taken to its ecological conclusion, a LETS system leads to a local currency that is viewed by local businesses and members of a community as being as valuable as the prevailing national currency. Though they may be tied to the value of the dollar, LETS currencies are often based on real resources like work hours. Residents of Ithaca, New York, for example, created a currency called Ithaca HOURS in honor of the length of time members of the community invest in creating a product or delivering a service. Because the value of an alternative currency is agreed upon by the community and no more of it is created than can be supported by the resource or valuation on which it is based, it is less likely than conventional currencies to inflate or deflate in value. Its value can be set at a level that allows locally produced goods and services to be affordable for locals.

Limits, also agreed upon by the community, are set on how much debt a LETS participant can accrue. Experience suggests that those limits are rarely exceeded. The members of a community know each other so well and their lives are so bound up in each others' successes and in the success of the community as a whole that they are disinclined to put their reputations on the line or their local economy at risk.

Adjustable local and regional currency valuing has the effect of undermining the advantage currently held by big-box purveyors of cheap imported goods and returning that advantage to local producers and merchants. Paul Glover, a community organizer, Temple University professor and creator of Ithaca's HOURS, highlighted the benefits of a metacurrency like HOURS to a local community. "We printed our own money because we watched federal dollars come to town, shake a few hands, then leave to buy rainforest lumber and fight wars. Ithaca's HOURS, by contrast, stay in our region to help us hire each other. While dollars make us increasingly dependent on multinational corporations and bankers, HOURS reinforce community trading and expand commerce that is more accountable to our concerns for ecology and social justice."[6]

Typically members of a community with an alternative currency choose to support it because it supports them. Using the local currency enriches a community's sense of pride in itself as well as its competence, confidence and actual prosperity. Susan Witt, one of the originators of BerkShares, has written that "small, slow exchanges [of local currencies] are balancing the abstract tendency of [funny] money by reconnecting financial transactions with the people, culture, and landscape of a particular place, while at the same time building the community wealth which is the foundation for a newly imagined economic system ... and a sustainable future."[7]

*Future Wealth* author James Robertson described "the monetary and financial system as a worldwide network of cash flows connecting people and organizations of all kinds." He has suggested that we conceive of a "multi-level structure of currencies — a world currency for use in international trading, national currencies for use in national trading, and local currencies for use in local trading, together with regional or continental currencies like the ecu (European currency unit) for use in

### Cash Flows

Alternative currency systems imagine that money works like water works in an ecosystem, that it's truly a "liquid" asset. Water vapor evaporates from bodies of water like lakes and oceans, is borne by wind over land where forest canopies and grasslands collect it in their leaves and distribute it slowly groundward. It falls as precipitation that either freezes and is withheld and distributed later or soaks into the ground where it recharges root systems, aquifers and groundwater. It also flows in streams and rivers and into wetlands and marshes and back into the lakes and oceans. Water, in other words, comes in a variety of forms at a number of scales from infinitesimal droplets to the wide Atlantic and Greenland ice cap. And it circulates through multiple levels of living systems from the smallest to the largest, accomplishing miracles of life giving at every level. Money can do the same thing.

regional or continental trading" — for as long as the latter continues to be viable.[8]

UK economist Richard Douthwaite suggested that "options run from group currencies such as LETS, through Swiss-style mutual credit systems for businesses and commodity-backed currencies, as in Exeter, New Hampshire, to money issued by local government like that in [the Isle of] Guernsey."[9] Transition Towns founder Rob Hopkins agrees with this staging of currencies for different purposes. "Relocalization is only possible with both a national currency and a local currency," for there will be trade among nations so long as there are nations. "But we will be increasingly moving toward a situation where more of our core needs are locally sourced rather than imported," and the transition from imports to local self-reliance can best be facilitated by the creation of local currencies to complement national currencies and international currency exchanges.[10]

Some local and regional currencies may be virtual, like the currencies that online gamers create to allow players to buy supplies for their avatars. After all, money is essentially information about the value of things and about who is "in possession" of that value. New forms of community money, like the funny-money they complement or replace, aim to more accurately track the value of things and share that value while giving consideration to the health and longevity of the human and natural communities in which they circulate. They may be exchanged in all the forms and on all the platforms in which information is exchanged.

The bottom line is that we need not be deterred by our present and perhaps permanent lack of sufficient conventional forms of money and their funny-money correlates from creating viable, locally self-reliant Earthological communities and circulating goods and services within and among them as living systems circulate water, information and air. We should be encouraged by the inequitable distribution, decreasing value and increasing scarcity of funny-money to seek alternatives over which we have control and that deliver to more of us more kinds of "bang for the buck." If governments can print money that's backed by nothing, surely as creator-participants in Earthological communities we can create money and monetary systems that are backed by our own efforts, actual human and natural resources, and Life.

## Addicted to Oil? Power Down ... Way Down

Alternative currencies and monetary systems and local money can help us get beyond funny-money. Can alternative energies get us beyond oil and other fossil fuels before we shoot past peak or they tilt the climate out of its tolerable range?

Maybe not beyond them, but at least ahead of them.

This can't be acknowledged too often: There will be no perfect solution to the peak oil problem, nor any other fuel or source of energy that did all that fossil fuels have done for us on the scale or in the way in which they've done it. Energy descent — a decline in the amount and kinds of energy we use — is a given. That being said, we need to come up with reasonably viable, life-sustaining (as opposed to global-economy-sustaining) solutions to the end of oil that prevent the descent from being a crash landing. Presuming changes in the scale and nature of our economic and provisional activities, we can.

Numerous national, international and supranational (transcending established national boundaries) plans for reducing oil dependency — because of the threat of peak oil or for the climate's sake or both — sit on desks and conference tables around the world. Many, if not most, are the equivalent of popcorn or white bread given to an AIDS patient with wasting disease. There is a strategy, however, that offers a stronger medicine. The Oil Depletion Protocol is intended to coordinate an international effort to reduce oil use fast enough that we can minimize climate instability and preserve remaining reserves longer into the future, but slowly enough so that reductions would be gradual, fair and predictable.[11] In particular, the Oil Depletion Protocol as described by Richard Heinberg would tie reductions in oil production and importation to the rate at which world reserves of oil are currently being depleted, about 3% per year. The protocol, explained in Heinberg's book and available online, is easy to understand and fair in its methods of enforcement. Under the terms of the protocol, "Nations, municipalities and businesses would be able to plan their economic futures with minimal concern for dramatic price variations."[12]

There's one potential weakness in the Oil Depletion Protocol, the same weakness that haunts all relatively ideal, large-scale solutions intended to address symptoms of Critical Mass. Like the Kyoto Protocol, which is intended to curb greenhouse gas emissions, the Oil Depletion Protocol will only be really effective if a critical mass of nations signs on to it and the signatories are able to hold each other's feet to the fire. Given the current focus on propping up the fossil-fueled global economy and the dependence of both oil-exporting and oil-importing economies on the continued flow of oil and oil price manipulations, it's difficult to imagine a consensus or concerted effort gathering around curtailing its retrieval and use. And the hard truth, as Heinberg himself recognizes, is that any method of weaning us from our addiction to oil will ultimately require every community, whether it's an Earthological community or not, to figure out how to wean its own economy from oil, and every member of every community must figure out how to do with less of it.

This reality gets us back to simplicity, restraint and downtimes, key Earthonomic practices of deeply green communities.

## Practicing Subtraction

In the decades since the end of World War II, the oil driven, fossil-fueled global economy has taken over functions that human and natural communities once fulfilled, to a great extent, for themselves. Because none of us alive now has lived in a world without oil, it's difficult for us to imagine what our lives would be like if it stopped fulfilling those functions or fulfilled them only occasionally.[13] So before we plan ways of systematically and individually cutting back and cutting out our use of oil and other fossil fuels, we need to get an up-close-and-personal sense of what peak everything fossil-fuel-wise would mean for our lives.

"At peak and just beyond, there is a massive potential for system failures of all kinds, social, economic, and political. Peak is quite literally a tipping point. Beyond peak, all bets are off about civilization's future."[14]

Passing peak to the point where we cannot pretend any longer that we haven't passed it will change everyone's lives dramatically, but it will change lives in prosperous nations more dramatically than it will change lives in parts of the world where Critical Mass has been a defining feature of life for decades and the benefits of cheap/easy oil, coal and gas have been mixed or limited. Why?

The world's less prosperous peoples are practiced in the arts of *subtraction* whereas those of us born since World War II in booming economies have grown up in decades of addition. Whatever our economic station, there has always been something else — some new or supposedly improved material good or service — that we could add to what we already had. Or that we could at least hope to add. In difficult economic times, there has always been something we could keep, which — given the subtractions many face in this bleak economic time — would feel, if not like addition, at least not like subtraction. And with very few exceptions, all of those things we've added and kept, whether they have been necessary or discretionary, have involved the use of oil or one of its kin or derivatives. How?

1) One or more of the variants of refined/processed oil are additives — ingredients, feedstock — in their manufacture, as is the case for plastics, synthetics, fertilizers and pharmaceuticals.

2) The manufacture, transportation and distribution of nearly everything we have requires the burning of gasoline, diesel, natural gas or coal — or the burning of oil or its derivatives or fossil-fuel substitutes to produce electricity.

3) Everything is conveyed to us by forms of transportation or infrastructure (electric utilities, for example) that are fueled by oil, gasoline, diesel, natural gas or coal.

Or, in the trifecta gamble that constitutes the ABCs of peak oil, getting the things we have added or kept has involved all three.

Passing peak oil without preparing for it will mean subtracting most of what we have added to our lives over the past century in the way of goods, services, conveniences and expectations. The following exercise is intended to help us learn subtraction, to imagine having a peak oil experience before we actually have one. Then critical masses of us may appreciate how important it is to avoid having a peak oil experience and to conserve fossil fuels for future vital purposes and use remaining fossil fuels to make the conversion to other forms of energy that will support Earthological communities sustainably.

At the level of the community and networks of communities, as well as at the national and international levels within which communities

# The ABCs of Peak Oil: An Exercise

What follows is a short exercise in subtraction. You may engage in it mentally or on paper, alone or with family, friends and colleagues.

Over the next several days, pay special attention to the objects around you in your kitchen, pantry, cupboards, garage, bathroom, closets and other rooms in the place you live in; in shops and stores; in your workplaces and places of entertainment; on the street and in your neighborhood and yard. Your first task is to mentally subtract from what you see and use everything that is

- made of or contains plastic

Then, in subsequent exercises, in the following order over a period of several days, mentally subtract everything that is

- packaged in plastic
- made of synthetics like nylon, rayon, acrylics, silicone, vinyl, or any of the "polys" like polyester, polypropylene and polyethylene
- contains oil- or coal-based feedstock — like solvents, paints, glues, building materials, insulation, lubricants, cleaners, medicines and cosmetics
- required oil, natural gas or coal for its manufacture
- comes from or originally came from more than 250 miles away
- runs on oil, gasoline, diesel, natural gas or coal

And, finally, subtract everything that

- requires electricity, including computers and the electro-gluttonous digital communications systems

As you pay attention to these things, you will doubtless discover that in nearly every category from food, clothing and furnishings to electronics, tools, appliances, transportation and electricity, most customary goods and services depend to some degree at some point on the availability of cheap/easy fossil fuels. ☞

In the worst case peak-everything scenario, everything in your list of subtractions would be subtracted from your life and world because it is not possible for a post-peak economy, or for locally self-reliant communities, in a period of Critical Mass to produce it. That world will not in any way resemble the one you live in now.

will still be operating for a time, curtailment, conservation and increased efficiency in the use of energy — getting more per buck and barrel of oil — will actually bring higher returns than spending oil and funny-money to suck and dredge the last gallons of expensive oil out of the Earth. And in a period in which conventional forms of financial support and buckets full of funny-money are in short supply, it may be that curtailment, conservation and increased efficiency — which, after all, add up to reduced need — are the energy/climate solutions in which we can still afford to engage at the local and regional level.

"Relying on widely agreed-upon figures, [Swiss] scientists estimated that two-thirds of all the primary energy consumed in the world today is wasted, mostly in the form of [cast-off] heat that nobody wants or uses.... This same paper concluded that, with currently available technologies, buildings could be made eighty percent more efficient, cars fifty percent more efficient, and motors twenty-five percent more efficient."[15]

Conservation and efficiency also make the alternatives to fossil fuels more viable. If buildings, businesses, food production, manufacturing and transportation can operate more efficiently, requiring less energy input, then alternative sources of energy have less slack to pick up. Conversely, they may be able to pick up the slack on goods and services that are basic and vital to our survival and well-being that do require the use of fossil fuels.

Some post-carbon strategists propose that the US, were it so inclined, could conserve its way out of dependence on foreign oil in a couple of decades.[16] Regional coalitions of communities (being able to adapt and change faster than larger, lumbering, cumbersome geopolitical entities like whole nations) might not need that long. Less prosperous nations and communities in those nations, having never had the luxury of using oil so extravagantly, could avoid arriving in the oil economy when it is most expensive and then having to figure out how to quit it again almost immediately. Statistics suggest that existing businesses and corporations could reduce their energy costs by as much as four times the cost of implementing the reduction. This is good news for locally focused manufacturers, corporations and businesses. It also suggests that new businesses in communities around the world could open and operate less expensively. More of them would be economically viable if they opened with Earthologic and energy efficiency in mind.

There is persuasive evidence that efficiency, conservation and the curtailing of our use of oil community by community could bring economic as well as Earthonomic benefits in a matter of a few years, in part because so much energy is currently wasted. Frances Moore Lappé reported, for example, that "Fifty-five percent of all energy in the US economy is wasted, according to the Lawrence Livermore National Laboratory. Other experts say it's even worse — with 87 percent wasted. These findings are less surprising if one considers that about two-thirds of energy entering most of the world's power plants — as coal or oil, for example — is released as waste heat."[17]

Billions of dollars, yen, yuan, pounds, pesos and euros can be saved — and a peso or pound saved is the equivalent of a peso or pound earned — and energy savings of 40% to 70% can be achieved "simply" by using energy more intelligently, carefully and not letting it literally go to waste.

## Acts of Efficiency, Conservation and Curtailment

An Earthological community's reduce/replace oil weaning process begins and ends with making and consuming less of everything. Or, as the logo for the Post-Carbon Institute frames it, "reduce consumption; produce locally." Toward this end, Earthological communities can:

• Retrofit existing structures and require new ones to use less heating, cooling and electric lighting.

- Stagger the hours of peak energy use and build downtimes — economic holidays — into manufacturing and retail systems.
- Turn off lights in empty buildings at night and reduce heating and cooling as feasible.
- Design and redesign local manufacturing systems so that heat is recycled through the system, for example, by a process called co-generation.
- Install compact fluorescent light bulbs in every fixture,[18] on-demand hot water systems, thermostat timers and timed off switches in continuous-drain electronics like TVs, DVDs, computers and printers.
- Persuade local appliance dealers to offer incentives to trade energy guzzling appliances for energy savers (while new appliances are still available) and reasonable fees for upgrading appliances that can be retroactively made more efficient.
- Legislate per person kilowatt caps, install indoor kilowatt meters and mandate that electric utilities do energy audits of consumers' buildings and (to the extent feasible) help pay for or otherwise facilitate retrofits. When most people "see" the energy they're consuming and mentally translate that into what it's costing them, they conserve energy voluntarily.
- Encourage a reduction in the number of automobiles in use by offering incentives for carpooling, shared car ownership and coordinated hitchhiking.
- limit ownership to one petroleum-powered car per household.
- Make driving and parking in the community less comfortable and convenient than using other forms of transportation.
- Encourage the transition to light weight, hybrid or electric vehicles.
- Ration or put ceilings on personal fossil fuel consumption, and tax those who exceed them.
- Upgrade electricity grids and retrofit them to receive inputs of energy from local producers of electricity.
- Hyper-tax gasoline-guzzling vehicles and McMansions (huge single-family homes) that are not super energy-efficient.
- Develop widely available, energy efficient and alternatively-fueled local and regional public transportation systems.

- Reduce the distances between homes, workplaces and shops by changing zoning regulations so that workplaces, clean factories, retail outlets,
  residences (both old and new), entertainment venues and restaurants,
  for example, can cluster in neighborhoods and communities (as they
  do in many cities) rather than sprawling between them.

"As Amory Lovins, one of the
world's most outspoken efficiency advocates, likes to point
out, 'just a 2.7 miles-per-gallon
gain in the fuel economy of
this country's light-vehicle [car]
fleet could displace Persian
Gulf imports entirely.'"[19]

Does doing any of these things at the
individual and community level make any
difference? *Plan C's* Pat Murphy thinks it
does. He proposed that just as we can now
learn our carbon and ecological footprints,
we can also now figure out the *barrels of oil
equivalent* (BOE) of the activities we engage
in and the goods and services we purchase.
We might think of BOE as being pronounced
like "boy," as in "Oh, boy, I just saved a lot of
oil and money." Getting a bead on our BOE
allows us to know how much of which kind of activities we should curtail
in order to help our communities become energy wise. We might take
knowing our BOE as seriously as we take knowing our blood type or
blood pressure.

Murphy's book offered some very discouraging statistics about the
ways in which humanity's food and transportation systems use and
waste oil energy. But his conclusion, at least in regard to the biggest oil
consuming economy, the US, was hopeful:

> Of the 57.8 BOE consumed per person [per year] in the
> US, the usages that are under our personal control take
> about 39 BOE — 10 BOE for food, 13.5 BOE for cars and
> 15.4 BOE for homes. This is about 67 percent of total per
> capita US energy consumption.[20]

As an indication that reducing this per capita BOE is feasible, the
per capita BOE in Germany and Japan is just over 30 and in the United
Kingdom just over 28. What we do as individuals does make a difference. But what we can do together as Earthological communities makes
a bigger difference.

Does efficiency, such as we're proposing now, lead to lower consumption of a fuel? That would, after all, be one of the primary reasons, along with saving money and maybe the climate, for increasing efficiency in our use of fossil fuel energies.

## The Jevons Paradox: A Warning against Great Expectations

Back around the end of the US Civil War, economist Stanley Jevons was trying to learn if the increased efficiency of steam engines, which caused them to use less coal, was resulting in actual reduced use of coal.

Jevons' conclusion was unexpected and discouraging. "It is a confusion of ideas," he wrote in 1865 in *The Coal Question*, "to suppose that economical use of a fuel is equivalent to reduced consumption."[21] Over a century later economists Daniel Khazoom and Leonard Brookes came to the same conclusion. The later-named Khazoom-Brookes Postulate states that "increased efficiency paradoxically leads to increased overall energy consumption."[22]

Architect and Earth alchemist Jeff Dardozzi explained "When you save money through improvements in efficiencies, such as with gas mileage or heating costs, invariably that savings has two effects. First, it decreases demand for an energy resource, which decreases the price of the resource. This then reveals a new layer of demand that, in turn, increases consumption of that resource. Such behavior can be found almost anywhere in the economy. In analyzing homes over the last 50 years we see efficiency in their energy use improved dramatically but the square footage more than doubled and the number of occupants more than halved." In other words, bigger houses with fewer people living in them equates to more per capita and overall consumption of energy, rather than less.

"The second effect resulting from efficiency improvements is that when you save money you usually spend it somewhere else," in the same viral global economic system of production, "and that translates into increased energy and resource consumption." You end up still supporting the system you were endeavoring to disempower and detach from.[23]

Bringing us full circle to simplicity, frugality, restraint and downtimes as keys to sustainability, Herman Daly wrote "Efficiency first doesn't give frugality second; it makes frugality less necessary. But if we seek frugality first we get efficiency second as an adaptation to scarcity."[24]

## Running Out of Oil? Power Up

To a limited extent we can overcome oil dependence and the problems associated with running out of cheap/easy oil by powering up on local and regional forms of inexhaustible energy. Communities and regions can produce some of their own energy and will need to very soon.

"Imagine," wrote Bill McKibben, "all the south facing roofs in your suburb sporting solar panels. Imagine a building code that requires all new construction to come with solar roof tiles and solar shutters. Imagine [small] windmills scattered around town in the gustier spots and heat pumps for extracting energy from the earth. Imagine all these pieces linked in a local grid, supplemented with small scale fuel-burning power plants that produce not just electricity but heat that can be pumped back out to local buildings."[25] Imagine that we use what funny-money and petroleum we still have to accomplish this transition. (Admittedly, without a generous flow of funny-money we will not be able to manifest this vision. No region possesses all the raw or recyclable materials that would be necessary to create a user-friendly energy system of this sort from scratch.)

Since funny-money for such projects is and may continue to be in short supply and unevenly distributed, energy descent, or "powering down," would also entail using more human and possibly animal energy than we're doing and, in general, less fuel-dependent energy of all kinds. A shift to small scale wind and solar energy would reduce dependence on firewood and charcoal as well as on oil and natural gas, which would allow forest restoration and would reduce pollution and greenhouse gas emissions. And if we are doing more of the work that oil and other fossil fuels have been doing, some

"Increasing awareness of global warming from burning fossil fuels coupled with decreasing renewable energy [RE] costs have contributed to the strong growth in the use of renewable energy. It will take a more explosive growth rate, similar to the recent exponential growth in Internet use, to radically reduce our dependence on fossil fuels and shift towards true sustainability."[26]

of the money that currently goes into the pockets of the purveyors of fossil-fueled energies would go into workers' pockets instead.

But reality requires me to repeat that, as George Monbiot, Pat Murphy and Richard Heinberg discovered in the process of writing *Heat, Plan C* and *The End of Growth*, no combination of energy alternatives is ever going to allow us to do all that we do now on the scale or with the ease that we do it. Or rather, on a scale and with the ease with which fossil fuels have been doing it for us. Powering down, curtailing, efficiency, subtracting, downsizing, doing more with less and conservation: these are still the most practical solutions to the energy dilemma. But some aspects of them will remain beyond local control and will not get done before the cheap oil, coal and gas run out. Rationing and restrictions, curbs and limits of some kind will be set by the world's leaders and will become routine; communities will have to adapt their economies and activities accordingly.

The leaders and Powers of most developed nations are not likely to require their people or businesses to cut back far enough. Leaders of presently-prosperous nations will not happily give up their American-style economies, particularly when those economies are already under duress. Nations that have recently become successful economically (like China, India and Brazil) and nations that are intractably impoverished will not willingly forego the dream of having American-style economies. Any significant changes in the kinds of energy we rely upon, where that energy comes from and how much we use will, by choice or default, occur locally and regionally at the level of the community and coalitions and networks of communities.

## Design. Period.

Clearly the conception, creation and maintenance of sustainable, Lifelike ecological communities will not happen by default but by design. "Design thinking can transform society," wrote *Business Week* columnist Bruce Nussbaum. As members of Earthological communities we will all be designers of our common future, though some of us may be more gifted at design or have more training than others. Professional designers, Nussbaum suggested, will design with the rest of us rather than only *for us*.

"Good design depends on a free and harmonious relationship to nature and people, in which careful observation and thoughtful interaction provide the design inspiration, repertoire and patterns. It is not something that is generated in isolation, but through continuous and reciprocal interaction with the subject," Life itself.

"Permaculture uses these conditions to consciously design our energy descent pathway."[27]

"Eco-restorative design makes use of buildings and their environs to help replenish Earth's ecosystems. Eco-restorative design integrates the language, methods and concepts of ecology with buildings, thus empowering designers to create humane architecture that rejuvenates the natural living systems of a building site and its environs."[28]

And among the things we will want them to design with us will be conceptual tools and templates that critical masses of us can use to do our own Earthological designing. "With more and more tools," Nussbaum explained, "we, the masses, want to design anything that touches us on the journey, the big journey through life. People want to participate in the design of their lives. They insist on being part of the conversation. Design democracy is the wave of the future."[29]

Paola Antonelli, curator of Architecture and Design at the Museum of Modern Art in New York calls this effort *organic design*. "Organic design," she wrote, "has had many connotations in history, but in most contemporary meaning it encompasses not only the enthusiastic exploration of natural forms and structures but also interpretations of nature's economical frameworks and systems."[30]

Green, eco-, permaculture, organic, restorative — whatever we call it, whatever compilation of techniques we choose — the creation of a sustainable future will be a design project. And organically democratic, sustainable communities and economies will be among its most significant creations.

But we will only succeed in these things if we and our communities, each in itself and all at the same time, share a common goal and follow common guidelines. To that end, we need a unifying human version, an expansion, of Life's prime directive: Live within Earth's means.

## When in Doubt, Remember the Earthological Prime Directive

Life values difference, diversity and uniqueness. Life as we know it has ruled that the economies of natural communities will be at least as different and unique as the species that create and manage them, the places they're located and the resources they're based on. But Life's prime directive is universal. "Live within Earth's means" applies everywhere. That means that it applies to us everywhere too. In a perfect world all of our diverse communities, or at least a critical mass of them, would at some point in time be living within Earth's means according to Life's Rules.

So, since it's not written in our blood and bones, we need the equivalent of a single commandment or law to:

1. Guide the mental transition from "live as far beyond your means as you can for as long as you can" to "live within Earth's means *where you are*."
2. Integrate our efforts in diverse places and conditions to do that.

We need a statement of principle that's pithy and universally applicable but not so pithy or universalized that it leaves too much room for interpretation.

There are many manifestos, charters, guidelines and sets of principles that fill in the details, but for the most part they too must be amended to lend themselves to Life's prime directive.[31]

## The Land Ethic as Guide

Back in the 1940s, US naturalist Aldo Leopold came up with a prime directive that he hoped would meet this need and, more specifically, would help his colleagues make good decisions as they entered what was then the new discipline and profession of ecology. Here's what he proposed in his essay "The Land Ethic":

> A thing is right when it tends to preserve the integrity, stability, and beauty of the biotic community. It is wrong when it tends otherwise.[32]

Simple, pithy and eloquent, Leopold's Land Ethic has inspired several generations of ecologists and environmentalists and, along with *A*

"Leopold's land ethic, or its equivalent, can be a Magna Charta for the land, freeing humanity to seek communities where the dream of sustainability can bond people to the land and to each other in a new way. We make no claim that this will come easily."[33]

*Sand County Almanac*, the book in which it first appeared, it has become a classic and staple of environmental literature. Leopold referred to "the biotic community"(the natural community) because it was clear those communities were increasingly at the mercy of human communities. He wanted, by giving humans an overarching ethic to live by, to abolish the disconnect in our thinking between human communities and natural communities. He wanted us to see that we are all members of the one largest community: Life.

"These two communities, the natural and human," wrote Wendell Berry, "support each other; each is the other's hope of a durable and livable life."[34] Leopold's "one community" idea was new and radical in the 1940s. For some of us it still is. Even the structure of our language makes it difficult for us to see human and natural communities as one community. That divisive "and" gets in between them. But this is an idea we have to get our heads around if we want to effectively treat Critical Mass. It has been us against or instead of them for too long. We need to consider us as part of "them." Earthological conscience must embrace both. *Consilience*, the coming together and reconciling of all forms of knowledge and all ways of knowing that biologist E. O. Wilson sought, happens when both the world and we are seen to be subject to "the same small number of natural laws:" Life's rules. "To the extent we banish the rest of life" from our consciousness and conscience, "we will impoverish our own species for all time."[35] Wilson recognized that with Life we don't get do-overs.

In the interim between Leopold's crafting of his poignant prime directive and our needing one to guide our efforts to survive Critical Mass, two of his terms — "stability" and "beauty" — have become less effective than they initially were at communicating his intent. Conventional conservation theory hadn't gotten around to complex, interdependent systems back in the 1940s.

"Quite clearly, natural systems are not geared toward change but towards the avoidance of change. Change occurs, not because it is desirable per se, but because in certain
conditions, it is judged to be necessary, as a means of preventing predictably larger and
more disruptive changes."[36]

## Stability

Ecologists and complex systems analysts have discovered since Leopold's
death in 1948 that living systems are not exactly steady state systems
and, though they aim for it, are rarely what we would consider to be
stable for very long. We tend to equate stability with stasis, to think of it
as a state that can be achieved once and for all after which nothing much
changes. At the level of the whole Earth — if you look at Life from the
outside — there's the appearance of stability over long stretches of time.
But looked at from the inside, at the level of ecosystems, species and
bodies, everything is always changing. The genius of living systems —
successful natural communities among them — is that they are always
adapting to what's going on in and around them, always in the process
of trying to achieve stability but never quite fully succeeding. It's that
dance of chaos with order that Dee Hock synthesized as chaordic. This
unending if unrequited pursuit of stability is thwarted at every turn by
the viral economy. Its chief impact on living systems is precisely constant
destabilization.

The ideal of stability has yielded somewhat in recent decades to the
ideals of *sustainability* and *resilience*. We've learned that what successful
natural communities have in common is not the achievement of some
ideal state of completion and permanence. What they have in common
is their ability to organize, reorganize when necessary, and regulate and
provide for themselves in ways that:

1. Do not destroy their environments or seriously destabilize the ecosystems of which they are a part — that's sustainability.
2. Allow them to recover when systemic changes and destabilization
   occur anyway — that's resilience.

## Beauty

Beauty is said to be in the eye of the beholder. Most of our eyes most of the time now behold things we humans have made. There are few if any coherent, let alone beautiful, natural communities in the world's cities, sprawling industrial parks and suburbs. "Beautiful" is as often applied now to things that destroy or replace natural communities as it is to anything that might generally be thought of as lovely in nature. An architecturally brilliant residential development that replaces a 100-acre wood and relocates or buries the streams that ran through it may be thought more beautiful than the woods and streams were. A technologically and architecturally brilliant dam that drowns millions of acres of land and all the natural communities on them, along with hundreds of human communities, may be said to be beautiful. And too, to be fair, most of us do not have Aldo Leopold's eye. There is much in nature that is necessary and Earthological but is not, to the average modern human eye, beautiful. Plague and placentas, slugs and swamps, disease and decomposition come to mind.

Half a century after Leopold conceived his version of an ecological prime directive, biological sciences writer Janine Benyus, who like Leopold "regarded organisms and natural systems as the ultimate teachers," hit on "'biomimicry,' the conscious emulation of Life's genius, doing it nature's way."[37] Biomimicry is the ultimate in organic design, deep Deep Green. To the Land Ethic's focus on Life appreciation and preservation she added Lifelikeness and gave us reason to adapt the ethic to read, perhaps, something like this:

### The Land Ethic, 2.0

A thing or activity is right when it works in ways that are Lifelike in order to preserve the integrity, adaptability, sustainability and resilience of the natural communities within which humans dwell. It is wrong when it does not.

This tentative revision of Leopold's classic will in its turn be revised, improved upon and doubtless rendered more eloquent. It is intended only to offer a starting point for thought. But as imperfect and incomplete as it is, if critical masses of us were to live as it directs, we'd live

"For the human necessity is not just to know but also to cherish and protect the things that are known, and to know the things that can be known only by cherishing. If we are to protect the world's multitude of places and creatures, then we must know them not just conceptually but imaginatively as well. They must be pictured in the mind and memory; they must be known with affection, 'by heart,' so that in seeing or remembering them the heart may be said to 'sing,' to make a music peculiar to its recognition of each particular place or creature that it knows well."[38]

within Earth's means. To fulfill its "Lifelike" qualification we'd have to do what Life does in the ways Life does.

## Deep Ecology and Eco-Spirituality

It has been a very long time since most humans were embedded in their natural communities and ecosystems. While a widely accepted directive like the Land Ethic can help to coordinate our efforts from community to community, it's a cognitive tool, useful for people who are persuaded by reason to behave in new ways. For those who are guided more by their own experience than by others', it's necessary to actually feel a connection with the other-than-human species and communities on which they depend. Most of us tend to take better care of and pay more attention to what we love than to what we only think about.

"If the Earth is no more than a bunch of wildlife programs we see on TV we'll never feel the kind of connection that motivates change," wrote English permaculture teacher Patrick Whitefield. "Only a relationship with an actual place can start to make that connection real, and understanding how our local landscape works is an important part of the relationship."[39]

But as Bill McKibben reminded us two decades ago in *The End of Nature*, there are so few places left where there is enough left of natural communities — of Nature unaffected by us — that it is difficult for most of us now to either learn about or feel for Life itself. Such natural communities as remain are often inhabited primarily by the sorts of opportunistic, invasive and hardy creatures that can survive almost any cataclysm, including the one we're causing. They are aggressive and headlong, more like us than they are like the kinds of healthy, diverse, democratic, mutually supportive natural communities and ecosystems from which we need to take our lessons.

> "As its name implies, ecopsychology (or ecological psychology) neatly explodes the age-old divide between mind and matter, between the psyche 'in here' and nature 'out there.' Ecopsychology suggests that the psyche cannot really be understood as a distinct dimension isolated from the sensuous world that materially enfolds us. . ."[40]

Allowing and encouraging the return of other species to our communities and restoring or healing natural systems that we have built over is a start on the path to rediscovering a feeling for the other-than-human. And the lifeways of remaining indigenous peoples and sources of information about now-lost indigenous traditions and economies offer a glimpse into models of embeddedness which we can adopt and adapt.

The principles and practices of Deep Ecology and Eco- or Environmental Spirituality complement the Land Ethic by offering us ways to feel deeply for and with the other-than-human beings with which we share our planet.

### Deep Ecology

Deep Ecology is a philosophy or worldview that considers humans in relationship to Life rather than apart from Life. "There is a basic intuition in deep ecology," wrote its founder Arne Naess, "that we have no right to destroy other living things without sufficient reason. Another norm is that, with maturity, humans will experience joy and sorrow when other life forms experience joy and sorrow. Not only will we feel sad when our brother or a dog or a cat feels sad, but we will grieve when living beings, including landscapes, are destroyed.

"The essence of deep ecology is to ask deeper questions. The adjective 'deep' stresses that we ask why and how, where others do not. For instance, ecology as a science does not ask what kind of a society would be best for maintaining a particular ecosystem—that is considered a question for value theory, for politics and economics, for ethics. As long as ecologists keep narrowly to their science, they do not ask such questions."[41]

Deep Ecology brings ecology (the study of our relationships with the wild worlds around us) together with psychology and philosophy (the studies of our relationships with our inner mental and shared moral and ethical worlds). The Land Ethic is a perfect example of a tenet of what its practitioners call ecopsychology.

The Deep Ecology movement with support groups and practitioners scattered around the world, uses philosophy, psychology, poetry, art, dance, film, journaling, photography, rituals, storytelling and natural history to immerse individuals and communities in Deep Green ways of thinking and being in the same way that shared sacred rituals, rites and seasonal routines immerse indigenous, or native, communities in place and in Life. Deep Ecology changes minds by touching hearts.

## *Eco-Spirituality*

Visionaries and Earth sages in every great spiritual and religious tradition are also striving to change our hearts by opening them to the sacredness of the manifest world, the world of things and beings we have not made and cannot make. Poet Mary Oliver calls Life "the other book of God." Christians call it "the Creation." Members of every kind of faith community have become environmental activists and educators in order to participate in preserving and serving the natural world which they perceive to be not only whole but also holy.

Practitioners of Environmental Spirituality teach awe, love, reverence and respect. In fact, the word "atonement," which is generally understood to mean making reparations for some harm that one has done and getting one's self right — again — with the source of one's life, evolved out of "at-one-ment," which means becoming again as one with that source of both one's own life and all of Life. Eco-spiritual principles and practices, many of which overlap with or complement Deep Ecological principles and practices, can help us to atone for the harm we've done to the natural communities and the immune system they comprise.

## Acknowledging the Rights of Other-Than-Human Beings

Taken to its logical conclusion the Land Ethic, in both versions, suggests that the other-than-human species that reside in, participate in and contribute to Life in the places where we live too are, in effect, residents of our communities and we are residents of theirs. But since they can't speak for themselves, they've been as easy to leave out of our consideration and to steal from as future generations of humans have been. Bringing other-than-human species into our consideration and erasing the legal distinctions between members of human and natural communities has been the purpose of a growing international movement to reform legal systems. Leaders in this movement advocate for *Wild Law* — a term coined by South African lawyer Cormac Cullinan in his book of that name — and *Earth Jurisprudence*, a concept introduced by Thomas Berry and developed at Centers for Earth Jurisprudence in London, England and in Florida.

"Trees have tree rights," Berry wrote, famously challenging our sense of superiority over other living things. "Insects have insect rights, mountains have mountain rights." On a finite and full planet, of necessity "All rights are limited and relative. So, too, with humans. We have human rights. We have rights to the nourishment and shelter we need. We have rights to habitat. But we have no rights to deprive other species of their proper habitat. We have no rights to interfere with their migration routes. We have no rights to disturb the basic functioning of the [living] systems of the planet. We cannot own Earth or any part of the Earth in any absolute manner. We [should] own property in accord with the well-being of the property and for the benefit of the larger life community as well as ourselves."[42] And while Berry, who died at 94 in June 2009, would have said that these are sacred truths to be held self-evident, they are also simply Earthological. As individuals we are impermanent. But most of us would like Life as we know it to be as permanent as it can be.

Growing out of this radically inclusive sense of community and of Earth as a commonwealth, Earth Jurisprudence refers to "the philosophy of law and human governance that is based on

"The distinctive features of Earth Jurisprudence are that it looks at law from the standpoint of the health of ecosystems and the role humans play as integral, interdependent members of a single, comprehensive Earth community. Earth Jurisprudence focuses on how legal norms may be established and disputes may be settled involving human-Earth relations."[43]

the belief that human societies should regulate themselves as members of the wider Earth community. This would require the development of laws and policies that ensure that people act in a way that is consistent with the fundamental 'laws' or principles of Nature that govern how the universe functions.... Earth Jurisprudence requires the expansion of our understanding of governance and democracy to embrace the whole Earth Community and not just humans."[44] Since our behavior is typically reined in and restrained only by the law and those who execute it, it may be that the only way we can be made to stop abusing other-than-human species and natural communities is if they are given rights and protections under human law that are equivalent to human rights.

## Earthological Citizenship: Granting Humans Rights

Other-than-human beings are not the only living things our top-down, money-based socio-political systems have written off the books. Nations customarily deny certain rights and benefits to those who are not, by conventional definition, citizens.

The conventional understanding of *citizenship* is that it belongs to us by birth or naturalization and by the fact that we have residence in and pay taxes to particular geopolitical entities like cities, states or nations. Citizenship carries with it the right to vote and privileges like police protection and access to health care and other public goods and services. Many enlightened nations have generously extended protection and services, without the other rights of citizenship, to such a large number of immigrants and their native-born children that they have strained their coffers to the breaking point.

Citizenship, on the other hand, carries with it almost no obligation except obedience to the law, payment of taxes and perhaps military service. And because the typical conception of citizenship demands so little of us, it gets little of real consequence from most of us. It perfectly suits orthodox concepts of democracy according to which democracy is variously a political system we're born into or a kind of government we live under. Either way, it's something that we are thought simply to have by default of living within certain borders.

But Lifelike, organic democracy — the kind of democracy we need to practice in order to cure ourselves of Critical Mass — is not something we have. It's something we do — together. Specifically, it's what we do together to make our lives work with Life in particular human and natural communities that are located in particular places, regardless of conventional geopolitical borders and boundaries. Whoever participates constructively in the life of those places and in their maintenance and well-being, whoever participates in activities that provision or protect a community as a whole as well as themselves and their family and friends, would be understood to be a member of that community. And members of communities are entitled to a fair share of the provisions and other benefits of membership.

If we take natural communities as our model, then anyone who lives in and helps to support a community is fulfilling the obligations we generally think of as defining citizenship. An inelegant toad or nematode is as much a member of and, in its own way, as necessary a participant in and provider for a forest community as the most elegant pine, oak, elk or deer and is, accordingly, a citizen of the forest.

Taken to its Earthological conclusion, those whom we presently call immigrants or seasonal migrants, and whom we designate and treat as non-citizens, might well be thought of as citizens of self-reliant communities and communities of communities. Though this was not her intent, journalist and filmmaker Julia Whitty makes the case for the citizenship status of immigrants and migrants in natural communities using butterflies as her example.

"Citizenship [is] the capacity to work together openly, cooperatively and democratically to achieve a community's shared visions, values and objectives. Citizenship is achieved through

- cooperation, the capacity to work together,
- humility, the capacity to pursue shared interests above individual ambitions,
- perseverance, the capacity to achieve long-term goals as well as short-term results, and
- inclusiveness, the capacity to welcome and work with all who agree to help achieve a community's vision."[45]

"Crossing prairies, mountains, deserts, rivers, wetlands and woodlands, the monarch [butterflies] connect these places to each other — changing locations they visit, being changed by them. Such transfluent energy is good for all parties involved, and satisfies a deep need of wild places [for diversity].... Thanks to the seasonal sanctuary, monarchs can complete the other phases of their lives, and in doing so cinch vast areas of North America from Canada to Mexico, literally connecting the landscape one milkweed bush at a time — helping milkweed to thrive. Species connected to the milkweed economy also prosper."[46] Similarly, the bear, herd of deer or flock of wild turkeys that moves into a forest and stays there or resides there seasonally on a regular basis contributes to the maintenance of the forest, gives to the community as much or more than it takes and takes no more than it needs, is, even by our usual reckoning, a member and citizen of the forest community.

Following this line, as monarchs follow theirs across dizzyingly different landscapes, it can be argued that immigrants and seasonal migrant workers accomplish the same things for the economies to which they currently contribute despite the tide of opinion against them. They might accomplish even more for themselves and for Earthological communities by which they would appropriately be considered valuable participants and therefore members: citizens. This is not an argument for open borders, unlimited immigration and instant citizenship. It puts new conditions on citizenship, Earthological conditions. Arguably, Earthologic would suggest we should withdraw citizenship from and perhaps ostracize those whose activities put our human and natural communities at risk of extinction. I mean here only to suggest a way in which immigrants and seasonal migrant workers might be viewed and treated differently by Earthological communities than they are and, perhaps, must be by money-based geopolitical units like nations.

Organically democratic communities with the aim of providing for themselves sustainably will, like natural communities, thrive on the kinds of diversity that people from other cultures, with other techniques, skills, intelligences and genetic inheritances bring to them. Though many ecological communities may begin as communities of tribal, ethnic, racial or cultural similarity and may have to deal with considerations of size because of space or resource limitations, they will, like natural communities, succeed to the extent they do not become inbred, rigid, closed and homogenous.

## Everything in This Book ...

... has been intended to show why preserving Life as we know it requires the expansion of our understanding of governance and democracy, economics and community to include the other-than-human species, natural communities and ecosystems on whose well-being our own depends, why we must make dramatic alterations in our way of thinking, living and being in the world. People who have HIV/AIDS have to live differently than they did before in order to live at all. People living on a planet that has the equivalent of HIV/AIDS must do the same.

Along with my mentors, predecessors and comrades in this problematic business of world saving, I have shown that we can do this, and even how we can do it. History suggests that, whether by choice — proactively — or by default, reactively — we just might do it.

# CHAPTER 15

# Precedents for Success

H UMANS ARE CAPABLE OF DRAMATICALLY CHANGING our minds about what works for our lives and then changing our lives and lifeways accordingly. As we're about to see, we have done this several times in the past — in response to geophysical pressures including other episodes of crippling Critical Mass. Pioneers in the study of human consciousness have identified anywhere between five and ten different stages in the evolution of human consciousness and have analyzed the various external pressures — geological, meteorological, social and political — that cause our minds to work differently from one period of time to the next.[1] According to organizational consultants Don Beck and Christopher Cowan, "The historic evidence is clear. New times produce new thinking."[2]

Humans have been able to make the necessary leaps in consciousness for a simple reason: Our brains function as democratically as every other organic system. Life really has built in

"The brain is what scientists call 'plastic' — it can reorganize itself. Not only are different regions of the brain engaged in ongoing communication with one another, with the body, and with the surrounding world; these relationships can be manipulated in ways that can reverse damage or dysfunction previously believed to be permanent."[3]

"In a dark time,
The eye begins to see."[4]
"In the middle of difficulty lies opportunity."[5]
"Evolution responds to big challenges with creative leaps — which usually wipe out something that seemed pretty solid before — and then provides ways to sustain its novel creations until they get challenged by some new circumstance. Consciousness goes through this same process. It is called 'learning.'"[6]

democracy everywhere. The diverse regions of the brain and the neural communities that compose them relate to each other and behave, as the participants in the immune system do, in ways that are organically democratic. They help each other to adapt to failures and successes. They learn from their mistakes and reorganize or regroup, creating new or reestablishing old coalitions when they are challenged or compromised. They share resources, work together and assign or yield leadership in a particular mental process to the part of the brain best equipped to deal with a particular kind of challenge. They experiment with Life's Rules but do not break them. Our brains and minds have changed in response to changing circumstances and that has allowed us to change, too. Our brains are, after all, complex systems.

Let's look at a few examples of occasions on which symptoms accompanying Critical Mass caused our minds to change, or us to change them.

## From Stone Throwers to Tool Makers

For most of our two million or so years on Earth, we humans made no tools more exciting than sharpened stones. Our lives as hunter-gatherers were limited to what we could do with stones. And according to theories of the evolution of human consciousness, we were embedded in natural communities and lived as one with the other-than-human-species we shared them with. In truth, it seems we had no concept of "other." We were simply part of all that was.

Then, beginning about 60,000 years ago in Southeast Asia and around 40,000 years ago in Europe and Africa — as if suddenly in each place — we began to make wooden, stone and bone tools that incorporated several components and different materials and that were designed to help us accomplish specific tasks. We built the first boats. We crafted fish hooks and nets, stone and spear throwers, flint knives with blades and handles of different shapes and sizes, pottery and baskets and all manner of things that made life easier and survival more likely in a wider range of places under a wider range of conditions.

What caused this sudden burst of creativity and innovation? A really severe, really long ice age seems to have forced us to find new ways to feed ourselves. Desperation and constant hunger pushed us to design different tools for different tasks — to see tools differently, to hunt and fish in coordinated teams farther and farther afield, to store food against an uncertain future, to work in more ways together. Long periods of trial and error, teaching and learning — and practice, practice, practice — gave us new survival skills. And those of us who survived using those skills thought differently about ourselves and each other and about how best to make our way together in the frigid world.

**Critical Mass forced critical masses of us to change our ways of thinking, behaving and living.**

Ironically, that breakthrough in mental facility, consciousness and manual dexterity — the sophistication of tool making that, along with speech, has been thought to distinguish us from other animals[7] — set us on the course that would lead to our capacity to break Life's Rules. We didn't have a concept of rules yet or of Life as a thing outside of or other than us. Even with these radical new mental breakthroughs, we were still simply doing what we could to survive. And we did it the same way, at the same primitive level, for a long time. But we also began to be able to get more out of Life than we put back.

## Practicing Magic, Inventing Art, Discovering the "Others"

In Europe around 30,000 years ago, in the very teeth of that long ice age, some of us holed up out of the cold in caves in southern France and northern Spain.

It was the first time we were contained for long periods within walls, living inside. We seem to have missed the wider worlds outside. Or perhaps we longed to stay connected with the larger Life within which we'd had our lives. Whatever the reason, we began for the first time to draw and sculpt the animals and plants that populated the worlds "out there" beyond the bright openings of our chilly caverns. We evidently spent a great deal of our time studying the habits, natures, lives and lifeways of animals, the locations and seasons of plants and the relationships of animals and insects to them.

We drew pictures of the hunt and the births and deaths of animals. We drew animals in repose and running away. We drew herds and birds and predators. We brought Life inside with us and into our collective memories. And when we ventured out to brave the cold, we hunted smarter and in larger teams.

We believed in magic and revered shamans who could "see" what most of us could not, work spells on our behalf and cause animals (or so it seemed to us back then) to volunteer to be killed and plants to yield themselves to feed us and heal our wounds.

As if suddenly, we seem to have become conscious of other living things as Others, others who had powers over us and others over whom we had some power, whose abilities we believed we could take into ourselves, and with whom we could trade places at will. When we put on the bear's skin we were the bear, could see, hear, smell, move and hunt as the bear. But when we took it off again we knew we were not the bear. We realized that we were differently gifted than the Others. That we were able to depict, summon and record them and their activities

"The anthropomorphic images and paintings of caves and rock shelters ... suggest that the earliest Stone Age hunter-gatherers had a similar attitude to the social and natural worlds: they were one and the same. One consequence, of benefit to us today, is that they expressed this view within their art....

"This collapse of the cognitive barrier between the social and natural worlds had significant consequences for their [Stone Age hunter-gatherers'] behavior, for it fundamentally changed their interaction with the natural world.... They seem to have been considerably more proficient at predicting game movements and planning complex hunting strategies."[8]

sometimes enabled us to outthink them. We could make things happen rather than only waiting for or allowing them to happen. We could choose how to respond to the snow, ice and cold, how to survive them.

What caused this dramatic change of mind? It would seem that the bitter cold had driven us inward, into our minds and imaginations, into deeper resonance with the members of our clans and deeper longing not to lose touch with the world and to better understand, adapt to and control our relationships with the wild "out there."

**Critical Mass forced critical masses of us to change our ways of thinking, behaving and living.**

We still did not have a concept of rules or laws, either Life's or our own, but we paid attention to Life's ways of doing things. It was useful to know when the herds came through our territory and that certain plants made visible seeds and others hid them in fruits, and some made us sick and others made us well. It saved time, effort and lives to know at least a little about what to expect from Life. Things we'd studied and learned were things that with practice, practice and more practice we could teach to our children. Cultures were born in that time. Cultures bound us together in time and between generations. But culture also separated us from other people with different cultures. Our new minds distinguished between us and them. They were Others, too. Competition got ritualized with that mind shift. We were much smarter hunters and gatherers and also less cooperative ones.

## Out of the Woods, into the Cities and Behind Walls

Yet again, 5,000 or so years ago — as if all of a sudden — humans did something brand new. In the region of the Middle East called Mesopotamia, which lay between the Tigris and Euphrates rivers in what is present-day Iraq, we invented civilization. What was the catalyst for cities and all their trappings, excesses and brilliance?

The intense final millennia of the last ice age — the Last Glacial Maximum — spread ice sheets so far south and built them so deep (two miles deep in some places) that a great deal of the Earth's finite supply of water got tied up in snow and ice. Drought was a norm at the equator and everywhere south. Some of that water had evaporated out of oceans, seas and lakes and not been returned. The Black Sea, for example, dried up, and the Persian Gulf retreated to what is now the narrow Strait of Hormuz. An amount of dry land equivalent in size to Africa was added to coastlines around the world.

During the several thousand years of excellent, moderate weather that followed the end of the Maximum, herds of wild grazing animals, flocks of birds and schools of fish increased in size. While some of us continued as hunters and gatherers of food, others learned to herd sheep and goats and to follow them as they followed the seasons of grass. Others learned to garden and to grow grains to feed growing populations. Humans moved out from Mesopotamia, established encampments and villages on the fertile exposed land in what had been the Black Sea and Persian Gulf. Given an abundance of good land and good weather we humans literally went forth and multiplied. It was, truly, Eden.

But then, in a very warm, very wet spell, the last of the snow and ice melted really fast. Rains came with a vengeance. All that rain and meltwater had to go somewhere. It went back where it had come from. The Black Sea filled so fast when the ridge of land that blocked it was breached, that scores of settlements were immersed in just months. The Persian Gulf rose and crested, again and again, lifting Noah's legendary ark and depositing it on top of a mountain. Rising waters drowned our Edenic settlements, slowly and persistently, burying thousands of square miles of hunting and grazing land and gardens. The water drove hunters

"By about 3000 BC in Mesopotamia and Egypt, a few hundred years later in the Indus Valley, a millennium or so later in China and another two millennia in the Americas, hierarchical, militaristic societies ruled by religious and political elites with immense powers of control over their populations were established.

"Various states and empires rose and fell without fundamentally altering this way of life.

"Their impact on their immediate environments was often far-reaching. They provide the first examples of intensive human alteration of the environment and of their major destructive impact. They also provide the first examples of societies that so damaged the environment as to bring about their own collapse."[9]

and gatherers, farmers and nomads alike before it and upon each other for several thousand years.

Shrunken landscapes, changing weather and ecosystems, fierce competition for land and resources between peoples with incompatible lifeways, methods of providing for themselves that no longer worked ... The inevitable result was chaos. The well-established order of agrarian, nomadic and hunting peoples was overturned. Regional Critical Mass forced us to change the way we lived.

We came out of our natural communities and forests and away from our half-wild settlements and built the first walled cities on land that the waters left us. Walls kept water and also the Others — who were now "the enemy" — out, and protected us and our food supply from them. Nomads fought farmers who fought back. City dwellers and their armies drove the last hunter-gatherers in the region into oblivion. Scribes wrote stories of combat, heroism and the rise and fall of kings and tribes and peoples into the first sacred and secular testaments of human history.

With practice, practice and more practice we learned how to use new materials — metals this time — and to make new tools that we put to new uses. Once again we conceived new techniques and technologies: large-scale farming and mining, navigation and wheeled transport, writing and mathematics, draft animals and slavery, laws and domination systems, empires, long-distance trade and money economies. These allowed more of us to live and some of us, the first true Powers, to live very well.

We became psychological beings, individuals, aware of and alternately happy with, anxious for and protective of our newly found "selves," increasingly frightened of and disconnected from the wild worlds outside our walls and of the others inside the walls with us. We discovered pyramids, power and the idea of power and the concept of time. We entered history, and then we began to make it.

### Critical Mass forced critical masses of us to change our ways of thinking, behaving and living.

Now, just because we could, and because we'd gotten creature proud and thought we had a right to, we began to break Life's Rules with a vengeance and to write laws that permitted and organized the breaking

of them. Embeddedness and reverence were replaced by a sense of superiority and hubris. Clan, tribe and village — community — gradually
yielded to fierce individualism: "we" gave way to "me."

## From Victims to Inducers of Critical Mass

Humans got through that series of regional climate-induced episodes
of Critical Mass and promptly, albeit unintentionally, learned how to
induce it ourselves. A millennium or two later (in an age called "Axial"
because our ways of thinking turned around in that time as the Earth
turns on its axis) came the Hindu Upanishads, Lao Tzu, the Tao Te
Ching and Confucius, the Babylonian Enuma Elish, Abraham, Socrates
and Plato, Moses, Jesus and Mohammad, the Jewish/Christian Bible and
the Koran. The world's great philosophies were conceived and its major
religious systems founded in a period of less than 2,000 years. Why then?

Regional Critical Mass was reached again, caused this time not by
cyclical climate instability but by the environmental excesses, economic
overreaching and social depredations of the first civilized domination
systems. Empires and Powers, slavery and crowding, crucifixions and
corruption, famine and pestilence — all the horrors of the Biblical
Old Testament — caused some of us, the sages and teachers, to think
differently about our lives and each other and how we might be more
harmless, kind and fair. The rest of us were given laws and spiritual exercises and new visions of more deeply humane relationships, the practice,
practice and further practice of which brought our minds and hearts and
some of us together in common cause.

> ### Critical Mass forced critical masses of us to change
> ### our ways of thinking, behaving and living.

Humans were still on a path away from Life's Rules and conscious
kinship with other-than-human living things, but God's laws and moral
law were teaching us conscious kinship with each other. And added to
our own and our communities' and cultures' memories, history was
beginning to teach us our place. Despite our moments of glory, triumph
and conquest we still were, as philosopher Pico Iyer has written, "tiny
figures in a larger frame, and all our small dramas [were] nothing next to
a higher logic enforced by Nature or Providence or Time."[10]

## From the Dark Ages to Organic Democracy

Joel Garreau, a *Washington Post* reporter and author of the book *Radical Evolution* points to the Renaissance and Enlightenment as evidence of human minds, behavior and ways of living changing yet again, this time in response to suffering caused by a bout of regional Critical Mass resulting from a combination of the Little Ice Age (lasting from 1300 to 1850, it doesn't seem so little to us); invasions by Asiatic barbarians (nomadic tribal peoples who were fleeing bitterly cold, dry weather in the steppes and mountains of their eastern homelands); repeated epidemics of the bubonic plague and the injustices of the Powers who ruled Europe in the Middle Ages.

"Looking at the future of the human race from the perspective of that time, you could be forgiven for thinking we were pretty much toast. You'd be seeing marauding hordes and plagues and all sorts of evil stuff. You'd probably be thinking 'This isn't going to end up well.' Then all of a sudden, in 1450, along came the printing press, and there was a new way of storing, sharing, collecting and distributing ideas that was previously unimaginable. This led to the Renaissance and Enlightenment, which gave birth to science, democracy and eventually to the world we have today....

"It was the collective action of millions of humans organizing themselves in a bottom-up way. They didn't wait for leaders to tell them what to do but changed their world to produce things as best they could."[11]

> **Critical Mass forced critical masses of us to change our ways of thinking, behaving and living.**

## Becoming a More Critical Mass in Our Time

Every episode of human-induced regional Critical Mass since the imperial civilizations of the Axial Age catalyzed antibodies in the form of world-changing spiritual teachers, has caused an increased expansiveness in human consciousness and in our collective conscience that has made us almost a new kind of creature. Every episode of human-induced Critical Mass has fomented a great turning in some of us away from empire and toward community, away from domination systems and toward democracy, away from Powers and toward interdependent self-reliance, away from trying to be larger than Life to becoming a partner with it, and with each other.

Critical Mass has come round again. And this time our global-scale economic overreaching, environmental depredations and social, political and economic ineptitude and injustices have caused it.

But we can choose to change our minds — and our behaviors and our relationships — yet again. We can choose to leave the Powers and their viral global economy behind. We can choose to obey Life's Rules and — with practice, practice and more practice — learn to live within Earth's means. We can choose to work as hard at restoring health to Earth's beleaguered immune system as the medical and scientific communities are working to learn how to restore health to the immune systems of patients with HIV/AIDS.

"The third dimension of the Great Turning [from Empire to Earth communities] involves a shift in consciousness. We can think of this shift as changing our mental map to one that puts the healing of our world at the very center of things. On this map, our community is all of life."[12]

A more critical mass of us can once again choose to change our ways of thinking, behaving and living.

Or Critical Mass will, once again, force us to change.

CHAPTER 16

# Dreaming Deep Green, Imagining the Ecozoic

I MAGINE HOMES, FACTORIES, schools and other kinds of buildings that breathe, heat and cool themselves, collect and store sunlight, produce food and recycle nearly all of their waste and water.[1] Imagine city sidewalks lined with nut and fruit trees under which grow raised beds of vegetables and berries; the front walls and windows of row houses are turned into hanging gardens and greenhouses. Empty shop spaces have turned into community canning and food drying operations, tool and equipment cooperatives. Imagine the basements of apartment buildings, offices and restaurants given over to vermiculture (worm-based) composting systems. Parking lots have become solar collectors and roofs water collectors.

Imagine vacant lots and even dumps turned into urban farmsteads or parks that recycle greywater, nurture chickens, geese, pigs and fish and produce gardens. Imagine living machines or bio-shelters like greenhouses that use aquatic plants to produce organic soil amendments, fish farms, irrigation water and electricity out of sewage. Imagine that temperate zone suburbs can produce 75% of the food, water and energy they consume.

Imagine shanty-towns and slums and schools and colleges establishing community gardens on local landfills, using methane from the fills to heat greenhouses and class and community rooms. Imagine buried non-toxic dumps becoming master gardener teaching centers.

Imagine residents of urban ghettoes transforming hundreds of blocks of hazardous waste sites, condemned buildings, vermin-infested, dilapidated housing, crack houses and closed businesses and vacant lots into urban eco-restorative villages: racially and ethnically diverse, neighborly communities that combine affordable housing, shops and community centers with pocket parks, urban organic farms and markets, environmental reclamation projects and community houses. Imagine city parks that feature wind generators, fruit orchards, fish ponds and community garden plots as well as concerts in summer and ice skating in winter.

Imagine that simulation games and computer models of human and natural communities can be used by neighborhoods, churches, schools and whole communities to create opportunities for community members to experiment with their present and future realities. Imagine that they can explore the options their landscapes and water resources offer, discover their physical limits, virtually raise and raze buildings, grow forests and mature them before actually planting trees and plot out the potential local and regional impact of climate change.

Imagine coliseums, movie theaters, stadiums, sports bars and Internet cafes as sights of Earthological design and innovation competitions.

Imagine that, because trial and error can be made virtual and time can be speeded up digitally, a community can make relatively appropriate and cautious decisions about and for itself in real time, and by that means over time avoid some of Life's more brutal paybacks.

Imagine that local cable channels and live-cast Internet sites are the equivalents of heavily trafficked public squares or community commons where members of a community bring their stories, work and opinions into the public realm; practitioners offer courses of study in eco-design, sustainable lifeways, consensus building or water quality monitoring. Imagine candidates for community council or representatives from surrounding communities introducing themselves and their ideas on live-cast as people gather to watch and discuss.

Imagine that churches, town halls, libraries, empty retail spaces and schools become open spaces for community big-screen local cable and movie viewing and for teleconferencing and discussion of local and cultural issues. Imagine that local programming enjoys an 80% audience share because it is genuine reality TV.

Imagine, as democracy guru Lloyd Wells has, that members of a community can signify in advance of receiving a tax bill their approval or disapproval of, interest or disinterest in local initiatives and expenditures by symbolically allotting their portion of local taxes to their preferred programs and projects on a mock-up of their tax bill that they receive in the mail or online. Local youths and adults film the flow of the seasons through their community, the shape of workers' days, the lives and quality of life of their human and natural communities, and they contribute in this way to the creation of a community memory.

Imagine schools and universities in which students raise their own food, process their own trash and waste, and are trained to compete in resource-watch and restoration and eco-design teams. Imagine empty big-box stores turned into community-owned libraries, community-built public housing and workshops; imagine small manufactories that produce fabrics from locally grown fibers like hemp, cotton, wool, cattail and flax; local businesses build furniture from recycled materials and sustainably harvested bamboo and timber.

Imagine that long buried watercourses are uncovered and allowed to flow through cities again. Depaved highways are turned into greenways that flow through and around them, too, allowing migratory animals and birds access to their whole range of ecosystems. Imagine that in places where there is no more nature, we invite nature back in.

All of these things are already being done somewhere. Hundreds of cities and suburbs around the world are bringing just such Earthological imaginings to life. But why stop here with our imaginings? Let's push beyond what's already being done. Let's imagine what isn't yet but could be.

## Imagining the Ecozoic

Imagine that the only thing we do on a global scale is share art, culture and information — about the status of our communities and environments, about survival strategies, inventions and innovations and about what worked for us and what didn't. Imagine that tribal desert dwellers in Africa, Mongolia and the Arabian Peninsula can teach us things we do not and cannot know if they don't teach us. That remnant populations of native peoples can teach us survival and subsistence techniques that make us competent and our communities sustainable in every kind of environment. That each generation of the world's children is more place-competent and Life-wise.

Imagine that everything doesn't always cost more and that nothing really important is scarce. That small *is* beautiful. That animals and plants and ecosystems become extinct only in the natural course of things. That — as if suddenly — the sky is once again darkened in spring and fall by clouds of butterflies and the migrations of birds. That you can hardly sleep in spring for the croaking of frogs. That salmon run thick in the world's rivers again, shrimp and lobsters crawl the continental shelves, polar bears aren't drowning or whales beaching or bees and bats dying. And color is coming back into the cheeks of paled coral.

Imagine that there are no world wars because there isn't enough funny-money or fossil fuels — or even the will or desire — to fight them. Imagine that human health improves because we're no longer poisoning ourselves, the air, water, soils and our food with derivatives of those fossil fuels. Imagine that the weather doesn't get any worse.

Imagine that as members of Earthological communities we really do have more control over our economic futures, more self-respect and respect for others than we do now, and a real sense of belonging. Imagine that as each new behavior leads Earthologically to the next, critical masses of us, somehow for the first time in eleven or twelve thousand years, manage together to bring our lifeways into line with Life's ways.

Imagine that what comes after Critical Mass is not collapse, a long emergency or the end of civilization, but something more like what Thomas Berry foresaw: a deeply green, Ecozoic Age. In this time ahead we do not live beyond Earth's means or behave as if we were larger than Life, but live within Earth's means with every other kind of living thing as if we were children of and partners with Life. We live in an age in which we have helped to restore health to Earth's immune system and learned how not to compromise it again.

Imagine that most of us are not unintelligent, inept, closed-minded, lazy, greedy or selfish as many self-styled "realists" say we are. Imagine that we simply need an occasion worth rising to. And that Critical Mass is such an occasion.

All this is possible.

# Notes

## Chapter 1: Diagnosing a Critical Condition

1.  I capitalize *Earth* in these pages to give it at least the importance we give to each other when we capitalize our names. It is, so far as we know, the only viable home for *Life* and, for now, the only viable home for us that we know of in our galaxy. I capitalize Life when it refers to the thin layer of living things that covers the Earth — the biosphere — in order to set it apart from any single individual life and, to a certain extent, from our collective lives as a species, and in order to remind us how utterly wonderful and necessary it is to us.

2.  "What is the Millennium Ecosystem Assessment (MA)." *Millennium Ecosystem Assessment*. [online]. [cited March 29, 2012]. maweb.org/en/About.aspx.

3.  Elizabeth Rosenthal. "Climate Fears Turn to Doubts Among Britons." *The New York Times*, May 24, 2010.

4.  Mohamed El-Erian. "Driving Without a Spare." *Secular Outlook*, May 2010. [online]. [cited February 27, 2012]. pimco.com/EN/Insights/Pages/Secular%20Outlook%20May%202010%20El-Erian.aspx.

5.  Marshall McLuhan and Quentin Fiore. *The Medium is the Massage: An Inventory of Effects*. Random House, 1967.

6.  If you need a sense of what our positive options look like before you're confronted further with the seriousness of our present circumstances, read Chapter 16 first.

7. Bill McKibben. *Eaarth: Making a Life on a Tough New Planet.* Times, 2010.
8. James Howard Kunstler. *The Long Emergency: Surviving the End of Oil, Climate Change, and Other Converging Catastrophes of the Twenty-First Century.* Atlantic Monthly, 2005, p. 5.
9. Paul Hawken. *Blessed Unrest: How the Largest Social Movement in History Is Restoring Grace, Justice, and Beauty to the World.* Viking, 2007, pp. 141–142.
10. Ervin Lazlo. *The Chaos Point: World at the Crossroads.* Hampton Roads, 2006, p. 87.
11. Avert.org. 1981 *History.* [online]. [cited February 28, 2012]. avert.org/aids-history-86.htm.
12. Marco A. Janssen. "An Immune System Perspective on Ecosystem Management." *Conservation Ecology,* Vol. 5#1 (2001). [online]. [cited February 28, 2012]. ecologyandsociety.org/articles/242.html.
13. *The American Heritage Dictionary.* Fourth Edition, s.v. "style."

## Chapter 2: Symptoms of Critical Mass — Making the Connections

1. Robert S. Porter, ed. *The Merck Manual of Diagnosis and Therapy,* 19th ed. Merck, 2011.
2. For updates and discussion of the symptoms of Critical Mass, their interactions and their implications, see the "Life Rules:the Blog" and "StartingPointNewsletter" tabs on my website: ellenlaconte.com.
3. Brecht Forum website. [online]. [cited April 3, 2012]. brechtforum.org/world-health-organization-estimates-13-world-population-well-fed-13-under-fed-and-13-starving.
4. The Hindu. "Number of hungry people in India rose by 65 mn between 1990–2005." May 31, 2011. [online]. [cited April 3, 2012]. thehindu.com/health/policy-and-issues/article2065723.ece; Swati Narayan. "India's battle against hunger." Poverty Matters blog, April 8, 2011. [online]. [cited April 3, 2012]. guardian.co.uk/global-development/poverty-matters/2011/apr/08/india-battle-against-hunger.
5. World Hunger Education Service. "2012 World Hunger and Poverty Facts and Statistics." Hunger Notes. [online]. [cited April 3, 2012]. worldhunger.org/articles/Learn/world%20hunger%20facts%202002.htm.
6. Donella Meadows, Dennis Meadows and Jørgen Randers. *Beyond the Limits: Confronting Global Collapse, Envisioning a Sustainable Future.* Chelsea Green, 1992, p. 52.

7. Michael Pollan. "Farmer in Chief." *The New York Times Sunday Magazine*, October 9, 2008. [online]. [cited April 4, 2012]. nytimes. com/2008/10/12/magazine/12policy-t.html?_r=1.

8. John Robbins. "2,500 Gallons All Wet?" Earthsave website. [online]. [cited April 3, 2012]. earthsave.org/environment/water.htm; "Our Message on WorldWaterDay2011." GlobalWaterPartnershipBlog. [online]. [citedApril 4, 2012] globalwaterpartnership.wordpress.com/2011/03/; Adam Shake. "1,000 Gallons Water Per 1 Gallon Ethanol — How Green is That?" Gas 2 website, October 16, 2008. [online]. [cited April 3, 2012]. gas2.org/2008/10/ 16/1000-gallons-water-per-1-gallon-ethanol-how-green-is-that/; Carl Bialik. "How Much Water Goes Into a Burger? Studies Find Different Answers." *Wall Street Journal,* January 11, 2008. [online]. [cited April 3, 2012]. online. wsj.com/article/SB120001666638282817.html; Matt McDermott. "From Lettuce to Beef, What's the Water Footprint of Your Food?" Treehugger website, June 11, 2009. [online]. [cited April, 3 2012]. treehugger.com/green-food/from-lettuce-to-beef-whats-the-water-footprint-of-your-food.html.

9. Global Change Program, University of Michigan. *Human Appropriation of the World's Fresh Water Supply.* January 4, 2006. [online]. [cited April 3, 2012]. globalchange.umich.edu/globalchange2/current/lectures/freshwater_ supply/freshwater.html.

10. Lester Brown. *Plan B 4.0: Mobilizing to Save Civilization.* Norton, 2009, pp. 51, 53.

11. Stewart Bum. "Water — The Global Challenge." Futureagenda website, September 24, 2009. [online]. [cited April, 3, 2012]. futureagenda.org/? p=246.

12. Magdalena Klocek. "Water for Life." *Contours,* Vol. 21#1 (March 2011), p. 5.

13. Bob Berwyn. "Ocean dead zones now spread over 95,000 square miles." *Summit County Citizens Voice,* January 21, 2011. [online]. [cited April 3, 2012]. summitcountyvoice.com/2011/01/21/ocean-dead-zones-now-spread-over-95000-square-miles/.

14. "Labor Statistics > Unemployment rate (most recent) by country." Nation Master website. [online]. [cited April, 3, 2012]. nationmaster.com/graph/ lab_une_rat-labor-unemployment-rate.

15. "Living on a Dollar a Day." *World Vision Report,* week of January 10, 2010. [online]. [cited April 3, 2012]. worldvisionreport.org/Stories/Week-of-January-2-2010/Living-on-a-Dollar-a-Day; Anup Shah. *Poverty Facts and Stats.* Global Issues website, September 20, 2010. [online]. [cited April 3, 2012]. globalissues.org/article/26/poverty-facts-and-stats.

16. "The Current Situation." World Health Organization, reported at *Need for TB Vaccines*. Aeras website. [online]. [cited April 3, 2012]. aeras.org/about-tb/need.php.
17. Overview of Global Issues — Environment and Sustainability. [online]. [cited April 3, 2012]. worldrevolution.org/projects/globalissuesoverview/overview2/EnvironmentNew.htm.
18. Stuart Heaslet. "Should We Save Our National Heritage?" for The Future Centre Trust, published in *Barbados Business*, February 14, 2011.
19. Michael T. Klare. *Resource Wars: The New Landscape of Global Conflict.* Metropolitan, 2001.
20. Roy Woodbridge. *The Next World War: Tribes, Cities, Nations, and Ecological Decline.* University of Toronto, 2004.
21. Thomas E. Lovejoy. "Will Unexpectedly the Top Blow Off?" *BioScience*, Vol. 38#10 (November 1988). [online]. [cited March 1, 2012]. shelf1.library.cmu.edu/cgi-bin/tiff2pdf/heinz/box00239/fld00037/bdl0003/doc0001/heinz.pdf.
22. Milton Leitenberg. "Deaths in Wars and Conflicts in the 20th Century." Cornell University Peace Studies Program, Occasional Paper #29, 3rd edition.
23. Rainforest Information Centre Educational Supplement. *Indigenous People of the Rainforest.* [online]. [cited April 4, 2012]. rainforestinfo.org.au/background/people.htm; Save the Rainforest. Facts About the Rainforest. [online]. savetherainforest.org/savetherainforest_007.htm
24. Brian Swimme and Thomas Berry. *The Universe Story: From the Primordial Flaring Forth to the Ecozoic Era — A Celebration of the Unfolding of the Cosmos.* Harper, 1992, p. 243.

## Chapter 3: Discovering the Coomon Cause

1. Michael C. Ruppert. *Confronting Collapse: The Crisis of Energy and Money in a Post Peak Oil World.* Chelsea Green, 2009, p. 31.
2. Richard J. Douthwaite. *Short Circuit: Strengthening Local Economies for Security in an Unstable World.* Chelsea Green, 1998, p. 179.
3. Jason Subik. "Forum sees oil peak as world crisis." *Daily Gazette*, June 7, 2008. [online]. [cited March 2, 2012]. dailygazette.com/news/2008/jun/07/0607_energyforum/?print.
4. I highly recommend any or all of Richard Heinberg's books on peak oil, natural gas and coal which consider in accessible prose the timing, implications for our lifeways, viability of various alternatives, ways of husbanding remaining fossil fuel resources for future generations and of protecting the climate from the potentially fatal consequences of continuing to burn

them. *The Party's Over: Oil, War and the Fate of Industrial Societies,* 2nd ed (New Society, 2005), *Powerdown: Options and Actions for a Post-Carbon World* (New Society, 2004). *Searching for a Miracle — Net energy Limits & The Fate of Industrial Society.* [online]. [cited March 2, 2012]. Searching_for_a_Miracle_web10nov09.pdf, for example, represent a crash course in post-carbon studies.

5. Mac Margolis. "Off the Deep End in Brazil." *Newsweek,* June 21, 2010, p. 4.

6. Efforts are underway to find methods of converting coal, of which there is still an abundance in the ground, into liquid form to stand in for oil. Caveat: The coal still in the ground is dirtier, of a lower quality and costlier to extract than in the past and there's not enough of it to do both what coal does and what oil has done. Peak coal is predicted to occur around 2020. Natural gas, the other touted substitute for oil, is slated to peak worldwide around the same time. Some of what remains is lost during oil and coal extraction; all of what remains is expensive and environmentally costly to retrieve or is located in Middle Eastern and Asian regions.

7. Kenneth S. Deffeyes. *Hubbert's Peak: The Impending World Oil Shortage.* Princeton, rev. ed., 2003 cited Heinberg, *The Party's Over,* p. 105.

8. Richard Heinberg. *Peak Everything: Waking Up to the Century of Declines.* New Society, 2009, pp. 6–7.

9. Roger A. Pielke, Sr. "Main Conclusions." *Pielke Research Group: News and Commentary.* [online]. [cited March 2, 2012]. pielkeclimatesci.wordpress.com/main-conclusions-2/.

10. Ross Gelbspan. *Boiling Point: How Politicians, Big Oil and Coal, Journalists, and Activists Have Fueled a Climate Crisis — And What We Can Do to Avert Disaster.* Basic, 2004, p.11.

11. World Meteorological Organization, various postings. [online]. [cited April 5, 2012]. See, for example: wmo.int/pages/mediacentre/press_releases/pr_904_en.html.

12. James Gustave Speth. *The Bridge at the Edge of the World: Capitalism, the Environment, and Crossing from Crisis to Sustainability.* Yale, 2008 cited in Gar Alperovitz. "The New-Economy Movement." New Economics Institute. [online]. [cited April 5, 2012]. neweconomicsinstitute.org/publications/new-economy-movement.

## Chapter 4: What's Wrong with a Global Economy?

1. Wendell Berry. "Solving for Pattern" in *The Gift of Good Land: Further Essays Cultural and Agricultural.* North Point, 1981, Chapter Nine. Cited

often, for example, in this context of Curitiba, Brazil where the concept has been used successfully: "Solving for Pattern." Edge::Regerate blog. [online]. [cited April 6, 2012]. edgeregenerate.com/?p=532.

2. Biocracy: a form of governance in which all life forms are recognized as participants and stakeholders; a concept that recognizes that Life rules, we don't.

3. Cited in Bill 6, 2010 of the Legislative Assembly of Ontario, Canada. "An act to increase awareness of climate change" [online]. [cited April 6, 2010]. ontla.on.ca/web/committee-proceedings/committee_business.do? BusinessType=Bill&BillID=2281&locale=en&ParlCommID=8856 and in Thomas L. Friedman. *Hot, Flat, and Crowded: Why We Need a Green Revolution and How It Can Renew America.* Farrar Straus, 2008, p. 139.

4. Keith Farnish. "If the Economy Doesn't Shrink, We're Finished!" *The Earth Blog,* December 31, 2008. [online]. [cited March 5, 2012]. earth-blog.bravejournal.com/entry/28508.

5. Minqi Li. *The Rise of China and the Demise of the Capitalist World-Economy.* Pluto, 2008, p. 177.

6. Suchitra Bajpai Chaudhary. "Making Changes." *Gulf News,* November 6, 2008. [online]. [cited April 6, 2012]. gulfnews.com/about-gulf-news/al-nisr-portfolio/friday/articles/making-changes-1.142247.

7. Mike Read. "High Frequency Trading, Flash Trading and Algo Trading: Interview With Peter Green." *HFT Review,* June 7, 2010. [online]. [Cited April 6, 2012]. hftreview.com/pg/blog/mike/read/5319/high-frequency-trading-flash-trading-and-algo-trading.

8. John Lanchester. "Euro Science." *The New Yorker,* October 10, 2011. [online]. [cited April 3, 2012]. newyorker.com/talk/comment/2011/10/10/111010taco_talk_lanchester.

9. Scott Baldauf. "In Zimbabwe, bread costs Z$10 million." *Christian Science Monitor,* March 25, 2008.

10. James Robertson. *Future Wealth: A New Economics For The 21st Century.* A TOES Book/TheBootstrap Press, 1990, p. 93. [online]. [cited March 5, 2012]. jamesrobertson.com/bookcontents.htm.

11. Charles Eisenstein. *Sacred Economics: Money, Gift, and Society in the Age of Transition.* Evolver, 2011, Kindle edition, Introduction.

12. Norman Myers. *Ultimate Security: The Environmental Basis of Political Stability.* Norton, 1993, p. 25.

13. William Catton. *Overshoot: The Ecological Basis of Revolutionary Change.* University of Illinois, 1982, p. 48.

14. James Hansen. *Storms of My Grandchildren: The Truth About the Coming Climate Catastrophe and Our Last Chance to Save Humanity.* Bloomsbury, 2009.

15. Derrick Jensen. *Listening to the Land: Conversations About Nature, Culture and Eros.* Chelsea Green, 2004, Chapter 13.

16. Derrick Jensen. *Endgame, Volume I: The Problem of Civilization.* Seven Stories Press, 2006, p. ix.

17. Keith Farnish. *Time's Up: An Uncivilized Solution to a Global Crisis.* Green, 2009, p. 220.

18. The Sustainable Scale Project. *The Ecological Footprint.* [online]. [cited April 3, 2012]. sustainablescale.org/conceptualframework/understanding scale/measuringscale/ecologicalfootprint.aspx; "Environment Statistics > Ecological footprint (most recent) by country." NationMaster website. [online]. [cited April 3, 2012]. nationmaster.com/graph/env_eco_foo-environment-ecological-footprint.

19. See, for example, the websites globalfootprint.org or redefiningprogress.org, to assess the size of your footprint or learn the footprints of nations. Or search "ecological footprints" for hundreds of other sources and resources.

20. Edward Goldsmith. *The Way: An Ecological World-View.* Univerity of Georgia, rev ed., 2008, p. 349.

21. Paul Ehrlich and Anne Ehrlich. *One With Nineveh: Politics, Consumption, and the Human Future.* Island Press, 2004, p. 24.

22. Population Reference Bureau. *2008 Annual Report.* [online]. [cited March 5, 2012]. prb.org/About/AnnualReports.aspx.

23. "Population and Energy Consumption." World Population Balance. [online]. [cited April 3, 2012]. worldpopulationbalance.org/population_energy.

24. Kirkpatrick Sale. *After Eden: The Evolution of Human Domination.* Duke, 2006, p. 1.

25. Father Xabier Gorostiaga of Nicaragua quoted in Peter Senge et al. *Presence: Human Purpose and the Field of the Future.* Society for Organizational Learning, 2004, p. 165.

26. Ronald Wright. *A Short History of Progress.* Carroll & Graf, 2004, p. 85.

## Chapter 5: How Did the Economy Get to Be Too Big *Not* to Fail?

1. David Rothkopf. *Superclass: The Global Power Elite and the World They Are Making.* Farrar Straus, 2008, jacket copy.

2. James K. Galbraith. *The Predator State: How Conservatives Abandoned the Free Market and Why Liberals Should Too.* Free Press, 2008, p. 126.

3. Tijn Touber. "Think global, act natural." *Ode* (July/August, 2006). [online]. [cited March 5, 2012]. odewire.com/52166/think-global-act-natural. html.

4. Laura Miller. "The rise of the superclass." *Salon*, March 14, 2008. [online]. [cited March 5, 2012]. salon.com/2008/03/14/superclass/.

5. Samuel Huntington. "Dead Souls: The Denationalization of the American Elite," *The National Interest* (Spring 2004). [online]. [cited March 5, 2012]. nationalinterest.org/article/dead-souls-the-denationalization-of-the-american-elite-620.

6. George Draffan. *The Elite Consensus: When Corporations Wield the Constitution.* Rowman & Littlefield, 2003, p. 1.

7. Richard Barnet and Ronald Müller. *Global Reach: The Power of the Multinational Corporations.* Touchstone, 1976. Cited in Tony Clarke. "The Mechanisms of Corporate Rule" in Edward Goldsmith and Jerry Mander. *The Case Against the Global Economy & for a Turn Towards Localization,* Sierra Club Books, 1996, p. 297.

8. Thom Hartmann. *Unequal Protection: The Rise of Corporate Dominance and the Theft of Human Rights.* Rodale, 2004, p. 91.

9. D. Ritz, (Ed). *Defying Corporations, Defining Democracy: A book of history & strategy.* Apex, 2001, p. xiv.

10. Clarke, "Mechanisms," p. 301.

11. John Rensenbrink. *Against All Odds: The Green Transformation of American Politics.* Leopold, 1999, p. 159.

12. Chris Hedges. "The Rise of Gonzo Porn is the Latest Sign of America's Cultural Apocalypse." AlterNet, July 31, 2009. [online]. [Cited April 11, 2012]. alternet.org/media/141675/the_rise_of_gonzo_porn_is_the_latest_sign_of_america%27s_cultural_apocalypse_/?page=1.

13. See, for example, Eduardo Porter. "Study Finds Wealth Inequality Is Widening Worldwide." *New York Times* (December 6, 2006). [online]. [cited March 5, 2012]. nytimes.com/2006/12/06/business/worldbusiness/06wealth.html.

14. Chris Hedges. "Zero Point of Systemic Collapse." *Adbusters* #88 (March/April 2010). [online]. [cited March 5, 2012]. adbusters.org/magazine/88/chris-hedges.html.

15. Robert B. Reich. *Supercapitalism: The Transformation of Business, Democracy, and Everyday Life.* Knopf, 2007, p. 131.

16. Frank Bures. "Access Denied." *Wired* (September 2007), pp. 60–61.

17. Edward Hoagland. "Curtain Calls: The fever called 'living' is conquered at last." *Harper's Magazine,* March 14, 2009.

18. Robert Reich. *The Precarious Jobs Recovery.* Daily Markets website, March 9, 2012. [online]. [cited April 4, 2012]. dailymarkets.com/economy/2012/03/09/the-precarious-jobs-recovery/.

19. Howard and Elizabeth Odum. *A Prosperous Way Down: Principles and Policies.* University of Colorado, 2008, p. 9.

20. David Wyss, Chief Economist, Standard & Poor's, quoted in Jeannine Aversa. "Global recession worst since Depression, IMF says." *Huffington Post,* April 22, 2009. [online]. [cited March 6, 2012]. huffingtonpost. com/2009/04/22/global-economy-may-shrink_n_190165.html.

21. James K. Glassman and Kevin A. Hassett. *Dow 36,000: The New Strategy for Profiting from the Coming Rise in the Stock Market.* Three Rivers, 2000.

22. Immanuel Wallerstein. "Globalization or the Age of Transition: A Long-Term View of the Trajectory of the World System." Paper in the archives at the Fernand Braudel Center at SUNY (State University of New York)/Binghamton.

23. Joseph A. Tainter. *The Collapse of Complex Societies.* Cambridge, 1988, p. 214.

24. Kirkpatrick Sale. *Human Scale.* New Catalyst, 2007, p. 59.

## Chapter 6: The Prognosis for Global Solutions Is Poor

1. Peter Boone and Simon Johnson. "Global Boom Builds for Epic Bust." *Bloomberg News,* January 5, 2010. [online]. [cited March 7, 2012]. bloomberg.com/apps/news?pid=newsarchive&sid=aKNBgGSnmi7c.

2. Ruppert, *Confronting Collapse,* p. 219.

3. William Greider. *The Soul of Capitalism: Opening Paths to a Moral Economy.* Simon & Schuster, 2003, Kindle edition, Chapter 6.

4. Speth, *The Bridge at the Edge of the World,* p. 218.

5. Brown, *Plan B 4.0,* p. 261.

6. Jean-Francois Rischard. *High Noon: 20 Global Problems, 20 Years to Solve Them.* Basic, 2003.

7. Brown, *Plan B 4.0,* pp. 221–222.

8. Ibid., p. 206.

9. Woodbridge, *The Next World War,* Kindle edition, Chapter 10.

10. Friedman, *Hot, Flat, and Crowded,* p. 244.

11. James Robertson. "The Twenty-first Century Crisis of World Development — The Central Role of Money Values: a metaproblem." *Development,* Vol. 53# 3 (September 2009). [online]. [cited March 7, 2012]. palgrave-journals. com/development/journal/v52/n3/pdf/dev200942a.pdf.

12. Jorge Buzaglo. "Global commons and common sense." *Real-World Economics Review* #51 (December 1, 2009). [online]. [cited March 7, 2012]. paecon.net/PAEReview/issue51/contents51.htm.
13. James Bernard Quilligan. "People Sharing Resources: Toward a New Multilateralism of the Global Commons." *Kosmos Journal* 36 (Fall/Winter 2009). [online]. [cited March 7, 2012]. kosmosjournal.org/articles/people-sharing-resources-toward-a-new-multilateralism-of-the-global-commons.
14. Set forth in 1984 by the Green Committees of Correspondence which formed the Green Party USA, these ten values have been adopted by the US national Green Party, most US state Green parties and many of the more than 100 variously named Green Parties around the world. See: Green Party of the United States. *Ten Key Values of the Green Party.* [online]. [Cited April 7, 2012]. gp.org/tenkey.shtml.
15. Duane Elgin. *Promise Ahead : A Vision of Hope and Action for Humanity's Future.* Morrow, 2000, pp. 197–198.
16. Steve McIntosh. *Integral Consciousness and the Future of Evolution.* Paragon, 2007, Kindle edition, Chapter 1.
17. James Surowiecki. "The Populism Problem." *The New Yorker,* February 15, 2010. [online]. [cited March 7, 2012]. newyorker.com/talk/financial/2010/02/15/100215ta_talk_surowiecki.
18. Richard Heinberg. *The Meaning of Copenhagen.* Museletter #212 (January 2010). [online]. [cited March 7, 2012]. richardheinberg.com/category/museletter/page/7.
19. Stefan Theil. "Greece is Far From the EU's Only Joker." *Newsweek/Daily Beast,* February 19, 2010.
20. Wendell Berry. "Out of Your Car, Off Your Horse: Twenty-Seven Propositions about Global Thinking and the Sustainability of Cities" in *Sex, Economy, Freedom, & Community: Eight Essays.* Pantheon, 1993. [online]. [cited March 8, 2012]. http://cupertino1985.blogspot.com/2009/01/wendell-berry-out-of-your-car-off-your.html.
21. Rischard, *High Noon,* p. 191.
22. Anthony Faiola. "Some World Bank Health Programs Ineffective, Report Says." *Washington Post,* May 1, 2009. [online]. [cited April 4, 2012]. washingtonpost.com/wp-dyn/content/article/2009/04/30/AR2009043003349.html.
23. Journal Wire Report, *Winston-Salem Journal.* "World has little to show for its fight on diseases." Drawn from World Health Organization Maximizing Positive Synergies Collaborative Group. "An assessment of interactions between global health initiatives and country health systems." *The Lancet,*

Vol. 373 #9681, June 20, 2009. [online]. [cited March 8, 2012]. thelancet. com/journals/lancet/article/PIIS0140-6736(09)60919-3/fulltext.

24. Paula Tejon Carbahal and David Kanter. "HFCs a Growing Threat to the Climate: The worst greenhouse gases you've *never* heard of." Greenpeace International, updated ed. December 2009. [online]. [cited April 4, 2012]. greenpeace.org/usa/PageFiles/58801/hfcs-a-growing-threat.pdf.

25. Mark Shapiro. "Conning the climate: Inside the carbon-trading shell game." *Harper's*, February 2010, p. 39.

26. Elizabeth Kolbert. "The Sixth Extinction?" *The New Yorker*, May 25, 2009, p. 54.

27. Michael Novacek. *Terra: Our 100-Million-Year-Old Ecosystem — and the Threats That Now Put It at Risk*. Farrar, Straus, 2007, p. 206.

28. Ibid., p. 220.

**Part II: How Life Deals with Critical Mass**

1. Kirkpatrick Sale. *Dwellers in the Land: The Bioregional Vision*. University of Georgia, 2000, p. 41.

**Chapter 7: Life's Steep Economic Learning Curve**

1. I use anthropomorphic language in this part of the book, language that makes it sound as if Life and living systems and other species behave or could behave like humans do. I do this strictly to make the way living systems and other-than-human beings behave easier to understand and to give them the importance to us they ought to have.

2. Lynn Margulis and Dorian Sagan. *What Is Life?* Simon and Schuster, 1995. p. 69.

3. Elisabet Sahtouris. *EarthDance: Living Systems in Evolution*. iUniverse, 2000, p. 9.

4. My understanding of ancient bacteria and ecology owes everything to the work of Lynn Margulis and Dorian Sagan, Elisabet Sahtoris, James Lovelock, Mahlon Hoagland, Franklin Harold, Fritjof Capra, Howard and Elizabeth Odum, Sir Edward Goldsmith, David Holmgren, Ian Mason, Janine Benyus, Brian Walker, David Salt, Michael Novacek, Tyler Volk, Connie Barlow, Stuart Kauffman, Craig Holdredge and Steve Talbot and to those whose work they synthesize and explain.

5. James Lovelock. *Gaia: A New Look at Life on Earth*. Oxford, 2000, p. 22.

6. Swimme and Berry, *The Universe Story*, p. 98.

7. Ibid.

8. Mahlon Hoagland. *The Way Life Works*. Crown, 1995, p. 8.

9. Margaret Wheatley and Myron Kellner-Rogers. *A Simpler Way.* Berrett-Koehler, 1996, p. 17.

10. Frank Herbert. "Appendix I: The Ecology of Dune" in *Dune.* Ace, 1990, p. 505.

## Chapter 8: Life is Earthonomical, Naturally

1. Hoagland, *The Way Life Works,* p. 23.

2. At the bottom of the deep-ocean food chain, several species of microbes have reverted to Life's first dietary regimen: They fuel up directly on chemicals released by seafloor vents, seeps and volcanoes. This process is called *chemosynthesis.* No sunlight is required.

3. Frans de Waal. *The Age of Empathy: Nature's Lessons for a Kinder Society.* Three Rivers, 2010, p. 36.

4. Janine M. Benyus. *Biomimicry: Innovation Inspired by Nature.* Harper, 2002, p. 248.

## Chapter 9: Life's Earthonomical Communities — Prototypes for Deep Green

1. D. Garneau. "Early Man 200,000 to 35,001 BC." European and Asian History. [online]. [cited April 5, 2012]. telusplanet.net/dgarneau/euro2. htm. An equivalent catastrophe today would reduce our numbers from nearly seven billion to less than three.

2. Margulis and Sagan, *What Is Life?,* p. 69.

3. Goldsmith, *The Way,* p. 328.

4. Christian de Quincey. *Consciousness from Zombies to Angels: The Shadow and the Light of Knowing Who You Are.* Park Street, 2009, p. 42. The term "interviduals" was coined by de Quincey's student, Andrew Miller.

5. Lovelock, *Gaia,* p. 43.

6. Fritjof Capra. *The Web of Life: A New Scientific Understanding of Living Systems.* Anchor, 1996, p. 34 .

7. Paul A. Weiss. *The Science of Life: The Living System — A System for Living.* Futura, 1973, pp. 74–75.

8. Robert Wright. *Non-Zero: The Logic of Human Destiny.* Pantheon, 2000, p. 251.

9. "Fish Symbiosis" (video). National Geographic Kids. [online]. [cited April, 5, 2012]. video.nationalgeographic.com/video/kids/animals-pets-kids/fish-kids/fish-symbiosis-kids/; "Rhinos graze with oxpeckers on board" (video). Earth-Touch.com. [online]. [cited April 5, 2012]. earth-touch.com/result.php?i=Rhinos-graze-with-oxpeckers-on-board..

10. Wendell Berry. "Solving for Pattern."

11. Goldsmith, *The Way*, p. 253.

12. There are as many as 7,000 species of green algae. They live in all kinds of aquatic settings in numbers that parallel the numbers of stars in the universe. You can't leave a puddle of water standing for very long without them colonizing it.

13. Margaret Wheatley and Deborah Frieze. "Using Emergence to Take Social Innovation to Scale." 2006. [online]. [cited March 13, 2012]. margaret wheatley.com/articles/emergence.html.

14. I first encountered this concept in Herman E. Daly and John B. Cobb's classic, seminal work *For the Common Good: Redirecting the Economy Toward Community, the Environment and a Sustainable Future*. Beacon, 1989. This is still one of the most complete and thoughtful books on the subjects of ecological communities and the ecologic of community.

15. Andreas Suchantke. *Eco-Geography: What We See When We Look at Landscapes*. Lindisfarne, 2001, p. 112.

16. *The American Heritage Dictionary*, Fourth edition, s.v. "ecosystem."

17. Lynn Margulis. "Gaia: The Living Earth" in Capra, *The Web of Life*, p. 106.

18. I borrowed this section title from Thomas Homer-Dixon's *The Upside of Down: Catastrophe, Creativity, and the Renewal of Civilization*. Island, 2006.

19. Hoagland, *The Way Life Works*, p. 21.

## Chapter 10: Life Is Organically Democratic

1. Gary Marcus. *Kluge: The Haphazard Construction of the Human Mind*. Houghton Mifflin, 2008, p. 2.

2. Larisssa Conradt and Tim Roper. "Consensus Decision Making in Animals." *Trends In Ecology and Evolution*, Vol. 20 #8 (August 2005). [online]. [cited April 6, 2012]. humancond.org/papers/conradt_consensus_animals?s []=consensus decision making in animals.

3. Ibid.

4. Tim Roper and L. Conradt. "Group Decision-Making in Animals." *Nature* 421 (January 2003), p. 155.

5. James Randerson. "Democracy beats despotism in the animal world." *New Scientist*, January 8, 2003. [online]. [cited April 6, 2012]. newscientist.com/article/dn3248-democracy-beats-despotism-in-the-animal-world.html.

6. de Waal, *The Age of Empathy*, Chapter 4.

7. Thom Hartmann. *What Would Jefferson Do?: A Return to Democracy*. Harmony, 2004, p. 141.

8. Werner Krieglstein. "How to Feel and Act Like an Amoeba." *Green Horizon Magazine*, Spring 2008.
9. Hoagland and Dodson, *The Way Life Works*, pp. 152–153.
10. Steve Talbott. "Can Biologists Speak of the 'Whole Organism'? A Conversation." *In Context* #22 (Fall 2009). The Nature Institute. [online]. [cited April 6, 2012]. natureinstitute.org/pub/ic/ic22/conversation.htm.
11. Stephen Johnson. *Emergence: The Connected Lifes of Ants, Brains, Cities and Software*. Scribner, 2001, p. 18.
12. Elisabet Sahtouris quoted in Tijn Touber, "Think global, act natural."
13. Lovelock, *Gaia*, p. 137.
14. Wright, *Non-Zero*, p. 250.
15. Margaret J. Wheatley. *Leadership and the New Science: Discovering Order in a Chaotic World*. Berrett-Koehler, 1999, p. 96.
16. Johnson, *Emergence*, p. 18.
17. Mark Slouka. "A Quibble." *Harper's Magazine*, February 2009.
18. See, for example: Wendell Berry. *The Way of Ignorance and Other Essays* (Counterpoint, 2006); Jared Diamond. *Collapse: How Societies Choose to Fail or Succeed* (Penguin, 2005); Tainter, *The Collapse of Complex Societies*; Thomas Homer-Dixon. *The Ingenuity Gap: Facing the Economic, Environmental, and Other Challenges of an Increasingly Complex and Unpredictable Future*, 2nd ed. (Knopf, 2000); Wright, *A Short History of Progress*.
19. See, for example: Johnson, *Emergence*; Bert Holdobbler and Edward O. Wilson. *The Ants* (Belknap, 1990) and John Whitfield. "E. O. Wilson Says Ants Live in Humanlike Civilizations." *Discover*, November 2008. [online]. [cited April 6, 2012]. discovermagazine.com/2008/nov/12-wilson-says-ants-live-in-humanlike-civilizations.
20. Dee Hock. *Birth of the Chaordic Age*. Berrett-Koehler, 2000, p. 209.
21. Hawken, *Blessed Unrest*, p. 143.
22. Heinz R. Pagels. *The Dream of Reason: The Computer and the Rise of the Sciences of Complexity*. Bantam, 1989, p. 127.
23. James Surowiecki. *The Wisdom of Crowds*. Anchor, 2005.
24. Donella H. Meadows. *Thinking in Systems: A Primer*. Chelsea Green, 2008.
25. Robert K. Greenleaf. *Servant Leadership: A Journey into the Nature of Legitimate Power and Greatness*. Paulist, 2002.
26. Mickey Z., Planet Green. *Green Glossary: Keystone Species*. [online]. [cited March 15, 2012]. animals.howstuffworks.com/endangered-species/green-glossary-keystone-species.htm.
27. Ken Thompson. *Bioteams: High Performance Teams Based on Nature's Most*

*Successful Designs.* Meghan Kiffer, 2008.

28. Brian Walker and David Salt. *Resilience Thinking: Sustaining Ecosystems and People in a Changing World.* Island, 2006, p. xiii.

29. Ibid., p. 38.

30. Animal Cannibalism: "Sharkland: Animal Cannibalism." *Nature.* [online]. [cited April 6, 2012].pbs.org/wnet/nature/episodes/sharkland/animal-cannibalism/1946/. Human cannibalism: Clive Ponting. *A New Green History of the World: The Environment and the Collapse of Great Civilizations.* Penguin, 2007, pp. 104–105. "While there might be 'survival of the fittest' within a given species, each species depends on the services provided by other species to ensure survival. It is a type of cooperation based on mutual survival and is often what a 'balanced ecosystem' refers to."; Anup Shah. "Why is biodiversity important? And who cares?" *Global Issues,* April 6, 2011. [online]. [cited April, 6, 2012] globalissues.org/article/170/why-is-biodiversity-important-who-cares#Ahealthybiodiversityoffersmanynatura lservices; Petr A. Kropotkin. *Mutual Aid: A Factor in Evolution.* [online]. [citedApril6,2012].gutenberg.org/catalog/world/readfile?fk_files=2138514.

31. Bonnie Bassler quoted in Natalie Angier. "Listening to Bacteria." *Smithsonian,* July/August 2010, p. 80.

32. Ibid., p. 78.

33. Scott Nearing. *Civilization & Beyond: Learning from History.* Social Science Institute, 1975, p. 255.

34. Jim Hightower. "To put the progress back in 'progressive,' we need a real populist movement." *The Hightower Lowdown,* Volume 12#6 (June 2010). [online]. [cited March 15, 2012]. hightowerlowdown.org/node/2357.

**The Heart of the Healing**

1. Sale, *Dwellers in the Land,* p. xix.

## Chapter 11: Mimicking Life's Economics — Improving the Odds and Our Lives

1. Geerat J. Vermeij. *Nature: An Economic History,* Princeton, 2006. Kindle edition, last page, Chapter 1.

2. John B. Cobb, Jr. *Sustaining the Common Good: A Christian Perspective on the Global Economy.* Pilgrim, 1994, p. 125.

3. International Council for Local Environmental Initiatives. *The Local Agenda 21 Planning Guide: An Introduction to Sustainable Development Plan.* International Development Research, 1996. [online]. [cited April 9, 2012]. web.idrc.ca/openebooks/448-2/.

4. G. E. Connell. "Letter to the Prime Minister" in *A Report to Canadians.*

National Round Table on the Environment and the Economy, 1991, p. 191.

5. Ervin Laszlo. *The Chaos Point: The World at the Crossroads.* Hampton Roads, 2006, p. 43.

6. "Ecological civilization." Opinion/Commentary, *China Daily,* October 24, 2007. [online]. [cited March 16, 2012]. chinadaily.com.cn/opinion/2007-10/24/content_6201964.htm.

7. *Beijing Forum Newsletter.* Volume 4#1 (2008). [online]. [cited April 10, 2012]. beijingforum.org/res/Home/report/bjn041en.pdf.

8. Critical Mass threatens to bring to an unpleasant end the present 60-million-year-old geological era, the Cenozoic. In the Cenozoic Era the continents took their present form, the cycle of ice ages began, and mammal, plant and bird species diversified and multiplied as never before, establishing mixed-species natural communities in every habitable place on Earth and laying the ground, literally, for Life as we know it.

9. Daniel Gross. "The Comeback Country." *Newsweek,* April 19, 2010.

10. Deep Green is also the name of Rex Wyler's column for Greenpeace and subheading for his blog, Ecolog. [online]. [cited March 16, 2012]. rexweyler.com. Originated by Derrick Jensen, Lierre Keith and Aric McBay, "Deep Green Resistance" named a burgeoning movement that challenges the industrial, corporate capitalist system and calls upon us to help topple it.

11. wiserearth.org and coalition-global-commons.org. [online]. [cited March 19, 2012].

12. Edmund Fowler. "The Life Force: Something Out of Nothing." *Green Horizon Magazine,* Spring 2009.

13. Transition Network. *Transition Initiatives Directory.* [online]. [cited April 10, 2012]. transitionnetwork.org/initiatives.

14. Richard Heinberg, from the Preface to the paperback edition of *Peak Everything: Waking Up to the Century of Declines.* New Society, 2010. [online]. [cited April 10, 2012]. richardheinberg.com/220-peak-everything.

15. Mark Roseland. *Toward Sustainable Communities: Resources for Citizens and Their Governments,* rev ed. New Society, 2005, p. 161.

16. Wes Jackson. *Becoming Native to This Place.* Counterpoint, 1996, p. 55.

17. Mary Douglas. "No Free Gifts." Foreword to Marcel Mauss. *The Gift: Forms and Functions of Exchange in Archaic Societies.* Norton, 2000.

18. Gifford Pinchot. "The Gift Economy." *In Context* #41 (Summer 1995).

19. Raj Patel. *The Value of Nothing: How to Reshape Market Society and Redefine Democracy.* Picador, 2010, p. 92.

20. James Bernard Quilligan. "People Sharing Resources — Toward a New Multilaterism of the Global Commons." *Kosmos,* Fall/Winter 2009.

[online]. [cited April 10, 2012]. kosmosjournal.org/articles/people-sharing-resources-toward-a-new-multilateralism-of-the-global-commons.

21. Commons Governance Work Group. [online]. [cited March 19, 2012]. wiserearth.org/group/commonsgroup.

22. John Robbins. *The New Good Life: Living Better Than Ever in an Age of Less.* Ballantine, 2010, p. xvi.

23. Wanda Urbanska, "Simple Living: Lessons from the World of Television" in Wanda Urbanska and Cecile Andrews, eds. *Less is More: Embracing Simplicity for a Healthy Planet, a Caring Economy and Lasting Happiness.* New Society, 2009, p. 9.

24. Jamaica Kincaid. "My Great Depression: Ten dispatches from the near future." *Harper's,* June 2009.

25. Alan AtKisson. "The Lagom Solution" in *Less is More,* p. 102.

26. Seven Stoll. "Fear of fallowing: The specter of a no-growth world." *Harper's,* March 2008.

27. Charles Siegel. "Robert Solow on the No-Growth Economy." Preservation Institute Blog, October 13, 2008. [online]. [cited March 20, 2012]. preservenet.blogspot.ca/2008_10_01_archive.html.

28. Richard Heinberg. "Life After Growth." MuseLetter #214, March 2010. [online]. [cited March 20, 2012]. richardheinberg.com/214-life-after-growth.

29. Eric W. Sanderson. *Mannahatta: A Natural History of New York City.* Abrams, 2009.

30. Richard Register. *EcoCities: Rebuilding Cities in Balance with Nature.* New Society, 2006, p. 178.

31. Pat Murphy. *Plan C: Community Survival Strategies for Peak Oil and Climate Change.* New Society, 2008, p.113.

32. Ibid., p. 116.

33. William McDonough and Michael Braungart. *Cradle to Cradle: Remaking the Way We Make Things.* North Point, 2002, p. 104.

34. Tom Vanderbilt. "Redesign Cities from Scratch." *Wired,* October 2008.

35. Woody Tasch. *Inquiries into the Nature of Slow Money: Investing as if Food, Farms, and Fertility Mattered.* Chelsea Green, 2008, p. 54.

36. David Orr. *Down to the Wire: Confronting Climate Collapse.* Oxford, 2009, p. 160.

37. A hectare is about two and a half acres.

38. Bill McKibben. *Deep Economy: The Wealth of Communities and the Durable Future.* Times, 2007, pp. 67, 68, 69.

39. Paul Hawken, Amory Lovins and L. Hunter Lovins. *Natural Capitalism: Creating the Next Industrial Revolution.* Little Brown, 1999, p. 210.

40. Ibid.
41. Richard Heinberg and Michael Bomford. *The Food and Farming Transition: Toward a Post Carbon Food System.* Post Carbon Institute, Spring 2009. [online]. [cited March 20, 2012]. richardheinberg.com/bookshelf.
42. Heather C. Flores. *Food Not Lawns: How to Turn Your Yard into a Garden And Your Neighborhood into a Community.* Chelsea Green , 2006.
43. Domenic Vitiello. "Growing Edible Cities" in Eugenie L. Birch and Susan M. Wachter, eds. *Growing Greener Cities: Urban Sustainability in the Twenty-First Century.* University of Pennsylvania, 2008, Chapter 14.
44. Clive Thompson. "Grow Your Own." *Wired,* September 2008.
45. McKibben, *Deep Economy,* p. 73–74, 75.
46. Shenzhen Government online. [online]. [cited April 10, 2012]. english. sz.gov.cn.
47. James Robertson. "Money: I, Thou and It" and "Work: The Right to Be Responsible" in *Beyond the Dependency Culture: People, Power and Responsibility.* Prager, 1998, pp. 103 and 71.
48. Kimberly Weisul. "Why More are Buying into 'Buy Local'." *Bloomsburg Business Week,* February 18, 2010. [online]. cited March 21, 2012]. businessweek.com/magazine/content/10_09/b4168057813351.htm.
49. Michael Shuman. *Going Local: Creating Self-Reliant Communities in a Global Age.* Routledge, 2000, pp. 6–7.
50. Nancy Jack Todd and John Todd. *Bioshelters, Ocean Arks, City Farming: Ecology as the Basis of Design.* Random, 1984, pp. 132.
51. Shuman, *Going Local,* p. 49.
52. Rob Hopkins. *The Transition Handbook: From oil dependency to local resilience.* Chelsea Green, 2008, pp. 68 and 69.
53. Adapted from *People Magazine,* April 6, 2009.
54. Adapted from Sarah James and Torbjörn Lahti. *The Natural Step for Communities: How Cities and Towns Can Change to Sustainable Practices.* New Society, 2004.
55. Richard Craver. "Boys and girls club buildings get facelift." *Winston-Salem Journal,* February 2010.

## Chapter 12: Mimicking Life's Politics — Organically Democratic Principles and Practices

1. Hock, *Birth of the Chaordic Age,* endpapers.
2. Sahtouris, *EarthDance,* p. 311.
3. Cited in Burton Egbert Stevenson. *The Home Book of Quotations, Classical and Modern,* tenth edition. Dodd Mead, 1984.

4. John Cavanagh and Jerry Mander, eds. *Alternatives to Economic Globalization: A Better World is Possible.* Berrett-Koehler, 2002, p. 110.
5. See, for example: C. Douglas Lummis. *Radical Democracy* (Cornell, 1996); Benjamin Barber. *Strong Democracy: Participatory Politics for A New Age* (University of California, 2004); Hartmann, *What Would Jefferson Do?*
6. Edmund Fowler. From Chapter Six of a book tentatively titled *From Galileo to the Greens: Our Escape From Mechanistic Thinking.*
7. See, for example [all cited April 16, 2012]: National Community Land Trust Network (cltnetwork.org/); the National Housing Trust's Institute for Community Economics (nhtinc.org/ice.php) and for an international perspective — the Canadian Land Trust Alliance (clta.ca/en/ ).
8. Shuman, *Going Local,* p. 192.
9. Adapted from Marie R. Jones and Helen Moak. "The Chestnut Hill Experiment" in Lloyd P. Wells and Larry Lemmel. *Recreating Democracy: Breathing New Life into American Communities.* Center for Consensual Democracy, 1998, pp. xv–xvi.
10. Hock, *Birth of the Chaordic Age,* p. 139.
11. Rensenbrink, *Against All Odds,* p. 22.
12. Shuman. *Going Local,* p. 128.
13. Ronald Reagan. "Address Before A Joint Session Of The Congress Reporting On The State Of The Union." January 25, 1984. [online]. [cited April 10, 2012]. reagan2020.us/speeches/state_of_the_union_1984.asp.
14. Shann Turnbull. "A New Way to Govern" in Roy Madrone and John Jopling. *Gaian Democracies: Redefining Globalisation and People-Power.* Green, 2003, p. 17.
15. *American Heritage Dictionary,* Fourth Edition, s.v. "conservative."
16. Andrew Sullivan. "Wanted: A Practical Guide to Saving the Planet." *The Sunday New York Times,* August 6, 2006.
17. David Jenkins. "Conservatism's Green Roots." *inFocus Quarterly,* Vol III#3 (Fall 2009). [online]. [cited March 22, 2012]. jewishpolicycenter. org/1417/conservatism-green-roots.
18. Adapted from Earthaven Ecovillage. [online]. [cited March 22, 2012]. Earthaven.org.
19. Queen Elizabeth II. "Address to the United Nations General Assembly," July 6, 2010. [online]. [cited April 10, 2012]. americanrhetoric.com/ speeches/queenelizabethunitednations.htm.
20. Greenleaf, *Servant Leadership,* pp. 38–39.
21 August T. Jaccaci. *General Periodicity: Nature's Creative Dynamics.* Fiddlehead Publishing/Unity Scholars Media, 2000, pp. 50, 51, 59, 63.

## Chapter 13: Setting a Good Example

1. Unless otherwise noted, all quotes for this section are taken from Wangari Maathai. *The Green Belt Movement.* Lantern, 2006.
2. Wangari Maathai. "The Green Belt Movement of Kenya." Keynote address, Bowdoin College Conference on Race, Justice and the Environment, February 2003. *Green Horizon Magazine,* Summer 2003.
3. John Rensenbrink. "Dispelling the Myths: Linking What Has Been Kept Separate." *Green Horizon Magazine,* Winter 2005.
4. Ibid.
5. P. Sainath. "Neo-Liberal Terrorism in India: The Largest Wave of Suicides in History." *Counterpunch,* February 12, 2009. [online]. [cited March 31, 2012]. counterpunch.org/2009/02/12/the-largest-wave-of-suicides-in-history/.
6. Vandana Shiva. "GM and The PM." *Navdanya's Diary,* March 28, 2012. [online]. [cited March 31, 2012]. navdanya.org/blog/.
7. Vandana Shiva. *Earth Democracy: Justice, Sustainability, and Peace.* South End, 2005, pp. 10 and 6.
8. Navdanya website. [online]. [cited March 2008]. navdanya.org.
9. The Swaraj Foundation. "What Is Swaraj?" [online]. [cited March 31, 2012]. swaraj.org/whatisswaraj.htm.
10. "Navdanya Trust." Hivos website. [online]. [cited March 31, 2012]. *hivos. nl/dut/community/partner/10000901.*
11. Navdanya website. [online]. [cited March 2008]. navdanya.org.
12. All quotes in this section are taken from Alan Weisman. *Gaviotas: A Village to Reinvent the World,* 10th anniversary edition. Chelsea Green, 2008. See also Friends of Gaviotas website. [online]. [cited April 2, 2012]. friendsof gaviotas.org/Friends_of_Gaviotas/Home.html.
13. Weisman, *Gaviotas,* pp. 112–113.
14. All quotes in this section are taken from Angus Wright and Wendy Wolford. *To Inherit the Earth: The Landless Movement and the Struggle for a New Brazil.* FoodFirst Books, 2003. See also Friends of the MST website. [online]. [cited April 2, 2012]. mstbrazil.org/.
15. Wright and Wolford, *To Inherit the Earth,* p. 321.
16. Most of the quotes and statistics for this section are taken from Leif Utne. "Don't Cry for Argentina." *Utne,* January/February 2003, p. 17–18; the video "Argentina's Economic Collapse 2001." [online]. [cited April 2, 2012]. democraticunderground.com/discuss/duboard.php?az=view_all& address=389x3650870; Federico Fuentes. "ARGENTINA: 'For a government of popular assemblies!'" *Green Left,* February 27, 2002. [online]. [cited April 2, 2012]. greenleft.org.au/node/25792.

17. Graceala Monteagudo. "The Argentinean Autonomist Movement and the Elections." *Synthesis/Regeneration* 32 (Fall 2003). [online]. [cited April 2, 2012]. greens.org/s-r/32/32-23.html.
18. Quotes for this section taken from Roy Morrison. *We Build the Road as We Travel*. New Society, 1991.
19. Georgia Kelly and Shaula Massena. "Mondragón Worker-Cooperatives Decide How to Ride Out A Downturn." *Yes!* Posted June 2, 2009. [online]. [cited April 2, 2012]. yesmagazine.org/issues/the-new-economy/mondragon-worker-cooperatives-decide-how-to-ride-out-a-downturn.
20. Quotes and statistics for this section taken from William A. Shutkin. *The Land That Could Be: Environmentalism and Democracy in the Twenty-First Century*. MIT, 2001; "Urban Agriculture in Boston's Dudley Neighborhood: A Modern Twist on Jefferson's Dream." (Chapter 4 in the same book); Dudley Street Neighborhood Initiative website. [online]. [cited April 2, 2012]. dsni.org/; "Dudley Street Neighborhood Initiative Creates an Urban Village." Civic Practices Network website. [online]. [cited April 2, 2012]. cpn.org/topics/community/dudly.html.
21. Quotes taken from Sarah James and Torbjörn Lahti. *The Natural Step for Communities: How Cities and Towns Can Change to Sustainable Practices*. New Society, 2004, pp. 104–105.

**Chapter 14: How to Become Deeply Green**

1. Richard Heinberg. "Timing and the Post Carbon Manifesto." MuseLetter #204 (April 2009). [online]. [cited March 26, 2012]. richardheinberg.com/204-timing-and-the-post-carbon-manifesto.
2. Susan Meeker-Lowry. "Community Money" in Jerry Mander and Edward Goldsmith, eds. *The Case Against the Global Economy: And for a Turn toward the Local*. Sierra Club, 1997, pp. 452–453.
3. Shuman, *Going Local*, p. 133. Shuman, the authors of *Building Sustainable Communities: Tools and Concepts for Self-Reliant Economic Change* (Bootstrap, 1989), New Society and Chelsea Green Publishers all provide information and resources about community banking and loan systems, community currencies and other aspects of monetary localization sufficient to get a community started on that path. Papers and books from the New Economics Institute are also invaluable. [online]. [cited March 26, 2012]. neweconomicsinstitute.org.
4. The Open Money Projects. [online]. [cited March 26, 2012]. openmoney.org/top/introduction.html.
5. Frances Moore Lappé. *Democracy's Edge: Choosing to Save Our Country by*

*Bringing Democracy to Life.* Jossey-Bass, 2005, p. 113.

6. Shuman, *Going Local,* p. 135.

7. E-mail, February 16, 2007.

8. James Robertson. *Future Wealth: A New Economics for the 21st Century.* Bootstrap, 1990, pp. 98 and 125.

9. Douthwaite, *Short Circuit,* p. v.

10. Hopkins, *Transition Handbook,* pp. 197 and 69.

11. *The Oil Depletion Protocol* itself has also been published under the names *Rimini Protocol* and *Uppsala Protocol,* as it was released at conferences in those European cities.

12. Richard Heinberg. *The Oil Depletion Protocol.* New Society, 2006, p. 33.

13. In his novel *World Made by Hand* (Grove, 2009), James Howard Kunstler has compellingly imagined for us what post-peak life might be like for the residents of a small town in upstate New York, with intimations of what it would be like for the rest of the US.

14. Kunstler, *The Long Emergency,* p. 65.

15. Elizabeth Kolbert. "The Island in the Wind: A Danish community's victory over carbon emissions." *The New Yorker,* July 7, 2008. [online]. [cited March 27, 2012]. newyorker.com/reporting/2008/07/07/080707fa_fact_kolbert.

16. "Post-carbon" refers to the period after we pass the peak in carbon-based fossil fuels including oil, coal and natural gas.

17. Frances Moore Lappé. *Eco-Mind: Changing the Way We Think, to Create the World We Want.* Nation, 2011, p. 21.

18. Changing bulbs is a "low-hanging-fruit" efficiency fix: easy, cheap, individualized and globalizable and therefore a first step. However, the CFL bulbs contain mercury, are dangerous when broken and hard to dispose of safely. No solution that permits us to continue to live large will meet all the terms of Life's Economic Survival Protocol.

19. Paul Roberts. *The End of Oil: On the Edge of a Perilous New World.* Houghton Mifflin, 2004, p. 220.

20. Murphy, *Plan C,* p. 141.

21. David Owen. "The Efficiency Dilemma." *The New Yorker,* December 20, 2010.

22. Ibid.

23. Jeff Dardozzi. "The Specter of Jevons' Paradox." *Synthesis/Regeneration* 47, Fall 2008.

24. Herman Daly in a book review of Polimeni et al., eds. *The Jevons' Paradox and the Myth of Resource Efficiency Improvements.* Earthscan, 2008.

25. Bill McKibben. *Deep Economy: The Wealth of Communities and the Durable*

*Future.* Times, 2007, p. 145.

26. Matthew Stein. *When Technology Fails: A Manual for Self-Reliance &
Planetary Survival.* Clear Light, 2000, p. 277.

27. David Holmgren. *Permaculture: Principles & Pathways Beyond Sustainability.*
Holmgren, 2002, p. 13.

28. Tim Watson. "Eco-Restorative Design: Applying Agrarian Earth Science
towards the Re-Greening America." January 25, 2009. [online]. [cited
March 27, 2012]. tlwarchitect.com/writings.html.

29. Bruce Nussbaum. "Are Designers the Enemy of Design?" *Business Week,*
March 18, 2007. [online]. [cited March 27, 2012]. businessweek.com/
innovate/NussbaumOnDesign/archives/2007/03/are_designers_t.html.

30. Paola Antonelli, ed. *Design and the Elastic Mind.* Museum of Modern Art,
2008, reprinted in *Seed,* March/April 2008.

31. See, for example, the UN Earth Charter (earthcharterinaction.org/content/
pages/Read-the-Charter.html), architect William McDonough's Hanover
Principles (mcdonough.com/principles.pdf) and Dr. Karl-Henrik Robèrt's
*Natural Step Framework for Long Term Sustainability* (naturalstepusa.org/
natural-step-framework/). [all online]. [all cited March 27, 2012].

32. Aldo Leopold. "The Land Ethic" in *A Sand County Almanac and Sketches
Here and There.* Oxford, 1968, pp. 224–225.

33. Ted Bernard and Jora Young. *The Ecology of Hope: Communities Collaborate
for Sustainability.* New Catalyst, 2008.

34. "Does Community Have Value?" in Wendell Berry. *Home Economics:
Fourteen Essays.* North Point, 1987, p. 192.

35. Edward O. Wilson. *Consilience: The Unity of Knowledge.* Knopf, 1998,
pp. 4 and 298.

36. Goldsmith, *The Way,* p. 137.

37. Benyus, *Biomimicry,* p. 2.

38. Wendell Berry. *Life is a Miracle: An Essay Against Modern Superstition.*
Counterpoint, 2001, p. 137.

39. Patrick Whitefield. "The Art of Reading the Landscape." *Permaculture
Magazine* #61 (Autumn 2009), pp. 36–37; excerpted from Patrick
Whitefield. *The Living Landscape: How to Read and Understand It.*
Permanent, 2009.

40. David Abrams. Foreword to Andy Fisher. *Radical Ecopsychology: Psychology
in the Service of Life.* SUNY, 2002, p. ix.

41. Arne Naess, from an interview conducted at the Zen Center in Los
Angeles in 1982, reprinted in Bill Devall and George Sessions. *Deep Ecology:
Living As if Nature Mattered.* Peregrine Smith, 1985, pp. 75 and 74.

42. Thomas Berry. *The Great Work: Our Way into the Future*. Harmony, 1999, p. 5.

43. Herman Greene & The Center for Earth Jurisprudence. *The Ecozoic,* No. 1 (2008).

44. "Wild Law." EnAct International website. [online]. [cited March 28, 2012]. enact-international.com/earth.htm.

45. Wells and Lemmel, *Recreating Democracy,* p. 163.

46. Julia Whitty. "By the end of the century half of all species will be gone." *Mother Jones,* May/June 2007, pp. 44 and 45.

## Chapter 15 Precedents for Success

1. See, for example: Merlin Donald. *Origins of the Modern Mind: Three Stages in the Evolution of Culture and Cognition* (Harvard, 1991); Steven Mithen. *The Prehistory of the Mind: The Cognitive Origins of Art, Religion and Science* (Thames & Hudson, 1996); Julian Jaynes. *The Origin of Consciousness in the Breakdown of the Bicameral Mind* (Houghton Mifflin, 1976); Mary E. Clark. *In Search of Human Nature* (Routledge, 2002); Daniel C. Dennett. *Consciousness Explained* (Little, Brown, 1991); Allan Combs. *The Radiance of Being: Understanding the Grand Integral Vision; Living the Integral Life,* 2nd ed. (Paragon, 2002); Jean Gebser. *The Ever-Present Origin, Part One: Foundations of the Aperspectival World and Part Two: Manifestations of the Aperspectival World* (Ohio, 1991).

2. Don Edward Beck and Christopher C. Cowan. *Spiral Dynamics: Mastering Values, Leadership, and Change.* Blackwell, 1996, p. 23.

3. John Colapinto. "Brain Games: The Marco Polo of neuroscience." *The New Yorker,* May 11, 2009. [online]. [cited March 28, 2012]. newyorker.com/reporting/2009/05/11/090511fa_fact_colapinto.

4. Theodore Roethke. "In A Dark Time." Poetry Foundation website. [online]. [cited April 12, 2012]. poetryfoundation.org/poem/172120.

5. Albert Einstein quoted in: Brook Noel. *Good Morning: 365 Positive Ways to Start Your Day.* Sourcebooks, 2008, pp. 32–33.

6. Tom Atlee. *Reflections on Evolutionary Activism: Essays, poems and prayers from an emerging field of sacred social change.* CreateSpace, 2009, p. 100. [online]. [cited April 12, 2012]. s3.amazonaws.com/evolutionaryactivism.wagn.org/card_files/2/EvolutionaryActivismAtlee.pdf.

7. We've learned that this is a false distinction. Though we do more with tools and speech than other animals, many other-than-human-species have rudimentary language capacities and use simple tools like sticks and stones, as we did early on.

8. Mithen. *The Prehistory of the Mind,* p. 167.
9. Ponting, *A New Green History of the World,* p. 67.
10. Pico Iyer. "Introduction" to Philip Zaleski, ed. *The Best Spiritual Writing 2010.* Penguin, 2010, p. xiv.
11. Joel Garreau in an interview with the editors of *EnlightenNext Magazine,* June-August 2009.
12. Joanna Macy and Chris Johnstone. *Active Hope: How to Face the Mess We're in without Going Crazy.* New World, 2012, p. 31.

**Chapter 16: Dreaming Deep Green, Imagining the Ecozoic**

1. One of the best compendiums of survival tools and techniques already in existence is: Alex Steffen, ed. *Worldchanging: A User's Guide for the 21st Century,* rev. and updated ed. Abrams, 2011. It covers topics ranging from shelter and community to cities, business and politics and offers examples and resources from around the world.

# Appendix: Suggestions for Further Reading

Bane, Peter. *The Permaculture Handbook: Garden Farming for Town and Country.* New Society, 2012.

Berry, Thomas. *The Great Work: Our Way into the Future.* Harmony, 1999.

Berry, Wendell. Any collection of his essays.

Catton, William. *Overshoot: The Ecological Basis of Revolutionary Change.* University of Illinois, 1982.

Cobb, John and Herman Daly. *For the Common Good: Redirecting the Economy Toward Community, the Environment and a Sustainable Future.* Beacon, 1989.

Edwards, Andreas. *The Sustainability Revolution: Portrait of a Paradigm Shift.* New Society, 2005.

Eisenstein, Charles. *Sacred Economics: Money, Gift and Society in the Age of Transition.* Evolver, 2011.

Foster, John Bellamy. *The Vulnerable Planet: A Short Economic History of the Environment.* Monthly Review, 1999.

Gilding, Paul. *The Great Disruption: Why the Climate Crisis Will Bring On the End of Shopping and the Birth of a New World.* Bloomsbury, 2012.

Goldsmith, Edward. *The Way: An Ecological World-View,* rev. ed. University of Georgia, 2008.

Goldsmith, Edward and Jerry Mander, eds. *The Case Against the Global Economy & for a Turn Toward Localization.* Sierra Club, 1996.

Greer, John Michael. *The Ecotechnic Future: Envisioning a Post-Peak World.* New Society, 2009.

Hawken, Paul. *Blessed Unrest: How the Largest Movement in History Is Restoring Grace, Justice, and Beauty to the World.* Viking, 2007.

Heinberg, Richard. *The End of Growth: Adapting to Our New Economic Reality.* New Society, 2011.

Holmgren, David. *Permaculture: Principles & Pathways Beyond Sustainability.* Holmgren, 2002.

Hopkins, Rob. *The Transition Handbook: From oil dependency to local resilience.* Chelsea Green, 2008.

James, Sarah and Torbjörn Lahti. *The Natural Step for Communities: How Cities and Towns Can Change to Sustainable Practices.* New Society, 2004.

Jensen, Derrick. *Endgame, Volume I: The Problem of Civilization.* Seven Stories, 2006.

Jensen, Derrick. *Endgame, Volume II: Resistance.* Seven Stories, 2006.

Korten, David. *The Great Turning: From Empire to Earth Community.* Berrett-Koehler/Kumarian, 2006.

Lewis, Michael and Pat Conaty. *The Resilience Imperative: Cooperative Transitions to a Steady-state Economy.* New Society, 2012.

Lipton, Bruce and Steve Bhaerman. *Spontaneous Evolution: Our Positive Future (And A Way to Get There from Here).* Hay House, 2009.

Macy, Joanna and Chris Johnstone. *Active Hope: How to Face the Mess We're In Without Going Crazy.* New World, 2012.

Madron, Roy and John Jopling. *Gaian Democracies: Redefining Globalisation and People-Power.* Green, 2003.

Bill McKibben. *Eaarth: Making a Life on a Tough New Planet.* Times, 2010.

McKibben, Bill. *Deep Economy: The Wealth of Communities and the Durable Future.* Times, 2007.

Meadows, Donella H. *Thinking in Systems: A Primer.* Chelsea Green, 2008.

Murphy, Pat. *Plan C: Community Survival Strategies for Peak Oil and Climate Change.* New Society, 2008.

Nickerson, Mike. *Life, Money and Illusion: Living on Earth as if we want to stay.* New Society, 2009.

Ophuls, William. *Plato's Revenge: Politics in the Age of Ecology.* MIT, 2011.

Orr, David. *Down to the Wire: Confronting Climate Collapse.* Oxford, 2009.

Ponting, Clive. *A New Green History of the World: The Environment and the Collapse of Great Civilizations.* Penguin, 2007.

Register, Richard. *Ecocities: Rebuilding Cities in Balance With Nature.* New Society, 2006.

Robbins, John. *The New Good Life: Living Better Than Ever in an Age of Less.* Ballentine, 2010.

Robertson, James. *Future Money: Breakdown or Breakthrough.* Green Books, 2012.

Roseland, Mark. *Toward Sustainable Communities: Resources for Citizens and Their Governments,* rev. ed. New Society, 2005.

Ruppert, Michael C. *Confronting Collapse: The Crisis of Energy and Money in a Post Peak Oil World.* Chelsea Green, 2009.

Sahtouris, Elisabet. *EarthDance: Living Systems in Evolution.* iUniverse, 2000.

Smiley, Tavis and Cornell West. *The Rich and the Rest of Us: A Poverty Manifesto.* Smiley Books, 2012.

Speth, James Gustav. *The Bridge at the Edge of the World: Capitalism, the Environment, and Crossing from Crisis to Sustainability.* Yale, 2008.

Vermeij, Geerat. *Nature: An Economic History.* Princeton, 2006.

Walker, Brian and David Salt. *Resilience Thinking: Sustaining Ecosystems and People in a Changing World.* Island, 2006.

Wilson, Edward O. *The Social Conquest of Earth.* Liveright, 2012.

Weiss, Paul. A. *The Science of Life: The Living System — A System for Living.* Futura, 1973.

Weston, Anthony. *How to Re-Imagine the World: A Pocket Guide for Practical Visionaries.* New Society, 2007.

# Index

**A**

acquired immune deficiency syndrome. *See* HIV/AIDS
AE (author), 125
aeroponics planters, 224
Africa
    disease management, 119
    Ecological Footprint, 76
    economic recovery, 102
    oil exports, 42
    water use, 22–23
*Against All Odds* (Rensenbrink), 93
agriculture
    corporate control of, 262–266
    industrialization of, 21–22
    land occupation, 247, 269–272
    pollution, 24
    water use, 22
AIDS (acquired immune deficiency syndrome). *See* HIV/AIDS
Airaudi, Oberto, 248
alternative energy, 296–297
Amazon rainforest, 156–157, 159
amoeba, 169
animal species
    common goods, 138
    democracy in, 166–168
    diversification of, 142–143
    extinction, 28, 32
    flagship species, 30, 179
    in hard times, 185–186
    keystone species, 180
    solar energy use, 137
    symbiotic relationships, 152
Antonelli, Paola, 298
ants, 168, 174
aquaponics, 224
Arcosanti, Arizona, 248
Arctic, 30, 39
Argentina, 247, 272–275
Arizmendiarrieta, José María, 248, 275–276
Asia, 20
asteroid crash, 122
asthma, 24
Atkins Community Development Corporation, 230
Atlee, Tom, 176, 235
Australia, 76

**B**

bacteria
    becoming sustainable, 132–134
    communication of, 187
    Critical Mass survival, 127–132
    diversification of, 142–143
    downsizing of, 141
    in entrepreneurship role, 179
    grassroots organization, 170–172
    information sharing, 174
    interdependence of, 150, 151
    merging of, 154
bad behavior, 238
Bailout Theory, 97–100

355

Barber, Benjamin, 237
Barclays, 120
barrels of oil equivalent (BOE), 294
barter, 65–66
basmati rice, 266
Bassler, Bonnie, 187
beauty, 302–303
Bechtel, 263
Beck, Don, 311
bees, 168
behaviors, democratic, 165–170
Beijing, 24
Benyus, Janine, 302
Berkeley, California, 248
Berks County, Pennsylvania, 224
BerkShares, 284
Berry, Thomas, 132, 200, 306, 324
Berry, Wendell, 153, 154, 300
BHP Billiton, 120
Big Five events, 122–123
biocracy, 79–81
biomimicry, 302
bioregions, 155–156
bird species, extinction, 28
Black Sea, 41
black-tailed prairie dogs, 180
*Blessed Unrest* (Hawken), 8, 197
BOE (barrels of oil equivalent), 294
Bombay, 24, 26
Boston, Massachusetts, 276–277
Brazil
    displaced farmers, 247, 269–272
    economic recovery, 102
    energy consumption, 78, 297
    poverty, 27
    tribal groups, 32
Bretton Woods, New Hampshire, 67, 90
British Petroleum (BP), 17
Brookes, Leonard, 295
Brown, Lester, 105, 106, 107, 109, 116–117
Bucks County, Pennsylvania, 224
*Building Cities That Work* (Fowler), 204
Buji Farm Produce Wholesale Market, 225
Bures, Frank, 94
Burlington, Vermont, 239
business incubators, 230
business parks, 229–230
*Business Week*, 297
businesses, 227–230
butterflies, 308–309
buy local, 227–230
C
campaign funding, 88–89
Campbell, Colin, 38
Canada
    Ecological Footprint, 76

fossil fuel conflicts, 40
    oil exports, 42
    tar sands, 39, 41
capitalism
    as cause of Critical Mass, 37–38, 55
    in democracy, 93–95
    without growth, 215
Capsian Sea, 42
Capuchin monkeys, 168
carbon dioxide (CO2)
    climate instability caused by, 130–131
    Earth's exchange system, 48–49
    sequestering of, 154
carbon trading, 120–121
Cargill, 120, 263
carrying capacity, 64–65, 70–73, 74, 99
catastrophe. *See* Critical Mass
Catton, William, 72, 95–96
CELs (Community Economic Laboratories), 204
Centers for Earth Jurisprudence, 306
Central Asia, 42
CFCs (chlorofluorocarbons), 120
*The Challenge of the Slums* (UN), 26
chaordic, 234–235, 301
chaos, 233, 234–235
charity, 207–208
Chelsea Green, 203
Chestnut Hill Community Association, 240–241, 248
China
    air pollution, 25
    city populations, 26
    Ecological Footprint, 76
    economic recovery, 102
    fossil fuel conflicts, 29, 40
    oil consumption, 42, 78, 297
    poverty, 27
    rise of, 38, 56
    urban agriculture, 225
*China Daily*, 199
choice, illusion of, 92
Christian, Diana Leaf, 247
Cincinnati, Ohio, 239
Citibank, 120
cities, local food production, 224
citizenship, 307–310
City Market, 228
Civic Economics, 227
civilizations
    conflicts and war, 29
    ecological, 200
    effect on ecosystems, 10
    importance of money, 65–70
    invention of, 315–318
    pyramidal structure, 80–81

sustainability of, 74–75
climate change. *See* climate instability
climate crisis, for bacteria, 130–131
climate instability
  as cause of Critical Mass, 38, 56
  complexity of climate, 46–48
  Earth as respiratory system, 48–49
  evidence of, 49–51
  human causes of, 52–54
  natural causes of, 51–52
  opinions on, 4–6
closed systems, 70–73
Club of Rome, 99
coal, 42, 295
*The Coal Question* (Jevons), 295
Coca-Cola, 263
code orange days, 24
collapse, use of term, 6–7
  *See also* Critical Mass
Colombia, 266–270
commodities, exchange of, 65–67
common goods, Earth as, 137–138
Commons Governance Work Group, 210
commons trusts, 109–110, 113
communities (human)
  agricultural settlements, 269–272
  democracy in, 235–236
  development of, 257–259
  governance, 238–243
  in hard times, 186
  importance of, 230–231
  integration with natural communities, 300
  learning of surroundings, 216–217
  local food production, 220–225
  mimicking Life, 196–199
  of place, 205–207
  possibilities, 323–324
  role of political parties, 243–244
  self-reliance, 266–270, 277–278
  for sustainable economies, 194–195
  urban village creation, 276–277
  *See also* natural communities
community associations, 239
community economics, 111
community gardens, 221
community land trusts (CLTs), 239
compassion, 251
competition, 153
complex systems, crisis multiplication, 15–17
conflict
  after collapse, 252
  avoidance of, 238
  disappearance of, 31
  as symptom of Critical Mass, 29–30
*Confronting Collapse* (Ruppert), 39, 102
Conradt, Larissa, 166–167

consciousness
  caused by Critical Mass, 313–315
  transformations in, 113–115
conserve-atism, 149, 182, 245–246
consumerism, 92, 95
Convention on Biological Diversity, 28
cooperation, 148–149
cooperatives, 275–276 229; 205
corporations, 86, 87–90
  *See also* global economy
Coutinho, Antonio, 175
Cowan, Christopher, 311
Cretaceous period, 122–123
crisis multiplication, 15–17
Critical Mass
  acknowledgement of, 33–35
  Big Five events, 122–123
  crisis multiplication, 15–17
  determining cause, 36, 37–38, 54–57
  downsizing by, 141
  effect of global economy, 63, 101–102
  effect on communities, 186–187
  effect on the Powers, 85–86
  evolution of, 8–11
  experience of bacteria, 127–134
  future possibilities, 324
  history of, 4
  human-induced, 319–320
  importance of community, 230–231
  as name for crisis, 6–8
  precedents for success following collapse,
    311–320
  religious development and, 318
  symptoms of, 13–15, 19–30
  timing of, 230–231
  transition to regional economies, 191
  treatment of symptoms, 30–32
Critical Mass (cyclist group), 7
Cuba, 224–225
Cullinan, Cormac, 306
curtailment, 218
D
da Silva, Arjuna, 247
Dahl, Robert A., 173
Dakha, Bangladesh, 26
Daly, Herman, 65, 67, 107, 213–214, 215–
  216, 295–296
Damanhur federation, 248
Dardozzi, Jeff, 295
Davis, Carol, 230
Davis, Mike, 26
de Quincey, Christian, 145
de Waal, Frans, 168
decentralization, 111, 181
Declaration of Independence, 253
Deep Ecology, 304–305

*Deep Economy* (McKibben), 221
Deep Green
    as cure, 201
    existing practices, 202–204
    possibilities, 321–324
    transition to, 199–202
Deepwater Horizon, 39, 40, 41
Deffeyes, Kenneth, 38
*Defying Corporations, Defining Democracy* (Ritz),
    89–90
degrowth of economies, 214–216
dematerializing, 218
democracy
    in Argentina, 272–275
    avoidance, 86–87
    in Brazil, 271–272
    built-in, 235–236
    capitalism and, 93–95
    challenge of mimicking, 237–238
    comparison to pyramidal structure, 188
    development of, 31
    of global economy, 79–81
    in India, 262–266
    information access in, 173–174
    in Kenya, 261–262
    in Life, 165–166
    organization of, 177–178
    participatory, 110, 307–310
    for subsistence farmers, 265
    turnover of, 182–184
    as verb, 242
denial, 4–6
Denmark, 40
depaving, 216
dependence, 150
design, 297–298, 312–313
developing nations. See poor nations
dictatorships, 31
*dictyostelium*, 169
digital democracy, 93–95
dinosaurs, 122
disease, 26–28, 119
dislocation, 26–28
diversity, 112, 142–143, 150
dolphins, 167–168
Doon Valley, India, 266
Dornhaus, Anna, 168
Douthwaite, Richard, 286
Dow Jones Industrial Average, 98
downsizing, 141, 214–216, 279–280 [160]
downtimes, 160–162, 211–214
Draffan, George, 86
Dudley Street Neighborhood Initiative (DSNI),
    276–277
*Dwellers in the Land* (Sale), 192

**E**
*Eaarth* (McKibben), 6
Earth
    bailouts, 97–98
    carrying capacity of, 64–65, 70–73, 74, 99
    as common inheritance, 137–138
    complexity of climate, 46–48
    depletion of resources, 3–6, 23
    downtimes, 160–162
    historic global catastrophes, 128–134
    living within the means of, 59–61, 299
    as respiratory system, 48–49
    support of Life on, 9
Earth Democracy, 263
Earth Jurisprudence, 306–307
Earthaven community, 247
Earthological, 60
Earthonomics
    avoidance of Critical Mass, 186–187
    comparison to pyramidal structure, 188
    of Life, 135–140
    survival protocol, 60
Earthscan, 203
*Ecocities* (Register), 248
ecological, use of term, 60
ecological civilization, 199–200
Ecological Footprint, 75–76
ecological wisdom, 110
economic summits, 84
Economic Survival Protocol
    as economic protocol, 60
    for human communities, 193–195, 219
    importance of all rules, 139–140, 235
    ten rules, 134
economics
    community-level, 111, 144–146
    of ecosystems, 157–160
    Life's survival protocol, 60
economies
    degrowth of, 214–216
    dependence of, 69–70, 95
    downsizing of, 198–199
    gift-based, 207–209
    interdependence of, 98
    measure of, 107–108
    of natural communities, 146–148
    obstacles to diversification, 279–280
    subsistence-based, 205–207
    for sustainable communities, 194–195
    taking charge of, 196–197
    tools for rebuilding, 90–91
    transition to regional, 191, 204–205
ecopsychology, 305
ecoregions, 155–156
Eco-Spirituality, 305
ecosystems

aging of, 182–184
collapse of, 28–29
definition, 157
economics of, 157–160
effect of civilizations on, 10
flagship species, 30
restoration of, 198
ecosystems services, 99
Ecozoic
    possibilities, 321–324
    transition to, 199–202
eggs, 71–72
Egypt
    acts of resistance, 253
    Ecological Footprint, 76
    pyramidal structure, 80
Eisenstein, Charles, 69
Elgin, Duane, 212
The Elite Consensus (Draffan), 86
Elizabeth II (Queen), 247, 249
Empire of Illusion (Hedges), 93
employment, 26–28, 225–227
The End of Growth (Heinberg), 297
The End of Nature (McKibben), 303
energy
    downsizing of systems, 198–199
    efficiency and consumption, 295–296
    local production, 296–297
    reduction in consumption, 292–295
    See also fossil fuels
energy crisis, for bacteria, 129–130
energy descent, 287–288
enlightenment, 113–115
Enlightenment, Age of, 319
entrepreneurship role, 179
Environmental Spirituality, 305
environments, partnerships with natural com-
    munities, 157–160
equal opportunities, 110–111
equality, 111–112
equilibrio, 275
Europe
    Ecological Footprint, 76
    fossil fuel conflicts, 40
    income, 78
    unemployment rates, 27
extinction, 28–29, 61
F
Fahnstrom, Dale, 236
fallowing, 214
Faneuil Hall Marketplace, 228
farms, 220–225
Farnish, Keith, 75, 91–93, 252
Financial Times, 26
flagship species, 30, 179
flash trading, 67–68

Fleming, David, 229
Flores, Heather, 223
food
    localization of production, 220–225
    as symptom of Critical Mass, 20–22
    water use, 22
Food Not Lawns (Flores), 223
Forbes 400, 84
Ford Motor Company, 229–230
forests, 259–262
Fosdick, Harry Emerson, 237
fossil fuels
    as cause of conflict, 29–30
    as cause of Critical Mass, 38, 55
    consumption, 78
    decline in use, 287–288
    effect of efficiency, 295–296
    effect on Earth's capacity, 10
    importance of oil, 20–22
    pollution from, 25
    reduction in consumption, 288–297
    See also peak oil
Fowler, Edmund, 204, 238
fracking, 42
France, 78
Franks, Nigel R., 168
Freecycle, 208
freedoms, 92
Freeling, Nicole Achs, 65
Fresh Kills landfill, 25, 220
Friedman, Tom, 108
frugality, 211–214
funny-money, 61–62, 65–70
future focus, 112
Future Wealth (Robertson), 285
G
Gaia, 176
"Gaia hypothesis," 8–9
Gandhi, Mahatma, 253, 265
Garreau, Joel, 319
Gaviotas, Colombia, 248, 266–270, 279
gender equality, 111–112
General Agreements on Trade and Tariffs
    (GATT), 90–91
General Periodicity (Jaccaci), 251
Georgescu-Rogen, Nicholas, 214
Germany, 78, 294
Ghana, 41
The Gift (Hyde), 207
gift economies, 207–209
global commons, 109–110, 113, 203, 209–211
global crises. See Critical Mass
global economy
    beneficiaries of, 104
    buying power of, 272, 274
    camouflage of, 91–93

as cause of Critical Mass, 54–57
checks on excess, 95–96
comparison to democratic communities, 188
comparison to HIV, 57–58
conflicts, 30
control of country's resources, 259–260
democracy of, 79–81
dependence on for provision, 61–63
equitability of, 77–79
goal of, 62
importance of peak oil, 44–46
information access in, 173–174, 176
as Juggernaut, 254–256
Life's economic rules and, 139–140
primary directive, 64
public holdings, 209–210
six degrees of separation, 191, 214
sustainability of provision, 64–77
too big to fail, 97–100
use of "green" terms, 201
*See also* industrialization
global solutions
commons trusts, 109–113
failure of, 115–117
impossibility of, 117–121
by Life, 121–123
in a perfect world, 104–109
strengthening global economy, 101–102
support for, 102–104
transformations in worldview, 113–115
Glover, Paul, 284–285
goby fish, 152
*Going Local* (Shuman), 228–229, 239
Goldman Sachs, 120
Goldsmith, Edward, 153
Goleman, Daniel, 217
Gore, Al, 97
governance
engagement in, 238–243
leaders and representatives, 242–243
in natural systems, 159
governments
chaos of, 234
function of, 86–87
local food production support, 222–223
provision by, 63
suppression of local alternatives, 274–275
working parallel to, 238–242
*gram swaraj*, 265
Grand Rapids, Michigan, 227
grassroots democracy, 110, 170–172
Great Depression, 98, 283
*The Great Turning* (Korten), 199
*The Great Work* (Berry), 200
"green," overuse of, 201
Green, Peter, 67–68

green algae, 154
Green Belt Movement, 248, 259–262
Green Books, 203
Green GDP (Gross Domestic Product),
107–108
Green Party
limitations of, 244–245
values, 110–113, 201
greenhouse gases, from agriculture, 21–22
Greenleaf, Robert, 179, 249–250
GreenZone, 229–230
Greer, John Michael, 199
group decision-making, 166–168
groupers, 152
Guahibos, 267
Gulf of Mexico, 17, 39, 42
**H**
Habitat for Humanity, 208
Haiti, 22
Hansen, James, 40, 72
hard times, 184–186
Hartmann, Thom, 87–88, 89, 168, 237
Hawken, Paul, 8–9, 197
hazardous wastes, 25–26
*The Heart of Simple Living* (Urbanska), 212
*Heat* (Monbiot), 297
heavy metals, 25
Hedges, Chris, 93–94
Heinberg, Richard, 38, 44, 204, 215, 287–288,
297
hierarchies, in natural communities, 177–178
*High Noon* (Rischard), 105, 119
Hightower, Jim, 189
Himalayas, 30
HIV/AIDS (human immunodeficiency virus/
acquired immune deficiency syndrome)
acknowledgement of, 33–35
carrying capacity of body, 65
comparison to viral global economy, 57–58
crisis multiplication, 15
Critical Mass as, 9–10
death of virus, 202
discovering cause, 35–36
history of, 11–13
limits to, 95–96
protein camouflage, 91
understanding symptoms of, 19
Hoagland, Edward, 95
Hoagland, Mahlon, 168–169, 182
Hobbes, Thomas, 186
Hock, Dee, 235, 242, 301
home study, 216–217
hope, illusion of, 93
Hopkins, Rob, 204, 249, 286
Hu Jintao, 199
human immunodeficiency virus. *See* HIV/AIDS

humans
 competition with other-than-human species,
 78–79
 effect on ecosystems, 9–10
 in hard times, 186
 organism metaphor, 9
 rights of, 307–310
 understanding our needs, 237–238
 See also civilizations; communities (human)
Huntington, Samuel, 84, 86
Hyde, Lewis, 207, 209
hydrogen, use by bacteria, 131–132
hyper-cities, 26–27
hyper-urbanization
 as cause of Critical Mass, 38, 55–56
 as symptom of Critical Mass, 26–28
Hyundai, 263
I
ice ages, 312–313, 315, 319
imagination, 313–315
immigrants, 308–309
immune system
 collective movement as, 9
 as distributed system, 181
 information sharing, 175, 236
 Life's version of, 9–10
India
 air pollution, 25
 corporate control of agriculture, 262–266
 Ecological Footprint, 76
 economic recovery, 102
 energy consumption, 42, 78, 297
 fossil fuel conflicts, 29
 hunger rates, 20
 poverty, 27
 water use, 22–23
indigenous peoples
 adaptation of, 9–10
 knowledge of, 323–324
 spirituality, 304
 sustainability of, 74
Indonesia
 economic recovery, 102
 fossil fuel conflicts, 30
 volcanic eruption, 141
Indus River, 30
industrial ecosystems, 201
industrialization
 of agriculture, 21–22
 as cause of Critical Mass, 38, 56
 effect of, 10
 pollution, 24
 sustainability of, 75
information sharing among natural communities, 172–177
Institute for Local Self-Reliance, 227

Institute of Community Economics, 239
Intellectual Property Rights, 263, 266
intelligence, sharing among natural communi-
 ties, 172–177
intentional communities, 247, 257
interdependence, 150–152
International Conference on Degrowth in the
 Americas, 214
International Energy Agency, 42
International Forum on Globalization, 237
International Monetary Fund (IMF), 90–91
The Interpreters (AE), 125
interregional networks, 241–242
Iran, 94, 253
Island Press, 203
Ithaca HOURS, 284
Iyer, Pico, 318
J
Jaccaci, August, 250–251
Jackson, Wes, 217
James, Sarah, 277
Japan
 barrels of oil equivalent, 294
 broadband services, 94
 Ecological Footprint, 76
 fossil fuel conflicts, 29, 40
 income, 78
Jenkins, David, 246
Jensen, Derrick, 75
Jevons, Stanley, 295
Joachim, Mitchell, 220
jobs, 26–28, 225–227
Johnson, Stephen, 170, 172
Johnstone, Chris, 258
Jordan River, 30
JP Morgan Chase, 120
Jubilee, 214, 256
Juggernaut, 254–256
K
Kangos, Sweden, 277–278
Kauffman, Stuart, 133
Kelly, Kevin, 176, 235
Kelly, Marjorie, 93
Kenya, 94, 259–262
keystone species, 179–180
Khazoom, Daniel, 295
Khazoom-Brookes Postulate, 295
Kinshasa, DRC, 26
Klare, Michael, 30
Klickitat County, Washington, 25
Kolbert, Elizabeth, 122
Korten, David C., 199
Krieglstein, Werner, 168–169
Kyoto Protocol, 287
L
lagom, 213

Lagos, Nigeria, 26
Lahti, Torbjörn, 277
Lancaster County, Pennsylvania, 224
The Land Ethic, 299–303, 305
"The Land Ethic" (Leopold), 299
Landless Workers' Movement, 247, 269–272
Lappé, Frances Moore, 292
Laszlo, Ervin, 199
Latin America, 20, 27
Lawrence Livermore National Laboratory, 292
leaders
    emergence of, 246–249
    in natural communities, 178–181
    support for solutions, 102–104
Leopold, Aldo, 299–300, 302
LETS (Local Exchange Trading System),
    281–286
liability, 250
Life
    checks on excess, 95–96
    communities, 144–146
    democracy in, 165–169
    downtimes, 160–162
    Economic Survival Protocol, 60, 134, 139–
        140, 193–195, 219, 235
    ecosystem turnover, 182–184
    evolution of Earth's immune system, 9–10
    experience of bacteria, 127–132
    mimicking democracy of, 237–238
    mimicking ways of, 196–199, 230–231
    politics of, 233–234
    primary directive, 59, 299
    solutions of for Critical Mass, 121–123
    spirituality, 303–305
    successful economies, 135–140
    survival techniques, 59–61
    threats to, 1
    tinkering by, 132–134, 142–143
limited liability institutions, 250
"The Limits to Growth" (Club of Rome), 99
Linton, Michael, 283
Little Ice Age, 319
living within our means, as economic protocol,
    60
local currencies, 281–286
Local Exchange Trading System (LETS),
    281–286
Local First, 227
localization. See relocalization
Los Angeles, 24
Louis Pasteur Institute, 35
love, 250–251
Lovelock, James, 8, 176
Lugari, Paolo, 248, 267, 279
Lummis, C. Douglas, 95, 237
Lundberg, Jan, 38

lung cancer, 24
**M**
Maathai, Wangari, 248, 259–262
Macy, Joanna, 199, 258
Malaysia, 29
manufacturing, 25
manure, 153–154
Marcellus field, 42
Margolis, Mac, 41–42
Margulis, Lynn, 136, 142, 152, 160
Marsh, Chuck, 247
McCallum, Ian, 217
McDonald's Restaurants, 229–230
McKibben, Bill, 6, 40, 221, 296, 303
McLuhan, Marshall, 5
Meadows, Donella, 178
Menem, Carlos, 273
*Merck Manual of Diagnosis and Therapy*, 19
Mesopotamia, 315
Mexico
    Ecological Footprint, 76
    fossil fuel conflicts, 29
    oil consumption, 78
Mexico City, 24
*Miami Herald*, 89
Middle Ages, 319
Middle East, 27, 42
migrants, 308–309
Miller, Laura, 86
MIT, 99
monarch butterflies, 308–309
Monbiot, George, 297
Mondragón cooperatives, 248–249, 275–276
money
    history of, 65–70
    local currencies, 281–286
    provision by, 61–62
monkeys, 168
Monsanto, 263
Monteagudo, Graceala, 274
Montreal Protocol, 119–120
Movimento dos Trabalhadores Rurais Sem-
    Terra (MST), 247, 269–272
Murphy, Pat, 218, 219, 294, 297
**N**
Naess, Arne, 304
NASA, 224
National Council of Women of Kenya, 260
National Oceanic and Atmospheric
    Administration (NOAA), 50
nations
community of, 116
solutions for, 107–109
*See also* poor nations; wealthy nations
*Natural Capitalism* (Hawken, Lovins, Lovins),
    222

natural communities
  comparison to global economy, 188
  cooperation, 148–149
  democracy in, 165–170, 187
  destruction of, 182–184
  disconnect from, 316–318
  in hard times, 184–186
  hierarchies, 177–178
  honoring, 198
  information sharing, 172–177
  integration with human communities, 300
  interactions of, 144–146
  interdependence of, 155–157
  leaders, 178–181
  partnership, 150–152, 157–160
  place-based economies, 146–148
  purpose, 162–163
  responsiveness of, 181
  spirituality, 303–305
  stability of, 301
natural gas, 42
Natural Step practices, 277
Navdanya, 249, 264–266
Nearing, Scott, 189, 205, 279
neem trees, 263, 266
Netherlands, 94–95
*The New Good Life* (Robbins), 211
New Society, 203
*New Yorker* magazine, 114, 122
*Newsweek*, 41, 116
*The Next World War* (Woodbridge), 30
niches, 163
Nigeria, 41
Nile River, 30
Nixon, Richard, 67
Noah's ark, 316
no-growth economies, 214–216
nonviolence, 111
North Korea, 30
North Sea oil fields, 42
Northern Africa, 27, 253
Norway, 40
Novacek, Michael, 122–123
Nussbaum, Bruce, 297
O
Oahu, Hawaii, 25
oak trees, 174, 176
Obama, Barack, 21
Odum, Eugene, 174
oil. *See* fossil fuels
Oil Depletion Protocol, 287–288
Oliver, Mary, 305
Ordovician period, 122
organic design, 298
organic farming, 222
organism metaphor, 9

Orinoco River, 41, 268
Orr, David, 217
other-than-human species
  competition with humans, 78–79
  consciousness of, 313–315
  democracy in, 166–169, 187
  grassroots organization, 171–172
  honoring, 198
  leaders, 178
  political activity of, 233–234
  rights of, 305–307
overpopulation, 37, 55
*Overshoot* (Catton), 72
Oxfam, 22
oxpecker birds, 152
oxygen
  Earth's exchange system, 48–49
  effect on bacteria, 131–132
ozone, depletion of, 119–120
P
Pacific Islands, 20
Pakistan, 95
Pan Yue, 199
paper economy, 65
parasitic relationships, 151
partnership
  communities of, 150–152
  in ecosystems, 157–160
  in solutions, 153–155
Passat, 157
Pauli, Gunter, 214
paving, 216
peak oil
  about, 38–40
  camouflages of, 43–44
  as cause of Critical Mass, 55
  date of, 41–42
  importance to global economy, 44–46
  practicing subtraction, 288–292
  terminology, 40–41
Peking University, 199
Pepsi, 263
Permian period, 122
Persian Gulf, 30
petroleum-based synthetics, 25
Philadelphia, 224, 240–241, 283
photosynthesis, 129–130
Pike Place Market, 228
pine trees, 268
pioneer species, 149
Pitt, Leonard, 89
place-based communities, 146–148, 205–207
*Plan B* (Brown), 106, 116–117
*Plan B 4.0* (Brown), 105, 117
*Plan C* (Murphy), 218, 219, 294, 297
*Planet of Slums* (Davis), 26

plankton, 142
plant species
    extinction, 28
    solar energy use, 136–137
plastic, 26
Pleistocene Overkill, 9
political parties, role of, 243–244
politics, current system of, 233–235
*The Politics of Simple Living* (Siegel), 215
Pollan, Michael, 21
pollution, 24–26, 31
pollution crisis, for bacteria, 131–132
poor nations
    Ecological Footprint, 76
    effect of Critical Mass, 14
    effect of economic tools, 90–91
    income, 78
Post-Carbon Institute, 292
potlatches, 208–209
poverty, 26–28
the Powers
    about, 83–84
    Critical Mass avoidance, 85–86
    delusions created by, 91–93
    democracy avoidance, 86–87
    energy consumption, 297
    as Juggernaut, 254–256
    keystone species comparison, 180
    opposition to change, 252
    reaction to resistance, 253
prairie dogs, 180
Pretty, Jules, 221
primary directives, 59, 64
private ownership, 209–211
protesting, 92
protocols, definition, 35
provisions, 61–63
Prygrocki, Greg, 236
public holdings, 209–211
public markets, 228
pyramid structure, 80–81, 188
Q
Quilligan, James Bernard, 109–110, 210
R
*Radical Evolution* (Garreau), 319
Rainforest Information Centre, 32
Reading Terminal Market, 228
Reagan, Ronald, 245
recycling, 135–136, 182
red deer, 167
redundancy, 163
Rees, William E., 75
refusal, 251–254
regional coalitions, 241–242
Register, Richard, 248
Reich, Robert, 94

relationships, democratic, 165–170
religions, 318
relocalization
    of businesses, 227–230
    currencies and, 286
    of employment, 225–227
    of food production, 220–225
    obstacles to, 279–280
    as solution, 204–205
rematerializing, 218
Renaissance, 319
Rensenbrink, John, 93, 262
Research Foundation for Science, Technology
    and Ecology, 265–266
resilience, 183, 301
resistance, 251–254
*Resource Wars* (Klare), 30
resources
    as common good, 137–138, 209–211
    corporate control of, 259–261, 262–266
    depletion of, 3–6
    in local area, 205
    place-based, 146–148, 205–207
    working within limits, 197–198, 217–220
respiratory system, 48–49
responsibility, personal, 112
restraint, 211–216
reuse, 135–136
(r)evolution, 251–254
Revolutionary Armed Forces of Colombia,
    268–269
rhinoceroses, 152
rice farmers, 159
Rischard, Jean-Francois, 105, 119
Ritz, Dean, 89–90
Robbins, John, 211
Roberts, Paul, 38
Robertson, James, 108, 226, 285
Rodale, 203
Roman Empire, 7
Roper, Tim, 167
Rothkopf, David, 84
rules, 60–61, 134
Ruppert, Michael, 38, 39, 102
Russia
    fossil fuel conflicts, 29, 40
    oil consumption, 78
S
*Sacred Economics* (Eisenstein), 69
Sagan, Dorian, 142
Sahara, 157
Sahel, Central Africa, 22
Sahtouris, Elisabet, 133, 145, 160, 237
Sale, Kirkpatrick, 191–192
Salt Spring Dollar, 284
Sámi, 277–278

San Francisco, 216
A Sand County Almanac (Leopold), 299–300
Sanderson, Eric, 216
Santa Clara County v. Southern Pacific, 87–90
Saudi Arabia, 42
scientific gifts, 209
seeds
  patents, 263
  of staple foods, 264–265
SeKom, 277–278
self-organization, 272–275
self-reliance
  funny-money and, 69–70
  obstacles to, 279–280
  popular assemblies, 272–275
  sustainable communities, 266–270,
  277–278
Servant Leadership (Greenleaf), 249–250
servant leadership role, 179, 247, 249–251
shale gas, 42
Shanghai, 26
Shapiro, Mark, 121
sharing, 207–209
Shenzhen, China, 225
Shiva, Vandana, 249, 263–266
Shuman, Michael, 228–229, 239, 244, 283
Siegel, Charles, 215
simplicity, 211–214
Six Degrees of Separation from the Global
  Economy, 191, 214
skills, 225–227
Slow Food Enterprises (SFEs), 221
Slow Money (Tasch), 221
social justice, 110–111
social structures, 80–81
socio-political systems, 86–87
solar energy, use by Life, 136–137
solid waste, 25
Solow, Robert, 215
solutions to multiple problems, 153
  See also global solutions
South Africa, 253
South Carolina, 227
South China Sea, 30
South End, 203
South Korea, 30, 94
South Sudan, 253
Southern Pacific, Santa Clara County v., 87–90
Soviet Union, 253
Spain, 275–276
specialization, 150
species. See animal species; humans; other-
  than-human species
Speth, James Gustave, 103
spirituality, 303–305
squirrels, 174

St. Paul, Minnesota, 216
stability, 301
Statoil, 229–230
stewardship, 246
Storms of My Grandchildren (Hansen), 72
Sub-Saharan Africa, 20, 27
subsistence, definition, 147–148
subsistence economies
  effect of global economy, 262–266
  natural economies as, 147
  transition to, 205–207
subtraction, of fossil fuel use, 288–295
Suchantke, Andreas, 156–157
Sullivan, Andrew, 246
Supercapitalism (Reich), 94
Superclass (Rothkopf), 84
Surowiecki, James, 114, 176, 235
survival, of Critical Mass, 6
sustainability
  Ecological Footprint, 75–76
  of global economy, 64–77
  goal of, 112
  Life's rules for, 64
  in natural communities, 301
swaraj, 265
Swimme, Brian, 132
symbiotic relationships, 151–152
Syria, 253
T
Tainter, Joseph, 81, 100
Taiwan, 29
Talbott, Steve, 169
tar sands, 39, 40, 41
Tasch, Woody, 221
teamwork, 143–144
technologies
  as cause of Critical Mass, 37, 55
  empowerment of, 94
  resource use and, 72
Tenino, Washington, 283
terrorism. See conflict
Theil, Stefan, 116
thinkering, 236
third world nations. See poor nations
Thompson, Ken, 180
Thoreau, Henry David, 212
Tigris-Euphrates River, 30
Time's Up (Farnish), 91–93
timing, 230–231
Tokyo, 26–27
tool making, 312–313
Tools of Disconnection, 91–93
Totnes, England, 249
Totnes Pound, 284
toxins, 25–26
trade, control of, 30

*The Transition Handbook* (Hopkins), 204
Transition Network, 249
Transition Towns Initiative, 204
trees, 259–262
Triangle Trade, 66
tribal groups, 32, 208
turnover, 182
U
Umeå, Sweden, 229–230
unemployment, 26–28
*Unequal Protection* (Hartmann), 87–88
UNICEF, 22
Union of Concerned Scientists, 28
United Kingdom
   barrels of oil equivalent, 294
   oil consumption, 78
   oil peak, 42
United Nations
   carbon emitters, 121
   disease management, 119
   role of, 106
UN Earth Charter, 106
UN Food and Agriculture Organization, 20
UN Human Settlements Program, 26
United States
   acts of resistance, 253
   barrels of oil equivalent, 294
   broadband services, 94
   consumerism, 95
   Ecological Footprint, 76
   energy consumption, 42, 78
   fossil fuel conflicts, 29, 40
   fossil fuel conservation, 291
   local currencies, 283
   water use, 22
US Department of Agriculture, 50
US Geological Survey, 42
USDA Census of Agriculture, 221
Urbanska, Wanda, 212
Utne, Leif, 273–274
V
Valchiusella Valley, Italy, 248
Varela, Francesco, 175
Venezuela, 41, 253
violence, 111
Vishnu, 254–256
Vivendi, 263
Vivero Organopónico Alamar, 224–225
*Voluntary Simplicity* (Elgin), 212

voting, 92
W
Wackernagel, Mathis, 75
Waite, Morris Remick, 89
Wallerstein, Immanuel, 99
Walsh, Colorado, 229
war. *See* conflict
*Washington Post*, 319
waste
   Earth's reuse, 135–136
   making less, 218–219
wasting diseases, 45
water
   corporate control of, 263
   effect of ice age, 315–316
   as symptom of Critical Mass, 22–24
   use by bacteria, 131–132
Watson, Tim, 198
wealthy nations
   Ecological Footprint, 76
   effect of economic tools, 90–91
   income, 78
Weisman, Alan, 268, 279
Weiss, Paul A., 150–151
Wells, Lloyd, 241, 248, 323
Westside Market, 228
Wheatley, Margaret, 172
Whitefield, Patrick, 303
Whitty, Julia, 308–309
*Wild Law* (Cullinan), 306
wildfires, 156
Wildwood, New Jersey, 283
Wilson, E. O., 300
*Wired* magazine, 94, 176
WiserEarth, 203
Witt, Susan, 282, 285
Wolford, Wendy, 271–272
Woodbridge, Roy, 30, 109
work, 26–28, 63, 225–227
World Bank, 90–91
World Health Organization, 119
World Meteorological Organization, 50
World Trade Organization (WTO), 91, 263
worldview, transformations in, 113–115
Wright, Angus, 271–272
Wright, Robert, 3
Wright, Ronald, 81
Z
Zimbabwe, 69

# About the Author

A FORMER EDITOR of *Farmstead* magazine and of the nationally sub-scribed newsletters *ForeFacts, Teaching Tomorrow Today* and *Starting Point*, Ellen LaConte is a contributing editor to *Green Horizon Magazine* and *The Ecozoic* and sits on the Advisory Board of the EarthWalk Alliance. Author of *Afton — A Novel* (in serial release online at www.ellenlaconte. com), *On Light Alone* and *Free Radical*, memoirs about influential home-steaders, social critics and bestselling *Living the Good Life* authors Helen and Scott Nearing, LaConte has been published in *The Sun, East/West Journal, Odyssey, New Perspectives, Country Journal, Countryside, Convergence, Gaia: A Literary & Environmental Journal* and in numerous trade journals. After 23 years homesteading, heating with wood, gardening organically and composting seaweed in Mid-Coast Maine, she relo-cated in 2001 and gardens and frequents farmers' markets now in the Yadkin River watershed of the Piedmont bioregion of North Carolina.

ellenlaconte.com

If you have enjoyed *Life Rules*, you might also enjoy other

# BOOKS TO BUILD A NEW SOCIETY

Our books provide positive solutions for people who
want to make a difference. We specialize in:

**Sustainable Living • Green Building • Peak Oil**
**Renewable Energy • Environment & Economy**
**Natural Building & Appropriate Technology**
**Progressive Leadership • Resistance and Community**
**Educational & Parenting Resources**

---

## New Society Publishers

### ENVIRONMENTAL BENEFITS STATEMENT

New Society Publishers has chosen to produce this book on recycled paper made
with **100% post consumer waste**, processed chlorine free, and old growth free.

For every 5,000 books printed, New Society saves the following resources:[1]

| | |
|---|---|
| 38 | Trees |
| 3,436 | Pounds of Solid Waste |
| 3,781 | Gallons of Water |
| 4,931 | Kilowatt Hours of Electricity |
| 6,246 | Pounds of Greenhouse Gases |
| 27 | Pounds of HAPs, VOCs, and AOX Combined |
| 9 | Cubic Yards of Landfill Space |

[1]Environmental benefits are calculated based on research done by the Environmental Defense Fund
and other members of the Paper Task Force who study the environmental impacts of the paper
industry.

---

*For a full list of NSP's titles, please call* 1-800-567-6772 *or check out our website* at:

**www.newsociety.com**